Taking Sides: Clashing Views
on Psychological Issues, 18e

by Brent Slife
Brigham Young University--Provo

http://create.mcgraw-hill.com

ISBN-10: 0078139619   ISBN-13: 9780078139611

Contents

Unit 7 227

Preface

Critical-thinking skills are a significant component of a meaningful education, and this book is specifically designed to stimulate critical thinking and initiate lively and informed dialogue on psychological issues. In this book I present 36 selections, arranged in pro and con pairs, that address a total of 18 different controversial issues in psychology. The opposing views demonstrate that even experts can derive conflicting conclusions and opinions from the same body of information.

A dialogue approach to learning is certainly not new. The Ancient Greek philosopher Socrates engaged in it with his students some 2400 years ago. His point-counterpoint procedure was termed a *dialectic*. Although Socrates and his companions hoped eventually to know the "truth" by this method, they did not see the dialectic as having a predetermined end. There were no right answers to know or facts to memorize. The emphasis in this learning method is on how to evaluate information—on developing reasoning skills.

It is in this dialectical spirit that *Taking Sides: Clashing Views on Psychological Issues* was originally compiled, and it has guided me through this edition as well. To encourage and stimulate discussion and to focus the debates in this volume, each issue is expressed in terms of a single question that is answered with two different points of view. But certainly the reader should not feel confined to adopt only one or the other of the positions presented. Readers' positions may fall between the views expressed or totally outside them, and I encourage readers to fashion their own conclusions.

Some of the questions raised in this volume go to the very heart of what psychology as a discipline is all about and the methods and manner in which psychologists work. Others address newly emerging concerns. In choosing readings I was guided by the following criteria: the readings had to be understandable to newcomers to psychology, they had to have academic substance, and they had to express markedly different points of view.

Plan of the book Each issue in this volume has an issue *introduction*, which defines each author's position and sets the stage for debate. Also provided is a set of point-counterpoint statements that pertain to the issue and that should help to get the dialogue off the ground. Each issue concludes with *challenge questions* to provoke further examination of the issue. The introduction and challenge questions are designed to assist the reader in achieving a critical and informed view on important psychological issues. Also, at the end of each issue is a list of Internet site addresses (URLs) that should prove useful as starting points for further research.

A word to the instructor An *Instructor's Resource Guide with Test Questions* (multiple-choice and essay) is available through the publisher for the instructor using *Taking Sides* in the classroom. A general guidebook, *Using Taking Sides in the Classroom,* which discusses methods and techniques for integrating the pro–con approach into any classroom setting, is also available. An online version of *Using Taking Sides in the Classroom* and a correspondence service for *Taking Sides* adopters can be found at www.mhhe.com/createcentral.

Taking Sides: Clashing Views in Psychological Issues is only one title in the *Taking Sides* series. If you are interested in seeing the table of contents for any of the other titles, please visit the *Taking Sides* website at www.mhhe.com/cls.

Editor of This Volume

BRENT SLIFE is currently a professor of psychology at Brigham Young University, where he chairs the doctoral program in theoretical and philosophical psychology and serves as a member of the doctoral program in clinical psychology. He has been honored recently with several awards for his scholarship and teaching, including the Eliza R. Snow Award (for research on the interface of science and religion), the Karl G. Maeser Award (top researcher at BYU), Circle of Honor Award (Student Honor Association), and both Teacher of the Year by the university and Most Outstanding Professor by the psychology student honorary, Psi Chi.

Slife moved from Baylor University, where he served as director of clinical training for many years and was honored there as Outstanding Research Professor. He also received the Circle of Achievement award for his teaching. The recipient of numerous grants (e.g., NSF, NEH), he is also listed in *Who's Who in the World, America, Science and Engineering,* and *Health and Medicine.* As a fellow of several professional organizations, including the American Psychological Association, he recently served as the president of the Society of Theoretical and Philosophical Psychology, and serves currently on the editorial boards of six journals: *Journal of Mind and Behavior, Journal of Theoretical and Philosophical Psychology, Humanistic Psychologist, Qualitative Research in Psychology, International Journal of Existential Psychology and Psychotherapy,* and *Terrorism Research.*

He has authored over 120 articles and six books, including *Taking Sides: Clashing Views on Psychological Issues* (2011, McGraw-Hill), *Critical Thinking About Psychology: Hidden Assumptions and Plausible Alternatives* (2005, APA Books), *Critical Issues in Psychotherapy: Translating New Ideas into Practice* (2001, Sage publications), *What's Behind the Research? Hidden Assumptions in*

the *Behavioral Sciences* (1995, Sage Publications), and
Time and Psychological Explanation (1993, SUNY Press).
Slife also continues his psychotherapy practice of over
25 years, where he specializes in marital and family
therapies. Please check his website, www.brentdslife.com,
for downloadable articles and links to his books.

Acknowledgments In working on this revision I received
useful suggestions from many of the users of the previous
edition, and I was able to incorporate many of their recommendations for new issues and new readings.

    In addition, special thanks to the McGraw-Hill staff
for their support and perspective.

Brent Slife
Brigham Young University

Academic Advisory Board Members

Members of the Academic Advisory Board are instrumental
in the final selection of articles for each edition of *Taking
Sides*. Their review of articles for content, level, and appro-
priateness provides critical direction to the editor and staff.
We think that you will find their careful consideration well
reflected in this volume.

Vincent Amato
*Suffolk County
Community College*

James Barnett
Lassen College

Sharon Boyd Jackson
Kean University

Deborah Briihl
Valdosta State University

Kimberly Brown
Ball State University

Raymond Brown
Keiser University

Bernardo J. Carducci
Indiana University Southeast

David Carroll
*University of
Wisconsin–Superior*

Cherie Clark
Queens University of Charlotte

Samuel L. Clay II
Brigham Young University, Idaho

Ellen Cole
Alaska Pacific University

Mala Datta
Dominican College

Peter Desberg
*California State
University, Long Beach*

Catherine DeSoto
*University of Northern
Iowa*

Jill Dominique
Capella University

Valeri Farmer-Dougan
Illinois State University

Edward Fernandes
East Carolina University

Kathy Firestine
Penn State Greater Alleghany

Christian Fossa-Andersen
DeVry South Florida

Edwin E. Gantt
Brigham Young University

Nicholas Greco IV
Adler School of Professional Psychology

Rick Herbert
South Plains College

Anthony Hermann
Willamette University

Julian Hertzog
William Woods University

Larry Hilgert
Valdosta State University

Harry Hughes
Salt Lake Community College

Matthew I. Isaak
University of Louisiana

David Jewett
University of Wisconsin

James C. Kaufman
CSU San Bernardino

William Kelemen
California State University

Barbara LaRue
Baker College–Port Huron

Elissa Litwin
Touro College

Michael Loftin
Belmont University

Rick Lupacchino
Strayer University

Donald Lynch
Unity College

Dawn McBride
Illinois State University

Douglas McKenzie
Grand Valley State University

Megan Meyer
Holy Family University

Robert Moore
*Marshalltown
Community College*

Correlation Guide

The *Taking Sides* series presents current issues in a debate-style format designed to stimulate student interest and develop critical thinking skills. Each issue is thoughtfully framed with an issue summary, an issue introduction, and a postscript. The pro and con essays—selected for their liveliness and substance—represent the arguments of leading scholars and commentators in their fields.

Taking Sides: Clashing Views on Psychological Issues, 18/e is an easy-to-use reader that presents issues on important topics such as *homosexuality, addiction, coercive interrogations,* and *scientific determinism.* For more information on *Taking Sides* and other *McGraw-Hill Create*™ titles, visit www.mcgrawhillcreate.com.

This convenient guide matches the issues in **Taking Sides: Psychological Issues, 18/e** with the corresponding chapters in three of our best-selling McGraw-Hill Psychology textbooks by Feldman, Lahey, and Feist/Rosenberg.

Taking Sides: Psychological Issues, 18/e	Psychology and Your Life, 2/e by Feldman	Psychology: An Introduction, 11/e by Lahey	Psychology: Perspectives & Connections, 2/e by Feist/Rosenberg
Does Learning Change the Structure of the Brain?	**Chapter 2**: Neuroscience and Behavior **Chapter 7**: Motivation and Emotion	**Chapter 3**: Biological Foundations in Behavior **Chapter 14**: Abnormal Behavior	**Chapter 3**: The Biology of Behavior **Chapter 16**: Treatment of Psychological Disorders
Is Evolution a Good Explanation for Psychological Concepts?	**Chapter 8**: Development **Chapter 9**: Personality and Individual Differences	**Chapter 3**: Biological Foundations in Behavior **Chapter 4**: Interplay of Nature and Nurture	**Chapter 5**: Human Development
Is Homosexuality Biologically Based?	**Chapter 1**: Introduction to Psychology	**Chapter 2**: Research Methods in Psychology	**Chapter 5**: Human Development
Is American Psychological Research Generalizable to Other Cultures?	**Chapter 1**: Introduction to Psychology **Chapter 9**: Personality and Individual Differences	**Chapter 1**: Introduction to Psychology **Chapter 2**: Research Methods in Psychology	**Chapter 1**: Introduction to Psychology **Chapter 2**: Conducting Research in Psychology
Are Traditional Empirical Methods Sufficient to Provide Evidence for Psychological Practice?	**Chapter 1**: Introduction to Psychology **Chapter 11**: Treatment of Psychological Disorders	**Chapter 1**: Introduction to Psychology **Chapter 2**: Research Methods in Psychology	**Chapter 1**: Introduction to Psychology **Chapter 2**: Conducting Research in Psychology
Should Neuroscience Research Be Used to Inform Public Policy?	**Chapter 12**: Social Psychology	**Chapter 1**: Introduction to Psychology **Chapter 2**: Research Methods in Psychology	**Chapter 1**: Introduction to Psychology **Chapter 2**: Conducting Research in Psychology
Are Violent Video Games Harmful to Children and Adolescents?	**Chapter 8**: Development **Chapter 9**: Personality and Individual Differences	**Chapter 11**: Motivation and Emotion **Chapter 12**: Personality	**Chapter 11**: Motivation and Emotion **Chapter 13**: Personality: The Uniqueness of the Individual **Chapter 14**: Social Behavior
Does Parent Sexual Orientation Affect Child Development?	**Chapter 8**: Development **Chapter 9**: Personality and Individual Differences **Chapter 12**: Social Psychology	**Chapter 3**: Biological Foundations in Behavior **Chapter 4**: Interplay of Nature and Nurture	**Chapter 5**: Human Development **Chapter 11**: Motivation and Emotion **Chapter 14**: Social Behavior **Chapter 15**: Psychological Disorders
Can Positive Psychology Make Us Happier?	**Chapter 2**: Neuroscience and Behavior **Chapter 7**: Motivation and Emotion **Chapter 8**: Development	**Chapter 10**: Developmental Psychology **Chapter 11**: Motivation and Emotion **Chapter 12**: Personality	**Chapter 5**: Human Development **Chapter 11**: Motivation and Emotion **Chapter 12**: Stress and Health **Chapter 13**: Personality: The Uniqueness of the Individual
Is Emotional Intelligence Valid?	**Chapter 2**: Neuroscience and Behavior **Chapter 7**: Motivation and Emotion	**Chapter 9**: Cognition, Language, and Intelligence **Chapter 11**: Motivation and Emotion	**Chapter 10**: Intelligence, Problem Solving, and Creativity **Chapter 11**: Motivation and Emotion

Taking Sides: Psychological Issues, 18/e	Psychology and Your Life, 2/e by Feldman	Psychology: An Introduction, 11/e by Lahey	Psychology: Perspectives & Connections, 2/e by Feist/ Rosenberg
Does an Elective Abortion Lead to Negative Psychological Effects?	**Chapter 2**: Neuroscience and Behavior **Chapter 7**: Motivation and Emotion **Chapter 12**: Social Psychology	**Chapter 3**: Biological Foundations in Behavior **Chapter 11**: Motivation and Emotion **Chapter 16**: Social Psychology	**Chapter 3**: The Biology of Behavior **Chapter 11**: Motivation and Emotion **Chapter 14**: Social Behavior
Is Attention-Deficit Hyperactivity Disorder (ADHD) a Real Disorder?	**Chapter 2**: Neuroscience and Behavior **Chapter 8**: Development **Chapter 10**: Psychological Disorders **Chapter 12**: Social Psychology	**Chapter 3**: Biological Foundations in Behavior **Chapter 10**: Developmental Psychology **Chapter 14**: Abnormal Behavior **Chapter 15**: Therapies **Chapter 16**: Social Psychology	**Chapter 3**: The Biology of Behavior **Chapter 8**: Learning **Chapter 14**: Social Behavior **Chapter 15**: Psychological Disorders **Chapter 16**: Treatment of Psychological Disorders
Are Fathers Necessary for Children's Well-Being?	**Chapter 12**: Social Psychology	**Chapter 16**: Social Psychology	**Chapter 14**: Social Behavior
Are All Psychotherapies Equally Effective?	**Chapter 11**: Treatment of Psychological Disorders	**Chapter 15**: Therapies	**Chapter 16**: Treatment of Psychological Disorders
Should Therapists Be Eclectic?	**Chapter 11**: Treatment of Psychological Disorders	**Chapter 15**: Therapies	**Chapter 16**: Treatment of Psychological Disorders
Can Psychotherapy Change Sexual Orientation?	**Chapter 11**: Treatment of Psychological Disorders	**Chapter 15**: Therapies	**Chapter 16**: Treatment of Psychological Disorders
Can Sex Be Addictive?	**Chapter 2**: Neuroscience and Behavior **Chapter 7**: Motivation and Emotion **Chapter 12**: Social Psychology	**Chapter 11**: Motivation and Emotion **Chapter 14**: Abnormal Behavior **Chapter 16**: Social Psychology	**Chapter 11**: Motivation and Emotion **Chapter 14**: Social Behavior **Chapter 15**: Psychological Disorders
Is Excessive Use of Facebook a Form of Narcissism?	**Chapter 8**: Development **Chapter 12**: Social Psychology	**Chapter 16**: Social Psychology	**Chapter 14**: Social Behavior

Topic Guide

This topic guide suggests how the selections in this book relate to the subjects covered in your course. You may want to use the topics listed on these pages to search the web more easily.

All issues that relate to each topic are listed below the bold-faced term.

Addiction

Can Sex Be Addictive?

Attention Deficit Disorder/Attention Deficit Hyperactivity Disorder

Is Attention-Deficit Hyperactivity Disorder (ADHD) a Real Disorder?

Behavior

Are Violent Video Games Harmful to Children and Adolescents?
Can Sex Be Addictive?
Does Learning Change the Structure of the Brain?
Are Fathers Necessary for Children's Well-Being?

Culture

Is Homosexuality Biologically Based?
Is American Psychological Research Generalizable to Other Cultures?
Is Excessive Use of Facebook a Form of Narcissism?

Emotions

Can Positive Psychology Make Us Happier?
Is Emotional Intelligence Valid?

Emotional Intelligence

Is Emotional Intelligence Valid?

Evolution/Evolutionary Psychology

Is Evolution a Good Explanation for Psychological Concepts?

Gender

Does Parent Sexual Orientation Affect Child Development?
Can Psychotherapy Change Sexual Orientation?

Happiness

Can Positive Psychology Make Us Happier?

Health

Does an Elective Abortion Lead to Negative Psychological Effects?

Internet

Is Excessive Use of Facebook a Form of Narcissism?

Personality

Should Therapists Be Eclectic?

Positive Psychology

Can Positive Psychology Make Us Happier?

Psychological Disorders

Does an Elective Abortion Lead to Negative Psychological Effects?
Is Attention-Deficit Hyperactivity Disorder (ADHD) a Real Disorder?

Psychotherapy/Psychological Treatment/Intervention

Are All Psychotherapies Equally Effective?
Should Therapists Be Eclectic?
Can Psychotherapy Change Sexual Orientation?

Research Issues

Is American Psychological Research Generalizable to Other Cultures?
Are Traditional Empirical Methods Sufficient to Provide Evidence for Psychological Practice?
Should Neuroscience Research Be Used to Inform Public Policy?

Self-Control

Can Sex Be Addictive?

Social Behaviors

Is Excessive Use of Facebook a Form of Narcissism?
Can Sex Be Addictive?
Does Learning Change the Structure of the Brain?
Are Fathers Necessary for Children's Well-Being?

Stress

Does an Elective Abortion Lead to Negative Psychological Effects?

Introduction

Why does psychology need a *Taking Sides* book? The expression "taking sides" implies that there are "controversial psychological issues," as the book title states. But how can there be controversial issues in a discipline that considers itself a science? Controversial issues would seem inherent in such disciplines as philosophy and religion, but wouldn't the issues of psychology be resolved by science—by finding out what is true and false through psychology's empirical methods? If so, are the "controversial issues" presented in this book only *temporary* issues waiting for empirical resolution? And if they are only temporary, why learn or argue about them? Why "take a side"?

As this introduction will argue, there are all sorts of reasons and opportunities to take a side in psychology. Scientific findings are not only decided by data—the information produced by scientific research—but they are also decided by theoretical allegiances, industry loyalties, and philosophical assumptions that are not themselves driven or resolved by data. These allegiances and assumptions allow for and even spawn controversial issues. Indeed, they form what some call the "disguised ideologies" of science (Bernstein, 1983; Richardson, Fowers, and Guignon, 1999): implicit worldviews or philosophies that guide what variables to select for research, what methods to use in these investigations, and what sense to make of the resulting data. As we will see, these are just a few of the many places in psychological research where the researcher's bias or ideology, and thus "controversial issues," can come into play.

Some may hold that the problem of bias affects only the "soft" sciences. They may believe that "hard" sciences, such as physics and chemistry, have essentially eliminated biases and ideologies. However, as we will show, both soft and hard sciences are subject to these ideologies and controversial issues. Indeed, one of the recent conclusions of physics is that the observer's "frame of reference" always affects what is observed (Einstein, 1990; Heisenberg, 1958; Wolf, 1981). In this introduction, we will point to dramatic examples of systematic biases in both types of sciences, showing how some of the most important research—research about health treatment—is substantially driven by factors outside the data per se.

Even so, some scientists will argue that these biases are miscarriages of science, that science conducted correctly would have no systematic ideologies. As we will attempt to describe, however, nothing could be further from the truth, because the scientific method is itself based on a philosophy. It is itself based on a broad ideology in this sense. This is not to say that science is *only* bias or that science is worthless. Indeed, we will argue that science is one of the best tools we have for helping to resolve

controversial issues. The main point of this introduction is that ideologies, biases, and "issues" are *never* avoided entirely and, indeed, play a *necessary* role in science. We believe this role is all the more reason to become aware of psychology's controversial issues, think them through, and, yes, even take a well-reasoned and well-informed "side."

Allegiance Effects in the Soft Sciences

Many examples of systematic bias in psychology exist (Slife, Reber, and Richardson, 2005), but Luborsky's theoretical (or ideological) "allegiance" is surely one of the more striking and significant (Luborsky, Diguer, Seligman, and colleagues, 1999; Luborsky and Barrett, in press). It is striking because theoretical allegiance is such an impressive predictor of psychological research, forecasting an unprecedented two-thirds of the variability in treatment outcomes, with correlations as high as 0.85 (Luborsky and Barrett, in press). We say "unprecedented" because correlations in psychology are rarely this high. Theoretical allegiance is also significant because it concerns the pivotal question: Which psychological treatment is best? In other words, this particular systematic bias is involved in deciding what actually works in psychology.

The term *allegiance* refers to a person's conscious or unconscious loyalty or commitment to a particular ideal, philosophy, or organization. In research on psychotherapy, Luborsky views theoretical allegiance as the degree of a researcher's loyalty to a specific theory of behavior change. The most common theories of psychotherapy, and thus types of theoretical loyalty, are the broad categories of dynamic, cognitive, behavioral, and pharmacological. Luborsky and Barrett (in press) essentially showed that a researcher's preference for one of these broad categories—as rated most accurately through reprints, self-ratings, and colleague ratings—correlates with the therapy found to be the best in the researcher's comparison of several therapies. In other words, whatever therapies or ideas researchers favor *before* their investigation are, with few exceptions, what the researchers "find" their results favoring *after* the investigation.

Luborsky found this correlation through "meta-analyses." Instead of a conventional analysis of one particular study, a meta-analysis is usually an analysis of many studies—an analysis of many conventional analyses. To understand what Luborsky's meta-analysis means, consider an example. Let us say that a particular researcher favors a certain theoretical approach, such as behavioral, and sets up a study comparing behavioral and pharmacological therapies.

Luborsky's analysis indicates that this study will probably favor behavioral therapies over pharmacological, even though the two might *really* be equivalent in effectiveness. According to Luborsky, "treatment benefits, as evidenced in comparative trials, are so influenced by the researcher's theoretical allegiance that in many comparisons differences between treatments lessen or become negligible when the influence of allegiance is considered" (Luborsky and Barrett, in press, p. 355).

Therefore, if we know the theoretical orientation of the researcher, we can predict with considerable accuracy the outcome of an empirical comparison among the various treatment approaches—without even making the comparison! Theoretical allegiance, in this sense, is a clear bias or ideology that is not being corrected by what is really happening in the treatment comparison.

Theoretical allegiances are occurring in spite of the controls instituted for subjective biases in these elaborate research designs. Although Luborsky believes that such allegiances should be controlled, conventional scientific methods are not currently doing so. In short, there are "controversial issues" that are not currently being resolved by the data. Also, as we will see (in the "What Is Happening?" section following), scientific research is conducted in a way that will never eliminate or resolve all the controversial issues.

Allegiance Effects in the Hard Sciences

Is this also true in the hard sciences, or do they avoid the ideas and ideologies that lead to controversial issues? As mentioned, physics has long recognized Heisenberg's (1958) "uncertainty principle" and Einstein's (1990) relativity of the "inertial frame of reference" as just two of the ways in which the observer is assumed to have an important impact on the observed (Bohm, 1980; Wolf, 1981). However, the hard sciences also have meta-analyses that are similar to Luborsky's. Findings in medicine, for example, parallel those we have just described in psychology. Here, *theoretical* allegiance is less of an issue, but *industry* allegiance is widely acknowledged as a potent bias in medical research (Bhandari and colleagues, 2004; Kjaergard and Als-Nielson, 2002; Lexchin and colleagues, 2003). Industry allegiance refers to the high correlations between the industry sponsor of research and the pro-industry outcome of this research.

Healy (1999), for instance, suggests that much of our current conception of the effectiveness of antidepressants is molded more by the marketing imperatives of the pharmaceutical industry than by the scientific findings. There is certainly no dispute that the pharmaceutical industry is the largest funder of medical research in North America, and this, as Valenstein (1998) notes, is "overwhelmingly true" for research on psychiatric drugs (p. 187). Indeed, Valenstein claims that these companies are unlikely to fund researchers who have been negative about drug effec-

tiveness. Still, it is one thing to point to this industry's massive funding efforts and profit motives, and quite another to claim that industry allegiance biases investigators. Is there evidence for this latter claim?

In fact, editorials in five different prestigious medical journals have all pointed to evidence that pharmaceutical funding has tainted the objectivity of these studies (Greenberg, 2001). Freemantle, Anderson, and Young (2000), for example, have recently shown in a meta-analysis of comparative studies that a sponsor's funding is the best predictor of whether studies will show the sponsor's drug to be effective. Similarly, Friedberg and colleagues (1999) have shown empirically that company-supported studies are more likely to report efficacy for the company's product than are independent studies of the same product. Bhandari and colleagues (2004) even report this effect for surgical interventions. Stern and Simes (1997) also found considerable evidence that studies that do not reflect positively on antidepressants are less likely to be published. Moncrieff (2001) reports that the problem of publication bias is even more pronounced with recent SSRI antidepressants because the majority of trials have been conducted by the pharmaceutical industry, which has no obligation to publish negative results and may see little advantage in doing so.

What Is Happening?

What is happening in the soft and hard sciences to produce these "allegiance" effects, either theoretical or industrial? There are issues, such as allegiance, that data never seem to determine or decide definitively. This suggests that some issues require old-fashioned discussion and debate among those in the discipline. It also indicates that scientific experiments alone will not always suffice. Why? Why can't data alone decide all the discipline's "controversial issues"? One of the primary reasons is a concept called *underdetermination*, which means that research data never *completely* determine the interpretation made of that data (Curd and Cover, 1998; Slife and Williams, 1995). The researcher always has a limited choice (within the parameters of the data) about which interpretation to use.

To begin to understand why this is true, consider that any set of data is meaningless without some interpretive framework for that data. In other words, a researcher must *add* his or her own organization or interpretation to the data for the results of any study to be meaningful findings. Even a quick scan of a (typical) data set reveals a bewildering array of numbers, especially if this scan lacks the researcher's explanation as to what specific categories of data and statistical results *mean* (or how they should be interpreted). (For an example, see Slife and Williams, 1995, pp. 5–6.) Researchers will often claim to "see" meanings in their data; this is not because the data *inherently* "mean" something, but because the researcher *already* has an interpretive framework, consciously or unconsciously, for the data in mind.

It is important to recognize that the interpretation selected must "fit" the data for the interpretation to be viable. In other words, not just any interpretation will do; meaningful interpretations must make sense of *all* the data. Nevertheless, more than one interpretation of all the data is always possible, with some potentially dramatic differences in these interpretations. This is what *underdetermination* means. (Please see Curd and Cover, 1998, and Slife and Williams, 1995, pp. 185–187, for the more technical considerations of this conception.) In this sense, a study's "findings" are never *merely* the data, because the data are not meaningful findings until the researcher organizes or interprets the data, allowing for systems of ideas, and thus "controversial issues," to enter the research picture.

Actually, data interpretation is just one of the many places where biases can creep into scientific research. Consider how researchers have all sorts of "subjective" choice points in their studies: first—what to study (what variables are crucial), second—how to study the variables (what operationalization and method design to use), third—how to analyze the study (what assumptions are met and statistics used), fourth—what the statistical results really mean (what interpretation to use), and fifth—what limits the study has (what study problems might impede certain interpretations). These choice points mean that subjective factors, such as allegiance, are inevitably part of any research study. Researchers, knowingly or unknowingly, are favoring their own ideologies through the decisions they make at these choice points. Part of the purpose of *Taking Sides* books, then, is to reveal and discuss these ideologies and to help students become aware of their impact on the discipline.

Science as Ideology

Many scientists will argue that influential ideological factors are not a necessary part of science—that the allegiance effects of psychology and medicine are examples of bad research. They may believe that good science occurs when all the systematic biases, and thus disguised ideologies, have been eliminated or controlled. However, as mentioned earlier, science itself is based on a broad ideology (or philosophy) about how science should be conducted. Moreover, this broad ideology could not itself have been scientifically derived because one would need the ideology (before its derivation) to conduct the scientific investigations to derive it. In short, *there is no empirical evidence for the philosophy of empiricism that underlies the scientific method.* Some may claim that this philosophy has been successful, but this is only a claim or an opinion, not a scientific fact. Even if we were to endorse this claim, which we would, it does not minimize the broad ideology of this philosophy of science, along with the biases and values it promotes.

Perhaps the most obvious bias or value of the philosophy of empiricism is the observability value. Because this philosophy assumes that sensory experience is the only really knowable experience, traditional science has based its doctrine of knowing on the sensory experience of vision or observability. For many students, this valuing of observability will not seem like a value (Slife, 2008). These students may have unknowingly (no pun intended) accepted this philosophy as their own, without critically examining it. In this case, the doctrine of observability will seem more like an axiom than a value.

To be a value rather than an axiom, observability must indicate not only what particular things have merit or worth but also what alternative things *could* be valued (Slife, 2008). Regarding the worth issue, it is probably obvious that traditional empiricism values, and thus selects, observable phenomena as having more merit or worth than nonobservable phenomena for scientific purposes. Perhaps the bigger hurdle for appreciating the value-ladenness of observability is understanding the possibility of alternatives—in this sense, the possibility of knowing *non*observables. Here, we could ask the empiricists if their doctrine of observability is itself observable. In other words, is the idea that "only the sensory can be known" *itself* observable? And if it is not, how then do we know that this idea is correct? Given that empiricists do not observe this idea, and given that they hold it to be correct, there must be other ways of knowing things than by observability.

We can at this point describe other philosophies (or epistemologies) of knowing that assert that many unobservable experiences are knowable, such as the feelings we have for someone or the thoughts we have about something. With the feelings of love, for example, we can surely observe someone who is "in love"—hugging and kissing or any specified observable factor (in research, these are called *operationalizations*). However, we would rarely assume that the feeling of love and these observables are identical. Hugs and kisses can occur without this feeling, and this feeling can occur without hugs and kisses. Therefore, studies of hugs and kisses (or any specified observable) are *not* studies of love. At the risk of noting the obvious, studies of observables are not studies of nonobservables. They may be studies of observables that are associated with nonobservables, but then if we cannot know the nonobservable, how can we know what is associated with them?

For this reason, traditional scientific methods selectively attend to, and thus value, one particular aspect of the world—observables over nonobservables. Indeed, this is part of the reason qualitative research methods were formulated and have become increasingly popular in psychology and other disciplines. They claim that they can investigate nonobservable experiences that are not strictly observable, such as meaning and emotion (cf. Denzin and Lincoln, 2000). If this is true, knowing nonobservables is possible, and the value-ladenness of only attending to observables is clear. Again, some may insist that only observables can be known, but this insistence is not itself a scientific claim because it cannot be decided through scientific observation (Slife, Wiggins, and Graham, 2005). It is a philosophical claim about how knowing occurs and is thus subject to comparison with other philosophical claims about knowing (other epistemologies).

Observability is not the only value of traditional scientific methods. Many of the customs and traditions of how one conducts and is supposed to conduct research originate from similarly unproven values and assumptions, including reductionism (Yanchar, 2005), instrumentalism (Richardson, 2005), naturalism (Richards and Bergin, 2005), and positivism (Slife and Williams, 1995). Indeed, the journal *Counseling and Values* (2008) devoted an entire issue to the topic of the values and assumptions of psychology's scientific methods, which are the hidden roots of some of today's "controversial issues."

The lesson here is that many values and unproven ideas are *inherent* in the system of science itself. Before a method is even formulated, the persons formulating the method must make assumptions about the world in which the method would be successful. The world cannot be known through the method, because the method has not been invented yet. Consequently, the assumptions and values used for its formulation have to be speculations and guesswork to some degree—in short, values and assumptions that are not themselves scientifically proven (Slife, 2008). Again, this does not make science wrong or bad. Indeed, these scientific values and assumptions have made science what it is, including any perceived effectiveness it has.

Still, the perceived effectiveness of the scientific enterprise does not mean that we can forget about these values. They are still unproven values, after all, and as such they can be either problematic or helpful, depending on the context in which they are used. As we described, they may be useful for observable aspects of the world but not so useful for nonobservable aspects of the world. In this sense, there will always be "controversial issues" in any scientific enterprise, hard or soft. Some will be resolved by data, but some will require other means of examination and debate.

Application to the Issues of This Book

The issues of this book are a wide assortment of both types: "empirical questions," which are primarily decided by research, and "philosophical questions," which are primarily decided by discussion and consensus or theoretical examination in relation to disciplinary values. Psychologists typically have the most skills in resolving empirical or research issues. They have been trained since their undergraduate days with multiple courses, such as "research methods" and "statistics," all in support of resolving empirical or research questions.

Psychologists are rarely as adept at philosophical questions, even though these questions pervade the discipline (as we have shown). Indeed, many psychologists may despair at such questions because they associate

philosophy with irresolvable issues—issues that seem interminable. We have sympathy for this attitude, yet we need to be careful not to "throw the baby out with the bathwater." In other words, just because there are seemingly interminable problems in philosophy does not mean that decisions and judgments cannot be made about the philosophical issues of a discipline such as psychology.[1] Many decisions and judgments have, of course, already been made. Otherwise, we would not have a philosophy that guides our science or a set of values that guides our ethics. As the issues of this book indicate, however, not all of these values and assumptions have been decided. Moreover, there is a case to be made that even the decided values should be continually explicated and reevaluated, as new research arenas and topics come to the fore.

Let us close this introduction, then, by pointing explicitly to how such philosophical issues may rear their ugly heads in a discipline such as psychology, and thus in this book. One way to categorize these issues is in terms of the *production* of research and the *outcome* of research. The first involves the many ways in which controversial ideas can enter the conducting of psychological investigations, whereas the second entails the many ways in which controversial ideas can enter the interpretation of a study's data or a program of research.

In the first case, controversial issues can arise when researchers have an allegiance or agenda in formulating and conducting their programs of research. This agenda does not have to be conscious, because loyalties can be influential—political or sociological, theoretical or organizational—whether or not they are known or articulated. They can influence what researchers consider important to study, along with the design, operational and analysis of the study. All these phases of a study, as we have just described, are choice points for researchers that allow for agendas to be revealed and loyalties to be identified. It would thus be important for students of "controversial issues" to try to discern these loyalties and agendas in the production of data. That is the reason there is often no substitute for studying the studies themselves.

Controversial issues can also result from interpretations of the existing data and studies. Perhaps the most striking example of this involves two sets of scholars—each well-trained and each looking at essentially the same data—coming to dramatically different conclusions. First, as we have noted, they can interpret the same data in two different ways (through the *underdetermination* of the data). Second, these interpretive frameworks can also lead researchers to weigh different sets of data differently. Although one set of investigators views certain studies as pivotal, another set considers the same studies deeply problematic, and thus gives them far less weight. In both cases, the interpretive framework of the researchers is part of the reason they "take the side" they do. There is no doubt that the data of the studies are important. Nevertheless, there is also no doubt that the sides taken and the interpretations made are not solely data driven.

Conclusion

The bottom line is that no science can avoid controversial issues. As long as humans are involved *as* scientists, allegiances and biases will be factors. There are just too many choice points for a scientist's ideologies, known or unknown, to seep into the methods employed. Truth be told, human beings are also the inventors and formulators of the methods of science. This means not only that these methods embody the biases and assumptions of the original inventors but also that subsequent changes in the philosophies that guide science will also stem from biased humans. In this sense, we will never be rid of controversial issues. Our job, then, is to expose them, discuss them, and take a well-informed "side" with respect to them.

Note

1. Likewise, we should not "throw out" the achievements of science just because they are not totally objective.

References

Bernstein, R. J. (1983). *Beyond objectivism and relativism.* Philadelphia: University of Pennsylvania Press.

Bhandari, M., et al. (2004). Association between industry fundings and statistically significant pro-industry findings in medical and surgical randomized trials. *Journal of the Canadian Medical Association, 170,* 477–480.

Bohm, D. (1980). *Wholeness and the implicate order.* London: Routledge & Kegan Paul.

Curd, M., & Cover, J. A. (1998). *Philosophy of science: The central issues.* New York: W. W. Norton & Company.

Denzin, N. K., & Lincoln, Y. S. (Eds.). (2000). *Handbook of qualitative methods.* Thousand Oaks, CA: Sage.

Einstein, A. (1961/1990). Relativity: The special and general theory. Translated by Robert W. Larson. In M. Adler (Ed.), *Great books of the Western world.* Chicago: University of Chicago Press.

Freemantle, N., Anderson, I. M., & Young, P. (2000). Predictive value of pharmacological activity for the relative efficacy of antidepressant drugs: Meta-regression analysis. *British Journal of Psychiatry, 177,* 292–302.

Friedberg, M., Saffran, B., Stinson, T. J., Nelson, W., & Bennett, C. L. (1999). Evaluation of conflict of interest in economic analyses of new drugs used in oncology. *Journal of the American Medical Association, 282,* 1453–1457.

Greenberg, R. (2001). Qualms about balms: Perspectives on antidepressants. *Journal of Nervous and Mental Disease, 189*(5), 296–298.

Greenberg, R. P., Bornstein, R. F., Greenberg, M. D., & Fisher, S. (1992). A meta-analysis of antidepressant outcome under "blinder" conditions. *Journal of Consulting & Clinical Psychology, 60,* 664–669.

Healy, D. (1999). The three faces of the antidepressants: A critical commentary on the clinical-economic context of diagnoses. *Journal of Nervous and Mental Disease, 187,* 174–180.

Heiman, G. W. (1995). *Research methods in psychology.* Boston: Houghton-Mifflin.

Heisenberg, W. (1958). *Physics and philosophy: The revolution of modern science.* New York: Harper Books.

Kjaergard, L. L., & Als-Nielson, B. (2002). Association between competing interests and authors' concluions: Epidemiological study of randomised clinical trials published in the BMJ. *British Medical Journal, 325,* 249–253.

Lexchin, J., Bero, L. A., Djulbegovic, B., & Clark, O. (2003). Pharmaceutical industry sponsorship and research outcome and quality: Systematic review. *British Medical Journal, 326,* 1167–1170.

Luborsky, L. B., & Barrett, M. S. (in press). Theoretical allegiance.

Luborsky, L., Diguer, L., Seligman, D. A., Rosenthal, R., Krause, E. D., Johnson, S., Halperin, G., Bishop, M., Berman, J. S., & Schweizer, E. (1999). The researcher's own therapy allegiances: A "wild card" in comparisons of treatment efficacy. *Clinical Psychology: Science and Practice, 6,* 95–132.

Moncrieff, J. (2001). Are antidepressants overrated? A review of methodological problems in antidepressant trials. *The Journal of Nervous and Mental Disease, 189,* 288–295.

Richardson, F. (2005). Psychotherapy and modern dilemmas. In B. Slife, J. Reber, & F. Richardson, (Eds.), *Critical thinking about psychology: Hidden assumptions and plausible alternatives* (pp. 17–38). Washington, DC: American Psychological Association Press.

Richards, P. S., & Bergin, A. E. (2005). *A spiritual strategy for counseling and psychotherapy* (2nd ed.). Washington, DC: American Psychological Association.

Richardson, F., Fowers, B., & Guignon, C. (1999). *Re-envisioning psychology: Moral dimensions of theory and practice.* San Francisco, CA: Jossey-Bass.

Slife, B. D. (2008). A primer of the values implicit in counseling research. *Counseling and Values, 53*(1), 8–21.

Slife, B. D., Reber, J., & Richardson, F. (2005). *Critical thinking about psychology: Hidden assumptions and plausible alternatives.* Washington, DC: American Psychological Association Press.

Slife, B. D., Wiggins, B. J., & Graham, J. T. (2005). Avoiding an EST monopoly: Toward a pluralism of methods and philosophies. *Journal of Contemporary Psychotherapy, 35,* 83–97.

Slife, B. D., & Williams, R. N. (1995). *What's behind the research? Discovering hidden assumptions in the behavioral sciences.* Thousand Oaks, CA: Sage.

Stern, J. M., & Simes, R. J. (1997). Publication bias: Evidence of delayed publication in a cohort study of clinical research projects. *British Medical Journal, 315,* 640–645.

Valenstein, E. S. (1998). *Blaming the brain: The truth about drugs and mental health.* New York: Free Press.

Wolf, F. A. (1981). *Taking the quantum leap.* San Francisco: Harper-Row.

Yanchar, S. (2005). A contextualist alternative to cognitive psychology. In B. Slife, J. Reber, & F. Richardson (Eds.), *Critical thinking about psychology: Hidden assumptions and plausible alternatives* (pp. 171–186). Washington, DC: American Psychological Association Press.

Unit 1

UNIT

Biological Issues

*O*ur biology is obviously a fundamental influence on behavior, one of the most important subject matters of psychology. But can we take biology's influence too far? Is it the basis or determinant for all behaviors, or is there room for personal decision making that is not completely forced by our biology? These are just some of the questions that arise in trying to understand behaviors such as addiction and homosexuality. Do people have a choice about their homosexual or addictive behaviors, or are they forced by their brain chemistry or genes to behave the way they do? Evolutionary theory is a prominent biological approach to explaining not only species changes but also social changes. Could it be another valid approach to understanding the biological influences in such behaviors as addiction and homosexuality?

Selected, Edited and with Issue Framing Material by:
Brent Slife, *Brigham Young University*

ISSUE

Does Learning Change the Structure of the Brain?

YES: R. Douglas Fields, from "Changes in Brain Structure during Learning: Fact or Artifact? Reply to Thomas and Baker," *NeuroImage* (2013)

NO: Cibu Thomas and Chris I. Baker, from "Teaching an Adult Brain New Tricks: A Critical Review of Evidence for Training-Dependent Structural Plasticity in Humans," *NeuroImage* (2013)

Learning Outcomes
After reading this issue, you should be able to:
• Decide if the research designs on neuroplasicity provide reliable data.
• Determine if alternative explanations of data invalidate study results.

ISSUE SUMMARY

YES: R. Douglas Fields, senior investigator at the National Institutes of Health, argues that there is sufficient evidence in the existing literature to support the notion that training and experience can change the structures of the brain.

NO: Cibu Thomas and Chris I. Baker, investigators at the National Institutes of Health, argue that methodological limitations prevent research from supporting the notion that training changes brain structure.

The decorated science columnist Sharon Begley recently reported an important change in the neuroscience literature: "For decades, the prevailing dogma in neuroscience was that the adult human brain is essentially immutable. . . . But research in the past few years has overthrown [this] dogma" (2007). The prevailing dogma that Begley is discussing here is the idea that the brain essentially stays the same once it is fully developed. However, the notion of *neuroplasticity*—the notion that the brain is "plastic" or malleable—tends to violate this dogma because it means the structure of the brain is capable of being reorganized through training and experience.

The notion of neuroplasticity has made possible a host of disciplines outside of neuroscience. New areas of research such as neuroanthropology and cultural neuroscience have recently emerged because they have a common interest in how culture shapes the brain (Chiao, 2009). These and similar emerging fields could also provide valuable information about the possible ramifications of treatments involving the brain. Instead of needing surgery or medication to treat a specific brain disease or disorder, psychotherapy could provide effective treatments that are less invasive with fewer negative side effects. For

example, mental disorders characterized by an inability to self-regulate (i.e., exert self-control) might be treated with certain therapies that are capable of altering areas of the brain related to this behavior, which could affect one's quality of life (e.g., Tang, Lu, Fan, Yang, & Posner, 2012). Yet, as important as neuroplasticity could be, researchers are still debating whether existing research supports this phenomenon and its implications.

In response, the author of the YES selection, R. Douglas Fields, argues that there is ample evidence for neuroplasticity in adults following training exercises. Fields offers a critique of Thomas and Baker's argument in the NO selection and describes what he views as the flaws in their logical argument. He contends that much of their arguments is weak because it relies heavily on the findings of just 1 of the 20 studies in their review. Fields points out that several of their analyses are based on what he considers to be misrepresentations of the methodological practices used in the studies featured in their review. With these and other criticisms, Fields believes that the phenomenon of neuroplasticity cannot be discounted. He concludes, ". . . there is strong evidence, from both animal and human studies, that experience can alter brain structure."

In the NO selection, Cibu Thomas and Chris I. Baker would seem to dispute all the implications of neuroplasticity. They argue that training does not change the structure of the adult brain because the existing research is laden with method limitations. Their argument is based on a review of 20 published studies that are directly related to neuroplasticity in adult populations. They call into question many of the methods used in these studies, including the use of MRI technology, statistic computations, and the use of control groups. They argue that many of these methods have not been used appropriately and that others are inadequate at producing reliable inferences. Based on their critical review, Thomas and Baker conclude, " . . . the current literature on training-dependent plasticity in adult humans does not provide unequivocal evidence for training-dependent structural changes. . . ."

References

Begley, S. (2007, January 19). The brain: How the brain rewires itself. *Time Magazine*. Retrieved from www.time.com/time/magazine/article/0,9171,1580438,00.html

Chiao, J. Y. (2009). Cultural neuroscience: A once and future discipline. *Progress in Brain Research, 178*, 287–304. dio:10.1016/S0079-6123(09)17821-4

Tang, Y., Lu, Q., Fan, M., Yang, Y., and Posner, M. I. (2012). Mechanisms of white matter changes induced by meditation. *Proceedings of the National Academy of Sciences of the United States of America, 109*, 10570–10574. doi:10.1073/pnas.1207817109

POINT

- The research designs of available research fail to provide consistent and reliable data.
- The majority of published studies do not use appropriate statistical analyses.
- Results from existing research can be explained by procedural artifact.
- The relationships between MRI changes and behavioral changes are inconsistent.

COUNTERPOINT

- Thomas and Baker misrepresent the methodology of several studies in their review.
- Statistical methodology is very much dictated by the context of research.
- Alternative explanations of data do not necessarily invalidate the results of a study.
- Assuming that MRI changes must correlate with behavioral changes is a misconception.

YES

R. Douglas Fields

Changes in Brain Structure during Learning: Fact or Artifact? Reply to Thomas and Baker

Introduction

. . . The review by Thomas and Baker (2012) express[es] misgivings about the simple two-sample experimental design and questions the large and diverse body of MRI data using various other experimental designs that find structural changes in the human brain after training. The thrust of the argument is that the studies showing structural changes in the human brain after training are unsound because MRI methodology lacks sufficient precision to detect the small changes produced relative to the experimental noise and errors introduced by procedures of analysis, and in their view, the authors of studies reporting positive findings have not designed their experiments correctly or analyzed their data with appropriate statistical methods. . . .

Proof by Consensus

A deep fault underlying the approach taken in this review is the "appeal to the majority" flawed logic that is applied. . . .

A faulty study does not invalidate the finding of a well-constructed study. Glossing over or mixing together such important differences among studies as the study objectives, experimental design, type of learning task involved, duration of training, age of subjects, time-points of analysis, measurement methods, replication, etc., makes cross-comparisons ambiguous.

The authors adopt the terminology of statistics, "robustness, strength, power, rigor, correlation, signal-to-noise, proof," but they use the words in the vernacular sense, rendering the arguments rhetorical and ambiguous. Statistics do not "prove" a hypothesis. Logic dictates that the only conclusion possible from a statistical analysis arises when the data disprove a hypothesis; typically that there is no difference between two or more sampled populations. The statistical analysis defines the probability that the differences in measurements obtained by sampling could have occurred by chance. A study that fails to reject the null hypothesis, e.g., Thomas et al. (2009), does not lead to any conclusion, other than a difference could not be detected. This outcome does not invalidate the conclusions of other studies that succeed. . . .

Favoring Type II Errors

The criticism in their review is a warning about the perils of committing a type I error (concluding a difference exists when there is none), and it offers detailed suggestions about how to design experiments to reduce type I errors in MRI studies of learning, but this well-intentioned and useful advice about reducing noise, dealing with small signals, how to design control groups, how much replication is necessary, the sensitivity and precision of the instruments, random errors and sources of systematic errors, artifacts, signal-to-noise issues, and covariance with other factors, is not pertinent. A false positive (type I error) is just as wrong as a false negative (type II error). The consequences of either error depend on context, and the threshold of committing a type I or type II error is controlled by setting the criterion probability value accepted for significance. Using a $p < 0.001$ will increase the likelihood of committing a type II error (false negative); using a $p < 0.05$ will increase the likelihood of committing a type I error (a false positive). This will obtain regardless of the experimental design or measurement method. Indeed, these conclusions are mathematically defined clear interpretations regardless of what experiments were performed, equipment used, or hypothesis that motivated the data sampling that generated the numbers.

Bias and Uncontrolled Variables and Measurement Error

That experimental data collection can be undermined by bias or subject to systematic errors is well appreciated. Certainly alternative interpretations for differences found to be statistically significant are always possible and important to consider, but this alternative interpretation is resolved by additional experiments to test a new specific hypothesis—either with new data or by reanalyzing the data sorted according to the new factor under consideration—not by the approach taken in their review. The criticism that differences between controls and experimental conditions may reflect more head motion in the controls because these subjects were less motivated than the experimental subjects, for example, is not a basis for rejecting the statistically defined difference between groups. Rather it requires accepting that the difference found by the experiment cannot be due to chance, but instead posits an alternative interpretation for the difference, which is testable. Unless the alternative factor can be identified in the experiment and eliminated, or the factor is examined separately in a different experiment, attacking studies on this basis is condemnation by innuendo.

> "... the changes in FA reported in participants who took part in integrative body-mind training rather than relaxation therapy ... could in principle arise from physiological changes (e.g. cardiac or respiration) induced in one of the groups following the training, rather than the specific meditation technique (p. 7)."

This alternative hypothesis could be tested experimentally, but without doing so this argument begs the question in rejecting the results of the original findings. . . .

If experimental errors and artifacts are distributed randomly, the finding of a statistically significant difference between groups justifies rejecting the null hypothesis. If these errors are not distributed randomly or biases influence the data collection or analysis, then the fundamental assumptions of any statistical analysis (or any experiment) are violated and no conclusion is possible. However, unless these assumptions are shown to have been violated, the results cannot be rejected by criticism that such things are possible.

Controls

> "Despite the importance of collecting control data, four of the 19 studies we identified did not include any control condition . . . making it impossible to assess the training-dependence of any reported effects (p. 4)."

This statement is not correct. These four studies used a repeated measures design in which changes were monitored in each individual after training, so that each subject was its own control, much as blood pressure changes might be measured in a person before and after taking medication for hypertension. Many of these studies said to lack a control also used correlation analysis showing strong and highly significant changes in MRI data with training and performance.

Correlation Between Behavioral Changes and Brain Structure

The authors would require that accepting the conclusion that structural changes in the brain accompany learning requires that behavioral measures of learning are also included in the study and found to correlate with the MRI changes. This thinking is a broken syllogism that fails to recognize the difference between necessity and sufficiency. There are many reasons to expect that behavioral measures (improved performance) might not require

structural changes or that such a correlation with MRI might not be found. Many factors are involved in performance of a complex task. Some are necessary but not sufficient for performance, and the same is likely to be the case for structural changes in the brain. Secondly, it is not clear which behavioral measure should correlate with a structural change observed—performance peak, speed of learning, amount of improvement, accuracy, practice time or specific aspects of the skill. Third, there are technical and biological reasons why MRI changes are seen in different brain regions at different times and ages, and associated with different aspects of tasks. Such correlations, or lack of them, are interesting and important questions in the field of learning, but this is a different issue from whether or not the MRI data are a measurement artifact.

The authors argue that the structural changes detected by MRI must be "specific to a given task not a general effect of any training (p. 4)." However, different parts of the brain are engaged at different times and for different purposes, and likely develop differently in people depending on their prior skill and learning strategy. Spatial information is moved from the hippocampus to the neocortex during slow wave sleep, for example. The cerebellum is involved in learning and in many other brain functions beyond motor control. As individuals develop specific skills the task becomes more automated and the cognitive process engages cortical regions to different extents or in different regions than when the task was a new challenge. These are questions at the forefront of information processing and learning, which MRI studies of human learning together with fMRI are beginning to answer. To presume the answers to these questions and then use them as a premise for testing the conclusion that structural changes in the brain accompany learning begs the question.

Conclusion

The review advances an opinion on an important subject that has been widely reviewed (Draganski and May, 2008; Fields, 2011; May, 2011; Zatorre et al., 2012), but the approach taken cannot lead to a certain conclusion, and the thesis advanced is undermined by internal inconsistency. . . .

Skepticism is vital in science. Publication bias toward positive results is appropriate and necessary because negative findings provide no logical conclusion. If through experimental bias incorrect results get published, as in the memory transfer experiments of the 1960s, they will be repudiated eventually (e.g., Luttges et al., 1966); this is the normal and healthy way that science should proceed. The future will no doubt find some studies in the field of brain imaging and learning flawed or wrong, but it is experimental data and adherence to the logic of the scientific method of hypothesis testing that brings answers. This holds whether using an MRI machine or a balance to investigate how experience alters brain structure.

References

Draganski, B., May, A, 2008. Training-induced structural changes in the adult human brain. Behav. Brain Res. 192, 137–142.

Fields, R.D., 2011. Imaging learning: the search for a memory trace. Neuroscientist 17, 185–196.

Luttges, M., Johnson, T., Buck, C., Holland, J., McGaugh, J., 1966. An examination of "transfer of learning" by nucleic acid. Science 151, 834–837.

May, A., 2011. Experience-dependent structural plasticity in the adult human brain. Trends Cogn. Sci. 15, 475–482.

Thomas, C., Baker, C.I., 2012. Teaching an adult brain new tricks: a critical review of evidence for training-dependent structural plasticity in humans. NeuroImage. (this issue).

Thomas, A.G., Marrett, S., Saad, Z.S., Ruff, D.A., Martin, A., Bandettini, P.A., 2009. Functional but not structural changes associated with learning: an exploration of longitudinal voxel-based morphometry (VBM). Neuroimage 48, 117–125.

Zatorre, R.J., Fields, R.D., Johansen-Berg, H., 2012. Plasticity in gray and white: neuroimaging changes in brain structure during learning. Nat. Neurosci. 15, 528–536.

R. DOUGLAS FIELDS is currently a senior investigator at the National Institutes of Health. He holds several leadership positions including head of the Neurocytology and Physiology Unit, NICHD, chief of the Nervous System Development and Plasticity Section, NICHD, and editor-in-chief of the journal *Neuron Glia Biology*. A primary focus of his lab at NIH is aimed at understanding how the brain and it structures develop through experience. He received his PhD from the University of California, San Diego.

Cibu Thomas and Chris I. Baker    **NO**

Teaching an Adult Brain New Tricks: A Critical Review of Evidence for Training-Dependent Structural Plasticity in Humans

Introduction

The relationship between brain structure and function has gained recent prominence in human neuroimaging. Studies have reported correlations between behavioral performance and localized brain structure (for a recent review, see Kanai and Rees, 2011) and have also identified possible training-dependent changes in structure (e.g. changes in measures of gray matter density or white matter integrity). Evidence for effects of training comes from both cross-sectional studies, comparing different groups of subjects with different experiences (e.g. musicians *versus* non-musicians (Bengtsson et al., 2005) or taxi *versus* bus drivers (Maguire et al., 2006)), as well as longitudinal studies, examining the effect of training over time in individuals (for a review see, Draganski and May, 2008; May and Gaser, 2006). . . .

Such MRI evidence for adult structural plasticity seems consistent with animal studies of experience-dependent plasticity (Draganski and May, 2008) and based on this apparent convergence, it has been proposed that changes in the MRI signal may reflect changes in axonal myelination, neurogenesis, angiogenesis, dendritic spine motility, glial cell proliferation, and synaptogenesis (Draganski and May, 2008; Scholz et al., 2009). However, while animal studies do suggest that experience-dependent structural plasticity in the adult brain persists throughout the life span (Fu and Zuo, 2011), it is highly constrained. . . .

Taking into account these considerations, we conducted a critical review of the evidence from all longitudinal studies of training-dependent structural plasticity in adult humans. . . .

Measuring Training-Dependent Structural Changes

. . . The most common techniques used in these studies to measure longitudinal structural changes are voxel-based morphometry (VBM) (Ashburner and Friston, 2000) and diffusion tensor imaging (DTI) (Basser et al., 1994). VBM is a whole-brain, automatic technique that enables voxel-wise statistical comparison of local gray matter volume (GMV) or gray matter density (GMD) between groups or time-points. . . . DTI is used specifically to detect differences in white matter microstructure. . . .

As with any MRI measure, the raw data from structural MRI scans reflect both the true underlying signal and noise. Further, the raw data are subjected to several stages of processing to remove potential artifacts and enable valid statistical inference (Ashburner and Friston, 2000; Pierpaoli, 2011), and the final outcome is far removed from the original data. At each stage, small biases can be inadvertently introduced in the processing pipeline, which can give rise to false positives (Jones et al., 2005; Thomas et al., 2009) and make it difficult to detect small changes in brain structure (Klauschen et al., 2009). . . .

Specificity

Training

Given the measurement error inherent even in structural imaging scans and the extensive pre-processing typically involved in assessing changes in brain structure, it is important to take into account the reliability of the structural measures used to assess the impact of training. Typically, this is done by collecting control data in the absence of the specific training protocol, often in a separate group of subjects. Such a control group is particularly important when studying older adults where there may be changes in structural properties over time in the absence of any training. Training-dependent structural plasticity is then evidenced by any MRI measurement that shows an interaction between group (training *versus* control) and time-point (pre- *versus* post-training), that is a larger difference between the two groups post- compared with pre-training. Despite the importance of collecting control data, four of the 20 studies we identified did not include any control condition (Driemeyer et al., 2008; Kwok et al., 2011; Landi et al., 2011; Takeuchi et al., 2010), making it impossible to assess the training-dependence of any reported effects. . . .

Thomas, Cibu; Baker, Chris I. From *NeuroImage*, vol. 73, June 2013, pp. 225–236 (Edited). Copyright © 2013 by Elsevier Health Sciences. Reprinted by permission via Rightslink.

Overall, the bulk of the evidence reporting training-dependent structural changes in adults does not appear to contain rigorous statistical evidence for specificity to training and the results should be interpreted with caution. In only five studies (Colcombe et al., 2006; Engvig et al., 2010, 2011; Erickson et al., 2011a; Schmidt-Wilcke et al., 2010) could we find any indication that the appropriate statistical tests to identify training-related structural changes were conducted. It is also worth noting that the study that employed a powerful within-subject control found no evidence for training-related structural plasticity (Thomas et al., 2009).

Task

While comparison of a trained group with an untrained group can provide evidence for specificity to training, the strongest test is to compare two groups who have been trained on different tasks and show that the changes are specific to a given task and not a general effect of any training. Such a comparison also makes it possible to determine what aspects of any given task are critical for inducing structural changes. Absence of a training task for the control group also raises an additional concern about the matching of the two groups of subjects. . . .

Among the 15 studies that included a control group/condition, only 3 employed a separate training task in the control condition. In two studies (Colcombe et al., 2006; Erickson et al., 2011a), the effect of aerobics exercise was investigated by comparing an aerobics group with an age-matched control group that practiced stretching exercises for the same training duration. Likewise, Tang et al. (2010) assigned different meditation techniques to the training and the control group and tested whether a specific type of meditation technique can induce significant structural changes. . . .

Replicability

Three-ball juggling has been used as the training task in four separate studies (see Table 1) allowing us to evaluate the replicability, of the structural changes reported. In the first of these studies, Draganski et al. (2004) reported changes in GMD bilaterally in the middle temporal region (visual motion area hMT/V5—although hMT was not functionally localized in this or later studies) and near the left posterior intra-parietal sulcus (IPS). Further, the increases observed with training over 3 months declined over the following 3 months without practice. However, as is evident from subsequent studies from the same research group showed limited replication of the location of the initially reported training-related peak changes (Thomas and Baker, 2012) and additionally revealed several regions not directly associated with processing visual motion including nucleus accumbens, hippocampus, as well as frontal and cingulate cortex. . . .

Overall, across all the studies that have reported training-dependent structural changes, there is limited evidence for replicability, the most fundamental criterion for the robustness of an effect. While the weak replicability across the juggling studies could in principle reflect real differences, it is important to take into account the concerns about the robustness of the statistical analyses in these studies described above.

Correlation with Behavior

Individual variations in GMD and white matter integrity have been reported to account for variance in behavioral measures (for a review, see Kanai and Rees, 2011). If the reported structural changes are the direct result of training, it seems reasonable to suppose that the change in structure should correlate with some measure of training behavior. Such a correlation is not necessary to conclude training-dependent structural changes but would significantly bolster support for this conclusion, and has been reported in some animal studies. . . .

While the original juggling study (Draganski et al., 2004) reported a close relationship between structural changes and juggling performance, no data or statistics were provided to support this assertion. Further, none of the later juggling studies found any significant correlation between change in brain structure and improvement in juggling performance (Boyke et al., 2008; Driemeyer et al., 2008; Scholz et al., 2009). A similar lack of correlation between behavioral and structural change was reported in three other studies using a range of different training tasks (Draganski et al., 2006; Lövdén et al., 2010; Schmidt-Wilcke et al., 2010). However, such negative results could simply reflect the fact that it is unclear which behavioral measure should correlate with the structural change (e.g. absolute performance at the end of training, relative task improvement, amount of practice). . . .

Robustness of Evidence

. . . Out of 20 studies, only one (Erickson et al., 2011a) demonstrates effects that are specific to training, task and brain region, with a significant correlation with behavioral performance (but see, Coen et al., 2011; Erickson et al., 2011b). Specifically, anterior, but not posterior, hippocampal volume was found to increase in elderly subjects trained to perform aerobic exercise compared with subjects performing stretching exercises. Further, the changes in hippocampal volume correlated with improvements in a spatial memory task. However, replication of this result would provide the strongest support for structural changes. While this study provides strong evidence for structural plasticity, the pre-defined ROI approach is limited by the focus on specific regions (Friston et al., 2006) (but see, Saxe et al., 2006) and does not capitalize on the ability to image the whole brain with MRI (but see, Colcombe et al., 2006). . . .

Table 1

Details of the Twenty Longitudinal Studies That Tested for Training-Related Structural Plasticity in the Adult Human Brain Using MRI Methods. The Studies Are Arranged in Chronological Order (# Approximate Mean Age of the Training Group, * Young Group, ^ Elderly Group).

Study	Method	Control condition	Sample		Mean age # (~years)	Task		Training duration (~days)
			Training	Control		Training	Control	
Draganski et al., 2004	VBM	Between subjects	12	12	22	Juggling	None	90
Colcombe et al., 2006	VBM	Between subjects	30	29	66	Aerobics	Stretching	120
Draganski et al., 2006	VBM	Between subjects	38	12	24	Learning abstract information	None	90
Boyke et al., 2008	VBM	Between subjects	25	25	60	Juggling	None	90
Ilg et al., 2008	VBM	Between subjects	18	18	24	Reading mirrored words	None	14
Driemeyer et al., 2008	VBM	None	20	None	27	Juggling	None	7
Thomas et al., 2009	VBM	Within subjects	12	12	33	Visuo-motor	None	14
Scholz et al., 2009	VBM and DTI	Between subjects	24	24	25	Juggling	None	45
Tang et al., 2010	VBM and DTI	Between subjects	22	23	21	Integrative body mind therapy	Relaxation therapy	30
Taubert et al., 2010	VBM and DTI	Between subjects	14	14	26	Whole body dynamic balancing	None	30
Schmidt-Wilcke et al., 2010	VBM	Between subjects	16	15	26	Decipher Morse code	None	120
Takeuchi et al., 2010	VBM and DTI	None	11	None	22	Working memory	None	60
Lövdén et al., 2010	DTI and volume analysis	Between subjects	32	23	25*, 69^	Working memory	None	101
Engvig et al., 2010	Cortical thickness	Between subjects	22	20	62	Memory	None	56
Erickson et al., 2011a	Volume analysis	Between subjects	60	60	67	Aerobics	Stretching	365
Kwok et al., 2011	VBM	None	19	None	20	Learning color names	None	3
Landi et al., 2011	VBM and DTI	None	12	None	26	Visuo-motor tracking	None	7
Bezzola et al., 2011	VBM	Between subjects	12	12	51	Golf	None	40
Engvig et al., 2011	DTI	Between subjects	21	20	62	Memory	None	56
Woollett and Maguire, 2011	VBM	Between subjects	39	31	38	Spatial memory	None	1095

Challenges in MRI Based Structural Imaging

Signal-to-Noise

The MR signal, which forms the basis for the structural images of the brain, is corrupted by various sources of noise that originate from the scanner (e.g. signal dropouts, eddy current distortions, susceptibility artifacts) or the subject (e.g. head motion, cardiac pulsation, respiration). These artifacts have a greater impact on DTI-based analysis (Basser and Jones, 2002; Pierpaoli, 2011) compared with VBM-based analysis because a reduction in SNR in diffusion MRI scan results in an artifactual increase in tensor-derived measures like FA (Farrell et al., 2007; Pierpaoli and Basser, 1996), the most widely used measure of microstructural integrity of white matter.

In the seven DTI studies we reviewed here, nearly all corrected for both head motion and eddy current distortions, although one study appeared to have corrected for head motion only (Taubert et al., 2010), and one did not report performing any corrections (Takeuchi et al., 2010). Importantly, none of the studies employed the correction techniques necessary for reducing the impact of physiological artifacts such as cardiac pulsation (Pierpaoli et al., 2003), which has been reported to cause significant artifactual changes in FA in several brain regions. Such outlier data points can be identified and removed from further analysis (Chang et al., 2005; Mangin et al., 2002). If not, they can manifest as significant group differences (Walker et al., 2011) that are unrelated to the experimental manipulation. For example, the changes in FA reported in participants who took part in integrative body-mind training rather than relaxation therapy (Tang et al., 2010) could in principle arise from physiological changes (e.g. cardiac or respiration) induced in one of the groups following the training, rather than the specific meditation technique. . . .

Conclusion

Based on our review of the literature and the limitations of MRI-based measures of structure, we conclude that the current literature on training-dependent plasticity in adult humans does not provide unequivocal evidence for training-dependent structural changes and more rigorous experimentation and statistical testing is required. . . .

Despite the numerous limitations of the studies reviewed here, we do not mean to suggest that the training protocols used in the human studies do not induce structural changes in the adult brain, nor do we mean to imply that MRI cannot be used to detect training-dependent structural changes in the adult brain. . . .

The challenge moving forward is to address the limitations of the existing studies and present the strongest possible evidence for training-dependent structural plasticity in the adult human brain. . . .

References

Ashburner, J., Friston, K.J., 2000. Voxel-based morphometry—the methods. NeuroImage 11, 805–821.

Basser, P.J., Jones, D.K., 2002. Diffusion tensor MRI: theory, experimental design and data analysis—a technical review. NMR Biomed. 15, 456–467.

Basser, P.J., Pierpaoli, C., 1996. Microstructural and physiological features of tissues elucidated by quantitative-diffusion-tensor MRI. J Magn Reson B 111, 209–219.

Bengtsson, S., Nagy, Z., Skare, S., Forsman, L., Forssberg, H., Ullén, F., 2005. Extensive piano practicing has regionally specific effects on white matter development. Nat. Neurosci. 8, 1148–1150.

Bezzola, L., Merillat, S., Gaser, C., Jäncke, L., 2011. Training-induced neural plasticity in golf novices. J. Neurosci. 31, 12444–12448.

Boyke, J., Driemeyer, J., Gaser, C., Buchel, C., May, A., 2008. Training-induced brain structure changes in the elderly. J. Neurosci. 28, 7031–7035.

Chang, L.C., Jones, D.K., Pierpaoli, C., 2005. RESTORE: robust estimation of tensors by outlier rejection. Magn. Reson. Med. 53, 1088–1095.

Coen, R.F., Lawlor, B.A., Kenny, R.A., 2011. Failure to demonstrate that memory improvement is due either to aerobic exercise or increased hippocampal volume. Proc. Natl. Acad. Sci. 108, E89.

Colcombe, S.J., Erickson, K.I., Scalf, P.E., Kim, J.S., Prakash, R., McAuley, E., Elavsky, S., Marquez, D.X., Hu, L., Kramer, A.F., 2006. Aerobic exercise training increases brain volume in aging humans. J. Gerontol. A Biol. Sci. Med. Sci. 61, 1166–1170.

Draganski, B., May, A., 2008. Training-induced structural changes in the adult human brain. Behav. Brain Res. 192, 137–142.

Draganski, B., Gaser, C., Busch, V., Schuierer, G., Bogdahn, U., May, A., 2004. Neuroplasticity: changes in grey matter induced by training. Nature 427, 311–312.

Draganski, B., Gaser, C., Kempermann, G., Kuhn, H., Winkler, J., Buchel, C., May, A., 2006. Temporal and spatial dynamics of brain structure changes during extensive learning. J. Neurosci. 26, 6314–6317.

Driemeyer, J., Boyke, J., Gaser, C., Büchel, C., May, A., 2008. Changes in gray matter induced by learning—revisited. PLoS One 3, e2669.

Engvig, A., Fjell, A.M., Westlye, L.T., Moberget, T., Sundseth, O., Larsen, V.A., Walhovd, K.B., 2010. Effects of memory training on cortical thickness in the elderly. NeuroImage 52, 1667–1676.

Engvig, A., Fjell, A.M., Westlye, L.T., Moberget, T., Sundseth, Y., Larsen, V.A., Walhovd, K.B., 2011. Memory training impacts short term changes in aging white matter: a longitudinal diffusion tensor imaging study. Hum. Brain Mapp. 32, 11–12.

Erickson, K.I., Voss, M.W., Prakash, R.S., Basak, C., Szabo, A., Chaddock, L., Kim, J.S., Heo, S., Alves, H., White, S.M., 2011a. Exercise training increases size of hippocampus and improves memory. Proc. Natl. Acad. Sci. U. S. A. 108, 3017–3022.

Erickson, K., Voss, M., Prakash, R., Basak, C., Szabo, A., Chaddock, L., White, S., Wojcicki, T., Mailey, E., McAuley, E., 2011b. Reply to Coen et al.: exercise, hippocampal volume, and memory. Proc. Natl. Acad. Sci. 108, E90.

Farrell, J.A.D., Landman, B.A., Jones, C.K., Smith, S.A., Prince, J.L., van Zijl, P., Mori, S., 2007. Effects of signal-to-noise ratio on the accuracy and reproducibility of diffusion tensor imaging-derived fractional anisotropy, mean diffusivity, and principal eigenvector measurements at 1.5 T. J. Magn. Reson. Imaging 26, 756–767.

Friston, K., Rotshtein, P., Geng, J., Sterzer, P., Henson, R., 2006. A critique of functional localisers. NeuroImage 30, 1077–1087.

Fu, M., Zuo, Y., 2011. Experience-dependent structural plasticity in the cortex. Trends Neurosci. 34, 177–187.

Ilg, R., Wohlschlager, A.M., Gaser, C., Liebau, Y., Dauner, R., Woller, A., Zimmer, C., Zihl, J., Muhlau, M., 2008. Gray matter increase induced by practice correlates with task-specific activation: a combined functional and morphometric magnetic resonance imaging study. J. Neurosci. 28, 4210–4215.

Kanai, R., Rees, G., 2011. The structural basis of interindividual differences in human behaviour and cognition. Nat. Rev. Neurosci. 12, 231–242.

Klauschen, F., Goldman, A., Barra, V., Meyer Lindenberg, A., Lundervold, A., 2009. Evaluation of automated brain MR image segmentation and volumetry methods. Hum. Brain Mapp. 30, 1310–1327.

Kwok, V., Niu, Z., Kay, P., Zhou, K., Mo, L., Jin, Z., So, K.F., Tan, L.H., 2011. Learning new color names produces rapid increase in gray matter in the intact adult human cortex. Proc. Natl. Acad. Sci. U. S. A. 108, 6686–6688.

Landi, S.M., Baguear, F., Della-Maggiore, V., 2011. One week of motor adaptation induces structural changes in primary motor cortex that predict long-term memory one year later. J. Neurosci. 31, 11808–11813.

Lövdén, M., Bodammer, N.C., Kühn, S., Kaufmann, J., Schütze, H., Tempelmann, C., Heinze, H.J., Düzel, E., Schmiedek, F., 2010. Experience-dependent plasticity of white-matter microstructure extends into old age. Neuropsychologia 48, 3878–3883.

Maguire, E., Woollett, K., Spiers, H., 2006. London taxi drivers and bus drivers: a structural MRI and neuropsychological analysis. Hippocampus 16, 1091–1101.

Mangin, J.F., Poupon, C., Clark, C., Le Bihan, D., Bloch, I., 2002. Distortion correction and robust tensor estimation for MR diffusion imaging. Med. Image Anal. 6, 191–198.

May, A., Gaser, C., 2006. Magnetic resonance-based morphometry: a window into structural plasticity of the brain. Curr. Opin. Neurol. 19, 407–411.

Pierpaoli, C., 2011. Artifacts in Diffusion MRI. Diffusion MRI Oxford Publications, pp. 303–318.

Pierpaoli, C., Basser, P.J., 1996. Toward a quantitative assessment of diffusion anisotropy. Magn. Reson. Med. 36, 893–906.

Pierpaoli, C., Marenco, S., Rohde, G.K., Jones, D.K., Barnett, A., 2003. Analyzing the contribution of cardiac pulsation to the variability of quantities derived from the diffusion tensor. Proc. Int. Soc. Magn. Reson. Med. 11, 70.

Saxe, R., Brett, M., Kanwisher, N., 2006. Divide and conquer: a defense of functional localizers. NeuroImage 30, 1088–1096.

Schmidt-Wilcke, T., Rosengarth, K., Luerding, R., Bogdahn, U., Greenlee, M., 2010. Distinct patterns of functional and structural neuroplasticity associated with learning Morse code. NeuroImage 51, 1234–1241.

Scholz, J., Klein, M., Behrens, T., Johansen-Berg, H., 2009. Training induces changes in white-matter architecture. Nat. Neurosci. 12, 1370–1371.

Takeuchi, H., Sekiguchi, A., Taki, Y., Yokoyama, S., Yomogida, Y., Komuro, N., Yamanouchi, T., Suzuki, S., Kawashima, R., 2010. Training of working memory impacts structural connectivity. J. Neurosci. 30, 3297–3303.

Tang, Y., Lu, Q., Geng, X., Stein, E., Yang, Y., Posner, M., 2010. Short-term meditation induces white matter changes in the anterior cingulate. Proc. Natl. Acad. Sci. U. S. A. 107, 15649–15652.

Taubert, M., Draganski, B., Anwander, A., Muller, K., Horstmann, A., Villringer, A., Ragert, P., 2010. Dynamic properties of human brain structure: learning-related changes in cortical areas and associated fiber connections. J. Neurosci. 30, 11670–11677.

Thomas, C., Baker, C.I., 2012. Remodeling human cortex through training: comment on May. Trends Cogn. Sci. 16, 96–97.

Thomas, A., Marrett, S., Saad, Z., Ruff, D., Martin, A., Bandettini, P., 2009. Functional but not structural changes associated with learning: an exploration of longitudinal voxel-based morphometry (VBM). NeuroImage 48, 117–125.

Walker, L., Chang, L.C., Koay, C.G., Sharma, N., Cohen, L., Verma, R., Pierpaoli, C., 2011. Effects of physiological noise in population analysis of diffusion tensor MRI data. NeuroImage 54, 1168–1177.

Woollett, K., Maguire, E.A., 2011. Acquiring "the knowledge" of London's layout drives structural brain changes. Curr. Biol. 21, 2109–2114.

CIBU THOMAS is a postdoctoral research fellow at the Center for Neuroscience and Regenerative Medicine and National Institutes of Health. His research focuses on the practical applications of functional MRI, developmental neurobiology, as well as neuroplasticity. He has served as an ad hoc reviewer for several journals including *Neuron*. He received his PhD from Carnegie Mellon University and Center for the Neural Basis of Cognition.

CHRIS I. BAKER is an investigator at the National Institutes of Health. He currently serves as a principal investigator in the Laboratory of Brain and Cognition, NIMH. His research focuses on the neural mechanisms of object recognition and the structural plasticity of the cortex following experience. He received his PhD from the University of St. Andrews.

EXPLORING THE ISSUE

Does Learning Change the Structure of the Brain?

Critical Thinking and Reflection

1. A major argument put forth by Thomas and Baker concerns the inconsistent evidence for a positive relationship between MRI changes and behavioral changes. Discuss whether or not this data is necessary to assess the issue of neuroplasticity.
2. Discuss the extent to which you agree with Fields' argument that Thomas and Baker do not accurately represent the existing literature.
3. What do Thomas and Baker suggest as a way to reduce bias in research design?
4. Choose a discipline of study not mentioned in the current selections and discuss the implications that neuroplasticity might have for it. Consider, for example, the emerging field of neuroanthropology as mentioned in the introduction.
5. State your position on this topic prior to reading this issue, and then state your position following your reading of this issue. Discuss how the arguments presented by the authors either successfully or unsuccessfully changed your position.

Create Central

www.mhhe.com/createcentral

Additional Resource

Kolb, B., and Gibb, R. (2010). Brain plasticity and behavior in the developing brain. *Journal of Canadian Academy of Child and Adolescent Psychiatry, 20* (4), 265–276. Retrieved from ww.ncbi.nlm.nih.gov/pmc/articles/PMC3222570/?report=classic

Internet References . . .

National Institutes of Health: Neuroplasticity

www.nichd.nih.gov/about/overview/50th/discoveries/Pages/neuroplasticity.aspx

Michael Merzenich: Growing Evidence of Brain Plasticity

www.ted.com/talks/michael_merzenich_on_the_elastic_brain.html

Selected, Edited and with Issue Framing Material by:
Brent Slife, *Brigham Young University*

ISSUE

Is Evolution a Good Explanation
for Psychological Concepts?

YES: **Glenn Geher,** from "Evolutionary Psychology Is Not Evil! (. . . and Here's Why . . .)," *Psychological Topics* (December 2006)

NO: **Edwin E. Gantt and Brent S. Melling,** from "Evolutionary Psychology Isn't Evil, It's Just Not Any Good" (An Original Essay Written for This Volume, 2009)

Learning Outcomes

After reading this issue, you should be able to:

- Evaluate the extent to which unreasonable bias against evolutionary psychology may or may not be present.
- Determine if evolutionary psychology needs to account for all aspects of psychology.

ISSUE SUMMARY

YES: Evolutionary psychologist Glenn Geher maintains that evolution provides the best meta-theory for explaining and understanding human psychology.

NO: Theoretical psychologists Edwin Gantt and Brent Melling argue that an evolutionary account of psychology omits many important and good things about humans.

Given the widespread success of evolutionary explanations in biology, many psychologists have suggested that these explanations can adequately and powerfully explain psychological and social behavior. Evolutionary psychology (EP) has become an increasingly recognized field, with numerous programs and institutes dedicated to researching its explanations. However, EP is not without its critics. Going beyond methodological issues those who are uncomfortable with EP argue that its philosophical assumptions ultimately deny important aspects of humanity, such as morality and personal responsibility. In response, evolutionary psychologists often observe that "evolution is not evil. . . ."

There's little argument that evolutionary explanations have been useful, and not "evil," in the biological sciences. Still, there is considerable debate about whether such an explanation can account for all facets of human experience and behavior. Can it explain, for example, the human sense of morality? Some scholars have held that morality itself is evolutionarily derived, with our own innate sense of rightness and goodness evolved from what is evolutionarily effective and efficient. On the other hand, critics argue that such a stance confuses morality

with biology and that morality involves much more than can be explained by biological mechanisms.

The author of the first article, Glenn Geher, disagrees. As the director of the Evolutionary Studies Program at the State University of New York at New Paltz, he argues that the best way to understand all psychological phenomena is to borrow evolutionary explanations from the biological sciences. EP makes the "modest" claim, according to Geher, that "minds are on the same footing as bodies where . . . natural selection is concerned." He maintains that evolutionary explanations do no harm, because they do not deny important human meanings or morality. Critics who see EP as "sexist, racist, [or] eugenicist" are misinformed about the point of EP. Evolutionary psychology merely tries to explain human behavior, not prescribe what humans *should* do.

Psychological researchers Edwin Gantt and Brent Melling argue that evolutionary psychology is not as innocent as it seems and, in fact, has major negative implications for the study of human behavior. They suggest that EP has a number of implicit biases that distort the world of human meaning but are rarely discussed in the EP literature. Despite claims to the contrary, for example, Gantt and Melling argue that EP presumes humans have no real choices about their behaviors, and thus no personal responsibility for them. For this reason and others, Gantt and Melling prompt caution in wholeheartedly accepting the latest scientific "facts" of EP. They note, instead, that scientific history is littered with "obvious facts that are later found to be not only questionable but on occasion outright false and misleading" (e.g., phlogiston, phrenology). Gantt and Melling conclude that such misleading facts and assumptions ultimately undermine the efforts of evolutionary psychologists to promote neutrality and morality.

POINT

- Critics have unreasonable or outmoded biases against evolutionary psychology (EP).
- EP research is objective and shows the world as it is.

- Evolutionary psychology is not evil.
- EP is a powerful tool for understanding all aspects of psychology.

COUNTERPOINT

- Rational, thoughtful individuals can have serious issues with evolutionary psychology (EP).
- EP has implicit biases that skew how researchers understand their data.
- EP denies the possibility of good or evil.
- EP cannot account for many important aspects of human psychology.

YES

Glenn Geher

Evolutionary Psychology Is Not Evil!
(. . . and Here's Why . . .)

Abstract

Evolutionary psychology has faced 'implacable hostility' (Dawkins, 2005) from a number of intellectual fronts. Critics of evolutionary psychology have tried to paint this perspective variously as reductionist and overly deterministic, at best, and as sexist, racist, and downright evil at worst. The current paper argues that all psychological frameworks which assume that human beings are the result of the organic evolutionary forces of natural and sexual selection are, essentially, evolutionary in nature (regardless of whether they traditionally fall under the label of evolutionary psychology). In other words, the perspective presented here argues that all psychology is evolutionary psychology. Two specific mis-characterizations of evolutionary psychology ((a) that it is eugenicist in nature and (b) that it is a fully non-situationist, immutable perspective on behavior) are addressed here with an eye toward elaborating on how these distorted conceptions of evolutionary psychology are non-constructive and non-progressive. A final section focuses on how the social sciences in general could benefit from being evolutionized.

"Evolutionary psychology (is) . . . subject to a level of implacable hostility which seems far out of proportion to anything even sober reason or common politeness might sanction."

If you are a modern scholar of human behavior who uses evolutionary theory to help guide your research and, accordingly, label yourself an evolutionary psychologist (as I do), you may find Dawkins' aforementioned quote as capturing the essence of how evolutionary psychology (EP) is perceived in many modern academic circles. In fact, based on my experiences, this quote captures the current state of affairs regarding EP in the broader landscape of academia in general so well that it is actually a bit unsettling.

Worded another way, this implacable hostility seems to result from scholars across disparate disciplines who conceptualize EP as downright evil. EP is often framed as evil by all sorts of people for all sorts of reasons. In terms of purely academic critiques, EP is often framed as overly deterministic and reductionistic while social critics of EP with more applied concerns paint EP as a sexist, racist, and even eugenicist doctrine designed with a hidden political agenda that should serve the status quo by, presumably, justifying such amoral acts as sexual harassment, murder, and war.

An unfortunate outcome regarding the current state of affairs pertains to the fact that EP is attacked from people holding political perspectives that span the spectrum of ideologies. Fundamentalist Christians, who necessarily reject ideas that are premised on evolution as an accepted theory of speciation, reject EP simply due to its reliance on evolutionary theory. This ideological hurdle is by no means small: A recent survey found that 87% of United States citizens do not believe that evolutionary forces in general (and natural selection, in particular), unaided by a supernatural deity, are responsible for human origins. Such individuals, whose numbers are, simply, daunting, are likely to reject EP as a sustainable perspective on any aspect of human functioning.

However, in addition to the resistance to EP presented by fundamentalist religious individuals, there is, in effect, a new kind of creationist, so to speak, rooted in secular intellectualism. These so-called new creationists are, in fact, very different from fundamentalist Christians in their ideological foundation. The new creationists may be conceptualized as academics and scholars who study varied aspects of human affairs from the perspective of the Standard Social Science Model, a model for understanding human behavior which is largely premised on the notion of the blank slate. The SSSM essentially conceives of human psychology as qualitatively different from the psychology of all other species. The SSSM presumes that there is no basic human nature—that the mind (and its corresponding physiological substrates) are fully malleable based on environmental stimuli and that all behavioral and psychological aspects of people are the result of experiences with environmental stimuli across ontogenetic time.

This denial of human nature, which is prevalent in many of the social sciences, has come to serve as the only politically acceptable paradigm in much of academia. Champions of this perspective are often more critical of EP than are adherents of fundamentalist Christianity. From the perspective of the SSSM, EP is problematic largely because its basic premises focus on understanding the nature of human nature.

Geher, Glenn. From *Psychological Topics (Psihologijske teme)*, vol. 15, no. 2, December 2006, pp. 181–189, 194–197 (excerpts). Copyright © 2006 by Psychological Topics. Reprinted by permission of the Faculty of Arts & Sciences, University of Rijeka, Croatia.

For instance, consider David Buss' work which revolves around understanding sex-differentiated mating strategies in humans from an evolutionary perspective. Research by Buss and his colleagues has documented many basic sex differences in the psychology of human mating. Several different studies, using varied methods, have replicated Buss' basic finding that men desire more lifetime sexual partners than do women. Buss' evolution-based explanation of these findings is rooted in Trivers' parental investment theory which suggests that males and females should differ in their mating tactics as a result of fundamentally different costs faced by each sex associated with bearing and raising children across the evolution of our species. From this perspective, women in our ancestral past who were driven to pursue short-term sexual strategies would have, on average, had less reproductive success compared with males pursuing similarly promiscuous strategies. A result of this sex-specific differential reproduction associated with variability in promiscuity over deep time would have led to sex-specific mating strategies (favoring promiscuity in males over females).

Critics of EP who may be thought to represent new creationism have tried hard to argue that findings which demonstrate such sex differences in mating strategies are based on flawed research. Further, such critics argue that even if such phenomena as sex differences in number of sex partners desired have been documented via sound research, these findings are best understood as resulting completely from environmental conditions during ontogenetic time. In other words, the SSSM perspective argues that all differences between the sexes in number of sexual partners desired results from males and females learning different messages about sexuality across their lifetimes. In short, this perspective argues that this phenomenon does not reflect basic and natural differences between male and female mating psychology—it only reflects differences in socialization between the sexes (differences that exist, in varying degrees, across human cultures).

Adherents of the SSSM perspective argue that appealing to evolutionarily shaped differences between the psychologies of men and women to explain something such as universal sex differences in desire for multiple sex partners is an inherently sexist approach. In short, these new creationists believe that any appeals to an evolutionarily shaped human nature to explain psychological phenomena (regardless of how well the said phenomena are documented) imply that human behavior is highly constrained by our nature, is genetically determined, and is, in effect, immutable. As such, adherents of the SSSM feel something of an obligation to fight EP, as they believe they are fighting an intellectual doctrine which sees human behavior as largely immutable and which ultimately provides a scholarly rationale for the status quo (which inherently treats people unfairly).

From the SSSM perspective, EP paints a picture of humans as fully under the control of genes. Further, the SSSM perspective sees EP as a doctrine that endorses all aspects of the status quo related to sexism. As seen through the lens of the SSSM, all phenomena documented by evolutionary psychologists and, subsequently, framed as resulting from evolutionary forces, are implicitly endorsed by evolutionary psychologists. As such, phenomena such as male promiscuity, filicide, rape, murder, and war are seen, from the SSSM perspective, as phenomena that are, essentially, supported, condoned, and, perhaps, encouraged by evolutionary psychologists as they are phenomena that evolutionary psychologists have studied from an evolutionary perspective and have tried to explain in terms of the nature of human nature.

Let me go on the record saying that I am very uncomfortable (on both moral and intellectual grounds) with any perspective that sees humans as fully incapable of choosing their own behaviors. Further, I am ardently opposed to sexism—ardently opposed to the idea that men and women (and boys and girls) should be treated differently by rules created by a society and should be given different opportunities within a society. I am, further, from a personal standpoint, not someone who encourages males to engage in promiscuous behavior and not someone who supports men who fly into violent jealous rages with females as targets of their anger and aggression. Additionally, I am strongly opposed to war, murder, rape, and filicide. I would feel a moral obligation to reject outright any doctrine which is inconsistent with these fundamental aspects of my belief system. In sum, I would see such a doctrine as downright evil.

So herein lies the problem, a problem which, as I see it, is largely one of perspective. If EP were the kind of intellectual doctrine that I describe in the prior paragraph, then it would be a morally disturbing framework. However, as several scholars have argued before me, EP is simply not such a doctrine. In the remainder of this paper, I argue that EP is the following:

A. A basic intellectual framework for understanding all psychological phenomena
B. A set of principles which, at its core, simply asserts that the human nervous system and resultant behavior are ultimately products of organic evolutionary processes
C. One of the most situationist/contextualist perspectives that exists within psychology writ large
D. A perspective that has the potential to serve as an underlying meta-theory to guide all the behavioral sciences in the future.

Evolutionary Psychology Is Not Evil

In engaging in the thought exercise of trying to empathize with academics who characterize EP as downright evil, I have concluded that the problem seems to lie largely in the naturalistic fallacy. Often, when people hear that some phenomenon is being framed as part of our nature, shaped by evolutionary forces across thousands of generations, they infer that the scientists who are documenting said evolutionarily shaped quality see this quality as something about us that should be the case. In other words, for instance, if one hears Daly, Wilson, and Weghorst argue that male sexual jealousy, and violence that has been directed toward countless women as a result of such jealousy, may be part of our evolutionary heritage, one may infer that these authors are arguing that men should show marked, intense, and emotional jealousy when faced with cheating partners and, further, that they should use violence against women as a solution to such problems.

Of course, Daly et al. believe nothing of the kind. Documenting that something is part of our nature is not synonymous with arguing that it should be condoned by society. Similarly, when David Buss argues that natural selection has shaped patterns of homicide and murder in a non-random way, such that our ancestors were most likely to murder when murder was likely to have increased the possibility of passing on genes of the murderer (i.e., under conditions in which murder had fitness benefits), he is not arguing that murder is good and/or that society should support murder. He is, rather, using evolutionary theory, the most powerful intellectual framework that exists in the life sciences, to help understand behaviors that are of high relevance to the functioning of society.

In sum, the naturalistic fallacy corresponds to conflating phenomena that naturally are with phenomena that should be. As evolutionary psychologists are charged with the task of understanding the nature of human psychological processes, they are at particular risk of having their work mis-characterized by others who are employing the reasoning that typifies the naturalistic fallacy. Further, for someone who is conflating some findings and ideas from EP with statements by evolutionary psychologists regarding how things should be, EP is likely to come across as appearing morally deficient and, yes, perhaps even evil!

What Evolutionary Psychology Is

While there are different brands of EP, with some variability in basic assertions, EP is, in its most basic form, simply an understanding of behavior that is guided by evolutionary theory. In the words of Richard Dawkins: "The central claim . . . (that evolutionary psychologists) . . . are making is not an extraordinary one. It amounts to the exceedingly modest assertion that minds are on the same footing as bodies where Darwinian natural selection is concerned."

As such, EP is an explanatory framework that has implications for understanding all psychological phenomena. It essentially conceptualizes humans as products of natural selection—thereby not conceiving of our species as somehow immune from the laws that govern the natural world. It is a humbling perspective in some respects.

In any case, this perspective is monistic at its core; it conceives of human behavior as resulting from the nervous system—including the brain—which was, according to this perspective (and to most modern scientists who study psychological phenomena), shaped by evolutionary processes such as natural selection.

If the nervous system were shaped by natural selection, then individual humans with certain neuronal qualities in our ancestral past (e.g., those with features of the autonomic nervous system) were more likely to survive and reproduce compared with conspecifics (other humans) with nervous systems that were less likely to ultimately lead to reproduction.

Ancestral humans with features of the autonomic nervous system were more likely to respond optimally to immediate threatening stimuli in requisite situations (e.g., running from a predator). Thus, they were more likely to survive than others with less advanced autonomic nervous systems. A simple logical truth is that being more likely to survive necessarily increases the likelihood of reproduction (corpses are not very good at successfully mating). As such, this (partly) genetically shaped feature of human anatomy (with integral implications for human behavior), the autonomic nervous system, was 'naturally selected' and has thereby come to typify our species.

This same reasoning applies to all domains of psychology. Human behavioral patterns are part of the natural world—and human beings are living organisms that have come about by evolutionary processes. As such, attempts at understanding such basic aspects of the human experience—mind and behavior—without understanding the broad evolutionary factors that have given rise to our species and, ultimately, to our psychology, is, from the perspective of EP, simply misguided. We can do better in understanding human psychology by understanding the nuances of evolutionary principles.

From my perspective, these are the basic ideas of EP. Note that I provide a list of resources (mostly developed by others; see Table 1) to introduce the reader to this field from various angles that fall under the general umbrella of EP. In sum, EP is simply a framework for understanding human behavior that has the capacity to unite all areas of psychology more so than any other paradigm that has existed in the history of psychology as a discipline. It is not driven by ideology; it is driven by the basic scientific motive of increasing understanding of the natural world.

Evolutionary Psychology Mischaracterized as an Immutable, Hyper-Dispositionist, Non-Situationist Perspective

One of the beliefs that many people tend to hold about EP is that it is a non-situationist doctrine, suggesting that organisms have just a few immutable, invariant ways of responding which are under the direct control of genes. This portrait of EP is simply inaccurate. EP posits that species-typical psychological design features with some heritable component have been shaped by natural and sexual selection. Often, many (but not all) evolutionary psychologists

Table 1

Web-Based Resources That Provide Basic Information About Evolutionary Psychology

1. Syllabus from Glenn Geher's section of Evolutionary Psychology taught at SUNY New Paltz:
   http://www.newpaltz.edu/~geherg/classes/fall08/syl307r.doc
2. The website for the international Evolutionary Studies (EvoS) Consortium:
   http://www.evostudies.org
3. Information on the Evolutionary Studies Program at the State University of New York at New Paltz
   http://www.newpaltz.edu/EvoS
4. Information on the Evolutionary Studies Program at Binghamton University
   http://evolution.binghamton.edu/evos/ directed by David Sloan Wilson (http://evolution.binghamton.edu/dswilson/)
5. Ed Hagen's Chapter on Controversies Surrounding Evolutionary Psychology (published in David Buss' Handbook of Evolutionary Psychology)
   http://itb.biologie.hu-berlin.de/%7Ehagen/papers/Controversies.pdf
6. Leda Cosmides and John Tooby's Introduction to the Field of Evolutionary Psychology
   http://www.psych.ucsb.edu/research/cep/primer.html
7. Ed Hagen's "Frequently Asked Questions about Evolutionary Psychology (e.g., "Is Evolutionary Psychology Sexist?")"
   http://www.anth.ucsb.edu/projects/human/evpsychfaq.html
8. Russil Durant and Bruce Ellis's Introduction to Evolutionary Psychology
   http://media.wiley.com/product_data/excerpt/38/04713840/0471384038.pdf
9. Human Behavior and Evolution Society page introducing the field:
   http://www.hbes.com/intro_to_field.htm
10. Personal Accounts about Applying for Academic Jobs While Branded as an Evolutionary Psychologist
   http://human-nature.com/ep/articles/ep02160173.html

will conceive of such design features as adaptations. In any case, such adaptations are rarely understood by evolutionary psychologists as being context-independent.

Evolutionary psychologists and biologists make an important distinction between non-conditional and conditional strategies that describe the phenotypes of different organisms. A classic example of a non-conditional, fully genetically determined (and immutable) strategy is found in male sunfish, which come in two varieties. The first variety includes large males who have the ability to acquire sufficient territories in intra-sexual competition. The second variety includes smaller, sneakier males, who are nearly indiscernible from females and who do not elicit aggressive responses from territory-holding males. While territory-holding males reproduce by honestly attracting females, sneaker males use a somewhat dishonest strategy: they blast their gametes after a female has released her eggs in a large male's territory, thereby using deception as a tool for reproduction. It turns out that the differences between these kinds of males is attributable to genetic differences. As such, the strategies employed are non-conditional.

The notion of conditional strategies, on the other hand, corresponds to situations in which an organism modifies its strategy *vis a vis* variability in situational factors. For instance, male tree frogs use strategies similar to

the male sunfish when it comes to mating. Sometimes, a male will carve out a territory and croak loudly. At other times, a male will hide near a territory-holding male and try to mate with females that are attracted to the croaking, territory-holding male. Importantly, in this species, males have been documented to show strategic pluralism; they modify their choice of strategy depending on the nature of such situational factors as the number of male territory-holders at a given time.

The use of a variety of strategies by male wood frogs does not suggest that their repertoire of mating behaviors is somehow outside the bounds of natural law or that these strategies are not designed with for 'purpose' of reproduction. Clearly, these mating strategies are related to optimal reproduction, a fact that speaks to their selection by evolutionary processes. As such, evolutionary geneticists and evolutionary psychologists have come to apply evolutionary reasoning to our understanding of mixed behavioral strategies that are highly context-sensitive.

In fact, modern-day EP is an extraordinarily situationist perspective. Consider, for instance, evolutionary informed research on homicide and familial violence. All of the most highly cited work in this area focuses on situational factors that underlie family violence. For instance, Daly and Wilson's often-cited work on violence toward children is all about contextual factors that covary with this atrocious act. Simply, the presence of a step-parent in a household has been shown to be the primary contextual factor that predicts fatal violence toward children. Another contextual factor that Daly and Wilson document as having a significant relationship with such violence has to do with the age of a given child (another contextual factor). In fact, their research, which is, in this regard, very prototypical of much work in EP overall, is all about contextual factors that underlie behaviors.

Consider, as another example, research on factors that predict promiscuous behavior on the part of women. Evolutionary psychologists have uncovered such important contextual factors as localized sex ratios, ovulation cycles, a woman's age, and the presence of children from prior mateships—each such contextual factor serving as an important statistical predictor of female promiscuity. In short, EP is, in fact, a highly situationist perspective, generally conceiving of human behavioral strategies as being extremely flexible and as falling within the realm of this general idea of strategic pluralism.

EP does not conceptualize humans as genetically guided automatons whose conscious decision-making processes are irrelevant or non-existent. Rather, this perspective sees humans as capable of extraordinary conscious decision-making. Further, with its roots in strategic pluralism, EP is situationist at its core. Importantly, EP has lessons to provide regarding the nature of situationism as an epistemological doctrine. While situationism in the social sciences is often framed as conceiving of human behavior as highly under the influence of situational influences (both small and large), this generic brand of situationism has generally been framed in a manner that is devoid of any insights into how important psychological design features have been ultimately shaped by evolutionary forces for the purpose of reproduction.

The kind of situationism that characterizes modern-day EP may be thought of as a sort of evolutionary situationism. This particular brand of situationism suggests that while human behavior is largely under the control of situational influences, the particular situational factors that should matter most in affecting behavior are ones that bear directly on factors associated with survival and reproductive success. As such, Daly and Wilson did not document just any factors that underlie familial violence—they specifically uncovered the role of step-parenting, a situational factor with clear and theoretically predictable relevance to issues tied to genetic fitness (from a strictly genetic-fitness perspective, a step-child shares no genes with a step-parent, and is, thus, costly).

Given the tremendous potential for EP to inform the search for contextual factors that underlie human psychological outcomes, this idea of evolutionary situationism has the potential to create extraordinary bridges between traditional social psychology and EP. . . .

The Future of Evolutionary Psychology

Evolutionary psychology has proven extremely powerful in (a) providing coherent explanations for many basic human behavioral patterns, (b) generating new research questions that simply would not be on the radar screen without EP as a guiding framework, and (c) generating novel findings about what it means to be human.

In terms of providing coherent explanations for basic psychological processes, consider Ekman and Friesen's landmark work demonstrating the universal nature of emotional expression. The evolutionary reasoning that these authors draw upon, arguing, essentially, that emotional-expression abilities must have been positively selected for across the evolution of our species due to the fitness-related benefits of such abilities, provides an extremely useful and coherent framework for understanding human emotion in general. I am fully confident that it is very much in the interest of all the behavioral sciences to ultimately support efforts designed to understand human behavioral patterns in light of our evolutionary history.

In generating novel research questions, consider Haselton and Miller's research demonstrating that women are particularly attracted to indices of creativity in potential mates during peaks in their ovulatory cycles. This research is excessively rooted in evolutionary ideas. First, the general idea that female mating psychology should vary as a function of variability in fertility across the ovulatory cycle is an idea that only makes sense when we think of psychological processes as being designed for the purposes of successfully reproducing. Additionally, the fact that this research focuses on attraction to indices of creative intelligence is rooted in Miller's theory of higher-order human cognitive abilities (such as creative intelligence) as having resulted from sexual selection pressures across evolutionary time and as serving the function of affording individuals benefits in the domain of intrasexual competition. Again, without guidance from EP, which suggests that basic psychological processes likely serve a reproductive function, the questions addressed in this research simply never would have made it onto the radar screen.

Just as EP allows novel questions to be asked, it allows such questions to be answered, thereby providing the world with all kinds of discoveries regarding our nature. While research in the domain of adaptations to ovulation strongly demonstrates several novel findings regarding human mating behavior, such research only provides the tip of the iceberg when it comes to novel findings obtained by evolutionary psychologists. In fact, evolutionary psychologists are responsible for uncovering novel findings across the entire range of psychological phenomena such as the inter-play between mating and homicide, the neuropsychological substrates underlying the detection of individuals who cheat in social-exchange situations the phenomenology of stranger anxiety experienced by babies, and the nature of altruistic tendencies across species.

(For a reader interested in reading more about the scientific utility of EP across the modern landscape of the behavioral sciences, I strongly recommend Ketelaar and Ellis' paper which conceives of EP as a meta-theory that guides research in a coherent manner and a paper by Schmitt and Pilcher which provides a model regarding the thorough methodology employed by evolutionary psychologists when they are at their best in trying to uncover human nature.)

In light of the powerful nature of EP in generating new questions and findings, I believe, strongly, that psychology writ large can only reach its potential by incorporating an evolutionary perspective across all its areas. Further, I believe that there is reason for optimism regarding the future of EP and the future of an evolutionarily informed psychology in general. Consider, for example, a recent analysis of articles published in a leading journal in the behavioral sciences, Behavioral and Brain Sciences, which revealed that more than 30% of articles published in the last decade include evolution in the title or as a keyword. These findings suggest that evolution is, in fact, making its way into the behavioral sciences.

However, with that said, an analysis regarding the education of the authors of these evolutionarily informed articles tells a different story. When authors of these articles were interviewed about their education, they generally reported being self-taught with regard to evolutionary principles. Such an effect is consistent with the portrait of academic institutions as less than fully embracing of the incorporation of evolution into the realm of human behavior.

Taken together, the different ideas presented in this section paint a variegated picture with regard to the inclusion of evolution into the behavioral sciences. On the one hand, a great deal of research on the evolutionary origins of human behavior and psychological processes is being conducted. This research is leading to novel findings regarding topics that cut across all areas within psychology. On the other hand, EP is a target of hostility from adherents of multiple political and ideological perspectives. Such implacable hostility emanates from characterizations of EP as overly deterministic, reductionistic, sexist, racist, and, simply, evil.

Importantly, there are several critiques of EP that are reasonable and that should be addressed. For instance, Panksepp and Panksepp, argue that evolutionary psychologists could improve their work by taking a less modularistic approach, working more closely on neurological substrates of behavior, and paying more attention to research regarding the neuroplasticity which seems to characterize much of the human brain. To be fair to these critics (and to others), I strongly believe that EP is not perfect and this approach to psychology has room for improvement. However, I see no reason to throw the baby out with the bath water. As Dawkins writes regarding recent critiques of EP: "Some individual evolutionary psychologists need to clean up their methodological act. Maybe many do. But that is true of scientists in all fields."

In short, EP has proven itself as having extraordinary abilities to (a) yield novel ways of thinking about who we are and to (b) generate new findings that shed light on the depths of our minds. While this approach may not be perfect, and while certain studies conducted under the general banner of EP may need improvement, the overall approach to understanding human behavior—focusing on understanding how basic psychological processes ultimately bear on issues tied to reproductive success—has an enormous capacity to improve our understanding of ourselves. I urge psychological researchers and students to go down the path of evolutionary enlightenment so as to allow psychology to realize its full potential—ultimately allowing our discipline to best help people deal with the many problems associated with what it means to be human.

Conclusion

My intellectual passions permeate my teaching and my research. After learning about applications of evolutionary theory to issues regarding behavior in Benjamin Sachs' Animal Behavior course in 1990 at the University of Connecticut, I came to see the evolutionary informed approach to psychology as the most coherent and powerful framework for understanding behavior across species (including *Homo Sapiens*). This intellectual approach to understanding psychology has permeated my teaching and my research since that time.

As stated prior, I do not believe that all EP is perfect. In the future, evolutionary approaches to psychology will surely benefit from better understanding the interrelationship between cultural and genetic forces that underlie behavior, studying the nature of neuroplasticity from an evolutionary perspective, teasing apart psychological qualities that were shaped for survival versus reproductive purposes, and addressing the interplay between behaviors that emerge in an ontogenetic timescale versus behaviors that are the result of thousands of generations of selection across our phylogenetic history. Further, I am certain that other improvements to an evolutionary approach to psychology are out there!

However—my student Warren Greig tells me that I need to be less apologetic when it comes to my passion for EP. And, as usual, he is right. As such, I end by making some simple points. First, EP is not an inherently evil approach to understanding human behavior. It is not overly immutable in its portrait of humans. It is, alternatively, one of the most situationistic/contextualistic doctrines that exists regarding human behavior. EP is not the new eugenics. In fact, EP and eugenics have virtually no commonalities whatsoever.

Evolutionary psychology is an extraordinarily coherent framework for understanding virtually all of human psychology. Its basic assumptions, suggesting (a) that fundamental human psychological processes were shaped by evolutionary forces and that (b) such psychological processes and behavioral patterns can be best understood in light of such evolutionary forces, are as solid and reasonable as the theory of evolution itself. Acknowledging this point is sure to benefit all work conducted in the realm of psychology.

GLENN GEHER is professor and director of evolutionary studies in the Department of Psychology at SUNY New Paltz. He received his PhD in social and personality psychology.

Edwin E. Gantt and Brent S. Melling

 **NO**

Evolutionary Psychology Isn't Evil, It's Just Not Any Good

"... **I**f there is a sure road to intellectual atrophy, it is paved with the complacent certainty that one's critics are deluded."

It is hard not to be amused when one hears advocates of evolutionary psychology (EP), such as Richard Dawkins, Daniel Dennett, and Glenn Geher, grumble that so many people take issue with their ideas. After all, couldn't one reasonably suspect that such firm believers in the universal truth of evolution would welcome the opportunity to see how their theories fare in the cutthroat competitive marketplace of ideas? Academics, red in tooth and claw, and all that? Certainly, if the theories of EP are true, they are strong enough to take on all comers and prove their hardiness by adapting to the challenges of lesser ideas. In the end, isn't that what evolutionary theory is all about anyway?

Oddly, most evolutionary psychologists seem to prefer to short-circuit critique instead of welcoming it, declaring critical examination to be off-limits at the outset. When not casting aspersions on critics by claiming they can only be motivated by unscientific or religious impulses, they treat objections to EP as though they were wholesale rejections of well-established Darwinian principles in biology. While this may be a clever debating move, and might win you a few points with the high school debating club, it is nonetheless pure sophistry and unworthy of the serious intellectual examination that science demands. Still, since Geher begins his defense of EP by chiding the motives of any who might venture a critique, it is important to be very clear at the outset here about what our response is NOT. What we have to say here is NOT some fundamentalist Christian rejection of evolutionary biology or Darwin's theories of natural selection. Neither is this article motivated by some desire to defend Creationism, Young Earth Theology, or Intelligent Design Theory. Although some of the controversies presently surrounding Darwinism in biology and its Intelligent Design rivals are thought-provoking, those issues are not our issues. The fact is that it is possible to be a strident and thoughtful critic of EP and have no commitment whatsoever to a religious worldview, fundamentalist or otherwise.

Additionally, this paper is in no way a defense of what evolutionary psychologists (EPs) like to call the "Standard Social Science Model (SSSM)" or "Secular Creationism." Indeed, despite all of the bluster to the contrary by folks like Geher, Steven Pinker, and others, it is hard to imagine that there is anyone in contemporary psychology who would defend what these people claim that advocates of the SSSM believe, especially given that "no serious figure embraces that view since, perhaps, John Watson in the early twentieth century." This "rhetoric of exclusion," whereby "whomever is not for the program is against Darwin," clearly owes more to hidebound dogmatism than it does to open-minded, scientific thinking.

What, then, is our purpose here? It is simply this: We seek to engage in a critical scientific and philosophical reflection about fundamental concepts in the social sciences, as well as consider of some of the implications of taking EP seriously. In short, what we propose to do here is a brief bit of critical thinking about some of the assumptions, implications, and claims of EP. We aim to show that EP is not nearly as coherent, obvious, or harmless as its defenders suggest.

Rhetoric, Values, and Ideology

In addition to the rhetoric of exclusion, EPs often employ the rhetoric of objectivism. Although there are various ways in which the term "objectivism" is defined, we will use it to refer to the assumption that one's methods are value-neutral and unbiased and, thus, that one's reporting of research findings is the reporting of objective facts about the world rather than particular interpretations of it. As is often the case in scientific research, the findings of EP researchers are usually presented as being objective in nature, the products of a value-neutral and unbiased mode of inquiry. For example, Geher offers up the research findings of many of his colleagues in order to support his contention about the significant contributions that EP is making to the study of human nature. While citing supporting research is necessary, it is important to note the language that Geher employs in so doing. Like other evolutionary psychologists, he frequently states that EP research has "documented" or is "demonstrating" some fact about human nature and the evolution of behavior. This rhetorical strategy helps paint a mental picture in which psychologists like Geher are engaged in simply observing the world of human behavior and documenting the facts of such behavior—facts that would be obvious to any rational being using the scientific method and not blinded by personal ambition, cultural shortsightedness, or religious bigotry. Likewise, when Geher maintains that EP is not "driven by ideology; it is driven by the basic scientific motive of increasing understanding of the natural world," he is invoking the authority of objectivism to persuade us that we can have confidence both in both his own claims and that of his EP colleagues because such claims are free of the self-serving and biasing influences of values and ideologies.

Unfortunately, Geher's confident assurances to the contrary, EP is inescapably undergirded with a variety of biases, values, and ideological commitments that serve not only to direct and shape EP's study of human behavior, but also provide the conceptual framework from within which data is interpreted. There are at least three such biases that often go unexamined or unacknowledged by EP theorists and researchers: objectivism, materialism, and instrumentalism. The first of these—objectivism—has already been discussed above in terms of its role in the rhetoric employed by advocates of EP. Objectivism is not just a rhetorical strategy, but is also a particular value—though rarely admitted as such. Objectivism is a bias not only in holding that the results of scientific research are value-neutral and free of the taint of human bias, but also in suggesting that the results of scientific investigation *ought to be* free of such flaws. Ironically, this claim that science "ought" to be objective to be good science is itself a subjective preference (or value) regarding how researchers should go about conducting their science and is not the only valid or possible perspective.

Likewise, materialism is a commonly taken-for-granted assumption in the natural and social sciences, particularly among EPs. Materialism is the notion that matter is the only reality and that everything, including thought, feeling, mind, and will, can be exhaustively explained in terms of matter and physical phenomena. This stance is not an incontrovertible fact of the universe conclusively demonstrated by scientific investigation but an assumption about the nature of reality that itself cannot be proven or disproven, especially by a materialist science that begins by assuming that materialism is true. In other words, materialism is a sort of faith, or set of beliefs and ideas that one assumes to be true but for which there is not—nor ever can be—conclusive proof. It is, in this way, clearly an ideology and not a demonstrated fact of the universe. Thus, EPs prefer materialist accounts of human behavior, not because such accounts have been *proven* in any way to be the best, the truest, or the most rational ones available, but rather because materialism is the ideology they have come to endorse for philosophical, theological, and/or cultural reasons.

Finally, EP accounts of human behavior assume instrumentalism, or the idea that all behavior is governed by some manner of calculative means-ends rationale, whereby any given behavior is best understood as just a means to attaining some other goal. In the case of EP, the ultimate goal or end toward which all behavior is striving is, of course, reproductive success. In fact, as Richard Dawkins has argued, from the EP perspective we are really just "survival machines" designed by our genes over eons of evolutionary history to ensure that these genes are able to continue on into future generations. "Their preservation," says Dawkins, "is the ultimate rationale for our existence." Thus, Geher speaks of "mating tactics" and "sexual strategies" and asserts that caring for step-children is "costly" because such children share no genes with the step-parent. Similarly, Robert Wright, another ardent advocate of EP, argues that "beneath the thoughts and feelings and temperamental differences marriage counselors spend their time sensitively assessing are the stratagems of the genes—cold hard equations composed of simple variables: social status, age of spouse, number of children, their ages, outside romantic opportunities, and so on." Nonetheless, even though EPs are strident and vocal in their assertion that all human behavior can be explained in terms of means-ends calculation, such claims are not based on any indisputable or documented fact but on certain philosophical assumptions about human nature and what constitutes the ultimate good in life. Even though instrumentalist assumptions may be so widely held in modern Western culture as to seem obvious, it is still the case that instrumental reasoning reflects a particular set of values arising from a particular ideology.

What the Data Says

Although their commitment to objectivism leads EPs to present their research findings as though the data is obvious and can only be explained from an evolutionary perspective, it is simply not the case that data ever speaks for itself. Data must always be interpreted in some way. Scientists must always provide some meaningful context within which particular findings can be understood and rendered sensible. Indeed, some authors have shown that not only does one's data require interpretation to be meaningful, but one's chosen method of investigation itself reflects an interpretation of the world that directs researchers to particular ways of making sense of one's data. Thus, no one is surprised when a feminist interprets an event as evidence of gender inequality, or by a Marxist who interprets the same event as the result of class-struggle. So we shouldn't be surprised when an evolutionary psychologist interprets the same event as a product of natural selection. None of these theorists use their particular explanatory framework because there is inherently more factual evidence for them—it is the framework itself that determines what counts as evidence and how it is to be interpreted. Thus, a feminist theorist will tend to see all situations as providing evidence of feminist assumptions, a Marxist will tend to see confirmation of Marxist assumptions, and an EP will tend to see evidence of evolutionary processes at work.

While most contemporary philosophers of science recognize that the interpretation of data requires an assumed framework, many EPs seem to think that their interpretive framework—or "meta-theory"—is inherently better because it is more parsimonious, more rational, or can explain all of the empirical data. What they seem to fail to realize is that all other reasonably sophisticated meta-theories can do the same. The ability to explain psychological phenomena by means of concepts borrowed from evolutionary biology is not testament to the fact that such explanations are true, only that evolution is a sophisticated and encompassing worldview—but, then again, so are many others.

Thus, while Geher cites the work of David Buss on mate-age selection as empirical proof that females select older men due the imperatives of natural selection, what is actually being offered is a particular way of interpreting the data at hand. Other interpretations are not only possible but viable. For example, rather than evidence of natural selection's instrumental operation for reproductive advantage, it could be that the age differential in mate-selection might reflect that women typically mature earlier than men and are more socially and verbally inclined. Thus, the observed age differences might simply reflect women's efforts to assure themselves of more socially skilled, verbally expressive, and interesting companions. Likewise, Geher offers up Daly and Wilson's research on domestic violence to demonstrate what has come to be known as the Cinderella Effect. Namely that children living with stepparents are about 100 times more likely to be fatally abused because natural selection shaped humans to take better care of our biological offspring than children with whom we do not share genes. Here too, alternative explanations are available that account for the data and are rationally defensible. A child is only going to be living with a stepparent if there has been some significant emotional, economic, and/or social disturbance of the family in the first place. Therefore, the social and relational problems that have contributed to the break-up of the original family are likely to continue with parents and children into subsequent family arrangements. It should be apparent that one need not invoke some powerful underlying genetic recognition and selection process to make adequate sense of this particular situation (for additional examples of alternative interpretations of EP research findings).

These examples of data reinterpretation aren't just interesting and clever intellectual exercises. Rather, we feel that they are important illustrations of critically reflecting on scientific knowledge claims, especially in terms of how data is interpreted and reported, for the history of science is replete with examples of researchers discovering and reporting presumably obvious facts that are later found to be not only questionable but on occasion outright false and misleading (e.g., phlogiston, phrenology, the geocentric theory of the universe, the Meckel-Serres Law, and classical Newtonian physics). The proper conduct of science requires, we believe, humility and continual critical self-reflection, not the dogmatic and repetitive assertion that one has found once and for all the indisputable truth of life, the universe, and everything.

Reductionism and Determinism

Another guiding ideology of EP is monism—the idea that all of reality is of the same kind, subject to the same rules and laws. The advantage to this position is that it avoids some of the tricky issues inherent in "the mind-body problem" (e.g., how do minds and bodies interact, how can mind be observed or measured, etc.). By starting from the assumption that "minds are on the same footing as bodies where Darwinian natural selection is concerned," EPs hope to sidestep the problem of how something seemingly immaterial, such as a thought or an emotion can have an effect on the material world. The way evolutionary psychologists achieve this monism, however, is by reducing one side of our experience (i.e., the immaterial side of minds, thoughts, and emotions) to another side of our experience (i.e., the material side of genes, brains, and bodies). As Geher states, the evolutionary perspective fundamentally "conceives of human behavior as resulting from the nervous system." In such a scheme, what we experience as immaterial (like feelings of love) is seen to be really nothing more than an expression of complicated physical realities (e.g., elevated hormones, particular neuronal firings, genetic tendencies and environmental conditions). Instead of integrating the immaterial and material into a meaningful whole, however, one facet of human experience is simply explained away by reducing it down to another. The end result of this sort of approach is not monism, but rather a "one-sided dualism" in which important but less easily or accurately measured features of the mind (i.e., thoughts, intentions, emotions, etc.) are ignored or discounted so that attention can be solely focused on the precisely measurable features of the brain such as synaptic activity and neurotransmitter levels. Unfortunately for EP, however, simply ignoring or discounting the essential nature of mental phenomena does little to actually explain how such things might arise out of one's genes or nervous system in the first place. After all, while a well-functioning nervous system may certainly be something that is necessary for having thoughts, making choices, and experiencing emotions, this does not mean that the nervous system is the only thing that one has to attend to when trying to make sense of where our thoughts, choices, and feelings come from or what they mean.

Unfortunately, this reductionism perpetuates the problems that evolutionary psychologists typically seek to avoid—a loss of meaning, morality, and choice. All of these things—though intangible in nature—are nonetheless real phenomena common to human experience that cannot be easily dismissed. By reducing mind to brain, however, EPs ultimately reduce the rich meanings of our lives and relationships into the merely mechanical happenings of our bodies. Instead of being human persons capable of making genuine choices, we become, as the novelist Terry Bisson once famously wrote, "Thinking meat! Conscious meat! Loving meat! Dreaming meat! The meat is the whole deal!" If we take EP seriously, our values and ethics are ultimately really nothing more than the chance result of a complicated interaction of genetic survival mechanisms and environmental happenstance. What is morally good in life, what is worthy and right is simply whatever increases our likelihood to survive, or at least pass on our genetic material to subsequent generations.

Evolutionary psychologists often protest these sorts of criticisms, arguing that they do not reduce all human activity to biology because other factors—such as culture and personal disposition—play a significant role in how our genetic predispositions are realized. However, when accounting for the origins of culture and its variations, EP ultimately falls back on biological reductionism. As Geher states, genetic shaping by natural selection (determinism) "applies to all domains of psychology" and any account that does not see how "the broad evolutionary factors that have given rise to our species and, ultimately, to our psychology, is . . . simply misguided." According to EP, culture is itself a product of natural selection and exists primarily to provide particular mating rituals that will help to ensure genetic fitness in our offspring. So, if complex social and cultural behaviors are part of the natural world and not immune from the laws that govern it, then it is hard to believe defenders of EP when they say that human beings are not determined by their biology. Granted, it is not a direct genetic determinism where "behavior is controlled exclusively by genes, with little or no role for environmental influence." But, such assurances provide little comfort in the face of EP's contention that our behavior is controlled *mutually* by our genes AND the cultural forces that genetic selection has produced. So, if Geher and other EPs are, in fact, "uncomfortable (on both moral and intellectual grounds) with any perspective that sees humans as fully incapable of choosing their own behaviors," then perhaps it is time for them to be a little more uncomfortable with evolutionary psychology's conception of human nature.

The Problem of Nihilism

Possibly the most troubling problem inherent to an EP approach is that it is fundamentally nihilistic. Nihilism is the notion that life is, at its root, without ultimate meaning or purpose, and that the genuine moral distinctions between good and bad, right and wrong, cannot be rationally defended. If all human behavior is just the causal outcome of the unthinking, undirected, mechanical processes of natural selection, then human actions are no longer meaningful in any real sense. In other words, if our behavior is something that is determined for us by something beyond of our control or active participation, then what we do or think or feel does not possess any intrinsic meaning.

For example, consider the day-long motion of blades of grass as they slowly bend and change position relative to the location of the sun. As a fundamentally biological

and determined event, this phenomenon is simply what it is, and has no intrinsic meaning. Granted, a golfer might attribute meaning to the "lean of the grass" while preparing to make a putt, but this attribution of meaning is merely subjective and, as such, does not reflect any real meaning in the events of the natural world taking place there on the green. Of course, if the golfer's subjective meaning is itself just the causal product of something going on in her brain, then that too would lack any genuine meaning and be basically the same as what is taking place with the grass. Only if there is the genuine possibility that a given event could be otherwise than it is does it make any sense to consider it to be genuinely meaningful (as opposed to merely subjectively meaningful).

Thus, if to be human is to be nothing more than a "gigantic lumbering robot" whose sole purpose for existing is the preservation of our genes, the meaning of our lives, our loves, our friends and families seems quite hollow. Sure, we may experience ourselves as being deeply in love with our spouse but such feelings are simply "illusions" caused by particularly complex biochemistry striving to get our body motivated enough to find a suitable mate for replicating our genes. All this romantic fuss is just so much clever claptrap meant to manipulate suitable others into sticking around long enough for successful reproduction. If EP is correct on this point, and matter is all that matters, then in the end nothing else about us *really* matters at all.

Given their commitment to objectivity, EP is typically presented as nothing more than an account of the "is" of human behavior. Advocates of EP, such as Geher, passionately reject any suggestion that their theories of human nature have anything whatsoever to say about how human behavior "ought" to be, claiming that such criticism simply reflects the naturalistic fallacy. However, if one of the most basic claims of EP is true (i.e., human nature is the causal product of material events and natural laws), and culture is itself just a byproduct of evolutionary forces acting on material events (i.e., brain function and genetic selection), then it makes little sense to say that there are any legitimate "oughts" in the world at all. If culture "originates in, is transmitted by, and is propagated through mental mechanisms that evolved through natural selection," and evolution through natural selection is fundamentally a purposeless, random process reliant on the chance interplay of natural events, then the "oughts" we experience and which constitute our cultural moral norms are really just accidental developments in the long march of human evolutionary history. If our fundamental sensibilities of right and wrong, good and evil are such accidents, then it makes no more sense to argue that murder or rape or theft is morally wrong than it does to claim that elephants should have smaller trunks or longer tusks. Unless morality is ultimately grounded in something a bit more solid and trustworthy than contingent evolutionary history, it is impossible to maintain that any particular way of life is really better or more meaningful than any other.

In closing, after all that has been said so far, one cannot help but wonder whether EP is ultimately not only an enemy of meaning and morality, but also of science and reason. A basic claim of EP—and one with which we have taken repeated issue in this brief essay—is materialism, or the notion that at the root of all of our thoughts and ideas there are really just the happenstance events of the brain and the genes. This truly startling claim has become so commonplace in our modern world that it's deeply disturbing implications for not only how we understand ourselves but also how we understand science typically go entirely unnoticed. We have tried to explore a few of those implications throughout this piece. There is, however, one last implication of this line of thinking that we would like mention before concluding.

Because of its fundamental commitment to materialism and determinism, EP claims that all of our thoughts, feelings, and behaviors are rooted in unthinking, non-rational, non-caring processes and causes aimed solely at ensuring successful reproduction. Therefore, because the driving purpose behind evolution is reproduction, not rationality, we cannot assume that the fruits of evolution, including human thought and culture, reflect the rise of anything inherently rational. Natural selection's fundamental aim, after all, is not to shape a human mind capable of producing true beliefs but to produce a mind whose beliefs motivate us toward reproductively advantageous behaviors, whether those beliefs are true or not. As Churchland, a prominent advocate of EP, has stated:

> "Looked at from an evolutionary point of view, the principal function of nervous systems is to enable the organism to move appropriately. Boiled down to essentials, a nervous system enables the organism to succeed in the four F's: feeding, fleeing, fighting, and reproducing. The principle chore of nervous systems is to get the body parts where they should be in order that the organism may survive. . . . Truth, whatever that is, definitely takes the hindmost."

There is more than a little irony in such a confident pronouncement, especially when the one making it is doing so in the name of scientific progress and truth. For, if our thoughts are simply the results of our biochemistry moving us toward reproduction, then the thought "evolutionary psychology is the best way to understand people" is itself not a rationally defensible or inherently true thought. Rather, it is simply something our brains make us think and say so that we might impress other reproductively viable members of our species in order to get them to mate with us.

The irony doesn't end here, though, for whether you accept the notion that evolutionary psychological theories of human behavior are true or reject them as pseudoscientific fables depends entirely on which genes are influencing your current neurological interactions with the environment AND NOT on whether you have been or could ever be persuaded by reasoned argument and the convincing power of truth. To put it another way, if EP is true, then the only reason anyone would advocate it is because (anyone, they) must do so given their evolutionary history and the particular mental mechanisms that their genes have provided them. Likewise, critics of the theory are only critics because they don't happen to possess the appropriate "evolutionary psychology is true" thought generating brain functions or genes. So much for reason, so much for science, so much for truth!

Ultimately, then, if EP is the "basic intellectual framework for understanding all psychological phenomena," as Geher argues, then natural selection is also the undergirding explanation for all of the activities and ideas of scientific researchers. The theories and conclusions of these scientists, including the evolutionary psychologist, are nothing more than the results of complex interactions between meaningless arrangements of matter and, as such, provide no assurance that they accurately reflect the truth of things. Indeed, if what Geher asserts is true, then his own scientific article is to be explained as really just an elaborate manipulation of his readers by his genes to maximize their chances of reproductive success. If EP is taken to its logical conclusion, then, there is nothing left of truth, meaning or morality in *any* human phenomenon, let alone the phenomenon of generating a scientific theory like EP and writing an article about it. In the end, we can't help but conclude that Geher is correct when he states that EP isn't evil—because from the EP perspective there is ultimately no such thing as good or evil, right or wrong, meaning or reason or truth. So, while its own perspective guarantees that EP cannot be evil, it also makes a pretty strong case that it isn't any good.

EDWIN E. GANTT is a professor of psychology at Brigham Young University. He received his PhD from Duquesne University. Dr. Gantt is interested in theory and philosophy of psychology and coedited *Psychology for the Other: Levinas, Ethics and the Practice of Psychology.*

BRENT S. MELLING is a doctoral candidate in theoretical and philosophical psychology at Brigham Young University. He holds a BS in bioinformatics.

EXPLORING THE ISSUE

Is Evolution a Good Explanation for Psychological Concepts?

Critical Thinking and Reflection

1. A major contention between these two positions is the objectivity of EP. Are evolutionary accounts of human behavior unbiased in their explanations? Should they be?
2. The authors of both articles agree that evolution is not evil, but for different reasons. What are these reasons? Do the articles differ about the "goodness" of EP? Why or why not?
3. Geher claims that EP works well for all aspects of psychology. How well does it account for the claims of humanistic or existential psychologists? If EP has trouble accounting for these claims, then what might this suggest about these schools of psychology? What does it suggest for EP?
4. What results have we gained from EP research? What would Gantt and Melling say about these results?
5. Geher suggests that EP is monism because the mind is governed by the same natural processes as the body. However, Gantt and Melling accuse this position of being a type of dualism. Which do you feel is correct on this issue, and why?
6. Geher suggests that EP is not overly deterministic because it takes account of environment and circumstance. Does this avoid the charge of determinism (i.e., all so-called human choices are determined by other factors and thus the person really has no true options)?

Create Central

www.mhhe.com/createcentral

Additional Resources

Bennett, M. D., and Hacker, P. (2007). The conceptual presuppositions of cognitive neuroscience. In *Neuroscience and Philosophy: Brain, Mind, and Language*, M. D. Bennett, D. Dennett, P. Hacker, and J. Searle (Eds.). New York, NY: Columbia University Press.

Cosmides, L., and Tooby, J. (1997). Evolutionary psychology: A primer. Retrieved from http://www.psych.ucsb.edu/research/cep/primer.htm. Accessed on February 16, 2010.

Ehrlich, P. R. (2000). http://news.stanford.edu/news/2000/september20/humans920.html

Internet Reference . . .

Wikipedia Entry on Criticism of Evolutionary Psychology

http://en.wikipedia.org/wiki/Criticism_of _evolutionary_psychology

Selected, Edited and with Issue Framing Material by:
Brent Slife, *Brigham Young University*

ISSUE

Is Homosexuality Biologically Based?

YES: Qazi Rahman, from "The Neurodevelopment of Human Sexual Orientation," *Neuroscience & Biobehavioral Reviews* (October 2005)

NO: Stanton L. Jones and Alex W. Kwee, from "Scientific Research, Homosexuality, and the Church's Moral Debate: An Update," *Journal of Psychology and Christianity* (Winter 2005)

Learning Outcomes
After reading this issue, you should be able to:
• Learn if current research supports biological determination of sexual orientation.
• Understand what evidence exists supporting the learning model of sexual orientation.

ISSUE SUMMARY

YES: Professor of psychobiology Qazi Rahman claims that the current research on the biology of homosexuality supports prenatal biological determination and refutes learning models of sexual orientation.

NO: Professor of psychology Stanton L. Jones and clinical psychologist Alex W. Kwee claim the current research on the biology of homosexuality provides no firm evidence for biological causation and leaves room for learning models of sexual orientation.

Many of the so-called "culture wars" in the United States have been fought over the issue of homosexuality. On one side of this "war" are those who claim that homosexuality is a moral issue, perhaps even a "sin." Yet, for this to be a moral issue, homosexuals would have to have some measure of control over or even a choice of their sexual orientation. Do they have such control? If this orientation is biologically determined, whether at birth or later, the control or choice necessary for sexual preference to be a "moral issue" would seem to be unavailable. If, on the other hand, homosexuals have made choices that lead them learn to "prefer" (choose) a certain type of sexual orientation, then a moral understanding of homosexuality could be justified.

Only relatively recently have psychologists and neuroscientists begun to conduct scientific research to address these issues. One of the earliest of these researchers, neuroscientist Simon LeVay, a self-declared gay person, found dramatic brain differences between gay and straight men. This investigation led many to speculate that sexual orientation was completely biological. Indeed, other scientific findings have been reported, especially as sensationalized by the media, that would seem to have confirmed this speculation. Do we now have enough evidence to conclude that homosexuality is completely biologically

based? Can we omit the role of learning factors in homosexuality altogether?

One of the foremost researchers in this area, Dr. Qazi Rahman, answers these questions in the first article by reviewing research on the neurodevelopment of human sexual orientation. He claims the research supports the proposal that homosexuality is biologically determined, even before birth. In support of his claim, he cites evidence from twin studies, genetic scanning, brain structure studies, and the fraternal birth order effect. He even refutes the idea that learning plays a role in the development of homosexuality by arguing that the theories which attempt to explain sexual orientation through cultural socialization, either by authority figures or peers, are simply "not supported."

In the second selection, on the other hand, noted psychologists Stanton Jones and Alex Kwee review much of the same research on the biology of homosexuality but come to very different conclusions. In discussing relevant twin studies, for example, they point to methodological weaknesses and side with one of the original studies' researchers that there is "no statistically significant indication of genetic influence on sexual orientation." While they agree that the research points to a correlation between biology and homosexuality, they contend that there is still no evidence of the cause of this correlation, whether learning from the environment or "hard-wiring" of the brain. They argue that there is still plenty of room for a learning model in the development of homosexual- ity by citing a recent study about the influence of parental socialization on homosexuality.

POINT

- Evidence from twin studies points to a genetically heritable homosexuality.
- Genetic scanning shows that homosexuality is correlated with several genes.
- The maternal immune theory is well established because it relies on the very reliable fraternal birth order effect.
- The fraternal birth order effect is accounted for in the prenatal environment.
- Brain structures differ between homosexual and heterosexual men.
- Research shows that learning plays no appreciable role in the development of sexual orientation.

COUNTERPOINT

- Twin studies suffer from methodological weaknesses that call into question the genetic influence on sexual orientation.
- Findings based on genetic scanning are ambiguous.
- The maternal immune theory relies on disputed findings regarding the fraternal birth order effect.
- The fraternal birth order effect can be accounted for in the postnatal social environment.
- Brain structure difference could be the effect rather than the cause of homosexuality.
- Research shows that learning plays a role in the development of sexual orientation.

YES

Qazi Rahman

The Neurodevelopment of Human Sexual Orientation

1. Introduction

Sexual orientation refers to a dispositional sexual attraction towards persons of the opposite sex or same sex. Sexual orientation appears 'dispositional' in that it comprises a target selection and preference mechanism sensitive to gender, motivational approach behaviours towards the preferred target, and internal cognitive processes biased towards the preferred target (such as sexual fantasies). In contrast, sexual orientation does not appear to be a matter of conscious self-labelling or past sexual activity because these are subject to contingent social pressures, such as the presence of linguistic descriptors and visible sexual minorities within an individual's culture, and the availability of preferred sexual partners. Therefore, in human investigations, sexual orientation is often assessed using self-report measures of 'sexual feelings' (i.e. sexual attraction and sexual fantasies) rather than self-labelling or past hetero- or homosexual activity.

Sexual orientation appears to be a dichotomous trait in males, with very few individuals demonstrating an intermediate (i.e. 'bisexual') preference. This is borne out by fine-grained analyses of self-reported heterosexual and homosexual orientation prevalence rates (using measures of sexual feelings) in population-level samples, and work on physiological genital arousal patterns (e.g. using penile plethysmography) in response to viewing preferred and non-preferred sexual imagery. Both lines of evidence consistently demonstrate a bimodal sexual orientation among men—heterosexual or homosexual, but rarely 'bisexual'. This is less so in the case among women. For example, Chivers et al. demonstrated a 'bisexual' genital arousal pattern among both heterosexual and lesbian women, suggesting a decoupling of self-reported sexual feelings (which appears broadly bimodal) from peripheral sexual arousal in women.

If sexual orientation among humans is a mostly bimodal trait, this implicates a canalization of development along a sex-typical route (heterosexual) or a sex-atypical (homosexual) route. Statistical taxometric procedures have confirmed this by demonstrating that latent taxa (i.e. non-arbitrary natural classes) underlie an opposite-sex, or same-sex, orientation in both men and women. Less well established are the factors that may be responsible for this 'shunting' of sexual orientation along two routes (the edges of which are fuzzier in women). These factors are the subject of the remaining discussion and it is suggested that they probably operate neurodevelopmentally before birth.

2. Behavioural and Molecular Genetics

A natural starting point for the neurodevelopment of physiological and behavioural traits must begin with the genetic level of investigation. Several family and twin studies provide clear evidence for a genetic component to both male and female sexual orientation. Family studies, using a range of ascertainment strategies, show increased rate of homosexuality among relatives of homosexual probands. There is also evidence for elevated maternal line transmission of male homosexuality, suggestive of X linkage, but other studies have not found such elevation relative to paternal transmission. Among females, transmission is complex, comprising autosomal and sex-linked routes. Twin studies in both community and population-level samples report moderate heritability estimates, the remaining variance being mopped up by non-shared environmental factors. Early attempts to map specific genetic loci responsible for sexual orientation using family pedigree linkage methods led to the discovery of markers on the Xq28 chromosomal region, with one subsequent replication limiting the effect to males only. However, there is at least one independent study which produced null findings, while a recent genome wide scan revealed no Xq28 linkage in a new sample of families but identified putative additional chromosomal sites (on 7q36, 8p12 and 10q26) which now require denser mapping investigations. These studies are limited by factors such as the unclear maternal versus paternal line transmission effects, possible autosomal transmission and measurement issues. Two candidate gene studies which explored the putative hormonal pathways in the neurodevelopment of sexual orientation (see Section 3): one on the androgen receptor gene and another on aromatase (CYP19A1) both produced null findings. . . .

3. The Fraternal Birth Order Effect and Maternal Immunity

The maternal immunity hypothesis is certainly the most revolutionary neurodevelopmental model of human sexual orientation. Empirically, it rests on one very reliable finding—the fraternal birth order effect (FBO): that is, homosexual men have a greater number of older brothers than heterosexual men do (and relative to any other category of sibling), in diverse community and population-level samples, and as early as they can be reliably surveyed. The estimated odds of being homosexual increase by around 33% with each older brother, and statistical modelling using epidemiological procedures suggest that approximately 1 in 7 homosexual men may owe their sexual orientation to the FBO effect. It has been suggested that the remaining proportions of homosexual men may owe their sexual orientation to other causes, such as differential prenatal androgen levels. Homosexual and heterosexual women do not differ in sibling sex composition or their birth order, thus any neurodevelopmental explanation for the FBO effect is limited to males. Importantly, recent work has demonstrated that homosexual males with older brothers have significantly lower birth weights compared to heterosexual males with older brothers. As birth weight is undeniably prenatally determined, some common developmental factor operating before birth must underlie FBO and sexual orientation among human males.

Specifically, investigators have proposed a role for the progressive immunization of some mothers to male-linked antigens produced by carrying each succeeding male foetus. That is, the maternal immune system 'sees' male-specific antigens as 'non-self' and begins producing antibodies against them. One possible group of antigens are the Y-linked minor histocompatibility antigens, specifically H–Y. The accumulating H–Y antibodies may divert male-typical sexual differentiation of the foetal brain, leading the individual to be sexually attracted to males. For example, male-specific antibodies may bind to, and inactivate, male-differentiating receptors located on the surface of foetal neurons thus preventing the morphogenesis of masculinized sexual preferences.

The maternal immunity theory is consistent with a number of observations: the number of older sisters is irrelevant to sexual orientation in later born males; the H–Y antigen is expressed by male foetuses only and thus the maternal immune system 'remembers' the number of males carried previously and may modulate its response; and H–Y antigens are strongly represented in neural tissue. Nonetheless, there is no data specifying a role for these particular antigens in sexual preferences among humans. There are several alternative candidate antigens to H–Y, including the distinct Y-linked protein families' *protocadherin* and *neuroligin*, both of which have been found in humans. These cell adhesion proteins are thought to influence cell–cell communication during early male-specific brain morphogenesis and may have male-typical behavioural consequences. Consistent with these studies is neurogenetic evidence for the direct transcription of Y-linked sex determination genes SRY and ZFY in the male human brain (including hypothalamus). The maternal immunity model may also explain the link between birth weight and sexual preferences: mouse models show that maternal immunization to male-derived antigens can affect foetal weight. Furthermore, male mice whose mothers are immunized to H–Y prior to pregnancy show reduced male-typical consummatory sexual behaviour towards receptive females.

The maternal immunity model implicitly relies on a non-hormonal immunologic neurodevelopmental explanation and thus cannot immediately explain the hyper-male features (e.g. 2D:4D and AEPs) associated with male homosexuality. It is possible that male-specific antibodies may interact with sexual differentiation processes controlled by sex hormones or be completely independent of them—this is unknown as yet. . . .

4. Neural Circuitry

Neurodevelopmental mechanisms must wire neural circuits differently in those with same-sex attractions from those with opposite-sex attractions, but we still know very little about this circuitry. The first indication for neural correlates of sexual partner preference came from Simon LeVay's autopsy study of the third interstitial nucleus of the anterior hypothalamus (INAH-3) which he found to be smaller in homosexual men than in presumed heterosexual men, and indistinguishable from presumed heterosexual women. Another study found a non-significant trend for a female-typical INAH-3 among homosexual men (and confirmed the heterosexual sex difference), but this was not evidenced the main sexually dimorphic parameter reported by this study (the total number of neurons). This preceding finding is noteworthy as a prediction from the prenatal androgen theory would be that a parameter which shows significant sexual dimorphism should also demonstrate within-sex variation attributable to sexual orientation. A conservative conclusion regarding these data is that while INAH-3 is larger in heterosexual men than in heterosexual women, and possibly smaller in homosexual men, structurally speaking this within-sex difference may not be very large at all.

One recent positron emission tomography study has demonstrated stronger hypothalamic response to serotonergic challenge in heterosexual than in homosexual men, and neuroimaging studies comparing heterosexual men and women while viewing preferred sexual imagery show significantly greater hypothalamic activation in heterosexual men. These findings, coupled with the anatomical findings described earlier, could be taken to suggest that there is a functionally distinct anterior hypothalamic substrate to sexual attraction towards women. This supposition is further supported by mammalian lesion models of the preoptic area (POA) of the anterior hypothalamus showing reduced appetitive responses towards female by male animals. Nevertheless, investigations comparing heterosexual and homosexual women are needed to support a role for this region in sexual preference towards females among humans.

While animal models point to a role for prenatal androgens in producing sexual variation in hypothalamic regions, a similar relationship in humans is unclear. One study found no sexual-orientation-related differences in the distribution of androgen receptors in sexually dimorphic hypothalamic regions. However, one animal model often overlooked by scientists may provide some guidance. Some males of certain species of sheep show an exclusive same-sex preference, and also how reduced aromatase activity and smaller ovine sexually dimorphic nuclei (a possible homolog to the human INAH-3) compared to female-oriented sheep. A role for aromatized metabolites of testosterone in underscoring possible hypothalamic variation related to human sexual orientation requires further study in light of these findings. Moreover, putative sexual orientation differences in aromatase activity in human males may go some way to explaining the 'mosaic' profile of hypo- and hyper-masculinized traits described earlier. For example, a reduction in aromatase activity in homosexual compared to heterosexual men (predicted from the Roselli findings) may lead to reduced availability of aromatized testosterone (i.e. estradiol) which typically masculinizes the male mammalian brain. This may lead to hypo-masculinized hypothalamic circuitry and yet leave excess non-aromatized testosterone to hyper-masculinize additional androgen sensitive traits (e.g. 2D:4D) through other metabolic pathways, such as 5-alpha reductase. Note, one mitigating piece of evidence with respect to these suggestions is the null finding of DuPree et al. regarding sexual-orientation-related variation in the aromatase gene. . . .

5. Is There a Role for Learning in the Development of Human Sexual Orientation?

The role of learning in the development of human sexual orientation has been the subject of much debate and controversy, most likely because it is erroneously believed to result in particular socio-political consequences associated with homosexuality. While data are a little thin on the ground, several lines of evidence mitigate the involvement of learning mechanisms. In animal models, there are documented effects of conditioning on sexual arousal, approach behaviour, sexual performance and strength of sexual preference towards opposite-sex targets, but no robust demonstrations of learning in the organization of same-sex preferences among males. Interestingly, one study in female rats demonstrated that the volume of the sexually dimorphic nucleus of the preoptic region was increased (male-typical) by testosterone administration coupled with same-sex sexual experience. This suggests that sexual experience may interact with steroid exposure to shape sexual partner preferences in females.

In humans, the extent of childhood or adolescent homosexual versus heterosexual activity does not appear to relate to eventual adult sexual orientation. Documented evidence regarding the situational or cultural 'initiation' of juvenile males into extensive same-sex experience (for example, in single-sex public schools in Britain or the obligatory homosexual activity required of young males in the Sambia tribe of New Guinea) does not result in elevated homosexuality in adulthood.

An alternative explanation for the FBO effect is that sexual interaction with older brothers during critical windows of sexual development predisposes towards a homosexual orientation. Studies in national probability samples show that sibling sex-play does not underscore the link between FBO and male sexual orientation, and that the sexual attraction component of sexual orientation, but not sexual activity, are best predicted by frequency of older brothers. In further support, same-sex play between pairs of gay brothers is also unrelated to adult homosexual attraction.

Perhaps parent–child interactions influence the sexual orientation of children? An informative test here is to examine the sexuality of children of homosexual parents because this type of familial dynamic could promote same-sex preferences through observational learning mechanisms. However, evidence from retrospective and prospective studies provides no support for this supposition. Nonetheless, one must bear in mind that if parental behaviour does determine offspring sexual orientation, it could be equally common in homosexual and heterosexual parents.

While a role for learning factors can never be entirely omitted, it is perplexing that several of the key routes by which these could have their effect, such as through sexual experience during childhood or adolescence, or through parental socialization, are not supported. Almost certainly the expression of homosexual *behaviour* has varied over time and across cultures, but there is little reason to think that dispositional homosexuality varies greatly cross-culturally or even historically. . . .

QAZI RAHMAN is a cognitive biologist at Queen Mary University of London. His research interests focus on the biological origin of sexual orientation in humans.

Stanton L. Jones and Alex W. Kwee

 **NO**

Scientific Research, Homosexuality, and the Church's Moral Debate: An Update

Etiological Research

Significant new research on etiology has emerged in six areas: 1) behavioral genetics; 2) genetic scanning, 3) human brain structure studies, 4) studies of "gay sheep" and "gay fruit flies," 5) fraternal birth order research, and 6) familial structure impact.

Behavioral Genetics

Bailey's behavioral genetics studies of sexual orientation in twins and other siblings seemed to provide solid evidence of a substantial degree of genetic influence on formation of homosexual orientation. Jones and Yarhouse criticized these studies severely, most importantly on the grounds that both studies were making population estimates of the degree of genetic influence on sexual orientation on *potentially biased samples*, samples recruited from advertisements in gay publications and hence potentially biased by differential volunteerism by subjects inclined to favor a genetic hypothesis for the causation of their orientation. Later research by Bailey and other associates with a truly representative sample of twins drawn from the Australian Twin Registry in fact refuted the earlier findings by failing to find a significant genetic effect in the causation of homosexual orientation.

Not included in our review was a major behavioral genetics study paralleling the work of Bailey: Kendler, Thornton, Gilman, and Kessler. This study is remarkable in two ways. First, it replicates almost exactly the findings of the earlier Bailey studies in reporting relatively strong probandwise concordances for homosexual monozygotic twins. Kendler et al. report their findings as pairwise concordances, but when the simple conversions to probandwise concordances are done, Kendler et al.'s 48% probandwise concordance for males and females together (reported as a 31.6% pairwise concordance) is remarkably similar to Bailey's reports of probandwise concordances of 52% for men and 48% for women.

Second, the Kendler et al. study is also remarkably similar to the earlier Bailey studies in its methodological weaknesses. Trumpeted as a study correcting the "unrepresentative and potentially biased samples" of the Bailey studies by using a "more representative sample," specifically a "U. S. national probability sample" (p. 1843), this

study appears actually to suffer all of the original problems of volunteer sample bias of the 1991 and 1993 Bailey studies. Further, the methodological problems give every sign of compounding one upon the next. The description of the methodology is confusing: Kendler et al. state that their sample comes from a MacArthur Foundation study of 3,032 representatively chosen respondents, but then they note that since this sample produced too few twins and almost no homosexual twins (as would be expected), they turned to a different sample of 50,000 households that searched for twins, and here the clear sampling problems begin: 14.8% of the households reported a twin among the siblings, but only 60% gave permission to contact the twin. There was further erosion of the sample as only 20.6% of the twins agreed to participate if the initial contact was with another family member, compared to 60.4% if the initial contact was a twin him- or herself (and given the lower likelihood of an initial contact being with a twin, this suggests a low response rate for twins overall). Yet further erosion may have occurred at the next step of seeking contact information of all siblings in the family; the write-up is confusing on this point. With all these potential sampling problems, it is then quite striking that the absolute number of identical/monozygotic twin pairs concordant for homosexuality were only 6 (out of a total of 19 pairs where at least one twin was "non-heterosexual"). With such a small absolute number of monozygotic twin pairs concordant for homosexuality, the smallest bias in the assembly of the sample would introduce problems in data interpretation; loss of just two concordant twin pairs would have wiped out the findings. It is remarkable that Kendler et al. give no explicit attention to these problems. Thus, we must regard this new study, promoted by some as a replication of Bailey's original 1991 and 1993 studies, as having the same fatal flaws as those earlier studies and as rightly superseded by Bailey's report in 2000 that there is no statistically significant indication of genetic influence on sexual orientation.

Genetic Scanning

Mustanski et al. reported on a "full genome scan of sexual orientation in men" (p. 272). This is the third study of genetics and homosexuality to emerge from the laboratory of the associates of Dean Hamer, and this study utilized

Jones, Stanton L.; Kwee, Alex W. From *Journal of Psychology and Christianity (JPC)*, vol. 24, no. 4, Winter 2005, pp. 304–307, 308–312 (excerpts). Copyright © 2005 by Christian Association for Psychological Studies, Inc. – CAPS. Reprinted by permission.

146 families; 73 families previously studied by either Hamer, Hu, Magnuson, Hu, and Pattatucci or Hu et al., and 73 new families not previously studied. The same sample limitations are present in these studies as were discussed in Jones and Yarhouse (pp. 79–83). If these studies were attempting to establish population estimates, these would constitute biased samples, but because they explicitly state that they are looking for genetic factors in a subpopulation of homosexual men predetermined to be more likely to manifest genetic factors, these are limitations and not methodological weaknesses. They obtained their sample through "advertisements in local and national homophile publications" and the "sole inclusion criterion was the presence of at least two self-acknowledged gay male siblings" (p. 273), a rare occurrence indeed.

Two findings are worth noting. First, the Mustanski et al. study continued the pattern of failing to replicate the original 1993 Hamer finding of an Xq28 region of the X chromosome being linked to male homosexuality, this despite somewhat heroic statistical focus in this study. This is yet another blow to the credibility of their original findings.

Second, while media outlets headlined the Mustanski et al. study as having found genes linked to homosexuality on chromosomes 7, 8, and 10, this is precisely what they did *not* find, but rather "we found one region of near significance and two regions close to the criteria for suggestive linkage" (p. 273). None of their findings, in other words, achieved statistical significance. It is hard to tell whether these findings represent a cluster of near false positives that will fail future replication, or clues that will lead to more fine-grained and statistically significant findings. If the latter, these genetic segments may be neither necessary nor sufficient to cause homosexual orientation, and may either contribute to the causation of the orientation directly or indirectly. This is an intriguing but ambiguous report.

Human Brain Structure Studies

New brain research allows us to expand the reported findings on the relationship of brain structure to sexual orientation, and to correct one element of our prior presentation of the data in this complex field. We duplicate [here] . . . (Table 1) part of the table summarizing brain findings from pages 68–69 of Jones and Yarhouse.

Our correction is to recategorize in Table 1 the findings of Swaab and Hoffman from our listing, following the original report, as from the SDNH or sexually differentiated nucleus of the hypothalamus to a finding reporting on the INAH1 or interstitial nucleus of the hypothalamus, area 1. The review of Byne et al. pointed out that the SDNH *is* the INAH1; Swaab's 1988 report was an extension of his earlier work and not an exploration of a new area. The new work of Byne et al. continued the pattern of refuting Swaab's reported findings.

The new findings reporting on brain structure and sexual orientation (summarized in Table 1) come from the respected laboratory of William Byne and his colleagues. We cited Byne heavily in our critique of the famous Simon LeVay studies of brain differences in the INAH3 region. Byne et al. replicated the previous findings of sexual dimorphism (male-female differences) in INAH3, and thus it is now safe to say that this is a stable finding. Further, Byne and his team have refined the analysis to be able to say, based on their 2000 study, that the INAH3 size difference by sex "was attributable to a sex difference in neuronal number and not in neuronal size or density." Simply put, the INAH3 area in women is, on average, smaller than it is in men, and this is because women have fewer neurons in this area, and *not* because their neurons are smaller or less dense.

This makes the findings of Byne et al. on sexual orientation yet more curious; they found the size (specifically, volume) of the INAH3s of homosexual males

Table 1

Summary of Brain Differences by Biological Sex and Sexual Orientation

Study	INAH1	INAH2	INAH3	INAH4
Swaab & Fliers (1985)	HetM > HetF			
Swaab & Hoffman (1988)	HetM = HomM; (HetM & HomM) > HetF			
Allen et al. (1989)	HetM = HetF	HetM > HetF	HetM > HetF	HetM = HetF
LeVay (1991)	HetM = HetF	HetM = HetF	HetM > (HetF & HomM)	HetM = HetF
Byne et al. (2000)	HetM = HetF	HetM = HetF	HetM > HetF	HetM = HetF
Byne et al. (2001)	HetM = HetF	HetM = HetF	HetM > HetF	HetM = HetF
			HetM = HomM in number of neurons	

HetM = heterosexual males; HetF = heterosexual females; HomM = homosexual males.

to be intermediate (to a statistically nonsignificant degree) between heterosexual males and heterosexual females. In other words, the volume of the INAH3s was, on average, between the average volumes of heterosexual males and heterosexual females such that the differences did not achieve statistical significance in comparison to either heterosexual males or females. Hence, "Sexual orientation cannot be reliably predicted on the basis of INAH3 volume alone." Further, and to complicate things more, they found that the nonsignificant difference noted between homosexual and heterosexual males was *not* attributable (as it was for the male-female difference) to numbers of neurons, as homosexual and heterosexual males were found to have comparable neuronal counts. So, there may be a difference between homosexual and heterosexual males, but if there is, it is not the same type of difference as that between males and females.

To complicate the analysis even further, Byne et al. point out that these differences, if they exist, are not proof of prenatal, biological determination of sexual orientation. While it is possible that differences in INHA3 may be strongly influenced by prenatal hormones, "In addition, sex related differences may also emerge later in development as the neurons that survive become part of functional circuits" (p. 91). Specifically, the difference in volume could be attributed to "a reduction in neuropil within the INAH3 in the homosexual group" (p. 91) as a result of "postnatal experience." In other words, if there are brain structure differences between homosexuals and heterosexuals, they could as well be the result rather than the cause of sexual behavior and sexual preference. (The same conclusion about directionality of causation can be drawn about the new study showing activation of sexual brain centers in response to female pheromones by male heterosexuals, and to male pheromones by female heterosexuals *and* male homosexuals. The authors themselves point out that these brain activations could be the result of learning as well as evidence of the "hard-wiring" of the brain.) . . .

Second, and in a rare admission for those advancing biological explanations of sexual orientation, Roselli et al. admit that the direction of causation is at this time completely unclear, in the process echoing the possible causal role of postnatal experience mentioned by Byne et al. above:

> However, the existing data do not reveal which is established first—oSDN size or mate preference. One might assume that the neural structure is determined first and that this, in turn, guides the development of sexual partner preference. However, it is equally possible that some other factor(s), including social influences or learned associations, might shape sexual partner preference first. Then, once a sexual partner preference is established, the continued experiences and/or behaviors associated with a given preference might affect the size of the oSDN. (p. 241)

A new study released in June, 2005 has ignited the latest frenzy about biological causation of sexual orientation. In response to this study, the president of the Human Rights Campaign ("the largest national lesbian, gay, bisexual and transgender political organization") stated that "Science is closing the door on right-wing distortions. . . . The growing body of scientific evidence continues to refute the opponents of equality who maintain that sexual orientation is a 'choice.'" Chairman of the Case Western Reserve University Department of Biochemistry Michael Weiss expressed for the *New York Times* his hope that this study "will take the discussion about sexual preferences out of the realm of morality and put it into the realm of science." Both quotes epitomize the over-interpretation and illogic of those anxious to press findings from science to moral conclusions.

The new study appears to be a strong piece of scientific research that will have important implications for our understanding of the biological bases of sexual behavior. The researchers generated a gene fragment (the *"fruitless (fru)"* allele) that was "constitutively spliced in either the male or the female mode" in the chromosomes of the opposite sex (i.e., male fruit flies had the allele inserted in a female mode and female fruit flies had the allele inserted in a male mode) with dramatic effects: "Forcing female splicing in the male results in a loss of male courtship behavior and orientation, confirming that male-specific splicing of *fru* is indeed essential for male behavior. More dramatically, females in which *fru* is spliced in the male mode behave as if they were males: they court other females" (p. 786). The results reported were indeed powerful; the behavioral distinctions in the modified fruit flies were almost unequivocal.

The authors of this study were reasonably circumspect in their report of the implications of their findings, though others were not as noted before. Three issues deserve attention. First, as in our discussion of "gay sheep," the differences between human and animal (or insect) mating patterns are enormous, and those differences limit application to the human situation. Demir and Dickson noted that male courtship of the female fruit fly is highly scripted, "largely a fixed-action pattern" (p. 785). The finding that the normal, almost robotic mating patterns of this creature are hard-wired is hardly surprising; in contrast, the enormous complexity of human sexual and romantic response indicates that such a finding will be challenging to apply to the human condition. Further, the interpretation that this study establishes a genetic base for "sexual orientation" in fruit flies is careless; the study rather finds genetic determination (to some degree) of an entire pattern of mating/reproductive behavior. The genetic control of mating behavior in this study is of something both more and less than sexual orientation as experienced by humans.

Second, we have plenty of existing data to indicate that no such encompassing genetic determination of sexual behavior exists in humans. The behavior genetics evidence of sexual orientation (see the earlier discussion of the Kendler et al. study) provides strong evidence that genetic factors provide (at most) incomplete determination of sexual orientation, even if genetic factors are part of a multivariant causal array.

Third, we must question the following claim of the authors:

> Thus, male-specific splicing of *fru* is both necessary and *sufficient* [emphasis added] to specify male courtship behavior and sexual orientation. A complex innate behavior is thus specified by the action of a single gene, demonstrating that behavioral switch genes do indeed exist and identifying *fru* as one such gene.

Strictly understood, the authors appear to be claiming that the presence of *fru* elicits, *necessarily and sufficiently*, stereotypical male courtship by males of female fruit flies, but a famous study from a decade before falsifies the sufficiency of *fru* causation. Zhang and Odenwald reported on genetic alterations in male fruit flies which produced "homosexual behavior" in the altered fruit flies. This study too resulted in many tabloid headlines heralding the creation of a "homosexual gene." Media reports failed to cite the other curious finding of the study: when genetically normal or "straight" fruit flies were introduced into the habitat of the "gay" flies without females present, the normal (genetically unaltered) male flies began engaging in the same type of "homosexual" behavior as the genetically altered flies. In other words, genetically normal ("straight") flies began to act like homosexual flies because of their *social environment*. Thus, in a most biological experiment, evidence of environmental ("psychological") influence emerged once again. So if the authors of the 2005 study are claiming that the presence of *fru* elicits (is sufficient to produce) stereotypical male courtship, that claim was falsified a decade before by the finding that normal male fruit flies (presumably with intact *fru* alleles), when exposed to certain social contexts ("gay" flies), engage in behavior that violates the stereotypical male courtship of females; other conditions—specifically, *social* conditions—are also sufficient to elicit homosexual behavior in fruit flies.

Together, these three issues suggest that, as powerful as the recent findings about fruit flies are, interpretive caution in application to humans is indicated.

Fraternal Birth Order Research

The fraternal birth order studies by Ray Blanchard, Anthony Bogaert, and various other researchers purport to show that sexual orientation in men correlates with an individual's number of older brothers. Specifically, it is claimed that male homosexuals tend to be born later in their sibships than male heterosexuals, and that male homosexuality is statistically (and causally) related to the number of older biological brothers (but not sisters) in the family. This purported relationship within the fraternal birth order is such that each additional older brother, it is claimed, increases the odds of homosexuality by 33%, and for gay men with approximately 2.5 older brothers, older brothers equal all the other causes of homosexuality combined.

Blanchard, Bogaert, and others advance the so-called maternal immune hypothesis to explain the fraternal birth order effect. According to this hypothesis, some mothers progressively produce, in response to each succeeding male fetus, antibodies to a substance called the H-Y antigen, which is produced by male fetuses and foreign to female bodies. The maternally produced anti-H-Y antibodies are thought to be passed on to the male fetus, preventing the fetal brain from developing in a male typical pattern, thereby causing the affected sons to develop homosexual orientations in later life. So much hyperbole surrounds the maternal immune causal hypothesis that it appears the assumption is simply being made that the fraternal birth order effect itself is indisputable when, in fact, it is not. We will direct the bulk of our critical attention to the birth order phenomenon. The maternal immune theory underlying the phenomenon can be quite readily dispatched at this point by stating that no direct evidence has ever been found for it, and so it remains purely speculative.

The major flaw of the fraternal birth order research is that the main studies were conducted on nonrepresentative samples. For example, one of the "landmark" studies that demonstrated the birth order effect recruited its sample from the 1994 Toronto Gay Pride Parade and several LGBT community organizations. Nonrepresentative samples are known to be vulnerable to a variety of selection biases. For instance, perhaps later-born gay men were overrepresented in this sample because they were more apt to be "out and proud," participate in Gay Pride events, and affiliate with overtly LGBT groups. If later born siblings tend to be less conventional and more rebellious as some research shows, later-born gay men, accordingly, may be less gender conforming and more likely to flaunt their sexual orientation. This may have resulted in an overrepresentation of later-born gay men and an underrepresentation of earlier-born gay men at Gay Pride events and within LGBT groups, which naturally exaggerated the fraternal birth order effect in this sample. This is just one of several possible selection biases which may have flawed Blanchard and Bogaert's sample.

To his credit, Bogaert attempted to correct for the methodological flaw of selection bias by examining national probability samples in the United States and Britain respectively. His study yielded a finding of fraternal birth order effects in both samples. While this may appear to replicate initial research results, we must question the size of the effects given the large samples involved—over 1,700 subjects in each of the samples. Bogaert did not clearly report the effect sizes he found. It is well known that using large enough samples, even small differences can be found to be statistically significant. Since statistical significance is a function of both sample size and effect size, and we really care about the effect size (and not merely that it is non-zero), Bogaert's findings are quite unhelpful.

In an even more recent study, Bogaert and Cairney attempted to answer the question of whether there is a fraternal birth order and parental age interaction effect in the prediction of sexual orientation. The researchers examined two samples—a U.S. national probability sample, and the flawed Canadian sample which we discussed above. The study based on the U.S. sample found an inter-action, but the data was so flawed—and acknowledged to be so by the authors themselves—that we cannot possibly take its conclusion seriously. Specifically, the preexisting U.S. data allowed for only an examination of absolute (not fraternal) birth order, surmised sexual orientation from behavior alone, and did not separate biological from non-biological siblings. The conclusion was counterintuitive in that while a positive association between (absolute) birth order and the likelihood of homosexuality was found, this association was weakened and in fact *reversed* with increasing maternal age. We believe that this conclusion highlights the problem of bias when researchers attempt to find putative phenomena in data to support a cherished theory. If one is trying to establish a link between mater-nal age and homosexuality, it seems counterintuitive that the likelihood of homosexuality weakens or is reversed with increasing maternal age. Of course, if there is no relationship between sexual orientation and maternal age (which we suspect), a finding of *any* relationship is prob-ably spurious and a methodological artifact. The research-ers acknowledge the counterintuitiveness of their result by stating that they "know of no evidence of a stronger maternal reaction [to the H-Y antigen] in younger (versus older) mothers" (p. 32), betraying their bias towards a theory for which no direct evidence has ever been estab-lished, and then calling for new research.

Turning to the Canadian sample, Bogaert and Cairney found a Parental Age x Birth Order interaction. Their weighted analysis (giving larger families a greater impact on the results) revealed that this interaction was carried by a Mother's Age x Older Sisters effect. This find-ing actually *undermines* the fraternal birth order theory because it provides some evidence that homosexuality is independent of the fraternal birth order effect. The authors acknowledge but downplay this, calling instead for the gathering of new data.

Other studies have falsified the fraternal birth order effect or showed no support for the maternal immune hypothesis. Using an enormous and nationally representa-tive sample of adolescents that we discuss fully below, Bearman and Brückner found "no evidence for a specula-tive evolutionary model of homosexual preference" (i.e., the older-brother findings; p. 1199).

Despite various methodological problems with the fraternal birth order research, we concede that the evidence as a whole points to some sort of relationship

between the number of older brothers and homosexuality. As responsible scientists, we should approach this body of research critically but not ignore the fact that it con-sistently shows some link between sexual orientation and fraternal but not sororal birth order. Research may well identify some pathway by which some men develop a sta-ble same-sex attraction that is linked to their placement in the birth order. However, those who argue that the mater-nal immunosensitivity theory explains the fraternal birth order effect run into the problem of having to show that the same hypothesis does not underlie pedophilia, sex-ual violence, and other forms of sexual deviancy. While Blanchard, Bogaert, and other researchers deny any link between fraternal birth order and pedophilia, or they believe that any such link exists only for pedophiles who are homosexual, other studies have demonstrated a link between fraternal birth order and general (pedophilic and non-pedophilic) sexual offending, raising the possibility that homosexuality shares a common pathway with some forms of sexual deviance.

Research has not clearly established what this path-way is. One of the most natural but politically divisive speculations, which cautiously raises its head in the lit-erature now and then, is that childhood sexualization and abuse has some causative relationship to homosexuality and pedophilia. This speculation is logical in relation to the fraternal birth order effect because younger brothers with higher fraternal birth order indices may have a higher probability of being victimized sexually by older brothers or otherwise experiencing same-sex sexualization. Pread-olescent sexualization and abuse underlie the post-natal learning theory of homosexuality and pedophilia, which most recently has been supported by James in his review of several major studies. However plausible this theory appears, it is based on inferences from other studies and the direct empirical evidence for it is extremely weak.

Familial Structure Impact

A particularly powerful study challenging all of the major paradigms asserting biological determination of sexual orientation, and of the claim that there is no meaningful evidence of psychological/experiential causation of ori-entation, was recently published. Bearman and Brückner reported on analyses of an enormous database of almost 30,000 sexuality interviews with adolescents, with fasci-nating findings on the determinants of same-sex attrac-tion for males (they found no evidence of significant determinants for females). Their summary of their find-ings merits citation in full:

> The findings presented here confirm some find-ings from previous research and stand in marked contrast to most previous research in a number of respects. First, we find no evidence for intrauter-ine transfer of hormone effects on social behavior. Second, we find no support for genetic influences on same-sex preference net of social structural

constraints. Third, we find no evidence for a speculative evolutionary model of homosexual preference. Finally, we find substantial indirect evidence in support of a socialization model at the individual level. (p. 1199)

Their second conclusion is a direct reference to the types of genetic influence posited by Bailey and others; the third conclusion a direct reference to the "older-brother" findings of Blanchard, Bogaert and others. But not only do their findings contradict other research, a new finding of socialization effects on same-sex attraction emerge from their data (see Table 2).

Bearman and Brückner found a single family constellation arrangement that significantly increased the likelihood that an adolescent male would report same-sex attraction, and that was when the adolescent male was a dizygotic (fraternal) twin whose co-twin is a sister (what they call "male opposite-sex twins"); in this arrangement, occurrence of same-sex attraction more than doubled over the base-rate of 7% to 8%: "we show that adolescent male opposite-sex twins are *twice as likely* as expected to report same-sex attraction, and that the pattern of concordance (similarity across pairs) of same-sex preference for sibling pairs does not suggest genetic influence independent of the social context" (p. 1181). They advance a socialization hypothesis to explain this finding, specifically proposing that sexual attraction is an outgrowth of gender socializa-

tion, and that no arrangement presents as much a challenge to parents to gender socialization than for a boy to be born simultaneous with a girl co-twin. In other words, they suggest that the parental task of accomplishing effective solidification of male sexual identity is challenged by parents having to handle a mixed-sex twin pair. The result of the diminished effectiveness of sexual identity formation in boys on average is the increased probability of same-sex attraction in the group of boys with twin sisters.

Bearman and Brückner go on to explore in their data the possibility that there could be a hormonal explanation for this finding: "Our data falsify the hormonal transfer hypothesis [i.e., the hypothesis posited to explain the fraternal birth order phenomenon], by isolating a single condition that eliminates the OS effect we observe—the presence of an older same-sex sibling" (p. 1181). Put simply, they found their effect disappeared when the boy with the twin sister was born into a family where there was already an older brother, an effect they attributed to the family already having grown accustomed to the process of establishing the sexual identity of a boy child; parents appear to be able to better handle the special challenges of a mixed-sex twin pair when they have already had some practice with an older brother. They firmly suggest that their "results support the hypothesis that less gendered socialization in early childhood and preadolescence shapes subsequent same-sex romantic preferences" (p. 1181). At a moment in time when it is common for many to deny that any firm evidence exists for the influence of non-biological causes on sexual orientation, these are remarkable findings (perhaps especially when the presence of an older brother decreases rather than increases the likelihood of homosexual orientation). . . .

Table 2

Core Findings of Bearman & Brückner

Relationship (Subject is a . . .)	% Reporting Same-Sex Attraction	N (all males)
Opposite Sex Dizygotic Twin	16.8%	185
Same Sex Dizygotic Twin	9.8%	276
Same Sex Monozygotic Twin	9.9%	262
Opposite Sex Full Sibling	7.3%	427
Same Sex Full Sibling	7.9%	596
Other (adopted non-related; half-sibling)	10.6%	832

STANTON L. JONES is a professor of psychology and provost at Wheaton College. He received his PhD in clinical psychology at Arizona State University and is the author of over 50 articles and book chapters.

ALEX W. KWEE is a licensed clinical psychologist and cofounder and president of Harmony Pacific Clinical Consultants (HPCC). He has published and presented internationally on various facets of cross-cultural psychology, values, and addiction.

EXPLORING THE ISSUE

Is Homosexuality Biologically Based?

Critical Thinking and Reflection

1. Is homosexuality a product of biology or learning? Support your claims with research evidence.
2. Many argue that if it were proven that homosexuality is biologically based, discrimination against homosexuals would decrease. Support this argument with research on discrimination and prejudice.
3. In Rahman's review of the research, he believes the evidence clearly points to a biological, prenatal based homosexuality. On the other hand, Jones and Kwee find the same research to be ambiguous and flawed. In fact, they interpret much of the same findings as evidence of a postnatal, learned homosexuality. What would convince you to take one side or the other? Provide reasons for your position.
4. Read the section from Rahman's controversial book *Born Gay* (co-authored with Glenn Wilson) about treating homosexuality. Also, find the full Jones and Kwee article and read the section entitled "Treatment Outcome Research." Each argues opposing viewpoints on the malleability of sexual orientation. Do you believe sexual orientation can be changed? Should we pursue such a research question?
5. Stanton Jones, the first author of the second article, has recently co-authored a book entitled *Ex-Gays?* In this book, he reports a complex research study that he argues is an indicator that homosexuals can change their sexual orientation. If this is true, what would this finding mean for the possibility of biological determination of sexual orientation?

Create Central

www.mhhe.com/createcentral

Additional Resource

Wilson, G., & Rahman, Q. (2008). *Born Gay: The Psychology of Sex Orientation*. Peter Owen Publishers London.

Internet References . . .

Evidence for God

www.godandscience.org/evolution/genetics_of_
homosexuality.html

Psychology Today

www.psychologytoday.com/blog/sexing-the-
body/201111/are-we-born-gay

Unit 2

UNIT

Research Issues

*R*esearch methods are the means by which psychologists test their ideas. Yet the way that psychologists conduct their research and interpret their findings is sometimes the subject of controversy. When, for example, are the findings sufficient to support a particular conclusion? Psychological practices, such as psychotherapy, are complicated phenomena, involving not only observable behaviors, the typical province of empirical methods, but also less observable client and therapist meanings. Also, how generalizable are such findings to other cultures? If American researchers dominate the research on a given topic, how applicable are these findings to other cultures, with different customs and social traditions? And what about specific research assumptions, such as scientific determinism, the notion that all things, including humans, are determined by causal forces outside their control? Could these assumptions, when taught to psychology students, affect them in unexpected ways?

Selected, Edited and with Issue Framing Material by:
Brent Slife, *Brigham Young University*

ISSUE

Is American Psychological Research Generalizable to Other Cultures?

YES: Gerald J. Haeffel, Erik D. Thiessen, Matthew W. Campbell, Michael P. Kaschak, and Nicole M. McNeil, from "Theory, Not Cultural Context, Will Advance American Psychology," *American Psychologist* (September 2009)

NO: Jeffrey Jensen Arnett, from "The Neglected 95%, a Challenge to Psychology's Philosophy of Science," *American Psychologist* (September 2009)

Learning Outcomes

After reading this issue, you should be able to:

- Describe some of the advantages and disadvantages of basic research compared to cross-culturally sensitive studies.
- Know what determines scientific progress and understanding.

ISSUE SUMMARY

YES: Gerald Haeffel and his colleagues believe that psychological studies of American people often generalize to people of other cultures, especially when basic processes are being studied.

NO: Jeffrey Arnett, psychological research professor, argues that culture is central to the functioning of humans and thus to psychological findings.

We live in a multicultural world, with important and substantial difference among cultures. Unfortunately, however, traditional psychological research has focused almost exclusively on a narrow portion of this multicultural world. Specifically, the majority of academic psychological investigations have been conducted using undergraduate American college students as participants (and generally those enrolled in psychology courses). While there are some variations within this subpopulation, college students are typically more homogenous than the wider population in categories like socioeconomic status, education, ethnicity, age, and values.

The major concern with studying such a narrow segment of the wider multicultural world is the question of *generalizability*—do studies of American college students actually tell us much about other populations in other circumstances? If they do not, then the findings of such research would not count as general knowledge. These findings would be viewed as more local, and thus not necessarily applicable to other populations. The primary issue in the generalizability question is whether contextual and cultural factors are *vital* to understanding humans. Are

these factors merely "add-ons," and humans are essentially the same the world over? If so, investigations of *any* humans, including American college students, tell us what is essential about all other humans. Alternatively, if situational and ethnic factors are required to understand the functioning of humans, then humans are not such interchangeable parts.

In the first article, Haeffel and his colleagues believe that concerns about the generalizability of American psychology are overstated. Although they agree that cultural factors are a valid concern for some research topics, such as gender roles and family structure, they consider these factors less relevant to "basic human processes," processes that are universal to all humans, such as perception and cognition. Haeffel and his colleagues also dispute the notion that these basic processes have no real-world implications. They cite several examples, which they believe illustrate the critical role of basic research, including the recent development of cognitive behavioral therapy from basic research on cognition. Science mainly progresses, they argue, on the basis of falsifiable theories that deal with core psychological processes. Cultural factors are important for understanding the particular manifestations of these universals, but these factors do not prevent the generalizability of research on these basic processes.

Psychological researcher Jeffrey Arnett argues that psychological investigations must become dramatically less American to truly make progress in understanding humans. By Arnett's calculations, psychologists conduct research on less than 5 percent of the world's population, and this selective group does *not* automatically represent the other 95 percent. Therefore, as Dr. Arnett maintains,

we should be more cautious about assuming the generalizability of psychological findings. Psychologists should do more to train investigators in multicultural issues; rigorous hypothesis testing alone is not sufficient to advance psychological knowledge. Only by broadening psychology's cultural horizons will the research become ecologically valid and truly contribute to an understanding of how people live their lives.

POINT

- Psychology should not focus primarily on culture and diversity issues
- Science progresses by rigorously testing falsifiable theories that include universals.
- Humans around the world have the same basic psychological processes.
- The careful control of variables through the scientific method will answer the basic questions of psychology.

COUNTERPOINT

- Psychology should step up its recognition and promotion of multicultural awareness, especially in research.
- Understanding cultural context is essential to the advancement of psychological science.
- The ways in which humans meaningfully carry out their activities are particular to their context.
- Laboratory control cannot answer many important questions about human nature, development, and experience.

YES

Gerald J. Haeffel et al.

Theory, Not Cultural Context, Will Advance American Psychology

In his recent article, "The Neglected 95%: Why American Psychology Needs to Become Less American," Arnett (October 2008) provided a thought-provoking analysis of the current state of psychology. He made two primary arguments: (a) Psychological research using American samples cannot generalize to the rest of the world, and (b) psychology's emphasis on basic processes should be replaced by an emphasis on context and culture. We agree with the author's call for greater attention to issues of context. However, we[1] fundamentally disagree with his position on issues related to generalizability and basic research. The goal of this comment is to provide a critical evaluation of Arnett's primary arguments as well as to offer alternative strategies for facilitating scientific progress on cultural and diversity issues.

Generalizability

Arnett's (2008) first argument is that American psychology does not represent people everywhere, and thus, its findings are not generalizable. This argument is a variation of the well-known "college sophomore problem." The argument is as follows: Research findings from a select sample such as college sophomores (or Americans, in this case) will not apply to other samples. This is a valid concern, and clearly there are situations in which research on select samples may not generalize. However, the problem of generalizability is often overstated. Studies using one sample of humans (e.g., Americans) often generalize to other samples of humans (e.g., Spaniards), particularly when basic processes[2] are being studied (e.g., Anderson, Lindsay, & Bushman, 1999). The results of studies investigating a wide range of psychological phenomena, including personality, information processing, aggression, and mental illness, tend to hold in a variety of contexts and with a variety of participant samples (see Stanovich, 2007, for review). The consistency of research findings across contexts and samples should not be surprising given that all humans, whether they live in America or a developing country, share a common genome, brain organization, and capacity for cognition, perception, and emotion.

The college sophomore problem is not new, and it is not clear that Arnett's (2008) discussion advances our understanding of the issue. His case is based largely on "straw man" arguments. He provided numerous examples of when differences between Americans and other samples would be expected, including gender roles, marital relations, family structure, and the nature of formal education. Although subjectively compelling, these examples do not address the issue of the generalizability of research on *basic processes*. The existence of cultural variation does not imply that there are no universals worth studying. The same basic process can generate different products depending on the structure of the environment in which that process operates. It is not enough to show that American culture is different from other cultures. This fact is not disputed. The critical question is what these differences mean for human psychology. That is, what do cultural differences (e.g., gender roles, family structure, formal mathematical skills) say about the basic human processes (e.g., perception, cognition, emotion) that played a role in the development of those differences?

Basic Research

Arnett's (2008) second argument is that psychological research should focus on culture and diversity rather than on basic processes. He went so far as to state, "At a time when there are numerous daunting international problems that psychological science could address, such as religious fundamentalism, terrorism, international ecological crises, war, the HIV pandemic, and growing poverty, the main thrust in American psychology continues to be a research focus on processes and principles that goes forward as if none of these issues existed" (p. 612). This statement demonstrates a fundamental misunderstanding about basic research. His statement is akin to asking why medical research continues to focus on growing stem cells when there are more daunting problems such as Alzheimer's and Parkinson's disease. Basic research in psychology has clear implications for real-world issues. For example, research on information processing and behavioral activation has led to the creation of highly effective treatments (e.g., cognitive behavior therapy) for disorders such as depression and anxiety. Similarly, research on early experience with binocular vision (e.g., Banks, Aslin, & Letson, 1975) demonstrated the critical need for early (as opposed to delayed) detection

Haeffel, Gerald J., et al. From *American Psychologist*, vol. 64, no. 6, September 2009, pp. 570–571. Copyright © 2009 by American Psychological Association. Reprinted by permission via Rightslink.

and treatment of conditions that cause abnormal binocular experience such as esotropia. In addition, research on obedience (e.g., the Milgram studies and Zimbardo's prison experiment) has important implications for understanding the sometimes atrocious behavior of humans (e.g., Abu Ghraib, terrorism, Nazi war crimes). These are just a few of many examples that illustrate the critical role of basic research (both human and animal[3]) in understanding, and creating solutions for, real-world issues.

Cultural Context—Where's the Theory?

Arnett's (2008) argument against basic research raises fundamental questions about how to define science (i.e., the problem of demarcation) and how to evaluate scientific progress. Following Arnett's reasoning, science is defined by its applicability to real-world problems, sample representativeness, and the use of nonexperimental designs. Thus, he concluded that psychological science is "incomplete" because of its focus on basic processes, American samples, and experimental designs. In contrast to Arnett, we subscribe to a philosophy of science described by philosophers such as Popper and Meehl. According to Popper (1959), science is characterized by the falsification of theories. If a theory is falsifiable, it is by definition scientific. Popper's definition of science does not depend on whether the work is basic or applied. It does not depend on the type of research design one uses (longitudinal, cross-sectional, experimental, quasi-experimental, etc). It does not depend on the sample (e.g., American or Nigerian). Science is characterized by testing and falsifying theories (Meehl, 1978).

In light of this philosophy, it is unclear why research on cultural context should be considered more scientifically progressive than research on basic processes. In fact, Arnett's (2008) description of cultural research raises concerns that it could actually slow progress in psychology. His vision of cultural psychology does not invoke theory or the importance of having testable hypotheses. Rather, cultural psychology appears to be exploratory and descriptive in nature. Will cultural psychology simply be an anecdotal record of cultural differences or a collection of replication studies? Will 100% of the world's population have to be studied before psychology can be considered a "complete science?" Arnett failed to provide any information about how cultural psychology will progress as a science.

From a philosophy of science perspective, Arnett's (2008) distinction between cultural context and basic processes is a false dichotomy. The problem with human psychology is not its focus on basic processes rather than cultural context; it is the lack of strong falsifiable theories (Meehl, 1978). Cultural context cannot exist in a vacuum isolated from basic processes such as cognition, perception, language, and so forth. If cultural research is to take hold in psychology, then it must be theory driven and integrated into work on basic processes. It is not enough to surmise that different cultures may lead to different outcomes. Researchers need to specify the conditions for when they would and would not expect culture to affect basic processes and behaviors.

Cultural context can serve an important purpose in psychological science: It will enable us to test hypotheses about which features of human behavior are acquired through experience and which are basic (or innate). Basic processes are mechanisms via which humans—and other animals—are able to respond adaptively to typical environments; however, these processes can be distinguished from another kind of adaptation, acquired associations or strategies (such as reading), which vary across situations and cultures. Within this framework, cultural adaptations can be thought to arise from the operation of basic processes, such as learning.[4] For example, at one time it was thought that language was acquired solely through imitation of and reinforcement by models within one's sociocultural context (e.g., Skinner's, 1957, *Verbal Behavior*), until Chomsky's synthesis of cross-cultural linguistic variation revealed important similarities across cultures, suggesting that language acquisition also depends on a more basic structure or process that all humans share. Similarly, conventional wisdom suggests that abstract mathematical concepts are learned through years of formal education and training; however, studies of hunter-gatherer cultures (e.g., the Pirahã; Gordon, 2004) and even of nonhuman animals (e.g., monkeys, rats, pigeons; Gallistel & Gelman, 2000) have shown that we all share a common system for representing the abstract concept of number. In clinical psychology, many assume that eating disorders such as anorexia nervosa and bulimia nervosa share a common genetic etiology. However, recent research suggests that the genetic diathesis for bulimia nervosa may exhibit greater pathoplasticity cross-culturally than the diathesis for anorexia nervosa; this finding indicates distinct etiologies for these disorders (Keel & Klump, 2003). These examples highlight the importance of using cultural context to test theories about basic and acquired human behavior.

Conclusion

Focusing on cultural context *rather* than basic processes is not going to advance American psychology, or psychology in general. Neither [is] having students travel abroad or take anthropology classes (as recommended by Arnett), in and of themselves. Rather, science will advance by developing and testing theories. We believe that psychological science can benefit most by using differences in culture and context to develop and test novel hypotheses about basic human processes.

Notes

1. The authors of this commentary represent a broad cross-section of psychological science including clinical, developmental, biological, and cognitive areas.

2. By basic processes, we mean those psychological or biological processes that are shared by all humans at appropriate developmental levels (e.g., cognition, perception, learning, brain organization, genome).

3. In addition to basic research on humans, there is also a large body of animal research to consider. For example, Michael Davis's research delineating the neural basis of fear and anxiety in rats led to the creation of a cognitive enhancer (D-cycloserine), which is currently being used to treat Iraq veterans with posttraumatic stress disorder (Davis, Myers, Ressler, & Rothbaum, 2005). Similarly, Michael Meaney's (2001) research on maternal care and gene expression in rats

has tremendous implications for understanding of human attachment, stress reactivity, and even developmental disorders such as autism.

4. Note that this formulation of the purpose of cross-cultural psychology differs markedly from Arnett's (2008), which espouses cultural representativeness as a goal unto itself.

GERALD J. HAEFFEL is an assistant professor of psychology at Notre Dame. His program of research is devoted to understanding the cognitive processes and products that contribute to risk and resilience for depression.

Jeffrey Jensen Arnett

 **NO**

The Neglected 95%, a Challenge to Psychology's Philosophy of Science

My goal in writing "The Neglected 95%: Why American Psychology Needs to Become Less American" (Arnett, October 2008) was to fuel a conversation in psychology about whether American psychological research should become more reflective of how human beings in different cultures around the world experience their lives. I am pleased to see that many of my colleagues have taken up this conversation, as represented in the four comments [in] *American Psychologist* . . . [published in September 2009]. The four comments were well chosen in that they represent quite different reactions to my article. Two of the comments were generally in support of my thesis that American psychology is too narrow culturally, and sought to provide additional information on the issues I raised. The other two comments were in opposition to my thesis and presented the grounds for their opposition. In this rejoinder I address the issues raised in [the second of the] opposing comments. Following this, I address the more general problem that cuts across the comments: American psychology's dominant philosophy of science. . . .

What Is Science? What Is Scientific Progress?

The most extensive of the four commentaries is the one offered by Haeffel, Thiessen, Campbell, Kaschak, and McNeil . . . [September 2009, *American Psychologist*], who took the position that "Theory, Not Cultural Context, Will Advance American Psychology" (p. 570). Their main goal was to defend the value of research on basic processes (e.g., cognition, perception, learning) and question the value of culturally diverse research.

Haeffel et al. (2009) are on shaky ground from the beginning. They showed the limits of their perceptions in asserting that "the problem of generalizability is often overstated" (p. 570), offering in support of this statement the assertion "Studies using one sample of humans (e.g., Americans) often generalize to other samples of humans (e.g., Spaniards)" (p. 570). Even adding Spaniards to Americans (and throwing in Canadians for good measure) still makes for less than 5% of the world's population. Psychologists are far too quick to jump from one study of Americans and one study of Spaniards to a declaration of

a universal psychological principle. It is not the problem of generalizability that is overstated but the research findings of psychologists based on a tiny and unusual segment of humanity.

There may be an effective case to be made for the value of psychological research on basic processes, but Haeffel and colleagues (2009) did not make it.[1] They claimed that I suffer from a "fundamental misunderstanding about basic research" and that my position is "akin to asking why medical research continues to focus on growing stem cells when there are more daunting problems such as Alzheimer's and Parkinson's disease" (p. 570). If only the connection between psychological research on basic processes and real-world human problems were as clear as the relation between stem cell research and diseases like Alzheimer's and Parkinson's! The relation between stem cell research and treatments for Alzheimer's and Parkinson's disease is evident even to the nonscientist. The relation between basic research in psychology and real human problems is far less clear even to a research psychologist. There may be value in psychological research on basic processes, especially when the results are linked to cultural contexts, as Haeffel et al. suggested. It is just that research on basic processes alone is not enough for a science of humanity. This approach to research leaves out too much about cultural beliefs, cultural practices, and social relations.

Haeffel et al. (2009) accurately identified the heart of the difference between my perspective and theirs as a divergence in views of "how to define science . . . and how to evaluate scientific progress" (p. 570). They hold to a philosophy of science they attribute to Popper (1959) and Meehl (1978): "If a theory is falsifiable, it is by definition scientific" (Haeffel et al., 2009, p. 570). To some extent, I agree with this view. Certainly testing falsifiable hypotheses is one part of psychological science. However, restricting research to falsifiable theories alone is far too narrow a view of psychology as a human science. A focus on falsifiable theories narrows psychology's intellectual and scientific scope mainly to the laboratory, where experimental situations can be carefully controlled. The problem with this focus is that laboratory studies are often ecologically invalid and have little relation to how people actually live and how they experience their lives. There are many aspects of human development, behavior, and experience that are worth investigating even if they cannot be reduced to falsifiable theories (Rogoff, 2003). Psychology needs to get over its "physics envy" and adapt its methods and theoretical approaches to its uniquely human topic, in all its cultural complexity and diversity, rather than endlessly and fruitlessly aping the natural sciences.

Toward a Broader Philosophy of Our Human Science

The four comments on my article (Arnett, 2008) are diverse, but together they suggest a need for a reexamination of psychology's dominant philosophy of science. Even the two comments that were sympathetic to my thesis did not fully grasp the crux of the problem. Both assumed that a cultural understanding of human psychology could be attained through cross-cultural research, not realizing how transporting American-based theories and methods to other cultures might result in missing the most distinctive and essential features of those cultures. The two opposing comments represented well the traditional approach to psychological research, with its confident assurance that progress in psychology is best served by following the model of the natural sciences, investigating basic processes in search of universal laws, with limited or no attention to that distracting variable, cultural context, that actually means the most to how people behave, how they function psychologically, and how they understand and interpret their lives.

I advocate a broader, more intellectually vibrant and inclusive philosophy of science. The goal of the human sciences should not be simply the pursuit of universal laws and the falsification of theories—no matter how dull or trivial the theory, no matter how little relation the theory has to how people experience life outside the laboratory. The goal of the human sciences should be to use the tools of the scientific method to illuminate our understanding of human behavior, human functioning, and human development. The tools of the scientific method in psychology should be construed broadly to include not just laboratory tasks but any systematic investigation of human phenomena. In this philosophy of science, the structured interview and the ethnography are no less legitimate as tools of the scientific method than are the laboratory or the questionnaire. Many diverse methods are welcome, and all contribute valuable pieces to the mosaic that makes up a full understanding of humanity.

That mosaic is still missing many large and essential pieces, over a century after psychology was first established as a field. However, many research psychologists are working daily to fill it in, using a wide range of theories and methods (Jensen, 2010). What we need now in American psychology is not a narrowing of theories and methods to those that seem best to mimic the methods of the natural sciences, but a wider range of new, creative theories and methods, synthesizing cultural perspectives from all over the world, that will broaden our understanding of the endlessly fascinating human experience.

Note

1. Haeffel et al. (2009) claimed, "Basic research in psychology has clear implications for real-world issues" (p. 570), but the examples they provided fall flat. Research on information processing and behavioral activation has not "led to the creation of highly effective treatments (e.g., cognitive behavior therapy) for disorders such as depression and anxiety" (p. 570). Cognitive behavior therapy was developed in the 1950s and 1960s by Albert Ellis and Aaron Beck, and its roots are in ancient Greek philosophy, not basic research on information processing and behavioral activation. To find an example of basic research related to any of the problems I suggested that psychology should address (e.g., religious fundamentalism, terrorism, international ecological crises, war), the authors are forced to go back half a century to Milgram's obedience studies and Zimbardo's prison experiment. I agree about the value of the Milgram and Zimbardo studies, and I regard it as a great pity that psychological research today is rarely as creative in its methods as those studies were. As for research on "abnormal binocular experience such as esotropia" (p. 570), this seems more in the realm of optometry than psychology.

Jeffrey Jensen Arnett is a psychological research professor in the Department of Psychology at Clark University. Dr. Arnett is the author of several books on adolescents.

EXPLORING THE ISSUE

Is American Psychological Research Generalizable to Other Cultures?

Critical Thinking and Reflection

1. Arnett accuses psychology of "physics envy" and suggests psychology should develop methods that better reflect the unique nature of humans. Why does he make this accusation, and what sorts of methods might be considered in this development?
2. Haeffel and colleagues make a distinction between "basic research" and the cross-cultural studies suggested by Arnett. What are the advantages and disadvantages of basic research compared to culturally sensitive studies? From your perspective, which is more needed in psychology, and why do you hold this position?
3. Why is generalizability such an important issue for some psychologists? Are there disadvantages to increasing generalizability through greater experimental control?
4. Both articles in this issue are written by scholars at American universities. How might their own cultural perspective inform or limit their view of this issue?
5. A central question debated in these two articles is what counts as scientific progress and understanding. What are the different understandings of these authors on the issue of progress, and how does this understanding impact their respective arguments?

Create Central

www.mhhe.com/createcentral

Additional Resources

Matsumoto, D., and Hwang, S. H. (2011). Reading facial expressions of emotion. Retrieved from www .apa.org/science/about/psa/2011/05/facial-expressions .aspx

Rubin, B., Gluck, M. E., Knoll, C. M., Lorence, M., and Geliebter, A. (2008). Comparison of eating disorders and body image disturbances between Eastern and Western countries. *Eating and Weight Disorders, 13* (2), 73–80.

Internet Reference . . .

Psychology Research Issues

www.academyprojects.org/est.htm

Selected, Edited and with Issue Framing Material by:
Brent Slife, *Brigham Young University*

ISSUE

Are Traditional Empirical Methods Sufficient to Provide Evidence for Psychological Practice?

YES: APA Presidential Task Force on Evidence-Based Practice, from "Report of the 2005 Presidential Task Force on Evidence-Based Practice," *American Psychologist* (May/June 2006)

NO: Brent D. Slife and Dennis C. Wendt, from "The Next Step in the Evidence-Based Practice Movement," APA Convention Presentation (August 2006)

Learning Outcomes
After reading this issue, you should be able to:
• Understand what has led to traditional empirical methods being considered sufficient evidence for psychological practices.

ISSUE SUMMARY

YES: The APA Presidential Task Force on Evidence-Based Practice assumes that a variety of traditional empirical methods is sufficient to provide evidence for psychological practices.

NO: Psychologist Brent D. Slife and researcher Dennis C. Wendt contend that traditional empirical methods are guided by a single philosophy that limits the diversity of methods.

Imagine that one of your family members needs to see a therapist for a severe depression. Of the two therapists available, the first therapist's practices are supported by evidence obtained through traditional scientific methods. The second therapist's practices are not. The latter's practices could be equally effective or even more effective than the first therapist's practices, but we do not know. Which therapist would you choose for this member of your family?

Most people would readily choose therapists who have scientific evidence for their interventions. They think of psychotherapy much like they think of medicine, with treatments that have stood the test of science. Just as physicians can provide evidence that pain relievers actually relieve pain, so too psychologists hope to provide evidence that their practices deliver their desired results. Because not all psychological treatments come with evidence to support their use, some psychologists worry that some treatments could actually do more harm than good. It is with this potential harm in mind that many psychologists banded together to establish empirically supported treatments (ESTs). The goal was to establish a list of ESTs for specific psychological disorders. Those involved in this movement (various task forces from different divisions

of the American Psychological Association) initially stressed the use of randomized clinical (or controlled) trials (RCTs)—a specific type of research design—to be sure that the scientific examination of these treatments was rigorous and thorough.

In the YES selection, however, the APA Presidential Task Force on Evidence-Based Practice questions whether too much emphasis has been placed on RCT research designs. This Task Force affirms the need for empirically based evidence in psychology but tries to reframe the notion of evidence-based practice so that a diversity of empirical methods, including correlational and even case study methods, are considered important for producing evidence. The Task Force calls for objectivity in gathering all forms of evidence. In fact, it still considers RCTs the most rigorous type of objective method. However, it also acknowledges that other empirical approaches to gathering information and evidence can and do have their place in deciding psychology's evidence-based practices.

In the NO selection, psychologist Brent D. Slife and researcher Dennis Wendt applaud the APA Task Force for taking important steps in the right direction. Nevertheless, they argue that the Task Force's statement is "ultimately and fundamentally inadequate." The Task Force correctly champions the objectivity and diversity of methods and evidence, in their view, but they contend that the Task Force is not objective and diverse enough. They claim that just as the EST movement restricted the gathering of evidence to a single method (RCTs), the Task Force's suggestions assume, but never justify, that evidence-based practice should be restricted to a single *epistemology* of method. They acknowledge that many psychologists view this empirical epistemology as not affecting the outcome of research, but they note that most practices that are considered evidence-based fit the biases of the philosophy of empiricism.

POINT

- Psychological treatments should be supported by evidence.
- Evidence should include RCTs as well as other empirical methods.
- Evidence should be both objective and diverse.
- Evidence should not be limited to a single method (RCT).

COUNTERPOINT

- Not all psychologists agree on what qualifies as evidence.
- Traditional empirical methods are not the only methods by which evidence can be obtained.
- Including only the "empirical" is neither objective nor diverse.
- Evidence should not be limited to a single methodology.

YES

Report of the 2005 Presidential Task Force on Evidence-Based Practice[1]

From the very first conceptions of applied psychology as articulated by Lightner Witmer, who formed the first psychological clinic in 1896, psychologists have been deeply and uniquely associated with an evidence-based approach to patient care. As Witmer pointed out, "the pure and the applied sciences advance in a single front. What retards the progress of one retards the progress of the other; what fosters one fosters the other." As early as 1947 the idea that doctoral psychologists should be trained as both scientists and practitioners became the American Psychological Association (APA) policy. Early practitioners such as Frederick C. Thorne articulated the methods by which psychological practitioners integrate science into their practice by . . . "increasing the application of the experimental approach to the individual case into the clinician's own experience." Thus, psychologists have been on the forefront of the development of evidence-based practice for decades.

Evidence-based practice in psychology is therefore consistent with the past twenty years of work in evidence-based medicine, which advocated for improved patient outcomes by informing clinical practice with relevant research. Sackett and colleagues describe evidence-based medicine as "the conscientious, explicit, and judicious use of current best evidence in making decisions about the care of individual patients." The use and misuse of evidence-based principles in the practice of health care has affected the dissemination of health care funds, but not always to the benefit of the patient. Therefore, psychologists, whose training is grounded in empirical methods, have an important role to play in the continuing development of evidence-based practice and its focus on improving patient care.

One approach to implementing evidence-based practice in health care systems has been through the development of guidelines for best practice. During the early part of the evidence-based practice movement, APA recognized the importance of a comprehensive approach to the conceptualization of guidelines. APA also recognized the risk that guidelines might be used inappropriately by commercial health care organizations not intimately familiar with the scientific basis of practice to dictate specific forms of treatment and restrict patient access to care. In 1992, APA formed a joint task force of the Board of Scientific Affairs (BSA), the Board of Professional Affairs (BPA), and the Committee for the Advancement of Professional Practice (CAPP). The document developed by this task force—the *Template for Developing Guidelines: Interventions for Mental Disorders and Psychosocial Aspects of Physical Disorders* (Template)—was approved by the APA Council of Representatives in 1995 (APA, 1995). The Template described the variety of evidence that should be considered in developing guidelines, and cautioned that any emerging clinical practice guidelines should be based on careful systematic weighing of research data and clinical expertise. . . .

Although the goal was to identify treatments with evidence for efficacy comparable to the evidence for the efficacy of medications, and hence to highlight the contribution of psychological treatments, the Division 12 Task Force report sparked a decade of both enthusiasm and controversy. The report increased recognition of demonstrably effective psychological treatments among the public, policymakers, and training programs. At the same time, many psychologists raised concerns about the exclusive focus on brief, manualized treatments; the emphasis on specific treatment effects as opposed to common factors that account for much of the variance in outcomes across disorders; and the applicability to a diverse range of patients varying in comorbidity, personality, race, ethnicity, and culture.

In response, several groups of psychologists, including other divisions of APA, offered additional frameworks for integrating the available research evidence. In 1999, APA Division 29 (Psychotherapy) established a task force to identify, operationalize, and disseminate information on empirically supported therapy relationships, given the powerful association between outcome and aspects of the therapeutic relationship such as the therapeutic alliance. Division 17 (Counseling Psychology) also undertook an examination of empirically supported treatments in counseling psychology. The Society of Behavioral Medicine, which is not a part of APA but which has significantly overlapping membership, has recently published criteria for examining the evidence base for behavioral medicine interventions. As of this writing, we are aware that task forces have been appointed to examine related issues by a large number of APA divisions concerned with practice issues. . . .

Definition

Based on its review of the literature and its deliberations, the Task Force agreed on the following definition:

> Evidence-based practice in psychology (EBPP) is the integration of the best available research with clinical expertise in the context of patient characteristics, culture, and preferences.

This definition of EBPP closely parallels the definition of evidence-based practice adopted by the Institute of Medicine as adapted from Sackett and colleagues: "Evidence-based practice is the integration of best research evidence with clinical expertise and patient values." Psychology builds on the IOM definition by deepening the examination of clinical expertise and broadening the consideration of patient characteristics. The purpose of EBPP is to promote effective psychological practice and enhance public health by applying empirically supported principles of psychological assessment, case formulation, therapeutic relationship, and intervention.

Psychological practice entails many types of interventions, in multiple settings, for a wide variety of potential patients. In this document, *intervention* refers to all direct services rendered by health care psychologists, including assessment, diagnosis, prevention, treatment, psychotherapy, and consultation. As is the case with most discussions of evidence-based practice, we focus on treatment. The same general principles apply to psychological assessment, which is essential to effective treatment. The settings include but are not limited to hospitals, clinics, independent practices, schools, military, public health, rehabilitation institutes, primary care, counseling centers, and nursing homes.

To be consistent with discussions of evidence-based practice in other areas of health care, we use the term *patient* in this document to refer to the child, adolescent, adult, older adult, couple, family, group, organization, community, or other populations receiving psychological services. However, we recognize that in many situations there are important and valid reasons for using such terms as *client, consumer,* or *person* in place of patient to describe the recipients of services. Further, psychologists target a variety of problems, including but not restricted to mental health, academic, vocational, relational, health, community, and other problems, in their professional practice.

It is important to clarify the relation between EBPP and ESTs (empirically supported treatments). EBPP is the more comprehensive concept. ESTs start with a treatment and ask whether it works for a certain disorder or problem under specified circumstances. EBPP starts with the patient and asks what research evidence (including relevant results from RCTs) will assist the psychologist to achieve the best outcome. In addition, ESTs are specific psychological treatments that have been shown to be efficacious in controlled clinical trials, whereas EBPP encompasses a broader range of clinical activities (e.g., psychological assessment, case formulation, therapy relationships). As such, EBPP articulates a decision making process for integrating multiple streams of research evidence, including but not limited to RCTs, into the intervention process.

The following sections explore in greater detail the three major components of this definition—best available research, clinical expertise, and patient characteristics—and their integration.

Best Available Research Evidence

A sizeable body of scientific evidence drawn from a variety of research designs and methodologies attests to the effectiveness of psychological practices. The research literature on the effect of psychological interventions indicates that these interventions are safe and effective for a large number of children and youth, adults and older adults across a wide range of psychological, addictive, health, and relational problems. More recent research indicates that compared to alternative approaches, such as medications, psychological treatments are particularly enduring. Further, research demonstrates that psychotherapy can and often does pay for itself in terms of medical costs offset, increased productivity, and life satisfaction.

Psychologists possess distinctive strengths in designing, conducting, and interpreting research studies that can guide evidence-based practice. Moreover, psychology—as a science and as a profession—is distinctive in combining scientific commitment with an emphasis on human relationships and individual differences. As such, psychology can help develop, broaden, and improve the research base for evidence-based practice.

There is broad consensus that psychological practice needs to be based on evidence, and that research needs to balance internal and external validity. Research will not always address all practice needs. Major issues in integrating research in day-to-day practice include: a) the relative weight to place on different research methods; b) the representativeness of research samples; c) whether research results should guide practice at the level of principles of change, intervention strategies, or specific protocols; d) the generalizability and transportability of treatments supported in controlled research to clinical practice settings; e) the extent to which judgments can be made about treatments of choice when the number and duration of treatments tested has been limited; and f) the degree to which the results of efficacy and effectiveness research can be generalized from primarily white samples to minority and marginalized populations. Nevertheless, research on practice has made progress in investigating these issues and is providing research evidence that is more responsive to day-to-day practice. There is sufficient consensus to move forward with the principles of EBPP.

Meta-analytic investigations since the 1970s have shown that most therapeutic practices in widespread clinical use are generally effective for treating a range of problems. In fact, the effect sizes for psychological interventions for children, adults and older adults rival, or exceed, those of widely accepted medical treatments. It is important not to assume that interventions that have not yet been studied in controlled trials are ineffective. Specific interventions that have not been subjected to systematic empirical testing for specific problems cannot be assumed to be either effective or ineffective; they are simply untested to date. Nonetheless, good practice and science call for the timely testing of psychological practices in a way that adequately operationalizes them using appropriate scientific methodology. Widely used psychological practices as well as innovations developed in the field or laboratory should be rigorously evaluated and barriers to conducting this research should be identified and addressed.

Multiple Types of Research Evidence

Best research evidence refers to scientific results related to intervention strategies, assessment, clinical problems, and patient populations in laboratory and field settings as well as to clinically relevant results of basic research in psychology and related fields. APA endorses multiple types of research evidence (e.g., efficacy, effectiveness, cost-effectiveness, cost-benefit, epidemiological, treatment utilization studies) that contribute to effective psychological practice.

Multiple research designs contribute to evidence-based practice, and different research designs are better suited to address different types of questions. These include:

- Clinical observation (including individual case studies) and basic psychological science are valuable sources of innovations and hypotheses (the context of scientific discovery).
- Qualitative research can be used to describe the subjective lived experience of people, including participants in psychotherapy.
- Systematic case studies are particularly useful when aggregated as in the form of practice research networks for comparing individual patients to others with similar characteristics.
- Single case experimental designs are particularly useful for establishing causal relationships in the context of an individual.
- Public health and ethnographic research are especially useful for tracking the availability, utilization, and acceptance of mental health treatments as well as suggesting ways of altering them to maximize their utility in a given social context.
- Process-outcome studies are especially valuable for identifying mechanisms of change.
- Studies of interventions as delivered in naturalistic settings (effectiveness research) are well suited for assessing the ecological validity of treatments.

- Randomized clinical trials and their logical equivalents (efficacy research) are the standard for drawing causal inferences about the effects of interventions (context of scientific verification).
- Meta-analysis is a systematic means to synthesize results from multiple studies, test hypotheses, and quantitatively estimate the size of effects.

With respect to evaluating research on specific interventions, current APA policy identifies two widely accepted dimensions. As stated in the *Criteria for Evaluating Treatment Guidelines*, "The first dimension is *treatment efficacy*, the systematic and scientific evaluation of whether a treatment works. The second dimension is *clinical utility*, the applicability, feasibility, and usefulness of the intervention in the local or specific setting where it is to be offered. This dimension also includes determination of the generalizability of an intervention whose efficacy has been established." Types of research evidence with regard to intervention research in ascending order as to their contribution to conclusions about efficacy include: clinical opinion, observation, and consensus among recognized experts representing the range of use in the field (Criterion 2.1); systematized clinical observation (Criterion 2.2); and sophisticated empirical methodologies, including quasi experiments and randomized controlled experiments or their logical equivalents (Criterion 2.3). Among sophisticated empirical methodologies, "randomized controlled experiments represent a more stringent way to evaluate treatment efficacy because they are the most effective way to rule out threats to internal validity in a single experiment."

Evidence on clinical utility is also crucial. As per established APA policy, at a minimum this includes attention to generality of effects across varying and diverse patients, therapists and settings and the interaction of these factors, the robustness of treatments across various modes of delivery, the feasibility with which treatments can be delivered to patients in real world settings, and the cost associated with treatments.

Evidence-based practice requires that psychologists recognize the strengths and limitations of evidence obtained from different types of research. Research has shown that the treatment method, the individual psychologist, the treatment relationship, and the patient are all vital contributors to the success of psychological practice. Comprehensive evidence-based practice will consider all of these determinants and their optimal combinations. Psychological practice is a complex relational and technical enterprise that requires clinical and research attention to multiple, interacting sources of treatment effectiveness. There remain many disorders, problem constellations, and clinical situations for which empirical data are sparse. In such instances, clinicians use their best clinical judgment and knowledge of the best available research evidence to develop coherent treatment strategies. Researchers and practitioners should join together to ensure that the research available on psychological practice is both clinically relevant and internally valid. . . .

Clinical Expertise[2]

Clinical expertise is essential for identifying and integrating the best research evidence with clinical data (e.g., information about the patient obtained over the course of treatment) in the context of the patient's characteristics and preferences to deliver services that have the highest probability of achieving the goals of therapy. Psychologists are trained as scientists as well as practitioners. An advantage of psychological training is that it fosters a clinical expertise informed by scientific expertise, allowing the psychologist to understand and integrate scientific literature as well as to frame and test hypotheses and interventions in practice as a "local clinical scientist."

Cognitive scientists have found consistent evidence of enduring and significant differences between experts and novices undertaking complex tasks in several domains. Experts recognize meaningful patterns and disregard irrelevant information, acquire extensive knowledge and organize it in ways that reflect a deep understanding of their domain, organize their knowledge using functional rather than descriptive features, retrieve knowledge relevant to the task at hand fluidly and automatically, adapt to new situations, self-monitor their knowledge and performance, know when their knowledge is inadequate, continue to learn, and generally attain outcomes commensurate with their expertise.

However, experts are not infallible. All humans are prone to errors and biases. Some of these stem from cognitive strategies and heuristics that are generally adaptive and efficient. Others stem from emotional reactions, which generally guide adaptive behavior as well but can also lead to biased or motivated reasoning. Whenever psychologists involved in research or practice move from observations to inferences and generalizations, there is inherent risk for idiosyncratic interpretations, overgeneralizations, confirmatory biases, and similar errors in judgment. Integral to clinical expertise is an awareness of the limits of one's knowledge and skills and attention to the heuristics and biases—both cognitive and affective—that can affect clinical judgment. Mechanisms such as consultation and systematic feedback from the patient can mitigate some of these biases.

The individual therapist has a substantial impact on outcomes, both in clinical trials and in practice settings. The fact that treatment outcomes are systematically related to the provider of the treatment (above and beyond the type of treatment) provides strong evidence for the importance of understanding expertise in clinical practice as a way of enhancing patient outcomes. . . .

Patient Characteristics, Culture, and Preferences

Normative data on "what works for whom" provide essential guides to effective practice. Nevertheless, psychological services are most likely to be effective when responsive to the patient's specific problems, strengths, personality, sociocultural context, and preferences. Psychology's long history of studying individual differences and developmental change, and its growing empirical literature related to human diversity (including culture[3] and psychotherapy), place it in a strong position to identify effective ways of integrating research and clinical expertise with an understanding of patient characteristics essential to EBPP. EBPP involves consideration of patients' values, religious beliefs, worldviews, goals, and preferences for treatment with the psychologist's experience and understanding of the available research.

Several questions frame current debates about the role of patient characteristics in EBPP. The first regards the extent to which cross-diagnostic patient characteristics, such as personality traits or constellations, moderate the impact of empirically tested interventions. A second, related question concerns the extent to which social factors and cultural differences necessitate different forms of treatment or whether interventions widely tested in majority populations can be readily adapted for patients with different ethnic or sociocultural backgrounds. A third question concerns maximizing the extent to which widely used interventions adequately attend to developmental considerations, both for children and adolescents and for older adults. A fourth question is the extent to which variable clinical presentations, such as comorbidity and polysymptomatic presentations, moderate the impact of interventions. Underlying all of these questions is the issue of how best to approach the treatment of patients whose characteristics (e.g., gender, gender identity, ethnicity, race, social class, disability status, sexual orientation) and problems (e.g., comorbidity) may differ from those of samples studied in research. This is a matter of active discussion in the field and there is increasing research attention to the generalizability and transportability of psychological interventions.

Available data indicate that a variety of patient-related variables influence outcomes, many of which are cross-diagnostic characteristics such as functional status, readiness to change, and level of social support. Other patient characteristics are essential to consider in forming and maintaining a treatment relationship and in implementing specific interventions. These include but are not limited to a) variations in presenting problems or disorders, etiology, concurrent symptoms or syndromes, and behavior; b) chronological age, developmental status, developmental history, and life stage; c) sociocultural and familial factors (e.g., gender, gender identity, ethnicity, race, social class, religion, disability status, family structure, and sexual orientation); d) current environmental context, stressors (e.g., unemployment or recent life event), and social factors (e.g., institutional racism and health care disparities); and e) personal preferences, values, and preferences related to treatment (e.g., goals, beliefs, worldviews, and treatment expectations). Available research on both patient matching and treatment failures in clinical trials of even highly efficacious interventions suggests that different strategies and relationships may prove better suited for different populations.

Many presenting symptoms—for example, depression, anxiety, school failure, bingeing and purging—are similar across patients. However, symptoms or disorders that are phenotypically similar are often heterogeneous with respect to etiology, prognosis, and the psychological processes that create or maintain them. Moreover, most patients present with multiple symptoms or syndromes rather than a single, discrete disorder. The presence of concurrent conditions may moderate treatment response, and interventions intended to treat one symptom often affect others. An emerging body of research also suggests that personality variables underlie many psychiatric syndromes and account for a substantial part of the comorbidity among syndromes widely documented in research. Psychologists must attend to the individual person to make the complex choices necessary to conceptualize, prioritize, and treat multiple symptoms. It is important to know the person who has the disorder in addition to knowing the disorder the person has.

EBPP also requires attention to factors related to the patient's development and life-stage. An enormous body of research exists on developmental processes (e.g., attachment, socialization, and cognitive, social-cognitive, gender, moral, and emotional development) that are essential in understanding adult psychopathology and particularly in treating children, adolescents, families, and older adults.

Evidence-based practice in psychology requires attention to many other patient characteristics, such as gender, gender identity, culture, ethnicity, race, age, family context, religious beliefs, and sexual orientation. These variables shape personality, values, worldviews, relationships, psychopathology, and attitudes toward treatment. A wide range of relevant research literature can inform psychological practice, including ethnography, cross-cultural psychology, psychological anthropology, and cultural psychotherapy. Culture influences not only the nature and expression of psychopathology but also the patient's understanding of psychological and physical health and illness. Cultural values and beliefs and social factors such as implicit racial biases also influence patterns of seeking, using, and receiving help; presentation and reporting of symptoms, fears and expectations about treatment, and desired outcomes. Psychologists also understand and reflect upon the ways their own characteristics, values, and context interact with those of the patient.

Race as a social construct is a way of grouping people into categories on the basis of perceived physical attributes, ancestry, and other factors. Race is also more broadly associated with power, status, and opportunity. In Western cultures, European or white "race" confers advantage and opportunity, even as improved social attitudes and public policies have reinforced social equality. Race is thus an interpersonal and political process with significant implications for clinical practice and health care quality. Patients and clinicians may "belong" to racial groups, as they choose to self-identify, but the importance of race in clinical practice is relational, rather than solely a patient or clinician attribute. Considerable evidence from many fields suggests that racial power differentials between clinicians and their patients, as well as systemic biases and implicit stereotypes based on race or ethnicity, contribute to the inequitable care that patients of color receive across health care services. Clinicians must carefully consider the impact of race, ethnicity, and culture on the treatment process, relationship, and outcome.

The patient's social and environmental context, including recent and chronic stressors, is also important in case formulation and treatment planning. Sociocultural and familial factors, social class, and broader social, economic, and situational factors (e.g., unemployment, family disruption, lack of insurance, recent losses, prejudice, or immigration status) can have an enormous influence on mental health, adaptive functioning, treatment seeking, and patient resources (psychological, social, and financial).

Psychotherapy is a collaborative enterprise, in which patients and clinicians negotiate ways of working together that are mutually agreeable and likely to lead to positive outcomes. Thus, patient values and preferences (e.g., goals, beliefs, and preferred modes of treatment) are a central component of EBPP. Patients can have strong preferences for types of treatment and desired outcomes, and these preferences are influenced by both their cultural context and individual factors. One role of the psychologist is to ensure that patients understand the costs and benefits of different practices and choices. Evidence-based practice in psychology seeks to maximize patient choice among effective alternative interventions. Effective practice requires balancing patient preferences and the psychologist's judgment, based on available evidence and clinical expertise, to determine the most appropriate treatment. . . .

Conclusions

Evidence-based practice in psychology is the integration of the best available research with clinical expertise in the context of patient characteristics, culture, and preferences. The purpose of EBPP is to promote effective psychological practice and enhance public health by applying empirically supported principles of psychological assessment, case formulation, therapeutic relationship, and intervention. Much has been learned over the past century from basic and applied psychological research as well as from observations and hypotheses developed in clinical practice. Many strategies for working with patients have emerged and been refined through the kind of trial and error and clinical hypothesis generation and testing that constitute the most scientific aspect of clinical practice. Yet clinical hypothesis testing has its limits, hence the need to integrate clinical expertise with best available research.

Perhaps the central message of this task force report, and one of the most heartening aspects of the process that led to it, is the consensus achieved among a diverse group of scientists, clinicians, and scientist-clinicians from multiple perspectives that EBPP requires an appreciation of the value of multiple sources of scientific evidence. In a given clinical circumstance, psychologists of good faith and good judgment may disagree about how best to weight different forms of evidence; over time, we presume that systematic and broad empirical inquiry—in the laboratory and in the clinic—will point the way toward best practice in integrating best evidence. What this document reflects, however, is a reassertion of what psychologists have known for a century: that the scientific method is a way of thinking and observing systematically and is the best tool we have for learning about what works for whom.

Clinical decisions should be made in collaboration with the patient, based on the best clinically relevant evidence, and with consideration for the probable costs, benefits, and available resources and options. It is the treating psychologist who makes the ultimate judgment regarding a particular intervention or treatment plan. The involvement of an active, informed patient is generally crucial to the success of psychological services. Treatment decisions should never be made by untrained persons unfamiliar with the specifics of the case.

The treating psychologist determines the applicability of research conclusions to a particular patient. Individual patients may require decisions and interventions not directly addressed by the available research. The application of research evidence to a given patient always involves probabilistic inferences. Therefore, ongoing monitoring of patient progress and adjustment of treatment as needed are essential to EBPP.

Moreover, psychologists must attend to a range of outcomes that may sometimes suggest one strategy and sometimes another and to the strengths and limitations of available research vis-à-vis these different ways of measuring success. Psychological outcomes may include not only symptom relief and prevention of future symptomatic episodes but also quality of life, adaptive functioning in work and relationships, ability to make satisfying life choices, personality change, and other goals arrived at in collaboration between patient and clinician.

EBPP is a means to enhance the delivery of services to patients within an atmosphere of mutual respect, open communication, and collaboration among all stakeholders, including practitioners, researchers, patients, health care managers, and policy-makers. Our goal in this document, and in the deliberations of the Task Force that led to it, was to set both an agenda and a tone for the next steps in the evolution of EBPP.

Notes

1. This document was received by the American Psychological Association (APA) Council of Representatives during its meeting of August, 2005. The report represents the conclusions of the Task Force and does not represent the official policy of the American Psychological Association. The Task Force wishes to thank John R. Weisz, PhD, ABPP for his assistance in drafting portions of this report related to children and youth. The Task Force also thanks James Mitchell and Omar Rehman, APA Professional Development interns, for their assistance throughout the work of the Task Force.

2. As it is used in this report, clinical expertise refers to competence attained by psychologists through education, training, and experience resulting in effective practice; clinical expertise is not meant to refer to extraordinary performance that might characterize an elite group (e.g., the top two percent) of clinicians.

3. Culture, in this context, is understood to encompass a broad array of phenomena (such as shared values, history, knowledge, rituals, and customs) that often result in a shared sense of identity. Racial and ethnic groups may have a shared culture, but those personal characteristics are not the only characteristics that define cultural groups (e.g., deaf culture, inner-city culture). Culture is a multifaceted construct, and cultural factors cannot be understood in isolation from social, class and personal characteristics that make each patient unique.

THE APA 2005 PRESIDENTIAL TASK FORCE ON EVIDENCE-BASED PRACTICE defines and discusses evidence-based practice in psychology (EBPP).

Brent D. Slife and Dennis C. Wendt

The Next Step in the Evidence-Based Practice Movement

Nearly everyone agrees that psychological practice should be informed by evidence (Westen & Bradley, 2005, p. 266; Norcross, Beutler, & Levant, 2006, p. 7). However, there is considerable disagreement about what qualifies as evidence (e.g., Reed, 2006; Kihlstrom, 2006; Messer, 2006; Westen, 2006; Stirman & DeRubeis, 2006). This disagreement is not a simple scientific dispute to be resolved in the laboratory, but rather a "culture war" between different worldviews (Messer, 2004, p. 580). As Carol Tavris (2003) put it, this "war" involves "deeply held beliefs, political passions, views of human nature and the nature of knowledge, and—as all wars ultimately involve—money, territory, and livelihoods" (as qtd. in Norcross et al., p. 8).

How does one address a cultural battle of deeply held worldviews and political passions? We believe the approaches that have tried to address it so far in psychology have been well-intended and even headed in the right direction, but are ultimately and fundamentally inadequate. We will first describe what we consider the two major steps in this regard, beginning with the empirically supported treatment (EST) movement, which still has considerable energy in the discipline, and then moving to the "common factors" approach, which recently culminated in a policy regarding evidence-based practice (EBP) in psychology from the American Psychological Association (APA, 2006). We specifically focus on the latter, extolling its goals, but noting their distinct lack of fulfillment. We then offer what seems to us the logical extension of these first two steps—what could be called "objective methodological pluralism" in the spirit of one of our discipline's founding parents, William James (1902/1985; 1907/1975).

The First Step: The EST Movement

Psychology's first step in addressing this evidence controversy involved a succession of APA Division 12 (Clinical) task forces. Beginning in 1993, these task forces have "constructed and elaborated a list of empirically supported, manualized psychological interventions for specific disorders" (Norcross et al., 2006, p. 5). In other words, this first step assumed that the battle of worldviews would be resolved through rigorous scientific evidence. "Rigorous evidence," in this case, was idealized as the randomized

clinical (or controlled) trial (RCT), widely esteemed as the gold standard of evidence in medicine. The advantages of this step were obvious. Third-party payers were familiar with this gold standard from medicine, and many psychologists believed that an EST list would provide a clear-cut index of "proven" treatments, not to mention greater respect from medicine.

Unfortunately, this seemingly rigorous, clear-cut approach has manifested more than a few problems (Westen & Bradley, 2005; Messer, 2004). Much like the testing movement in education, where teachers found themselves "teaching to the test," psychologists found their practices being shaped by the RCT "test." The critics of the RCT showed how professional practices were conforming, consciously or unconsciously, to the RCT worldview in order to make the EST list. In other words, the practices being studied tended to accommodate the particular RCT perspective on treatments, therapists, and patients.

With regard to treatments, this medical-model worldview of the RCT is biased toward "packaged" treatments for well-defined, compartmentalized disorders (e.g., Bohart, O'Hara, & Leitner, 1998). This model of treatment took its cues from the pharmaceutical industry, where "one must specify the treatment and make sure it is being applied correctly" (p. 143). According to this model, every patient would receive the same thing, and it is this thing, not the therapist or patient, that is considered the agent of change. Critics have argued that this view of treatment undermined many types of therapy, such as humanistic or psychodynamic therapies, in which "treatment" does not entail a manualized set of principles (e.g., Bohart et al.; Safran, 2001).

A related argument against this packaged view of treatment concerned the role of therapists. The assumptions or worldview of the RCT, these critics contended, turned the therapist into an interchangeable part, discounting the importance of the therapist's distinctive personality, practical wisdom, and unique relationship with the patient. Many researchers have worried, to use the words of Allen Bergin (1997), that the RCT manualization of treatments turned therapists into "cookie cutters" and researchers into "mechanotropes" (pp. 85–86). This worry has been validated by research suggesting that manualization often hinders important therapeutic factors, such as the therapeutic alliance and the therapist's genuineness, creativity, motivation, and emotional involvement (Duncan & Miller, 2006; Piper & Ogrodniczuk, 1999).

→ Third, critics have noted that the biases of RCTs shaped one's view of the patient, assuming that researchers and clinicians work with pure patient pathologies only. According to this argument, RCTs are limited to patients with textbook symptoms of a single DSM disorder; thus, their results "may apply only to a narrow and homogeneous group of patients" (Butcher, Mineka, & Hooley, 2004, p. 563). This limitation is no small problem, critics have warned, because the vast majority of U.S. patients are not pathologically "pure" in this narrow RCT sense. Rather, they are co- or "multi"-morbid in the sense that they are an amalgam of disorders (Morrison, Bradley, & Westen, 2003; Westen & Bradley, 2005). The prevalence of these "messy" patients is corroborated by the 35%–70% exclusion rates of RCTs for major disorders (Morrison et al., p. 110).

The common theme behind the above criticisms is that the biases of the EST movement stem from its narrow framework for validating evidence. Thus, it is not mere coincidence, critics have argued, that therapies that exemplify this type of treatment (e.g., behavioral or cognitive-behavioral treatments) are the most frequently listed as ESTs (Messer, 2004). The exclusion of other types of therapy (e.g., humanistic and psychodynamic therapies) has prompted critics to contend that the EST movement constitutes a methodological bias toward behavioral and cognitive-behavioral therapies (e.g., Slife, Wiggins, & Graham; Messer, 2004). If this first step has taught psychologists anything, it has taught that what the evidence seems to say has a great deal to do with what one considers evidence.

The Second Step: The Common Factors Movement

The second step—the common factors movement—was, in part, an attempt to learn from the shortcomings of the EST movement. Common factors advocates have argued that a focus on specific, "packaged" treatments for specific disorders is a narrow way of conceptualizing psychological research and practice (e.g., Westen & Bradley, 2005; Bohart et al., 1998). An alternative approach is to discover and validate factors of therapeutic change that are common across treatments. In this way, responsibility for change is not just attributed to the treatment, as in ESTs. Change is considered the result of a dynamic relationship among the "common factors" of therapy, which include the therapist, patient, and technique (APA, 2006, p. 275).

A common factors approach is especially appealing to the majority of practitioners, who consider themselves eclectics or integrationists. Its popularity has helped it to play a significant role in shaping APA's (2006) new policy statement on evidence-based practice. For this policy statement, evidence was liberalized not only to include studies of therapist and patient variables but also to include other methods than RCTs for conducting these studies (pp. 274–75). The main guideposts for selecting these methods, according to the underlying rationale of the APA policy, were their objectivity and their diversity. Methods should be *objective* to prevent the intrusion of human error and bias that would distort the findings (p. 276), and they should be *diverse* to prevent the shaping of practice that a focus on only one method might produce, such as the problems created by RCTs (pp. 272–74).

The problem, from our perspective, is that the APA culmination of this common factors approach is not objective and diverse enough. In other words, we applaud the goals but criticize the implementation. The APA policy is a clear step forward, in our view, but its conceptions of objectivity and diversity are inadequate. As we will attempt to show, this inadequacy means that the lessons of the EST movement have not been sufficiently learned. Recall that this first step restricted itself to a single ideal of evidence, the RCT, and thus disallowed any true diversity of methods. Recall also that several biases resulted from this restriction, obviating objectivity and shaping practice even before investigation. As we will argue, this same lack of diversity and objectivity has continued into the second approach to the evidence controversy.

Our basic criticism is this: Just as an EST framework uncritically restricts acceptable evidence to a *single method* ideal (the RCT), so does the APA policy uncritically restrict acceptable evidence to a *single epistemology*. By "epistemology" we mean the philosophy of knowing that provides the logic and guides the conduct of a group of methods (Slife & Williams, 1995). Although the EST framework is biased toward a certain *method*, the common factors framework is biased toward a certain *methodology*—a narrow brand of *empiricism*.

According to this empiricist epistemology, "we can only know, or know best, those aspects of our experience that are sensory" (Slife, Wiggins, & Graham, 2005, p. 84). This narrow conception of empiricism is fairly traditional in psychology. More liberal usages of empiricism differ substantially, such as William James' radical empiricism. James' empiricism encompasses "the whole of experience," including *non*-sensory experiences such as thoughts, emotions, and even spiritual experiences (James, 1902/1985; 1907/1975). Still, psychologists have interpreted the natural sciences to be grounded in the narrow empiricism. Historically, psychologists have wanted to be both rigorously scientific and comparable to medicine, leading them to embrace the narrower empiricism. As we will attempt to show, however, this restriction to a single epistemology is not based on evidence. Analogous to the EST restriction to a single method, the APA policy merely assumes and never justifies empiricism as the only appropriate epistemology for evidence-based practice, in spite of other promising epistemologies.

The reason for this lack of justification seems clear. Throughout much of the history of psychology, empiricism has been mistakenly understood not as a *particular* philosophy of science, but as a *non*-philosophy that makes reality transparent. Analogous to the way in which many EST proponents view RCTs, empiricism is not *a* way to understand evidence, but *the* way. Consequently, nowhere in the APA policy or its underlying report is a rationale provided for a commitment to empirical research, and nowhere is a consideration given for even the possibility of a "non-empirical" contribution to evidence-based practice.

This equation of evidence with empiricism is directly parallel to the EST movement's equation of evidence with RCT findings. Just as Westen and Bradley (2005) noted that "EBP > EST" (p. 271), we note that EBP > empirical. After all, there is no empirical evidence for empiricism, or for RCTs, for that matter. Both sets of methods spring from the human invention of philosophers and other humanists. Moses did not descend Mt. Sinai with the Ten Commandments in one hand and the principles of science in the other. Moreover, these principles could not have been scientifically derived, because one would need the principles (before their derivation) to conduct the scientific investigations to derive them.

Indeed, the irony of this epistemology's popularity is that many observers of psychology have long considered empiricism to be deeply problematic for psychological research. Again, the parallel to the dominance of RCTs is striking. Just as the majority of real-world patients, therapists, and treatments were perceived to defy RCT categories, so too the majority of real-world phenomena can be perceived to defy empirical categories. Indeed, many of the common factors for evidence-based practice are not, strictly speaking, empirical at all. Rather, they are experiences and meanings that are not sensory, and thus not observable, in nature (Slife et al., 2005, p. 88).

Consider, for example, the efforts of APA Division 29 (Psychotherapy) to provide empirical support for therapy relationships, such as therapeutic alliance and group cohesion (Norcross, 2001; APA, 2006, p. 272). Although patients and therapists probably experience this alliance and cohesion, these relationships literally never fall on their retinas. The people involved in these relationships are observable in this sense, to be sure, but the "betweenness" of these relations—the actual alliance or cohesion themselves—never are. Their unobservability means, according to the method requirements of empiricism, that they must be operationalized, or made observable. Thus, it is not surprising, given its commitment to a narrow empiricism, that the APA policy report presumes that operationalization is a requirement of method (p. 274).

The problem with this requirement, however, is that any specified operationalization, such as a patient's feelings about the relationship (e.g., Norcross, 2002), can occur without the therapeutic alliance, and any such alliance can occur without the specified operationalization. The upshot is that the construct (e.g., alliance) and the operationalization are two different things, yet the operationalization is the only thing studied in traditional research. Moreover, one can never know empirically the relation between the construct and its operationalization because pivotal aspects of this relation—the construct and relation itself—are never observable. Thus, APA's policy runs the risk of making psychotherapy research a compendium of operationalizations without any knowledge of how they relate to what psychologists want to study.

Problems such as these are the reason that alternative philosophies of science, such as qualitative methods, were formulated. Many qualitative methods were specifically formulated to investigate unobservable, but experienced, meanings of the world (Denzin & Lincoln, 2000; Patton, 1990; Slife & Gantt, 1999). The existence of this alternative philosophy of science implies another problem with the unjustified empiricist framework of the APA policy report—it runs roughshod over alternative frameworks, such as qualitative methods. Although the policy includes qualitative research on its list of acceptable methods (APA, p. 274), it fails to understand and value qualitative research as a different philosophy of science.

A clear indication of this failure is the use of the word "subjective" when the report describes the purpose of qualitative research (p. 274). In the midst of a report that extols "objective" inquiry, relegating only qualitative methods to the "subjective" is second-class citizenship, at best. More importantly, this relegation only makes sense within an empiricist framework. In non-empiricist philosophies, such as those underlying many qualitative methods, the notions of "objective" and "subjective" are largely irrelevant because most non-empiricist conceptions of science do not assume the dualism of a subjective and objective realm (Slife, 2005).

The bottom line is that a common factors approach to the evidence controversy is a clear advancement of the EBP project, but it is not an unqualified advance. Indeed, it recapitulates some of the same problems that it is attempting to correct. In both the EST and the common factors approaches, criteria for what is evidence shape not only the studies conducted but also the practices considered supported. Indeed, we would contend there is no method or methodology that is not ultimately biased in this regard. As philosophers of science have long taught, all methods of investigation must make assumptions about the world *before* it is investigated (Curd & Cover, 1998). The question remains, however, whether there can be a framework for understanding evidence that does not *automatically* shape practice before it is investigated.

Presaging the Next Step: The Ideas of William James

The answer, we believe, is "yes," and we do not have to reinvent the wheel to formulate this alternative. One of the intellectual parents of our discipline, William James, has already pointed the way. Consequently, we will first briefly describe three of James' pivotal ideas: his radical empiricism, his pluralism, and his pragmatism. Then, we will apply these ideas to the evidence-based practice issue, deriving our alternative to the current monopoly of empiricism—objective methodological pluralism.

James was actually quite critical of what psychologists consider empirical today. As mentioned above, his radical empiricism embraces the whole of experience, including non-sensory experiences such as thoughts, emotions, and spiritual experiences (James, 1902/1985; 1907/1975). His position implies, as he explicitly recognizes, that there are several epistemologies of investigation ("ways of knowing") rather than just one. As James (1909/1977) put it, "nothing includes everything" (p. 145). In other words, no philosophy of science is sufficient to understand everything.

Psychology needs, instead, a *pluralism* of such philosophies, which is the second of James's ideas and an intriguing way to actualize APA's desire for diversity. In other words, we not only need a diversity of methods, which the APA report (2006) clearly concedes (p. 274), we also need a diversity of *methodologies* or philosophies underlying these methods. It is not coincidental, in this regard, that James (1902/1985) used qualitative methods to investigate spiritual meanings in his famous work, *Varieties of Religious Experiences*. His pluralism of methods dictated that he should not change or operationalize his phenomena of study to fit the method, but that he should change his method to best illuminate the phenomena—spiritual phenomena, in this case.

This approach to method implies the third of James's ideas—his pragmatism. According to James:

> Rationalism sticks to logic and . . . empiricism sticks to the external senses. Pragmatism is willing to take anything, to follow either logic or the senses and to count the humblest and most personal of experiences. [Pragmatism] will count mystical experiences if they have practical consequences. (James, 1907/1975, p. 61)

As James implies, the heart of pragmatism is the notion that one should never approach the study or understanding of anything with fixed schemes and methods. There is too much danger that the method will distort understanding of the phenomena being studied. This is not to say that one can or should approach such phenomena without some method or interpretive framework. Yet this framework does not have to be cast in stone; psychologists should allow the phenomenon itself to guide the methods we choose to study it.

This pragmatism may sound complicated, but it is not significantly different from what good carpenters do at every job—they let the task dictate the tools they use. They have a pluralism of tools or methods, rather than just one, because many tasks cannot be done with just one tool, such as a hammer. Moreover, not every carpentry job can be "operationalized" into a set of "nails." As Dupré

(1993) and others (e.g., Feyerabend, 1975; Viney, 2004) have noted, this pragmatism is the informal meta-method of physics, where the object of study is the primary consideration, and the method of studying it is a secondary consideration.

By contrast, APA's version of evidence-based practice is method-driven rather than object-driven. That is to say, psychologists have decided the logic of their investigation before they even consider what they are studying. If the object of study does not fit this logic, they have no choice but to modify it to fit this logic through operationalization. For example, an unobservable feeling, such as sadness, becomes operationalized as an observable behavior, such as crying.

The irony of this familiar research practice is that psychologists are driven more by an unrecognized and unexamined philosophy of science, as manifested through their methods, than by the objects they are studying. Indeed, they are changing their object of study—from sadness to crying—to accommodate this philosophy. We believe that this accommodation is contrary to good science, where everything including the philosophies that ground one's methods, should be subject to examination and comparison.

The Next Step: Objective Methodological Pluralism

This description of James' three pivotal ideas—his radical empiricism, pluralism, and pragmatism—sets the stage for our proposal on evidence-based practice: "objective methodological pluralism." First, this pluralism assumes a broader empiricism, in the spirit of James. To value only sensory experiences, as does the conventional empiricist, is to affirm a value that is itself unproven and non-empirical. There simply is no conceptual or empirical necessity to value only the sensory. We recognize that many would claim the success of this value in science, but we also recognize that no scientific comparison between such philosophical values has occurred. These claims of success, then, are merely opinion, uninformed by scientific findings.

In practical terms, this move from conventional empiricism to radical empiricism means that alternative methods, such as qualitative methods, are no longer second class citizens. They are no longer "subjective" and experimental methods considered "objective," because all methods ultimately depend on experiences of one sort or another. This creates more of a level playing field for methods—a pluralism—and allows for an even-handed assessment of each method's advantages and disadvantages.

Unlike the APA policy's conception, the criteria of this assessment are not already controlled by one, unexamined philosophy of science. They are guided, instead, by the object of one's study. This is the reason for the term "objective" in our alternative, *objective* methodological pluralism. Methods, we believe, should be driven not by some philosophy of method that is deemed to be correct *before* the object of study has even been considered. Methods should be driven by consideration of the objects themselves.

This consideration is itself evaluated pragmatically, in terms of the practical differences it makes in the lives of patients. As James realized, any evaluation of practical significance begs the question of "significant to what?" In other words, any methodological pluralism requires thoughtful disciplinary discussion of the moral issues of psychology, a discussion that has begun in a limited way in positive psychology (Seligman, 2002): What is the good life for a patient? When is a life truly flourishing? Such questions cannot be derived from the "is" of research; they must be discussed as the "ought" that guides this research and determines what practical significance really means.

Obviously, much remains to be worked out with a Jamesian pluralism. Still, we believe that this particular "working out" is not only possible but also necessary. The monopoly and problems of empiricism—the lessons of

our first two steps in the evidence controversy—do not go away with a rejection of this pluralism. This is the reason we titled this article "the next step"—the difficulties with empiricism and APA's desire for diversity lead us logically, we believe, to this next general step. Admittedly, this kind of pluralism is a challenging prospect. Still, if carpenters can do it in a less complex enterprise, surely psychologists can. In any case, it is high time that psychologists face up to the challenge, because ignoring it will not make it go away.

BRENT D. SLIFE is currently a professor of psychology at Brigham Young University, where he chairs the doctoral program in theoretical and philosophical psychology and serves as a member of the doctoral program in clinical psychology.

DENNIS C. WENDT is a predoctoral fellow for the University of Michigan Substance Abuse Research Center (UMSARC), funded through a NIDA training grant.

If the only tool you have is a hammer every problem looks like a nail

- step away from medical model towards dimensional?

EXPLORING THE ISSUE

Are Traditional Empirical Methods Sufficient to Provide Evidence for Psychological Practice?

Critical Thinking and Reflection

1. The label "objective" is typically used only in reference to empirical evidence. Why is this typical, and what would Slife and Wendt say about this practice?
2. The APA Task Force bases its definition of evidence-based practice on a conception formulated by the Institute of Medicine. Find out what this definition is and form your own informed opinion about its relevance or irrelevance to psychotherapy. Support your answer.
3. Many people think they would feel safer if their therapist used practices that have been validated by science. Explain what it is about science that leads people to feel this way.
4. William James is known as the father of American psychology. Why do you think the APA has largely neglected to take his pluralism into consideration?
5. Slife and Wendt believe that the methods of psychology (and any other science, for that matter) are based on and guided by philosophies, yet few psychology texts discuss these philosophies. Why do you feel that this is the case, and is the absence of this discussion justified?

Create Central

www.mhhe.com/createcentral

Additional Resource

James, W. (2006, November 15). A pluralistic universe. *BiblioBazaar*. Retrieved from www.gutenberg .org/ebooks/11984

Internet Reference . . .

Journal of Mind and Behavior

www.umaine.edu/jmb/archives/volume29/v30n3.htm

Selected, Edited and with Issue Framing Material by:
Brent Slife, *Brigham Young University*

ISSUE

Should Neuroscience Research Be Used to Inform Public Policy?

YES: **Sonia K. Kang, Michael Inzlicht, and Belle Derks,** from "Social Neuroscience and Public Policy on Intergroup Relations: A Hegelian Analysis," *Journal of Social Issues* (vol. 66, no. 3, pp. 586–591, 2010)

NO: **Sonia K. Kang, Michael Inzlicht, and Belle Derks,** from "Social Neuroscience and Public Policy on Intergroup Relations: A Hegelian Analysis," *Journal of Social Issues* (vol. 66, no. 3, pp. 591–596)

Learning Outcomes

After reading this issue, you should be able to:

- Understand what it means to understand human thought and behavior at the point of "unification."
- Determine if policymakers place too much emphasis on the influence of neuroscience research on public policy.

ISSUE SUMMARY

YES: Sonia K. Kang, assistant professor of organizational behavior and human resource management at the University of Toronto, Michael Inzlicht, associate professor of psychology at the University of Toronto, and Belle Derks, professor of psychology at Leiden University, argue that because neuroscience research is the most valid and reliable source of information concerning the ways in which human beings interact with one another, it is a sound foundation for public policy.

NO: Sonia K. Kang, assistant professor of organizational behavior and human resource management at the University of Toronto, Michael Inzlicht, associate professor of psychology at the University of Toronto, and Belle Derks, professor of psychology at Leiden University, contest that because neuroscience research faces various theoretical and practical limitations, it is an unsound foundation for public policy.

Psychologists take pride in producing objective information about a host of topics, from criminality to gay marriage to abortion. Is this important information for public policy? Public policy is where lawmakers and government officials look to scientists for valid information to help guide their efforts in formulating new laws and regulations. Psychologists, in particular, are often relied upon when policymakers need information about how humans act and react. If psychological research, for example, shows that video games make adolescents more aggressive, as many psychologists have shown, then policymakers may want to censor or even eliminate these games. In other words, the policy stakes are often very high, and valid scientific information is vital.

The problem in the field of psychology is constantly evolving, with ever new findings and discoveries. In some

cases, these new findings and discoveries—often to the embarrassment of researchers—seem to discredit what were once thought to be hard-fast empirical truths. To take the media aggression issue just a bit further, several psychological researchers believe that their own research *does not* show that media games cause violence. These researchers may hold the minority view, but what do policymakers do with this type of scientific disagreement? Does the change, evolution, or general disagreement in psychological findings mean that these findings are problematic sources of information for the makers of public policy?

The YES and NO selections specifically address the validity of *neuroscience* research for informing public policy in this regard. Kang, Inzlicht, and Derks are the authors of both selections in this issue. They argue for an approach they consider to be Hegelian. Hegelian means here that they make a case for *both* sides of the issue before combining the two sides to form a "synthesis" or a compromise between the two positions. (See the original text for the authors' synthesis of the two sides of the issue.)

The authors begin by arguing that neuroscience research should be used to inform public policy. To justify this claim, they cite three major reasons to support that neuroscience is the best source of information concerning human beings. First, neuroscience is able to address the multiplicity of factors and variables that influence human thought and behavior by investigating human thought and behavior at the point of "unification" (i.e., in the processes of the brain). Second, neuroscience is able to address *implicit* thoughts and behaviors. These are thoughts and behaviors that people aren't consciously aware of and, therefore, are unable to account for on their own. And finally, neuroscience is able to address the extent to which the choices people make are made freely, which has important implications for legal systems where culpability and punishment require an individual to have been capable of *choosing* not to commit a crime.

The authors then argue in the NO selection that neuroscience research should not be used to inform public policy. To support this claim, the authors focus their attention on the limits of neuroscience. They begin by addressing the ultimate inability of neuroscience to fully account for psychological events with biological events—a form of materialistic reductionism. They then explain that neuroscience has been unable to provide society with "incremental utility"—failing to demonstrate its own practical usefulness. Lastly, they argue that the public views neuroscience research as being far more absolute than the research actually justifies—suggesting that whether or not the research is valid, policymakers are likely to put far more trust in the research than they should.

POINT

- Neuroscience accounts for the entirety of human experience.
- Neuroscience addresses implicit aspects of human thought and behavior.
- Neuroscience can determine whether natural law governs mental processes.
- Human experience can be understood by examining brain processes.

COUNTERPOINT

- Neuroscience is unable to account for human experience.
- Neuroscience fails to demonstrate its own practical usefulness.
- Neuroscience cannot provide compelling evidence for its claims.
- Human experience cannot be reduced to physiological processes.

YES

Sonia K. Kang, Michael Inzlicht,
and Belle Derks

Social Neuroscience and Public Policy on Intergroup Relations: A Hegelian Analysis

Neuroscience Should Inform Public Policy

One goal of the Society for the Psychological Study of Social Issues is to bring empirically sound research findings to bear on public policy. Neuroscience contributes to this goal by strengthening the empirical foundation upon which effective public policy is built. We will review three paths through which neuroscience strengthens social psychological research in general and research on intergroup relations in particular. First, neuroscience works to extend knowledge to another, biological, level of analysis. Second, neuroscience allows for the examination of implicit or automatic cognitive processes previously beyond the realm of measurement. Third, social neuroscience can influence policy by clarifying our notions of free will and determinism.

The unification of knowledge. The unification of knowledge across multiple levels of analysis, or *consilience*, is a fundamental goal of scientific inquiry (Wilson, 1998). Wilson points to William Whewell's first explanation of consilience: "consilience . . . takes place when an Induction, obtained from one class of facts, coincides with an Induction, obtained from another different class. This consilience is a test of the truth of the Theory in which it occurs" (Wilson, 1998, pp. 8–9). Neuroscience contributes to the consilience of psychological theories, and therefore the strength of the policies they inform, by increasing our understanding of the combination of physiological processes underlying psychological phenomena. In this context, neuroscience is but one piece of the overall enterprise of psychological science. When combined with standard cognitive and behavioral methodologies, neuroscience promises to reveal the biological underpinnings of social behavior. Integrating findings from these different levels of analysis refines and constrains psychological theories (e.g., Cacioppo, 2004; Cacioppo, Berntson, & Nusbaum, 2008).

As an example, consider recent functional magnetic resonance imaging (fMRI) investigations of women experiencing stereotype threat (Krendl, Richeson, Kelley, & Heatherton, 2008; Wraga, Helt, Jacobs, & Sullivan, 2007). These women showed heightened activity in the rostral-ventral anterior cingulate cortex (ACC), a brain area associated with emotion regulation, and reduced activity in

neural regions associated with high performance in math and spatial ability. Importantly, analyses linked this pattern of brain activation to impaired performance under stereotype threat, thus lending biological support to behavioral theories that coping with negative stereotype-related emotions uses up cognitive resources that could otherwise be applied to cognitive tasks (Schmader & Johns, 2003; Schmader, Johns, & Forbes, 2008). Whereas previous behavioral studies focused on only one mediator at a time, these neuroscience studies examined the diverse biological mechanisms that interactively produce the stereotype threat effect, showing that stereotype threat leads simultaneously to reductions in cognitive efficiency and increases in processing of negative affective reactions. From a policy-making standpoint, this suggests that interventions aimed at improving experiences for women in science and math must be multipronged. Interventions aimed simply at improving math skills, for example, are not enough. Instead, policy makers should move toward interventions that also teach women to effectively cope with stigma-related anxiety, for example, by teaching about stereotype threat (Johns, Schmader, & Martens, 2005). Indeed, as Johns and his colleagues note, knowing about stereotype threat is half the battle—which is as of yet absent from intervention-based policies related to gender issues in math and the sciences.

Beyond just this example, consilience is important for the process of policy making more broadly speaking. Policy making, implementation, and change are costly endeavors, and it is in everyone's best interest that policies are effective from their inception. Consilience is a helpful predictor of efficacy; if the results of many studies using many different methods point to the same finding, policies based on this finding are likely a better investment than policies based on findings without converging support. Given that policy makers are looking for research findings that will lead to policies that will give them the most bang for their policy buck, it is more likely that findings that have reached consilience (e.g., behavioral and neuroscience studies showing the same effects) will be implemented into policy. As such, from a scientist's perspective, striving for behavioral and neural consilience increases the chances that research findings will find their way into effective public policy.

Social neuroscience is particularly helpful because using a new method allows us to move beyond some of the method invariance issues that arise when the same behavioral measures (e.g., reaction time, self-report or peer report) are used again and again. Of course, the same could be said if, for example, social neuroscience methods had been used for years before the advent of reaction time measurement. If that were the case, it would be important to complement social neuroscience work with reaction time work to more fully understand results independent from any method invariance inherent in social neuroscience measures. As such, consilience can only be achieved with multiple levels of analysis. Repeated demonstrations of a finding using the same method or at the same level of analyses are useful, but examining this finding with another method or another level of analysis—unifying our knowledge—is even better. Unifying behavioral and biological levels of analysis provides a detailed picture of the processes and mechanisms underlying social problems and the policies that will change them for the better. Going back to our example, now that the emotional coping-based theory of stereotype threat has achieved consilience, both scientists and the public can feel confident about dedicating resources toward interventions aimed at helping individuals cope more effectively with stereotype-related negative emotions.

Measuring implicit processes. In addition to increasing the consilience of social psychological theories, neuroscience allows for the direct and unobtrusive measurement of nonconscious and automatic processes that are impossible to assess with self-report and reaction time measures alone. This ability is of great import, as many cognitive operations occur automatically, outside of awareness and conscious control (Bargh, 1994). Further, some of the phenomena of interest to social psychologists, prejudiced attitudes for example, are susceptible to biased reporting, and adding a lower-level analysis provides a more accurate view of these phenomena than behavioral measures alone. Thus, neuroscience offers more direct measures of cognitive operations than the methods that are currently available.

For example, the event-related potential technique (ERP) allows us to measure implicit processes (e.g., racial and gender categorization, implicit evaluations, control processes) that occur very early in information processing (Correll, Urland, & Ito, 2006; Ito, Thompson, & Cacioppo, 2004; Ito & Urland, 2003, 2005; Kubota & Ito, 2007; Willadsen-Jensen & Ito, 2006). This research shows that racial categorization occurs within 200 milliseconds, and that this automatic racial categorization mediates the relationship between explicit cultural stereotypes and behavioral racial bias (Correll et al., 2006). Moreover, ERP measures show that, within 500 milliseconds, individuals exhibit more negative implicit evaluations of Black than White individuals (Ito et al., 2004). Importantly, the late positive potential, a specific ERP-component indicating implicit evaluation, has been related to modern racism

scores (Ito et al., 2004), and is unaffected by instructions to misreport one's attitudes. ERP studies have also shed light on the automatic control processes that allow people to control their racial bias (Amodio, Devine, & Harmon-Jones, 2008; Amodio et al., 2004). While behavioral research had already revealed that people who are internally rather than externally motivated to behave unprejudiced display less prejudice (Devine, Plant, Amodio, Harmon-Jones, & Vance, 2002), it was not until control processes were measured neurally that the cognitive mechanisms underlying control of racial bias were revealed. These ERP experiments show that people who are internally motivated to respond without prejudice are capable of automatically detecting situations that call for inhibition of stereotyping. As a result, these individuals are better able to inhibit prejudiced responses than individuals who are externally motivated to respond without bias.

As such, measures of brain activity provide a relatively more reliable view of separate cognitive operations (e.g., categorization, evaluation, cognitive control) that occur during person perception than is possible with traditional measures like the implicit association test (Greenwald, McGhee, & Schwarz, 1998). Although useful in their own right, behavioral measures tend to confound several mental operations (e.g., attention, categorization, response selection), whereas the ERP technique allows for a more direct, pinpointed measure of the operation of interest. This is not to say that ERPs give us absolute insight into true attitudes or perception, but just that they provide insight into the ways in which very early processing operations might affect behavior and the circumstances that influence these early processes.

As we have alluded to, neuroscience methodology holds the promise of measuring and disentangling separate implicit cognitive operations independent of controlled processes. In so doing, social neuroscience can help inform public policy by showing which processes are malleable and changeable and which are not, and thus help policy makers decide where resources should and should not be directed. For example, neuroscience research on racial categorization indicates that this categorization is automatic (Dickter & Bartholow, 2007; Ito et al., 2004; Ito & Urland, 2003, 2005), suggesting that public policy directed at reducing social categorization (e.g., color-blind policies and school uniforms in high schools) is unlikely to improve intergroup relations (Richeson et al., 2003; Richeson & Nussbaum, 2004; Schofield, 2001; Wolsko, Park, Judd, & Wittenbrink, 2000). On the other hand, neuroscience research has also indicated that responding to members of the outgroup can change depending on a person's processing goals and motivation to respond without prejudice (Amodio et al., 2008; Wheeler & Fiske, 2005), suggesting that public policy aimed at, for example, increasing egalitarian motives and teaching people what kind of situations call for control of racial biases has a good chance of succeeding (e.g., Amodio, 2008; Correll et al., 2007).

Clarifying free will. The final argument that we will offer for why neuroscience should inform public policy is a provocative one, and we present it here in hopes of sparking discussion and debate. Specifically, we argue that policy makers should pay attention to social neuroscience because by allowing us to actually witness the biological machinery underlying our actions, it has the power to reawaken and perhaps transform our moral intuitions about free will and responsibility (Greene & Cohen, 2004). A cursory examination of our current legal and moral systems reveals an emphasis on blameworthiness and responsibility. In essence, a legal or moral transgression can only be officially deemed as such if two elements are present: a guilty act, or *actus rea*, and an accompanying guilty mind, or *mens rea*. The capacity to possess a guilty mind is regarded as something of a privilege; among others, children and mentally disabled individuals are generally judged as unable to take responsibility for their actions. Because their guilty actions cannot be accompanied by a sound guilty mind, these individuals are seldom punished in the legal system. Such notions of mind and free will have lead to a criminal-justice system directed by a delimited idea of retribution—namely, that criminals deserve to be punished only when they have freely chosen to commit an immoral act. However, recent neuroscience findings conflict with ideas of free will, suggesting that the activity in our own brains actually makes us less "free" than we would like to think. Instead, these findings suggest that the neural hardwiring of our brains—based largely upon the environments of our evolutionary predecessors—governs our actions in an uncontrollable, even deterministic, fashion (Greene, 2003; Greene, Nystrom, Engell, Darley, & Cohen, 2004; Greene, Sommerville, Nystrom, Darley, & Cohen, 2001). Basically, the argument here is that what we previously thought of as free will is really not so free; "free will" appears to be determined by processes that neuroscience methods are only now allowing us to see with our own eyes.

These ideas about free will are starting to have an impact upon the legal system in the United States. For example, in the 2005 Supreme Court case Roper versus Simmons, the court held that it is unconstitutional to impose capital punishment on an adolescent. During this case, neuroscientific evidence was presented to the court suggesting that adolescents should not be held responsible for their actions because of the developmental immaturity of brain regions associated with cognitive control and decision making. Thus, it was argued, adolescents cannot be held fully accountable for their actions, as the neural capacity to behave otherwise was not in place. The problem with this argument, of course, is that although all adolescents share this immature neuroanatomy, not all adolescents commit such crimes. What is at stake here is the broader issue of legal responsibility. Just as personal responsibility has been challenged by examinations of the social and structural factors that contribute to criminality, neuroscience has been similarly used to remove any sense of choice from the individual. If this argument is taken to

its logical conclusion, any crime could be forgiven because of the lack of choice involved. As a consequence, our legal system must adopt new ideas about freedom, responsibility, and retribution if it is to effectively deal with contemporary challenges. In particular, less emphasis should be placed on the punishment of undesired behavior and more resources should be devoted toward initiatives designed to prevent future problems from occurring in the first place.

Given that neuroscience has begun to creep into the legal system, it will likely not be long before decisions about neural evidence are the subject of heated debate among legal policy makers and the lay public alike. New ideas about free will and responsibility garnered from neuroscience will also likely have an impact upon public policy makers. For example, will we allow a racist manager who turns down a Black employee for promotion hide behind the defense that his brain made him do it? Will we stop pushing for the patching of the leaky pipeline which keeps women out of top positions in math and science because the brains of their male colleagues will not allow them to accept women into their coterie? The answer to both of these questions is (hopefully) no. However, questions like these force us to reconsider our ostensibly outdated notions of free will and strike to the heart of the issue of what we evaluate as unequivocally right or wrong. Those with a vested interest in intergroup relations should pay careful attention to the ways in which neuroscience is reshaping ideas of free will and responsibility and, in combination with what we already know from social psychology, make suggestions for the most appropriate application of neuroscience to public policy. For example, although a move away from retribution-based policy (e.g., imprisoning someone who commits a hate crime) toward a consequentialist framework (e.g., teaching about multiculturalism and tolerance in schools) as suggested by Greene and Cohen (2004) may be an appropriate application, blindly pardoning those who transgress against intergroup harmony because their actions have been deemed to be out of their control is not. Neuroscience studies on racial bias not only reveal neurological processes that limit our notion of free will (e.g., the spontaneous activation of stereotypes, activation of emotion regulation in stereotype threat settings), but also indicate that our motivations impact the selection of behavioral responses (e.g., automatic control processes that limit racial bias among people who are internally motivated to respond without prejudice). Considering these new ideas from social neuroscience has the potential to shake up the field of intergroup research, to really encourage thought and debate about our stand on various issues and, hopefully, translate these shared beliefs into policy.

SONIA K. KANG is an assistant professor of organizational behavior and human resource management at the University of Toronto. Among other awards, she has received the Ken Dion Most Outstanding Social/Personality Graduate

Student Award, an SSHRC Postdoctoral Fellowship, and the Sir James Lougheed Award of Distinction. She has received a PhD in psychology at the University of Toronto.

MICHAEL INZLICHT is an associate professor of psychology at the University of Toronto and is an associate scientist at Rotman Research Institute. He was a fellow of the Society for Experimental Social Psychology, as well as the National Academy of Education. He was given the Most Valuable Professor award by the Psychology Graduate Student Association (University of Toronto) and the Louise Kidder Early Career Award by the Society for the Psychological Study of Social Issues. He has received a PhD in experimental psychology at Brown University.

BELLE DERKS is an assistant professor of social and organizational psychology at Leiden University. She has received a PhD in psychology at Leiden University.

Sonia K. Kang, Michael Inzlicht,
and Belle Derks

Social Neuroscience and Public Policy on Intergroup Relations: A Hegelian Analysis

Neuroscience Should Not Inform Public Policy

In the previous section, we spent some time highlighting the ways in which neuroscience research can inform the public policy of intergroup relations. In this section, we take the reverse position, our antithesis, and contend that neuroscience has little to offer policy makers. In particular we argue that, at best, neuroscience cannot inform policy because the brain cannot describe the mind and has actually taught us very little that we did not already know and, at worst, should not inform policy because it presents persuasive arguments that could lead to misguided conclusions. Please note that our antithesis is not based on a criticism of methods in neuroscience, which although considerable, have been discussed extensively by others (e.g., Miller, 2008).

The limits of reductionism. Despite claims to the contrary (e.g., Harmon-Jones & Winkielman, 2007), there can be no doubt that social neuroscience is at its core an exercise in reductionism. Reductionism is a framework whereby phenomena at one level are explained completely in terms of other, more fundamental phenomena. Any social neuroscience approach reduces psychological phenomena to basic neurobiological ones. In terms of stigma, we are in danger of losing rich information about the complex, lived experience of stigma at the macrolevel (e.g., Chaudoir & Quinn, this issue; Jahoda, Wilson, Stalker, & Cairney, this issue; van Laar, Derks, Ellemers, & Bleeker, this issue), and replacing this with a more mundane understanding of physiological effects at the microlevel. When we declare that coping with a stigmatized identity can lead to increases in levels of blood cortisol and blood pressure (e.g., Blascovich, Spencer, Quinn, & Steele, 2001), we reduce the lived experience of stress to physiology. When we show that the experience of stereotype threat is associated with activity in the brain's prefrontal cortex (Krendl et al., 2008; Wraga et al., 2007), we are reducing the psychological experience of fear and apprehension to neurology.

There is nothing wrong with reductionism per se; reductionist methods are the basis for many well developed fields of scientific inquiry, including physics, chemistry, and cell biology. As psychologists, we regularly use reductionist logic when we search for the basic cognitive mechanisms and processes that underlie our favorite phenomena. The field believes, for example, that stereotype threat is an interaction between emotional arousal and cognitive distraction (Johns, Inzlicht, & Schmader, 2008; Schmader et al., 2008) because of reductionist methods. The problems with reductionism arise when we consider large-scale fields such as psychology, sociology, or economics. Behavior can be described by a hierarchy of organization, and while describing it one level down the hierarchy is desirable (Dawkins, 1986), any attempt to reduce complex phenomenon down many levels of the hierarchy is to abandon psychology altogether (Dennett, 1969). The further down this hierarchy we go in search of basic elements, the further we are from our phenomena of interest, which, because of their complexity, may be governed by an entirely different set of emergent principles than are the basic elements. Although neuroscience may be useful to social psychology when studying a certain class of intra-individual phenomena (e.g., social cognition), it may be less useful when trying to reduce other, more complex social phenomena to the brain (Dovidio et al., 2008). For example, if one was interested in understanding how a nation can best integrate its immigrant populations, it would make little sense to analyze this in terms of an interaction between this and that brain area, just as it would make little sense to analyze it in terms of the physical and mathematical laws governing nerve cell conduction. A more useful approach would be to recognize the impact of all factors, including those that are structural and situational, and these factors may not be decomposable into basic elements in the brain. The point here is that although reductionism helps us to understand phenomena at adjacent levels of the explanatory hierarchy, it becomes problematic when we go too far down.

Even if we could provide explanations for the mind from low-level analyses of the brain, we need to ask if these explanations are good, or if there are better ones available. Philosopher Hilary Putnam once stated that the laws of particle physics could not provide a good explanation of why a square peg would not fit into a round hole (Putnam, 1975). Although an invocation of quantum electrodynamics could provide some sort of deduction, it would provide a terrible explanation—and who needs terrible explanations when a simple and elegant explanation is readily available?—that the round hole is smaller than the cross-section of the square peg. Along similar lines, is the link between stereotype threat and the ACC (Derks et al., 2008) an explanation of stereotype threat or is it merely a description? And if it is an explanation, isn't an explanation based on stress and distraction better? When explaining psychological phenomena, especially higher-order ones, we may be better served by psychological explanations than neurological ones. Mind, after all, is not the same as brain. Perhaps because the connection between mind and brain is unclear, the actual utility of social neuroscience for policy makers is also unclear.

Reductionism-related problems for social neuroscience are true not only for understanding process, but also for our efforts to develop interventions. Intervention is a major goal of policy, but reductionism to brain processes is not intervention friendly, particularly policy related to intergroup issues. For example, we now know that the amygdala is implicated in stereotyping (e.g., Cunningham et al., 2004), but is intervening at the level of the amygdala really a viable solution for reducing prejudice? Intervening at this level would be expensive, invasive, and, frankly, seems a bit absurd (take this pill once a day and your prejudice will disappear!), not to mention nonspecific. For example, taking a drug or using electricity to stimulate or subdue the amygdala would be highly undesirable, given that the amygdala is involved in a host of other brain processes, many of which we are not even aware of at this point. Interventions for social problems seem better suited to the societal—or at the very least, individual—level, not the physiological level. When we think about it this way, learning more and more about the brain's role in stigma-related processes does not necessarily bring us any closer to designing interventions to improve the lives of stigmatized individuals. Again, we are confronted with the problems that arise when we attempt to go too far down the explanatory hierarchy.

Incremental utility. Whereas the preceding section was concerned with theoretical questions perhaps best left to philosophers, what follows is nothing if not practical. A number of researchers have argued that social neuroscience would lead to groundbreaking discoveries that could make novel theoretical contributions to social psychology (e.g., Cacioppo & Berntson, 2002; Ochsner & Lieberman, 2001). Neuroscience, it was claimed, would also constrain psychological theorizing to what is physically and biologically possible (e.g., Cacioppo & Berntson, 2002; Ochsner, 2007). In our view, however, social neuroscience has fallen short of this enormous promise. A quick scan of the—admittedly, still very young—social neuroscience literature reveals very few instances of real progress or theoretical innovations. From the perspective of social psychology, neuroscience methods have actually added very little new information beyond what was already known from pure behavioral methods (Dovidio et al., 2008). Some have gone so far as to claim that

neuroscientific findings have never constrained social-psychological theory (Kihlstrom, 2006).

Let us return to the neuroscientific study of prejudice and discrimination to illustrate this point. As mentioned above, neuroimaging has implicated the orbital gyrus and ACC in the experience of social identity threat (Wraga et al., 2007). Although these results are interesting and we have frequently cited these findings in our own work, we wonder how informative this is for social psychologists. After all, these findings did not actually expand our knowledge of stereotype threat; rather, they confirmed what the field had already uncovered with simple behavioral measures—that stereotype threat involves heightened arousal and executive control depletion (e.g., Ben-Zeev, Fein, & Inzlicht, 2005; Schmader & Johns, 2003). This type of research may be more relevant to neuroscientists interested in the ACC than to social psychologists. It seems, then, that social neuroscience—at least so far—has offered little in the way of incremental utility for social psychologist and, perhaps, policy makers. Far from constraining social psychological theory, it appears that social psychological theory has constrained our interpretations of neuroscience (Kihlstrom, 2006). In short, the relationship between social psychology and neuroscience may be asymmetrical, with social psychology offering a framework to understand and interpret brain data, but with the brain data offering little to social psychologists or policy makers in return.

The seductive brain. Whereas issues of ontological reductionism and incremental utility suggest that social neuroscience cannot inform public policy, a number of other factors—related mostly to the way neuroscience is perceived by lay audiences—suggest that it should not inform policy. Very few scientific endeavors have garnered as much public and media attention as studies that show the human brain "in action." Yet brain data—and especially brain images—have a power to persuade that reaches far beyond their power to explain.

A recent study suggests that people are more likely to believe a bad explanation for a phenomenon when it is accompanied by irrelevant neuroscientific explanation than without the brain data (Weisberg, Keil, Goodstein, Rawson, & Gray, 2008). Neuroscience explanations, that is, seem to mask otherwise salient logical inconsistencies in an argument. And concrete brain images are even more seductive. In a recent paper by McCabe and Castel (2008), participants had to evaluate the scientific reasoning of, in one study, newspaper reports of a brain imaging study, and in a second study, a real journal article reporting brain data. Participants saw one of three versions of these articles: in one condition the brain data were described in the text, in a second there was the text plus a bar-graph summary of the brain data, and in a third there was the text plus an fMRI-style brain image summarizing the data. Results revealed that those who saw the brain image rated the scientific reasoning of both the newspaper and journal article as more compelling than did the others even though the images themselves added no new relevant information beyond the text. Clearly people are too easily convinced by brain data and brain images; readers may be left with the false impression that they are learning something more scientific because of the inclusion of images showing the physical brain "in action." It is thus important that researchers and audiences do not privilege neuroscience data and make sure to hold it to the same statistical and interpretational standards as behavioral data (Cacioppo et al., 2003; Dovidio et al., 2008).

This issue makes brain data dangerous—especially to policy makers. In the hands of people who have only limited knowledge of neuroscience, brain data could be used to advocate or defend this or that social policy despite only weak scientific evidence for it. For example, in 2007 the *New York Times* ran an op-ed piece that reported on an fMRI study that could "reveal some voter impressions on which [the 2008 US Presidential] election may well turn" (Iacobini et al., 2007). The study (and op-ed piece) was widely criticized by the neuroscientific community, which bristled at a design that relied so heavily on reverse inference and was described as little data and lots of storytelling (Miller, 2008). The lay public however, may not understand the scientific problems of the study and instead become mesmerized by the idea of a "bona fide pipeline" to voter intentions. Policy makers may be equally impressed and start advocating for positions that "voters' brains" really want. The bottom line is that there is a real danger that the public (including judges and juries, policy makers, employers, insurers, etc.) will ignore the complexities of neuroscience and treat brain images as a kind of indisputable truth. It is for this reason that the field of "neuroethics" was born, with a new Neuroethics Society, a new *Neuroethics* journal, and a number of neuroethics centers worldwide safeguarding against this possibility.

The brain is so seductive, in fact, that it may distract us from important research that does not employ neuroscientific methodology. If we continue to place so much emphasis on brain data, what becomes of psychological effects that have not yet or cannot ever be shown on a neural level? It is important to remember that the types of studies that are possible with current neuroscience methods are quite constrained and, as such, neuroscience must be viewed as an added tool, not a necessary step, in testing the validity of social psychological research. For example, we do not yet have the technology or perhaps even the resources to truly examine what happens when many brains are put together in vivo, or even what happens when one brain is put into a real social context. These are important limitations to keep in mind as we continue to move forward with the social neuroscience approach.

References

Amodio, D. M. (2008). The social neuroscience of intergroup relations. *European Review of Social Psychology, 19*, 1–54.

Amodio, D. M., Devine, P. G., & Harmon-Jones, E. (2008). Individual differences in the regulation of intergroup bias: The role of conflict monitoring and neural signals for control. *Journal of Personality and Social Psychology, 94*, 60–74.

Amodio, D. M., Harmon-Jones, E., Devine, P. G., Curtin, J. J., Hartley, S. L., & Covert, A. E. (2004). Neural signals for the detection of unintentional race bias. *Psychological Science, 15*, 88–93.

Bargh, J. A. (1994). The four horsemen of automaticity: Awareness, intention, efficiency, and control in social cognition. In R. Wyer Jr. & T. Srull (Eds.), *Handbook of social cognition* (Vol. 1, pp. 1–40). Hillsdale, NJ: Lawrence Erlbaum Associates.

Ben-Zeev, T., Fein, S., & Inzlicht, M. (2005). Stereotype threat and arousal. *Journal of Experimental Social Psychology, 41*, 174–181.

Blascovich, J., Spencer, S. J., Quinn, D. M., & Steele, C. M. (2001). African-Americans and high blood pressure: The role of stereotype threat. *Psychological Science, 12*, 225–229.

Cacioppo, J. T. (2004). Common sense, intuition, and theory in personality and social psychology. *Personality and Social Psychology Review, 8*, 114–122.

Cacioppo, J. T., & Berntson, G. G. (2002). Social neuroscience. In J. T Cacioppo, G. G. Berntson, R. Adolphs, C. S. Carter, R. J. Davidson, M. K. McClintock, et al. (Eds.), *Foundations in social neuroscience* (pp. 1–9). Cambridge, MA: MIT Press.

Cacioppo, J. T., Berntson, G. G., Lorig, T. S., Norris, C. J., Rickett, E., & Nusbaum, H. (2003). Just because you're imaging the brain doesn't mean you can stop using your head: A primer and set of first principles. *Journal of Personality and Social Psychology, 85*, 650–661.

Cacioppo J. T., Berntson, G. G., & Nusbaum, H. C. (2008). Neuroimaging as a new tool in the toolbox of psychological science. *Current Directions in Psychological Science, 17*, 62–67.

Correll, J., Park, B., Judd, C. M., Wittenbrink, B., Sadler, M. S., & Keesee, T. (2007). Across the thin blue line: Police officers and racial bias in the decision to shoot. *Journal of Personality & Social Psychology, 92*, 1006–1023.

Correll, J., Urland, G. L., & Ito, T. A. (2006). Event-related potentials and the decision to shoot: The role of threat perception and cognitive control. *Journal of Experimental Social Psychology, 42*, 120–128.

Cunningham, W. A., Johnson, M. K., Raye, C. L., Gatenby, J. C., Gore, J. C., & Banaji, M. R. (2004). Separable neural components in the processing of Black and White faces. *Psychological Science, 15*, 806–813.

Dawkins, R. (1986). *The blind watchmaker.* New York: Norton & Company, Inc.

Devine, P. G., Plant, E. A., Amodio, D. M., Harmon-Jones, E., & Vance, S. L. (2002). The regulation of explicit and implicit race bias: The role of motivations to respond without prejudice. *Journal of Personality and Social Psychology, 82*, 835–848.

Dennett, D. (1969). Personal and subpersonal levels of explanation. In J. L. Bermudez (Ed.), *Philosophy and psychology* (pp. 17–21). New York: Routledge.

Derks, B., Inzlicht, M., & Kang, S. (2008). The neuroscience of stigma and stereotype threat. *Group Processes & Intergroup Relations, 11*, 163–181.

Dickter, C. L., & Bartholow, B. D. (2007). Racial ingroup and outgroup attention biases revealed by event-related brain potentials. *Social, Cognitive, and Affective Neuroscience, 2*, 189–198.

Dovidio, J. F., Pearson, A. R., & Orr, P. (2008). Social psychology and neuroscience: Strange bedfellows or a healthy marriage. *Group Processes & Intergroup Relations, 11*, 247–263.

Greene, J. D. (2003). From neural "is" to moral "ought": What are the moral implications of neuroscientific moral psychology? *Nature Reviews Neuroscience, 4*, 847–850.

Greene, J. D., & Cohen J. D. (2004). For the law, neuroscience changes nothing and everything. *Philosophical Transactions of the Royal Society of London B, 359*, 1775–1785.

Greene, J. D., Nystrom, L. E., Engell, A. D., Darley, J. M., & Cohen, J. D. (2004). The neural bases of cognitive conflict and control in moral judgment. *Neuron, 44*, 389–400.

Greene, J. D., Sommerville, R. B., Nystrom, L. E., Darley, J. M., & Cohen, J. D. (2001). An fMRI investigation of emotional engagement in moral judgment. *Science, 293*, 2105–2108.

Greenwald, A. G., McGhee, D. E., & Schwartz, J. K. L. (1998). Measuring individual differences in implicit cognition: The implicit association test. *Journal of Personality and Social Psychology, 74*, 1464–1480.

Harmon-Jones, E., & Winkielman, P. (2007). A brief overview of social neuroscience. In E. Harmon-Jones & P. Winkielman (Eds.), *Social Neuroscience: Integrating biological and psychological explanations of social behavior* (pp. 3–11). New York: Guilford Press.

Iacobini, M., Freedman, J., Kaplan, J., Hall Jamieson, K., Freedman, T., Knapp B., & Fitzgerald K. (2007). *This is your brain on politics*. Retrieved on September 12, 2008, from www.nytimes.com/2007/11/11/opinion/11freedman.html?_r=2&pagewanted=1sq=Marco%20lacobini&st=nyt&scp=1&oref=slogin.

Ito, T. A., Thompson, E., & Cacioppo, J. T. (2004). Tracking the timecourse of social perception: The effects of racial cues on event-related brain potentials. *Personality and Social Psychology Bulletin, 30*, 1267–1280.

Ito, T. A., & Urland, G. R. (2003). Race and gender on the brain: Electrocortical measures of attention to race and gender of multiply categorizable individuals. *Journal of Personality and Social Psychology, 85*, 616–626.

Ito, T. A., & Urland, G. R. (2005). The influence of processing objectives on the perception of faces: An ERP study of race and gender perception. *Cognitive, Affective and Behavioral Neuroscience, 5*, 21–36.

Johns, M., Inzlicht, M., & Schmader, T. (2008). Stereotype threat and executive resource depletion: The influence of emotion regulation. *Journal of Experimental Psychology: General, 137*, 691–705.

Johns, M., Schmader, T., & Martens, A. (2005). Knowing is half the battle: Teaching stereotype threat as a means of improving women's math performance. *Psychological Science, 16*, 175–179.

Kihlstrom, J. F. (2006). Does neuroscience constrain social-psychological theory? *SPSP Dialogue, 21*, 26–27.

Krendl, A. C., Richeson, J. A., Kelley, W. M., & Heatherton, T. F. (2008). The negative consequences of threat: An fMRI investigation of the neural mechanisms underlying women's underperformance in math. *Psychological Science, 19*, 168–175.

Kubota, J. T., & Ito, T. A. (2007). Multiple cues in social perception: The time course of processing race and facial expression. *Journal of Experimental Social Psychology, 43*, 738–752.

McCabe, D. P., & Castel, A. D. (2008). Seeing is believing: The effect of brain images on judgments of scientific reasoning. *Cognition, 107*, 343–352.

Miller, G. (2008). Growing Pains for fMRI. *Science, 320*, 1412–1414.

Ochsner, K. N. (2007). Social cognitive neuroscience: Historical development, core principles, and future promise. In A. Kruglanksi & E. T. Higgins (Eds.), *Social psychology: A handbook of basic principles* (2nd ed., pp. 39–66). New York: Guilford Press.

Ochsner, K. N., & Lieberman, M. D. (2001). The emergence of social cognitive neuroscience. *American Psychologist, 56*, 717–734.

Putnam, H. (1975). The meaning of "meaning." In H. Putnam (Ed.), *Philosophical papers: Volume 2, mind, language and reality* (pp. 291–303). Cambridge, UK: Cambridge University Press.

Richeson, J. A., Baird, A. A., Gordon, H. L., Heatherton, T. F., Wyland, C. L., Trawalter, S., et al. (2003). An fMRI examination of the impact of interracial contact on executive function. *Nature Neuroscience, 6*, 1323–1328.

Richeson, J. A., & Nussbaum, R. J. (2004). The impact of multiculturalism versus color blindness on racial bias. *Journal of Experimental Social Psychology, 40,* 417–423.

Schmader, T., & Johns, M. (2003). Converging evidence that stereotype threat reduces working memory capacity. *Journal of Personality and Social Psychology, 85,* 440–452.

Schmader, T., Johns, M., & Forbes, C. (2008). An integrated process model of stereotype threat effects on performance. *Psychological Review, 115,* 336–356.

Schofield, J. W. (2001). The colorblind perspective in school: Causes and consequences. In J. A. Banks & C. A. McGee Banks (Eds.), *Multicultural education. Issues and perspectives* (4th ed., pp. 247–267). New York: Wiley.

Weisberg, D. S., Keil, F. C., Goodstein, J., Rawson, E., & Gray, J. R. (2008). The seductive allure of neuroscience explanations. *Journal of Cognitive Neuroscience, 20,* 470–477.

Wheeler, M. E., & Fiske, S. T. (2005). Controlling racial prejudice: Social-cognitive goals affect amygdala and stereotype activation. *Psychological Science, 16,* 56–63.

Willadsen-Jensen, E. C., & Ito, T. A. (2006). Ambiguity and the timecourse of racial categorization. *Social Cognition, 24,* 580–606.

Wolsko, C., Park, B., Judd, C. M., & Wittenbrink, B. (2000). Framing interethnic ideology: Effects of multicultural and colorblind perspectives of judgments of groups and individuals. *Journal of Personality and Social Psychology, 78,* 635–654.

Wraga, M., Helt, M., Jacobs, E., & Sullivan, K. (2007). Neural basis of stereotype-induced shifts in women's mental rotation performance. *Social Cognitive and Affective Neuroscience, 2,* 12–19.

SONIA K. KANG is an assistant professor of organizational behavior and human resource management at the University of Toronto. Among other awards, she has received the Ken Dion Most Outstanding Social/Personality Graduate Student Award, an SSHRC Postdoctoral Fellowship, and the Sir James Lougheed Award of Distinction. She has received a PhD in psychology at the University of Toronto.

MICHAEL INZLICHT is an associate professor of psychology at the University of Toronto and is an associate scientist at Rotman Research Institute. He was a fellow of the Society for Experimental Social Psychology, as well as the National Academy of Education. He was given the Most Valuable Professor award by the Psychology Graduate Student Association (University of Toronto) and the Louise Kidder Early Career Award by the Society for the Psychological Study of Social Issues. He has received a PhD in experimental psychology at Brown University.

BELLE DERKS is an assistant professor of social and organizational psychology at Leiden University. She has received a PhD in psychology at Leiden University.

EXPLORING THE ISSUE

Should Neuroscience Research Be Used to Inform Public Policy?

Critical Thinking and Reflection

1. What was the authors' goal in presenting both sides of the issue?
2. In the "Incremental Utility" section (found in the NO selection), what evidence do the authors give to support their claim that neuroscience shouldn't be used to inform public policy?
3. In both the YES and NO selections, the authors focus on neuroscience research. How might their arguments (for both sides of the issue) apply to psychological research in general?
4. Pick a side of the issue. How might psychologists respond to the critiques that the authors present?
5. In the YES selection, what do the authors mean when they say that neuroscience represents the "unification of knowledge"?

Create Central

www.mhhe.com/createcentral

Additional Resource

Brooks, D. (2013, January 10). Beware stubby glasses. *The New York Times*. Retrieved from www.nytimes.com/2013/01/11/opinion/brooks-beware-stubby-glasses.html?smid=pl-share&_r=0

Internet References . . .

The Legislative Process—House.gov

www.house.gov/content/learn/legislative_process/

Psychological Research and Public Policy: Bridging the Gap

www.yale.edu/intergroup/Dovidio_Esses_2007.pdf

Unit 3

UNIT

Development Issues

*T*he objective of most developmental psychologists is to document the course of physical, social, and cognitive changes over the entire span of our lives. But what has the greatest influence on human development? Some have said that today's youth have been raised with such material affluence and parental indulgence that they have learned to become self-centered rather than other-centered. Is that true? Moreover, the amount of time spent online has led some psychological researchers to be curious about the effect of digital social connections, such as online friendships, on development. How are these online friendships affecting today's youth? Are they different from the youth of a generation ago?

Selected, Edited and with Issue Framing Material by:
Brent Slife, *Brigham Young University*

ISSUE

Are Violent Video Games Harmful to Children and Adolescents?

YES: Steven F. Gruel, from "Brief of *Amicus Curiae* in Case of *Brown v. Entertainment Merchants Association*,"
U.S. Supreme Court, No. 08-1448 (2010)

NO: Patricia A. Millett, from "Brief of *Amici Curiae* in Case of *Brown v. Entertainment Merchants Association*,"
U.S. Supreme Court, No. 08-1448 (2010)

Learning Outcomes

After reading this issue, you should be able to:

- Discuss and critically evaluate the arguments about the strength of scientific evidence that either supports or discredits the relationship between playing violent video games and engaging in aggressive behavior among youth.
- Understand the ways in which playing video games can influence neurological structure and functioning.
- Evaluate the extent to which playing violent video games by young people can lead to academic problems.
- Compare the rationale used by the government to regulate other media such as television and radio and the arguments made for and against the regulation of violent video game sales to children.
- Consider the similarities and differences between passively watching a violent movie and actively participating in a violent video game.

ISSUE SUMMARY

YES: Prosecutor Steven F. Gruel, in arguing before the Supreme Court, cites what he says is an overwhelming amount of research support to conclude that viewing violence causes children to act more violently.

NO: Defense attorney Patricia A. Millett argues before the Supreme Court that psychological research about the effects of media violence on children is inconclusive, with these researchers making claims about causation that cannot be substantiated.

With the introduction of any new media—film, television, Internet—its dangers and benefits are inevitably debated. Video games, the newest such technology, are no exception. Advances in video game graphics, as well as an increasing mass-market appeal, have resulted in larger numbers of gamers and more lifelike depictions of simulated violence. These large numbers and lifelike depictions have led, in turn, to some parents and policymakers raising concerns about the potential for real-life violence, what some have called "murder simulators." These concerns seemed to come to a head, at least legally, when a California law that would ban the sale of violent video games to minors was recently proposed.

The possibility of legal restrictions mobilized video game enthusiasts and free-speech supporters. They bristled

at not only the restrictions but also the implication that video games controlled their actions. When the California law came before the U.S. Supreme Court, psychological research was called upon to help decide the issue. Both sides seemed to focus on neuroscience research, which some consider a specialty of psychology, as ammunition for their arguments. Eventually the Court ruled the law unconstitutional on the grounds that it limited free speech. However, the battle over the ultimate effects of media violence continues.

In the YES selection Steven F. Gruel probably represents those who consider video games a danger. A former federal prosecutor and lead legal counsel for the case before the Supreme Court, Gruel claims that neuroscience research indicates that playing video games increases violent behavior, and thus presents a clear risk to the nation's youth. He believes that a general conclusion from the scientific literature "can be drawn without any reasonable doubt": video game use is a "causal risk factor" resulting in several negative outcomes, including physically aggressive behavior, lowered school performance, loss of "proactive control" to inhibit impulsive actions, damaged higher level thinking, and decreased emotional control. From Gruel's perspective, "the scientific debate about whether exposure to media violence causes increases in aggressive behavior is over."

In the NO selection, however, Patricia A. Millett, counsel of record for opponents to the California law, argues that this debate is *not* over. She says that the conclusion of the opposition "is based on profoundly flawed research." Millett rejects this research on the basis of its methodological limitations, noting that it not only fails to show causation but also is suspect even as a correlation. She criticizes the research for relying on "proxies for aggression that do not correlate with aggressive behavior in the real world." Millett argues that whatever correlations may or may not be in play between video game use and violent behavior, there are other, more relevant variables that confound the research, such as family violence at home, antisocial personality tendencies, and the influence of peers.

POINT

- The scientific community has come to an overwhelming consensus about the effects of violent video games on children.

- Studies show that exposure to simulated violence increases aggression in children.
- Numerous studies show a significant correlation between viewing and then performing aggressive acts.

- Neuroscience research shows that playing violent video games rewires the brain for later physical violence.

COUNTERPOINT

- No such consensus exists, and there is much research arguing that there is no negative effect of violent video games on children's behavior.
- Previous studies have used poor definitions of aggression, which do not correlate with real-world behavior.
- Correlation can never be causation, which means that other factors can account for violent behavior, such as violence at home.
- Neuroscience studies describe changes in the brain, but cannot adequately address the causes of those changes.

YES

Steven F. Gruel

Brief of *Amicus Curiae* in Case of *Brown v. Entertainment Merchants Association*

I. Science Confirms That Violent Video Games Are Harmful to Minors Allowing the State Clear Justification in Regulating Children's Access to These Materials

. . .

1. A Minor's Exposure to Violent Video Games—More Time Spent Playing Games With Increasing Graphic Violence

A minor's exposure to the avalance of violent video games is staggering. Video games first emerged in the 1970s, but it was during the 1990s that violent games truly came of age. In 1992, *Wolfenstein 3D*, the first major "first-person shooter" game was released. In a first-person shooter, one "sees" the video game world through the eyes of the player, rather than seeing it as if looking on from afar. The player is the one fighting, killing, and being killed. Video game historian Steven Kent noted that "part of *Wolfenstein 3D* popularity sprang from its shock value. In *Wolfenstein 3D*, enemies fell and bled on the floor."

With ever changing advancements in technology, the dramatic increases in speed and graphic capability have resulted in more realistic violence. As an example, in the video game *Soldier of Fortune*, the player/shooter can wound an enemy causing exposed bone and sinew.

As the video games became more graphically violent, the average time children played these games continued to climb. In the book, *Violent Video Game Effects on Children and Adolescents*, the authors note that in the early 1990s, boys averaged 4 hours a week and girls 2 hours a week playing video games. In a few years these averages jumped to 7.1 and 4.5, respectively. In a recent survey of over 600 eighth and ninth-grade students, children averaged 9 hours per week with boys averaging 13 hours per week and girls averaging 5 hours per week.

In 1993, United States Senators Joseph Lieberman and Herbert Kohl noticed the increasing violence in video games and held hearings to examine the issue. Although there was much less research on the effects of violent video games, the senators put pressure on the video game industry to create a rating system. The goal of the rating system was to provide information to parents about the content of games so that they could make informed decisions about which games their children could play. However, these industry "voluntary" labels rating video games are inherently flawed and have failed due to "invalid assumptions about what is safe versus harmful."

In 2003, more than 239 million computer and video games were sold in the United States; that is almost two games for every household in the United States. More than 90% of all U.S. children and adolescents play video games. The National Youth Violence Prevention Resource Center has stated that a 2001 review of the 70 top-selling video games found 49% contained serious violence. In 41% of the games, violence was necessary for the protagonists to achieve their goals. There is no doubt, violent video games are among the most popular entertainment products for teens and adolescents, especially for boys.

New generation violent video games contain substantial amounts of increasingly realistic portrayals of violence. Elaborate content analyses revealed that the favored narrative is a "human perpetrator engaging in repeated acts of justified violence involving weapons that results in some bloodshed to the victim."

2. Scientific Studies Confirm that Violent Video Games Have Harmful Effects Minors

In a nutshell, teens and adolescents play video games frequently, and a significant portion of the games contain increasingly realistic portrayals of violence. Viewing violence increases aggression and greater exposure to media violence is strongly linked to increases in aggression.

Playing a lot of violent games is unlikely to turn a normal youth with zero, one or even two other risk factors into a killer. But regardless of how many other risk factors are present in a youth's life, playing a lot of violent games is likely to increase the frequency and the seriousness of his or her physical aggression, both in the short term and over time as the youth grows up. These long-term effects are a consequence of powerful observational learning and desensitization processes that neuroscientists and psychologists now understand to occur automatically in the human child. Simply stated, "adolescents who expose themselves to greater amounts of video game violence were more hostile, reported getting into arguments with teachers more frequently, were more likely to be involved in physical fights, and performed more poorly in school.

In a recent book, researchers once again concluded that the "active participation" in all aspects of violence: decision-making and carrying out the violent act, result in a greater effect from violent video games than a violent movie. Unlike a passive observer in movie watching, in first-person shooter and third-person shooter games, you're the one who decides whether to pull the trigger or not and whether to kill or not. After conducting three very different kinds of studies (experimental, a cross-sectional correlational study, and a longitudinal study) the results confirmed that violent games contribute to violent behavior.

The relationship between media violence and real-life aggression is nearly as strong as the impact of cigarette smoking and lung cancer: not everyone who smokes will get lung cancer, and not everyone who views media violence will become aggressive themselves. However, the connection is significant.

In an upcoming publication concerning children and violent video games, three complementary theoretical perspectives are discussed when contemplating the effects of playing video games. The *General Aggression Model* and its offshoot the *General Learning Model* describe the basic learning processes and effects involved in both short-term and long-term effects of playing various types of games. The *Five Dimensions of Video Game Effects* perspective describes different aspects of video games and video game play that influence the specific effects likely to occur. The *Risk and Resilience* perspective describes the effects of video game play—prosocial, antisocial, and other—take place within a complex set of social and biological factors, each of which contribute[s] to development of the individual's thoughts, feelings, and behaviors.

The main findings can be succinctly summarized: playing violent video games causes an increase in the likelihood of physically aggressive behavior, aggressive thinking, aggressive affect, physiological arousal, and desensitization/low empathy. It also decreases helpful or prosocial behavior. With the exception of physiological arousal (for which there are no cross-sectional or longitudinal studies), all of the outcome variables showed the same effects in experimental, cross-sectional, and longitudinal studies. The main effects occurred for both males and females, for participants from low-violence collectivistic type Eastern countries (*e.g.*, Japan), and from high-violence individualistic type Western countries (*e.g.*, USA, Europe).

Research also indicates that the aggression carried out by video game characters is usually portrayed as justified, retributional, necessary to complete the game, rewarded and followed by unrealistic consequences. The overall level and realism of violent depictions, use of guns and likelihood of being killed by a gun has risen substantially over time; additionally, female victims and police officer victims rose significantly across time.

Many researchers have begun studying the concept of video game "addiction" and most researchers studying the pathological use of computer or video games have defined it similarly to how pathological gambling is defined—based on damage to family, social, school, occupational, and psychological functioning. The pace of studies has increased greatly in the past decade. In 2007, the American Medical Association released a report on the "addictive potential" of video games. The report concluded with a recommendation that the "AMA strongly encourage the consideration and inclusion of 'Internet/video game addiction' as a formal diagnostic disorder in the upcoming revision of the *Diagnostic and Statistical Manual of Mental Disorders*-IV."

The most comprehensive study to date in the US used a national sample of over 1,100 youth aged 8 to 18, in which 8.5% of video game players were classified as pathological demonstrates that it is not a trivial number of people who are suffering damage to their lives because of their game play.

School Performance

Several studies have documented a negative relation between amount of time playing video games and school performance among children, adolescents, and college students. The displacement hypothesis, that games displace time on other activities, is the most typical explanation for this relation. It could be argued, however, that the relation might be due to the children themselves, rather than to game time. It is highly likely that children who perform more poorly at school are likely to spend more time playing games, where they may feel a sense of mastery that eludes them at school. Nevertheless, each hour a child spends playing entertainment games (in contrast to educational games, which have been demonstrated to have educational benefits) is an hour not spent on homework, reading, exploring, creating, or other things that might have more educational benefit. Some evidence has been found to support the displacement hypothesis. In one nationally representative US sample of 1,491 youth between 10 and 19, gamers spent 30% less time reading and 34% less time doing homework. Therefore, even if poor school performance tends to cause increases in time playing video games, large amounts of video game play are likely to further hurt their school performance.

In short, the recent explosion in research on video game effects has greatly improved our understanding of how this medium affects its consumers. Several conclusions can be drawn without any reasonable doubt. First, there are many different effects of playing video games on the player. Some of these are short term, whereas others are long term. Second, the specific effects depend on a host of factors, including the content, structure, and context of the game. Third, the same game can have multiple effects on the same person, some of which may be generally beneficial whereas others may be detrimental. Fourth, playing violent video games is a causal risk factor for a host of detrimental effects in both the short and the long term[s], including increasing the likelihood of physically aggressive behavior.

Negative Effects on the Brain

Studies have shown evidence that exposure to violent video games reduces the player's use of some brain areas involved in higher order thought and impulse control.

In addition to behavioral–psychological theories explaining the relationship between media violence exposure and aggressive behavior, recently attention has turned to neuro-psychological theories. These theories attempt to identify areas of brain functioning that may be affected by media violence exposure and that may underlie aggressive behavior.

As recently as June 2010, another study of violent video game effects on frontal lobe activity was published wherein it was concluded that playing a violent video game for only 30 minutes immediately produced lower activity levels (compared to a nonviolent video game) in prefrontal regions thought to be involved in cognitive inhibition. This study shows that playing a violent video game for 30 minutes causes a decrease in brain activity in a region of the frontal lobe that is known to be important in the ability to inhibit impulsive behavior. The study also suggested that . . . violent games may also impair emotional functioning when it noted that "an impaired role of DLPFC (dorsolateral prefrontal cortex) in inhibition, therefore, may yield impaired emotional functioning following violent video game play."

Other studies of the neurological underpinnings of aggressive behavior, for example, indicate that a neural circuit that includes parts of the frontal cortex, amygdale, and temporal lobes is important in emotional regulation and violence. Research strongly suggests an underactivity of brain inhibitory mechanisms in the frontal cortex and striatum, coupled with hyperarousal of the amygdala and temporal lobe regions, is responsible for chronic, explosive, and/or severe aggressive behavior.

Research clearly indicates that areas in the frontal lobe and amygdale may be activated by viewing violent television and playing violent video games.

With the use of functional magnetic resonance imaging (fMRI), research has shown a direct alteration in brain functioning from exposure to media violence. Researchers found that teenagers who played a violent videogame exhibited increased activity in a part of the brain that governs emotional arousal and the same teenagers showed decreased activity in the parts of the brain involved in focus, inhibition, and concentration.

Youth who play a lot of violent video games (but who have not been diagnosed with a behavioral disorder) show a similar pattern of brain activity when doing complex executive control tasks as youth who have been diagnosed with some type of aggression-related behavior disorder. This pattern is very different from control-group youth who do not play a lot of violent games (and who have not been diagnosed with a behavioral disorder).

Youth who play a lot of violent video games show a deficit in a specific type of executive control known as proactive control. Proactive control is seen as necessary to inhibit impulsive reactions. This difference shows up in the brain wave patterns as well as in behavioral reactions.

Additionally, video game violence exposure and aggressive behavior to brain processes have been linked reflecting a desensitization in the aversive motivational system. Repeated exposure to media violence reduces its psychological impact and eventually produced aggressive approach-related motivational states theoretically leading to a stable increase in aggression.

Finally, in a functional magnetic resonance imaging study on players of the first-shooter game *Tactical Ops: Assault on Terror*, the violent portions of a video game activated the regions in the brain known to be active in fight-or-flight situations. In other words, the brain reacted to the fictional violence of a video game in much the same way as it reacts to real violence.

In short, neuroscience research supports a critical link between perpetration of virtual violence with reduced activation of a neural mechanism known to be important for self-control and for evaluation of affect. These findings strongly suggest that focusing on the activity of prefrontal cortical structures important for executive control could provide important mediational links in the relationship between exposure to violent media and increased aggression.

3. Recent Studies and Researchers Continue to Find Harmful Effects To Minors From Playing Violent Video Games

In March 2010, leading researchers in the area of media violence from the United States and Japan worked together to conduct a meta-analytic procedure testing the effects of violent games on aggressive behavior, aggressive cognition, aggressive affect, physiological arousal, empathy/desensitization, and prosocial behavior. In conducting their meta-analysis on the effects of video game violence, these researchers retrieved over 130 research reports which entailed scientific tests on over 130,000 participants. This study has been described as "probably about as exhaustive a sampling of the pre-2009 research literature as one could obtain and far more than that used in any other review of violent video game effects."

This extensive meta-analysis of the effects of violent video games confirms what many theories predicted and what prior research about other violent mass media found: that violent video games stimulate aggression in the players in the short run and increase the risk for aggression behaviors by the players later in life. The effects occur for males and females and for children growing up in Eastern and Western cultures. Also, the effects were stronger for more violent than less violent outcomes.

From their overarching analysis, these researchers concluded that the scientific debate should move beyond the simple question whether violent video game play is a causal risk factor for behavior because: "scientific literature has effectively and clearly shown the answer to be 'yes.'"

Regardless of research method (experimental, correlational, or longitudinal) and regardless of cultures tested (East and West) the same effects are proven: exposure to violent video games is a causal risk factor for aggressive thoughts and behavior, and decreased empathy and prosocial behavior in youths. In fact, Dr. Anderson, one of three 2010 American Psychological Association Distinguished Scientist Lecturers, has stated that this recent meta-analysis on violent video games may be his last because of its "definitive findings."

4. The Shortcomings of Purported "Research" Contesting the Scientific Studies Showing the Harmful Effects to Minors Playing Violent Video Games

The Video Software Dealers Association and the Entertainment Software Association will likely contest the science showing the harmful effects of violent video games on minors. Apart from the self-serving motive for such opposition, one need only consider a professional organization that clearly does not doubt the serious aggression-teaching abilities of violent video games—the United States Department of Defense. Both the U.S. Army and U.S. Marines have their own video games used to train soldiers as tactical "first-person shooters" leading teams in "close-quarters urban combat." Many of these military combat training videos, such as *Full Spectrum Warrior* and *First To Fight* have been adapted and placed on the commercial market for minors to play.

Also, alleged "scientific" studies may be suggested by Respondents to argue that there are no harmful effects from violent video game playing. These "findings" can be explained by small sample size, poor test conditions, and chance. The simple response to these studies is the recent and clear findings of the meta-analysis comprising 130 studies of the effects of violent video games showing the like between violent video games and aggression.

II. Conclusion

The scientific debate about whether exposure to media violence causes increases in aggressive behavior is over. All major types of research methodologies have been used, including experiments, cross-sectional correlational studies, longitudinal studies, intervention studies, and meta-analyses. For each category exposure to media violence was significantly associated with increased aggressions or violence. Likewise, the harmful effects on minors from playing violent video games are documented and not seriously contested.

Much research over several decades documents how witnessing violence and aggression leads to a range of negative outcomes for children. Negative outcomes result both from witnessing real violence [and] from viewing media violence. The most recent comprehensive review of the media violence literature documents the ". . . unequivocal evidence that media violence increases the likelihood of aggressive and violent behavior in both immediate and long-term contexts."

In the end, we need only to circle back from this rising ocean of research and return to simple commonsense. Society has a direct, rational, and compelling reason in marginally restricting a minor's access to violent video games. . . .

STEVEN F. GRUEL is a practicing criminal defense attorney and former federal prosecutor with over 25 years of experience. Voted California's top "SuperLawyer" for 3 consecutive years, he was previously the chief of the Major Crimes Section in the U.S. Attorney's office. He has received a law degree from the University of Wisconsin Law School.

Patricia A. Millett

Brief of *Amici Curiae* in Case of *Brown v. Entertainment Merchants Association*

Introduction and Summary of Argument

As respondents explain, California's ban on the sale and rental of certain video games to minors is subject to strict scrutiny because it directly regulates video games based on the content of a game, i.e., whether the game is deemed "violent." California asserts that its law is necessary to "prevent[] psychological or neurological harm to minors who play violent video games." Under strict scrutiny, California must both provide "substantial evidence" that the video games it regulates cause psychological or neurological harm to minors who play them, and demonstrate that the restriction will "alleviate these harms in a direct and material way."

California has done neither. Indeed, California does not offer any reliable evidence, let alone substantial evidence, that playing violent video games causes psychological or neurological harm to minors. California confesses it cannot prove causation, but points to studies that it says show a "correlation" between the two. But the evidence does not even do that.

California and Senator Yee also cite studies that purport to show a link between the playing of violent video games and violent, aggressive, and antisocial behavior by minors. But in the court of appeals, California expressly disclaimed any interest in regulating video games sales and rentals to minors to prevent such conduct, and therefore these studies are waived because the argument was waived. The studies are of no help to California in any event because they document neither a causal connection nor a correlation between the playing of violent video games and violent, aggressive, or antisocial behavior.

Indeed, whether attempting to link violent video games with psychological and neurological harm or with violent, aggressive, and antisocial behavior, all of the studies that California and Senator Yee cite suffer from inherent and fundamental methodological flaws.

- The survey of aggressive behavior. The courts below carefully considered this survey and correctly discredited it because the questions it posed are simply not valid indicators for actual violent or aggressive behavior and because it fails to account or control for other variables that have been proven to affect the behavior of minors.
- The laboratory experimental study of aggression. This study, too, was rightly discounted by the courts below because it relies on proxies for aggression that do not correlate with aggressive behavior in the real world.
- The "meta-analysis" of video game violence research. A meta-analysis combines the results of many other studies on a particular subject. But the accuracy and utility of any meta-analysis depends on the quality of the underlying studies themselves. Put another way a meta-analysis of scientifically unreliable studies cannot cure the studies' flaws. Here, the meta-analysis on which Senator Yee relies was compromised because it was based on studies that used invalid measures of aggression.
- "Longitudinal" studies of aggression. A longitudinal study analyzes participants on many occasions over an extended period. The studies that Senator Yee cites are not longitudinal because they observed participants on only a few occasions and over just a short period of time. Additionally, those studies both failed to account for other variables that may explain aggressive behavior and used invalid measures of aggression.
- Neuroscience studies. These studies supposedly show a connection between playing violent video games and altered brain activity. The courts below properly concluded that they do not. Further, the neuroscience studies are rooted in fundamentally flawed statistical methodologies and do not address the cause of brain activation and deactivation in children.

Methodological flaws are only the beginning of the studies' problems. Both California and Senator Yee repeatedly exaggerate the statistical significance of the studies' findings, failing to inform the Court of express disclaimers and cautionary statements in the studies about the nature of their findings.

Finally, California and Senator Yee ignore a weighty body of scholarship, undertaken with established and reliable scientific methodologies, debunking the claim that the video games California seeks to regulate have harmful effects on minors.

Argument

I. California's Asserted Interest in Preventing Psychological and Neurological Harm to Minors Is Not Supported by Any Reliable, Let Alone, Substantial Evidence

A. California's Studies Do Not Show a Causal Link, or Even a Correlation, Between Playing Violent Video Games and Psychological or Neurological Harm to Minors

California's ban on the sale and rental of violent video games to minors rests on the same flawed studies that court after court has rejected.

The courts were right to reject these studies because they do not even establish the "correlation" between violent video games and psychological harm to minors that California says exists, let alone the causation of harm that, as respondent explains, the First Amendment requires. Nor do the studies show a connection between playing violent video games and violent or aggressive behavior of minors, which explains why California disclaimed that interest below.

First, California points to a 2004 study by Douglas Gentile of approximately 600 eighth and ninth-grade students. These students completed surveys that asked questions about the types of video games they preferred and how "violent" they were. (The survey did not provide any definition of "violent.") The survey also recorded how often the students played the games; the students' hostility level; how often they had argued with teachers during the past year; their average grades; and whether they had been in a physical fight in the past year. From the survey answers, Gentile concluded that "[a]dolescents who expose themselves to greater amounts of video game violence" were more hostile and reported getting into more arguments with teachers and physical fights and performing poorly in school.

Although California relies heavily on the Gentile survey, it has absolutely no relevance here. The survey examines only the purported connection between video game violence and "aggressive behavior" or "physical aggression" towards third parties. It does not study, and says nothing about, the psychological or neurological harm allegedly caused to those who play violent video games, which is the only interest that California defended below and thus is the only interest that is properly before this Court.

Even if the Gentile survey were relevant, it simply does not say what California says it does. California states that the survey "suggest[s] a causal connection between playing violent video games and aggressive behavior." It does no such thing. The survey makes absolutely no finding that exposure to violent video games leads to physical aggression. To the contrary, it explicitly cautions against making that inference: "It is important to note . . . that this study is limited by its correlational nature. Inferences about causal direction should be viewed with caution." ("Are young adolescents more hostile and aggressive because they expose themselves to media violence, or do previously hostile adolescents prefer violent media? Due to the correlational nature of this study, we cannot answer this question directly.").

Beyond that, the Gentile survey is rife with methodological flaws that undermine even the suggested correlation. For example, the measures of "aggressive behavior" that Gentile employed are highly suspect. Having an argument with a teacher—without any further exploration into the nature of the event—does not even suggest violent or aggressive behavior. And simply asking students whether they had been in a fight—again, without any further analysis of the event—is not a valid indicator for violent or aggressive behavior.

Additionally, there are many factors that may influence youth violence or aggressive behavior, including: family violence, antisocial personality traits, and association with delinquent peers. . . . Because Gentile's survey failed to control for, or even consider, those other variables, its conclusion that there is a correlation between video games and hostility to third parties lacks scientific grounding. In fact, controlling for gender alone removes most of the variance from which Gentile finds a correlation. In other words, the correlation Gentile claims to find is equally explainable by the effect of gender: boys tend to play more violent video games and tend to be more aggressive.

Second, California points to a 2004 study of 130 college students by Craig Anderson. That study measured the blood pressure of students before, during, and after playing selected video games and had students take a "word completion" test after playing selected video games. Based on the resulting measurements, Anderson concluded that the students' blood pressure increased while playing certain video games he labeled "violent" and that game play "increase[d] . . . the accessibility of aggressive thoughts."

The Anderson study is no help to California, because it does not show that a rise in students' blood pressure has any relationship to whether violent video games cause psychological or neurological harm. Nor does California show how "aggressive thoughts" leads to psychological harm.

Laboratory experiments, like Anderson's, that measure aggression immediately following the playing of a video game are common in the field of media effects research. And like Anderson's, these experiments rely on proxies for real aggressive or violent behavior, such as the participants' willingness to administer blasts of white noise against an unseen (and non-existent opponent). The problem is that the proxies bear no relationship to whether someone is going to act aggressively or violently in the real world. Similarly giving participants words with blank spaces and evaluating whether they make "aggressive" or "non-aggressive" words with the letters they fill in (i.e., "explo_e" could be completed as "explore" or "explode"), as Anderson did in his experiment, has no known validity for measuring aggressive behavior (or even aggressive thinking).

Third, California points to a 2004 study of fourth and fifth grade students by Jeanne Funk, and claims it "found that playing violent video games was correlated with lower empathy as well as stronger pro-violence attitudes." But the Funk study specifically disclaimed any proof of causality. As Funk admitted, the children in her study whose scores indicated lower empathy or stronger pro-violence attitudes may simply have been drawn to violent video games. Moreover, the small sample size—just 150 children—and the failure to control for or consider any other variables undermine even the study's tentative conclusion of a correlation between violent video games and pro-violence attitudes. . . .

B. California and Senator Yee Ignore the Large Body of Empirical Evidence That Shows No Causal Connection, or Even a Correlation, Between Violent Video Games and Harm to Minors

California and Senator Yee ignore a wealth of recent empirical evidence disabusing the notion that violent video games are harmful to minors. Here is just a snapshot of that body of scholarship:

- A study of 603 Hispanic youths (ages ten to fourteen), recently published in The Journal of Pediatrics, examined various risk factors for youth violence, including video game violence, delinquent peer association, family conflict, depression, and others. The children listed television shows and video games and rated how often they viewed or played the media—a reliable and valid method of evaluating violent media exposure. The children were then evaluated using the Child Behavior Checklist, a well-researched and well-validated tool for measuring behavioral problems in children and adolescents. A statistical analysis of the results revealed that exposure to video games had a negligible effect size and was not predictive of youth violence and aggression.
- A study of 1,254 seventh and eighth-grade students examined the influence of exposure to violent video games on delinquency and bullying behavior. The Entertainment Software Ratings Board ratings were employed as a standardized measure of participants' exposure to violence in video games. The study applied a multivariate statistical method that considered other factors that might be predictive of aggressive behavior (such as level of parental involvement, support from others, and stress). This study did not use abstract measures of aggression, but instead focused on specific negative behaviors such as delinquency and bullying. A statistical analysis revealed insignificant effect sizes between exposure to violent video games and delinquency or bullying. The

authors accordingly concluded that exposure to such games was not predictive of delinquency or bullying.
- A study of 213 participants examined the influence of violent video game play on aggressive behavior. The 213 participants were divided into a 75-person treatment group that played a single game, Asheron's Call 2, a type of "massively multi-player online role-playing game" that is "highly violent" and has "a sustained pattern of violence," for at least five hours over a one-month period, and a 138-person control group that did not play the game. Participants then completed self-reported questionnaires that included a range of demographic, behavioral, and personality variables. Aggression-related beliefs were measured according to the Normative Beliefs in Aggression general scale, a well-validated scale for measuring beliefs about the acceptability of aggression, and aggressive social interactions were measured using specific behavioral questions. Both measurement techniques had been successfully used in previous studies of violent television and video game effects. The results of this study found no effects associated with aggression caused by playing violent video games.

These studies are just the tip of the iceberg. They rate barely a mention in Senator Yee's brief, which disparages them as "alleged 'scientific studies'" that involved "small sample size, poor test conditions and chance." That is wrong. The studies employed large sample sizes, longstanding and validated measures of aggression, and superior statistical controls. Ironically, the studies also include the work of researchers whom California and Senator Yee cite favorably. For example, as noted above, California relies on the research of Jeanne Funk. But, in a separate study that California does not mention, Funk "fail[ed] to find" even a correlation between violent video games and aggressive emotions and behavior. Notably, this second Funk study employed the Child Behavior Checklist, which is a better validated measure of aggression than measures utilized in the studies on which California and Senator Yee rely.

At minimum, the scholarship that California and Senator Yee ignore belies the notion that the "substantial evidence of causation" standard imposes an "insurmountable hurdle" on science or legislatures. These studies show unequivocally that the causation research can be done, and, indeed, has been done. The problem confronting California and Senator Yee thus is not the constitutional standard; it is simply their inability to meet that standard in this case because validated scientific studies prove the opposite, leaving no empirical foundation for the assertion that playing violent video games causes harm to minors.

PATRICIA A. MILLETT has argued more than 30 cases before the Supreme Court, and was named one of the 100 most influential lawyers by the *National Law Journal*. She graduated summa cum laude from Harvard Law School.

EXPLORING THE ISSUE

Are Violent Video Games Harmful to Children and Adolescents?

Critical Thinking and Reflection

1. Imagine that you have to argue this case before the Supreme Court, based on the evidence cited. What in your view is the most convincing piece of research evidence for or against violent video games as a danger to children? Why is this study so convincing to you?
2. What is the difference between correlation and causation in psychological research? Could a study determine causation conclusively? If so, describe what would be required for such a study. If not, explain why.
3. Gruel argues his point based on the methodological strengths of longitudinal research and meta-analyses, while Millett attempts to undermine that argument by exposing flaws in the methodologies of those studies. How important is methodology in rating the worth of a study? Why?
4. Both sides of the debate cited neuroscience research as an important part of their arguments. What can descriptions of the physical brain tell you about psychological concepts such as aggression? What can they not tell you?
5. Based on the arguments given by both sides, how much agreement is there in the psychological community about this topic? What would be needed to reach a consensus?

Create Central

www.mhhe.com/createcentral

Additional Resources

Kutner, L., and Olson, C. K. (2011). *Grand theft childhood: The surprising truth about violent video games and what parents can do.* New York: Simon & Schuster.

Nije Bijvank, M., Konijn, E. A., and Bushman, B. J. (2012). "We don't need no education": Video game preferences, video game motivations, and aggressiveness among adolescent boys of different educational ability levels. *Journal of Adolescence, 35*(1), 153–162. doi:10.1016/j.adolescence.2011.04.001

Polman, H., de Castro, B., and van Aken, M. G. (2008). Experimental study of the differential effects of playing versus watching violent video games on children's aggressive behavior. *Aggressive Behavior, 34*(3), 256–264. Retrieved from web.ebscohost.com.silk.library.umass.edu/ehost/detail?vid=7&hid=7&sid=0e2bl9af-8751-4d92-826d-7fc8403f873%40sessionmgrl5&bdata=JnNpdGU9ZWhvc3OtbG12ZSZzY29wZTlzaXRl#db=a ph&AN=31875598

Sacks, D. P., Bushman, B. J., and Anderson, C. A. (2011). Do violent video games harm children? Comparing the scientific amicus curiae "experts" in *Brown v. Entertainment Merchants Association, Northwestern Law Review, 106*, 1–12.

Internet References . . .

Quarterly Newsletter of the Entertainment Merchants Association

www.entmerch.org/government-relations/ema-v -schwarzenegger-faqs.html

Research Findings Suggesting That Video Games Encourage Moral Disengagement

www.ncbi.nlm.nih.gov/pubmed/22766175

A Satirical View of Various Societal Problems for Which Video Games Are Blamed

www.wired.com/geekdad/2013/01/video-games -violence/

Selected, Edited and with Issue Framing Material by:
Brent Slife, *Brigham Young University*

ISSUE

Does Parent Sexual Orientation Affect Child Development?

YES: Mark Regnerus, from "How Different Are the Adult Children of Parents Who Have Same-Sex Relationships? Findings from the New Family Structures Study," *Social Science Research* (vol. 41, pp. 752–770, July 2012)

NO: Alicia Crowl, Soyeon Ahn, and Jean Baker, from "A Meta-Analysis of Developmental Outcomes for Children of Same-Sex and Heterosexual Parents," *Journal of GLBT Family Studies* (vol. 4, pp. 385–407, October 2008)

Learning Outcomes

After reading this issue, you should be able to:

- Understand how the influence of same-sex couples on the development of their child might differ from heterosexual parents.
- Discuss the problems one may encounter in trying to research this issue.

ISSUE SUMMARY

YES: Mark Regnerus, associate professor of sociology at University of Texas at Austin and research associate at Population Research Center, contends that notable developmental differences exist among children reared by same-sex couples compared to heterosexual couples.

NO: Alicia Crowl, former doctoral student in the Department of School Psychology at Michigan State University; Soyeon Ahn, former doctoral student of measurement and quantitative methods at Michigan State University; and Jean Baker (deceased), former associate professor of school psychology at Michigan State University, argue that there are essentially no developmental differences between children reared by same-sex couples when compared with heterosexual couples.

In 2011 Zach Whals, the 19-year-old son of two lesbian women, testified before the Iowa House of Representatives stating, "The sexual orientation of my parents has had no effect on the content of my character" (Whals, 2011). Whals' testimony reflects one side of a major issue confronting psychologists—the question that titles this issue. As sincere as Whal's testimony apparently was, testimony is not the same as scientific evidence. Part of the job of psychologists is to systematically and scientifically investigate such issues, especially given the significance of this one. In fact, the political and public discourse surrounding same-sex marriage has recently intensified with the passing of California's Proposition 8. This proposition could be viewed as one aspect of the "other" side of the issue, since it proposed that only a man and woman can legitimately practice marriage. Underlying each of these "sides" is the well-being of the children reared by such couples, so a lot

is at stake. Can psychologists help to resolve this important issue?

The research addressing this question so far has focused almost exclusively on determining the effects of parents' sexual orientation on child development. These investigations have assessed a variety of vital aspects of the controversy, including depression, gender identity, and education attainment, to name but a few. To date, psychologists are divided on the issue, with some echoing Whals' (2011) claims—children reared by same-sex couples are "no different" from those reared by heterosexual couples on developmental outcomes. Yet other investigators assert that their results indicate the opposite of these claims, suggesting that there are notable "differences" with significant negative consequences. This controversy also involves mutual critiques, with each side repeatedly describing flaws in their opponents' research methodology.

The articles included here are representative of the controversy. In the second article, Alicia Crowl, Soyeon Ahn, and Jean Baker (2008) argue that parent sexual orientation does not negatively affect a child's well-being. Crowl and colleagues approach the issue through a comprehensive analysis of existing research, known as a *meta-analysis*. Their meta-analysis included 19 studies comparing children reared by same-sex and heterosexual couples on six different developmental outcomes: child gender role behavior, gender identity, sexual orientation, cognitive functioning, psychological adjustment, and quality of parent–child relationship. They believe their analysis shows that "children raised by same-sex and heterosexual parents were found not to differ significantly" (p. 398) on five of the six outcome measures, with the only outcome that differed showing that same-sex parents were better.

On the other hand, Mark Regnerus (2012) argues in the first article that there are indeed developmental negative differences in children raised by same-sex couples compared to heterosexual couples. He cites data that originate from a large probability sample, a technique used to avoid sampling bias and obtain more accurate data. His analysis compared eight different family structures including intact biological families, mother with a same-sex romantic relationship, father with a same-sex romantic relationship, and several others on 40 different outcome measures. Regnerus concludes that despite previous research "the basic statistical comparisons between [children of same-sex couples] and those of others, especially biologically intact, mother/father families, suggests that notable [unfavorable] differences on many outcomes do in fact exist" (p. 765).

Reference

Whals, Z. (2011). Zach Whals speaks about family. Retrieved from www.youtube.com/watch?v=yMLZO-sObzQ

POINT

- Research indicates that parent sexual orientation does not affect child development.
- Crowl et al.'s study offers an in-depth analysis of children's developmental outcomes.
- Crowl et al.'s statistics reduce the chance of omitting group differences when one exists.
- Crowl et al.'s results continue to support the findings from the existing body of research.

COUNTERPOINT

- The existing research on this topic is laden with limitations.
- The Regnerus data is a more accurate representation of the American population.
- The studies included by Crowl et al. contain biased self-reported data.
- Regnerus' study provides evidence that is contrary to previous studies.

YES ↵

Mark Regnerus

How Different Are the Adult Children of Parents Who Have Same-Sex Relationships? Findings from the New Family Structures Study

Introduction

Sampling Concerns in Previous Surveys

Concern has arisen . . . about the methodological quality of many studies focusing on same-sex parents. In particular, most are based on non-random, non-representative data often employing small samples that do not allow for generalization to the larger population of gay and lesbian families (Nock, 2001; Perrin and Committee on Psychosocial Aspects of Child and Family Health, 2002; Redding, 2008). For instance, many published studies on the children of same-sex parents collect data from "snowball" or convenience samples (e.g., Bos et al., 2007; Brewaeys et al., 1997; Fulcher et al., 2008; Sirota, 2009; Vanfraussen et al., 2003). One notable example of this is the National Longitudinal Lesbian Family Study, analyses of which were prominently featured in the media in 2011 (e.g., *Huffington Post*, 2011). The NLLFS employs a convenience sample, recruited entirely by self-selection from announcements posted "at lesbian events, in women's bookstores, and in lesbian newspapers" in Boston, Washington, and San Francisco. While I do not wish to downplay the significance of such a longitudinal study—it is itself quite a feat—this sampling approach is a problem when the goal (or in this case, the practical result and conventional use of its findings) is to generalize to a population. All such samples are biased, often in unknown ways. As a formal sampling method, "snowball sampling is known to have some serious problems," one expert asserts (Snijders, 1992, p. 59). Indeed, such samples are likely biased toward "inclusion of those who have many interrelationships with, or are coupled to, a large number of other individuals" (Berg, 1988, p. 531). But apart from the knowledge of individuals' inclusion probability, unbiased estimation is not possible. . . .

Are There Notable Differences?

The "no differences" paradigm suggests that children from same-sex families display no notable disadvantages when compared to children from other family forms. This suggestion has increasingly come to include even comparisons with intact biological, two-parent families, the form most associated with stability and developmental benefits for children (McLanahan and Sandefur, 1994; Moore et al., 2002). . . .

Much early research on gay parents typically compared the child development outcomes of divorced lesbian mothers with those of divorced heterosexual mothers (Patterson, 1997). This was also the strategy employed by psychologist Fiona Tasker (2005), who compared lesbian mothers with single, divorced heterosexual mothers and found "no systematic differences between the quality of family relationships" therein. Wainright et al. (2004), using 44 cases in the nationally-representative Add Health data, reported that teenagers living with female same-sex parents displayed comparable self-esteem, psychological adjustment, academic achievement, delinquency, substance use, and family relationship quality to 44 demographically "matched" cases of adolescents with opposite-sex parents, suggesting that here too the comparisons were not likely made with respondents from stable, biologically-intact, married families.

However, small sample sizes can contribute to "no differences" conclusions. It is not surprising that statistically-significant differences would *not* emerge in studies employing as few as 18 or 33 or 44 cases of respondents with same-sex parents, respectively (Fulcher et al., 2008; Golombok et al., 2003; Wainright and Patterson, 2006). Even analyzing matched samples, as a variety of studies have done, fails to mitigate the challenge of locating statistically-significant differences when the sample size is small. This is a concern in all of social science, but one that is doubly important when there may be motivation to confirm the null hypothesis (that is, that there are in fact no statistically-significant differences between groups). . . .

More recently, however, the tone about "no differences" has shifted some toward the assertion of differences, and that same-sex parents appear to be *more* competent than heterosexual parents (Biblarz and Stacey, 2010; Crowl et al., 2008). . . .

Another meta-analysis asserts that non-heterosexual parents, on average, enjoy significantly better

Regnerus, Mark. From *Social Science Research*, vol. 41, no. 4, July 2012, pp. 752–770. Copyright © 2012 by Elsevier Health Sciences. Reprinted by permission via Rightslink.

relationships with their children than do heterosexual parents, together with no differences in the domains of cognitive development, psychological adjustment, gender identity, and sexual partner preference (Crowl et al., 2008).

However, the meta-analysis reinforces the profound importance of *who* is doing the reporting—nearly always volunteers for small studies on a group whose claims about documentable parenting successes are very relevant in recent legislative and judicial debates over rights and legal statuses. Tasker (2010, p. 36) suggests caution. . . .

Regardless of sampling strategy, scholars also know much less about the lives of *young-adult* children of gay and lesbian parents, or how their experiences and accomplishments as adults compare with others who experienced different sorts of household arrangements during their youth. Most contemporary studies of gay parenting processes have focused on the present—what is going on inside the household when children are still under parental care (Tasker, 2005; Bos and Sandfort, 2010; Brewaeys et al., 1997). Moreover, such research tends to emphasize *parent-reported* outcomes like parental divisions of labor, parent-child closeness, daily interaction patterns, gender roles, and disciplinary habits. While such information is important to learn, it means we know far more about the *current* experience of *parents* in households with children than we do about young adults who have already moved through their childhood and now speak for themselves. Studies on family structure, however, serve scholars and family practitioners best when they span into adulthood. Do the children of gay and lesbian parents look comparable to those of their heterosexual counterparts? The NFSS is poised to address this question about the lives of young adults between the ages of 18 and 39, but not about children or adolescents. While the NFSS is not the answer to all of this domain's methodological challenges, it is a notable contribution in important ways. . . .

The Data Collection Process

The data collection was conducted by Knowledge Networks (or KN), a research firm with a very strong record of generating high-quality data for academic projects. Knowledge Networks recruited the first online research panel, dubbed the KnowledgePanel®, that is representative of the US population. Members of the KnowledgePanel® are randomly recruited by telephone and mail surveys, and households are provided with access to the Internet and computer hardware if needed. Unlike other Internet research panels sampling only individuals with Internet access who volunteer for research, the KnowledgePanel® is based on a sampling frame which includes both listed and unlisted numbers, those without a landline telephone and is not limited to current Internet users or computer owners, and does not accept self-selected volunteers. As a result, it is a random, nationally-representative sample of the American population. . . .

The Structure and Experience of Respondents' Families of Origin

. . . For this particular study, I compare outcomes across eight different types of family-of-origin structure and/or experience. They were constructed from the answers to several questions both in the screener survey and the full survey. It should be noted, however, that their construction reflects an unusual combination of interests—the same-sex romantic behavior of parents, and the experience of household stability or disruption. The eight groups or household settings (with an acronym or short descriptive title) evaluated here, followed by their maximum unweighted analytic sample size, are:

1. IBF: Lived in intact biological family (with mother and father) from 0 to 18, and parents are still married at present ($N = 919$).
2. LM: R reported R's mother had a same-sex romantic (lesbian) relationship with a woman, regardless of any other household transitions ($N = 163$).
3. GF: R reported R's father had a same-sex romantic (gay) relationship with a man, regardless of any other household transitions ($N = 73$).
4. Adopted: R was adopted by one or two strangers at birth or before age 2 ($N = 101$).
5. Divorced later or had joint custody: R reported living with biological mother and father from birth to age 18, but parents are not married at present ($N = 116$).
6. Stepfamily: Biological parents were either never married or else divorced, and R's primary custodial parent *was* married to someone else before R turned 18 ($N= 394$).
7. Single parent: Biological parents were either never married or else divorced, and R's primary custodial parent did *not* marry (or remarry) before R turned 18 ($N = 816$).
8. All others: Includes all other family structure/ event combinations, such as respondents with a deceased parent ($N = 406$). . . .

Outcomes of Interest

This study presents an overview of 40 outcome measures. . . . I elected to report here an overview of those outcomes, seeking to include common and oft-studied variables of interest from a variety of different domains. I include all of the particular indexes we sought to evaluate, and a broad list of outcomes from the emotional, relational, and social domains. . . .

Discussion

Just how different are the adult children of men and women who pursue same-sex romantic (i.e., gay and lesbian) relationships, when evaluated using population-based estimates from a random sample? The answer, as might be expected, depends on to whom you compare them. When compared with children who grew up in biologically (still) intact, mother–father families, the children of women who reported a same-sex relationship look markedly different on numerous outcomes, including many that are obviously suboptimal (such as education, depression, employment status, or marijuana use). On 25 of 40 outcomes (or 63%) evaluated here, there are bivariate statistically-significant ($p < 0.05$) differences between children from still-intact, mother/father families and those whose mother reported a lesbian relationship. On 11 of 40 outcomes (or 28%) evaluated here, there are bivariate statistically-significant ($p < 0.05$) differences between children from still-intact, mother/father families and those whose father reported a gay relationship. Hence, there are differences in both comparisons, but there are many more differences by any method of analysis in comparisons between young-adult children of IBFs and LMs than between IBFs and GFs. . . .

Given that the characteristics of the NFSS's sample of children of LMs and GFs are close to estimates of the same offered by demographers using the American Community Study, one conclusion from the analyses herein is merited: the sample-selection bias problem in very many studies of gay and lesbian parenting is not incidental, but likely profound, rendering the ability of much past research to offer valid interpretations of *average* household experiences of children with a lesbian or gay parent suspect at best. Most snowball-sample-based research has, instead, shed light on *above-average* household experiences. . . .

Nevertheless, to claim that there are few meaningful statistical differences between the different groups evaluated here would be to state something that is empirically inaccurate. Minimally, the population-based estimates presented here suggest that a good deal more attention must be paid to the real diversity among gay and lesbian parent experiences in America, just as it long has been among heterosexual households. Child outcomes in stable, "planned" GLB families and those that are the product of previous heterosexual unions are quite likely distinctive, as previous studies' conclusions would suggest. Yet as demographers of gay and lesbian America continue to note—and as the NFSS reinforces—planned GLB households only comprise a portion (and an unknown one at that) of all GLB households with children. . . .

Appendix [A]. Construction of Outcome Indexes

CES-D (Depression) Index (8 Items, $\alpha = 0.87$)

Respondents were asked to think about the past 7 days, and assess how often each of the following things were true about them. Answer categories ranged from "never or rarely" (0) to "most of the time or all of the time" (3).

Some items were reverse-coded for the index variable (e.g., "You felt happy."):

1. You were bothered by things that usually do not bother you.
2. You could not shake off the blues, even with help from your family and your friends.
3. You felt you were just as good as other people.
4. You had trouble keeping your mind on what you were doing.
5. You felt depressed.
6. You felt happy.
7. You enjoyed life.
8. You felt sad.

Current Romantic Relationship Quality (6 Items, $\alpha = 0.96$)

Respondents were asked to assess their current romantic relationship. Answer categories ranged from strongly disagree (1) to strongly agree (5):

1. We have a good relationship.
2. My relationship with my partner is very healthy.
3. Our relationship is strong.
4. My relationship with my partner makes me happy.
5. I really feel like part of a team with my partner.
6. Our relationship is pretty much perfect.

Family-of-Origin Relationship Safety/Security (4 Items, $\alpha = 0.90$)

Respondents were asked to evaluate the overall atmosphere in their family while growing up by responding to four statements whose answer categories ranged from strongly disagree (1) to strongly agree (5):

1. My family relationships were safe, secure, and a source of comfort.
2. We had a loving atmosphere in our family.
3. All things considered, my childhood years were happy.
4. My family relationships were confusing, inconsistent, and unpredictable.

Family-of-Origin Negative Impact (3 Items, $\alpha = 0.74$)

Respondents were asked to evaluate the present-day impact of their family-of-origin experiences by responding to three statements whose answer categories ranged from strongly disagree (1) to strongly agree (5):

1. There are matters from my family experience that I am still having trouble dealing with or coming to terms with.

2. There are matters from my family experience that negatively affect my ability to form close relationships.
3. I feel at peace about anything negative that happened to me in the family in which I grew up.

Impulsivity (4 Items, $\alpha = 0.76$)

Respondents were asked to respond to four statements about their decision-making, especially as it concerns risk-taking and new experiences. Answer categories ranged from 1 (never or rarely) to 4 (most or all of the time):

1. When making a decision, I go with my 'gut feeling' and do not think much about the consequences of each alternative.
2. I like new and exciting experiences, even if I have to break the rules.
3. I am an impulsive person.
4. I like to take risks.

Closeness to Biological Mother and Father (6 Items, $\alpha = 0.89$ and 0.92)

Respondents were asked to evaluate their current relationship with up to four parent figures—who they reported living with for at least 3 years when they were 0–18 years old—by reporting the frequency of six parent–child interactions. For each parent figure, these six items were coded and summed into a parental closeness index. From these, I derived indices of closeness to the respondent's biological mother and biological father. Response categories ranged from never (1) to always (5):

1. How often do you talk openly with your parent about things that are important to you?
2. How often does your parent really listen to you when you want to talk?
3. How often does your parent explicitly express affection or love for you?
4. Would your parent help you if you had a problem?
5. If you needed money, would you ask your parent for it?
6. How often is your parent interested in the things you do?

Attachment (Depend, 6 Items, $\alpha = 0.80$; Anxiety, 6 Items, $\alpha = 0.82$)

For a pair of attachment measures, respondents were asked to rate their general feelings about romantic relationships, both past and present, in response to 12 items. Response categories ranged from "not at all characteristic of me" (1) to "very characteristic of me" (5). Items 1–6 were coded and summed into a "depend" scale, with higher scores denoting greater comfort with depending upon others. Items 7–12 were coded and summed into an anxiety scale,

with higher scores denoting greater anxiety in close relationships, in keeping with the original Adult Attachment Scale developed by Collins and Read (1990). The measures employed were:

1. I find it difficult to allow myself to depend on others.
2. I am comfortable depending on others.
3. I find that people are never there when you need them.
4. I know that people will be there when I need them.
5. I find it difficult to trust others completely.
6. I am not sure that I can always depend on others to be there when I need them.
7. I do not worry about being abandoned.
8. In relationships, I often worry that my partner does not really love me.
9. I find that others are reluctant to get as close as I would like.
10. In relationships, I often worry that my partner will not want to stay with me.
11. I want to merge completely with another person.
12. My desire to merge sometimes scares people away.

References

Berg, Sven, 1988. Snowball sampling. In: Kotz, Samuel, Johnson, Norman L. (Eds.), Encyclopedia of Statistical Sciences, vol. 8. Wiley-Interscience, New York.

Biblarz, Timothy J., Stacey, Judith, 2010. How does the gender of parents matter? Journal of Marriage and Family 72 (1), 3–22.

Bos, Henny M.W., Sandfort, Theo G.M., 2010. Children's gender identity in lesbian and heterosexual two-parent families. Sex Roles 62, 114–126.

Bos, Henny M.W., van Balen, Frank, van den Boom, Dymphna C., 2007. Child adjustment and parenting in planned lesbian parent families. American Journal of Orthopsychiatry 77, 38–48.

Brewaeys, Anne, Ponjaert, Ingrid, Van Hall, Eylard V., Golombok, Susan, 1997. Donor insemination: child development and family functioning in lesbian mother families. Human Reproduction 12, 1349–1359.

Busby, Dean M., Holman, Thomas B., Taniguchi, Narumi, 2001. RELATE: relationship evaluation of the individual, family, cultural, and couple contexts. Family Relations 50, 308–316.

Collins, Nancy L., Read, Stephen J., 1990. Adult attachment, working models, and relationship quality in dating couples. Journal of Personality and Social Psychology 58, 644–663.

Crowl, Alicia L., Ahn, Soyeon, Baker, Jean, 2008. A meta-analysis of developmental outcomes for children of same-sex and heterosexual parents. Journal of GLBT Family Sciences 4 (3), 385–407.

Finer, Lawrence B., Henshaw, Stanley K., 2006. Disparities in rates of unintended pregnancy in the United States, 1994 and 2001. Perspectives on Sexual and Reproductive Health 38, 90–96.

Fulcher, Megan, Sutfin, Erin L., Patterson, Charlotte J., 2008. Individual differences in gender development: associations with parental sexual orientation, attitudes, and division of labor. Sex Roles 57, 330–341.

Golombok, Susan, Perry, Beth, Burston, Amanda, Murray, Clare, Mooney-Somers, Julie, Stevens, Madeleine, Golding, Jean, 2003. Children with lesbian parents: a community study. Developmental Psychology 39, 20–33.

Huffington Post: Healthy Living, 2011. Child Abuse Rate at Zero Percent in Lesbian Households, New Report Finds. The Huffington Post. <http://www.huffingtonpost.com/2010/11/10/lesbians-child-abuse-0-percent_n_781624.html> (accessed 01.13.12).

McLanahan, Sara, Sandefur, Gary, 1994. Growing Up with a Single Parent: What Hurts, What Helps. Harvard University Press, Cambridge.

Moore, Kristin Anderson, Jekielek, Susan M., Emig, Carol, 2002. Marriage from a Child's Perspective: How Does Family Structure Affect Children, and What Can We Do About It? Child Trends Research Brief, Child Trends, Washington, DC.

Nock, Steven L., 2001. Affidavit of Steven Nock. Halpern et al. v. Canada and MCCT v. Canada. ON S.C.D.C. <http://marriagelaw.cua.edu/Law/cases/Canada/ontario/halpern/aff_nock.pdf> (accessed 12.20.11).

Patterson, Charlotte J., 1997. Children of lesbian and gay parents. In: Ollendick, Thomas H., Prinz, Ronald J. (Eds.), Advances in Clinical Child Psychology, vol. 19. Plenum, New York.

Patterson, Charlotte J., 2006. Children of lesbian and gay parents. Current Directions in Psychological Science 15 (5), 241–244.

Perrin, Ellen C., Committee on Psychosocial Aspects of Child and Family Health, 2002. Technical report: coparent or second-parent adoption by same-sex partners. Pediatrics 109, 341–344.

Redding, Richard R., 2008. It's really about sex: same-sex marriage, lesbigay parenting, and the psychology of disgust. Duke Journal of Gender Law and Policy 16, 127–193.

Sirota, Theodora, 2009. Adult attachment style dimensions in women who have gay or bisexual fathers. Archives of Psychiatric Nursing 23 (4), 289–297.

Snijders, Tom A.B., 1992. Estimation on the basis of snowball samples: how to weight? Bulletin de Méthodologie Sociologique 36, 59–70.

Tasker, Fiona, 2005. Lesbian mothers, gay fathers, and their children: a review. Developmental and Behavioral Pediatrics 26 (3), 224–240.

Tasker, Fiona, 2010. Same-sex parenting and child development: reviewing the contribution of parental gender. Journal of Marriage and Family 72, 35–40.

Vanfraussen, Katrien, Ponjaert-Kristoffersen, Ingrid, Brewaeys, Anne, 2003. Family functioning in lesbian families created by donor insemination. American Journal of Orthopsychiatry 73 (1), 78–90.

Wainright, Jennifer L., Patterson, Charlotte J., 2006. Delinquency, victimization, and substance use among adolescents with female same-sex parents. Journal of Family Psychology 20 (3), 526–530.

Wainright, Jennifer L., Russell, Stephen T., Patterson, Charlotte J., 2004. Psychosocial adjustment, school outcomes, and romantic relationships of adolescents with same-sex parents. Child Development 75 (6), 1886–1898.

Mark Regnerus is an associate professor in the Department of Sociology at the University of Texas at Austin. His research is primarily concerned with religion, family, and adult sexual behavior and he has published numerous articles and book chapters relating to these areas. He has been the recipient of the Best Article Award twice by the American Sociological Society and oversees the New Family Structure Study (NFSS). He received his PhD from the University of North Carolina, Chapel Hill.

Alicia Crowl, Soyeon Ahn, and Jean Baker

 **NO**

A Meta-Analysis of Developmental Outcomes for Children of Same-Sex and Heterosexual Parents

Gay and lesbian parenting is a topic that evokes feelings of opposition and disdain as well as acceptance and pride. . . .

The existing body of research comparing gay and lesbian parents with heterosexual parents has shown that parent sexual orientation is not related to negative psychological adjustment or overall negative developmental outcomes in children (Allen & Burrell, 1996, 2002; Anderssen, Amlie, & Ytteroy, 2002; Lambert, 2005). Despite the consistent message borne out by these studies, however, most gay and lesbian families frequently face discrimination both within and outside of the schools (Ryan & Martin, 2000), and many gay and lesbian parents continue to lose custody of their children (Stacey & Biblarz, 2001). . . .

The American Psychological Association's (2002) "Ethical Principles of Psychologists and Code of Conduct" mandates that professionals ". . . provide services, teach, and conduct research with populations and in areas only within the boundaries of their competence . . . " (2.01a, p. 1063). It is clear from the research, however, that few psychologists are trained and prepared to work with same-sex families (Pilkington & Cantor, 1996). . . . Thus, gaining an understanding of children's development in the context of being raised with gay or lesbian parents challenges professionals' own views about same-sex parenting, meeting the American Psychological Association (2002) standards for professionals to critically examine biases and prejudices held of particular groups. . . .

It is difficult to estimate the number of children raised by a same-sex parent because many gay and lesbian individuals do not reveal their sexual orientation. Prevalence estimates range from 2 to 14 million children depending on the criteria specified in the study. These figures, however, may not accurately represent the diverse and sometimes informal caregiving arrangements in many same-sex families (Tasker, 2005). In other words, studies investigating the prevalence of same-sex parenting have yet to reveal the complex family constellations that are unique to gay and lesbian parents, thereby underestimating the number of children brought up with a gay or lesbian parent.

While there has been a recent upsurge in the number of studies related to children raised by gay and lesbian parents, the literature in this area continues to be small and wrought with limitations (Schumm, 2004; Stacey & Biblarz, 2001). In a critique of the studies done on the outcomes of children with same-sex parents, Schumm (2004) provides several limitations that underlie this line of research and that he believes researchers and policymakers should take into account when interpreting the absence of significant differences between children raised by heterosexual versus same-sex parents. First, it is difficult to obtain a random, representative sample of gay and lesbian parents. Because many same-sex parents are not open about their sexual orientation, it is often necessary to rely on volunteer participants, who may differ in important ways from gay and lesbian individuals unwilling to expose their sexual identities, thus resulting in biased samples. Second, much of the research conducted in this area is based on fairly small sample sizes since it is difficult to obtain subjects who are willing to participate in studies assessing the impact of their sexual orientation on their children's development. A small sample necessarily leads to low statistical power, increasing the likelihood of failing to reject null hypotheses (Schumm, 2004). Because the samples tend to be small, they also tend to look fairly homogeneous: Caucasian, female, middle-class, urban, and well-educated. Few studies have included a diverse group of individuals, whether by race, class, or gender. The majority of the research conducted on children with same-sex parents is done primarily with lesbian mothers since they tend to have not only custody of the child but are often the primary caretakers as well—gay fathers are much less likely to be custodial parents (Bozett, 1987). And still other researchers have argued that there are meaningful differences, especially with respect to gender role development when children are raised by same-sex parents, and that researchers have downplayed the importance of these differences (Stacey & Biblarz, 2001).

Critics of the research performed with gay and lesbian parents, therefore, argue that the current data are not sufficient to make any conclusions regarding the effect of sexual orientation on various child outcomes (Belcastro,

Gramlich, Nicholson, Price, & Wilson, 1993; Cameron & Cameron, 1997). Clearly, there is a need for more research aimed at understanding the lives of children who grow up in this type of nontraditional family setting. A quantitative synthesis of research of the effects of parent sexual orientation on child developmental outcomes would allow for a comparison that is more statistically powerful (Lipsey & Wilson, 2001), addressing a major limitation inherent in the studies that define this area of research.

Although there have been two previous meta-analyses investigating the effect of parent sexual orientation on child developmental outcomes (Allen & Burrell, 1996, 2002), there were several reasons for conducting the current study. Firstly, the Allen and Burrell (1996, 2002) meta-analyses were limited to studying the effects of parent sexual orientation on child psychological adjustment and child sexual orientation. The present study, however, examined the differences between children raised with same-sex parents and children raised with heterosexual parents on six outcomes. Secondly, since the publication of the most recent meta-analysis, there have been a number of published studies (two of which included the first random samples in this body of research) comparing the effect of parent sexual orientation on various child outcomes that enhanced the accuracy of the current meta-analysis. Thus, there was a need to review the literature through quantitative means to ascertain whether differences in developmental outcomes exist between children raised with heterosexual or same-sex parents. Not only does meta-analysis allow for the reduction of Type II error by compensating for the small samples that define this body of research (Lipsey & Wilson, 2001) but it also enables others to replicate the analysis to further validate the study's findings (Allen & Burrell, 2002).

Therefore, to address the needs of professionals working with gay and lesbian parents within the schools and to add to the existing body of research examining the differences between children raised by same-sex parents and children raised by heterosexual parents, a comprehensive meta-analysis was conducted for the current study. Two questions were addressed in the analyses: (a) Does a child's developmental well-being, i.e., child gender role behavior, gender identity, sexual orientation, cognitive functioning, and psychological adjustment, or quality of parent–child relationship, vary by parents' sexual orientation? and (b) If there are between-study or between-group variations among outcome effect sizes, is it possible to explain these variations using different moderators such as children's gender, children's age, perspective of outcome, ethnicity, sampling method of study, and/or matching of participant characteristics? . . .

Discussion

. . . With respect to the first question, results of this study confirmed previous findings regarding associations between parent sexual orientation and child developmental outcomes, namely that parent sexual orientation was not a salient predictor for children's development (Fitzgerald, 1999; Lambert, 2005; Tasker, 2005). However, because there were significant differences between groups on the outcome of parent–child relationship, it was necessary to account for possible moderators in the relationship between parent sexual orientation and developmental outcomes. Thus, for the second question addressed in this study, we found that the perspective of the data moderated the relationship between parent sexual orientation and the quality of parent–child relationship. No moderator accounted for the variance among studies on the outcome of gender role behavior, however.

In sum, children raised by same-sex and heterosexual parents were found to not differ significantly in terms of their cognitive development, gender role behavior, gender identity, psychological adjustment, or sexual preferences. For the outcome that was significantly different between children of same-sex and heterosexual parents, the finding was in favor of same-sex parents. For the outcome of parent–child relationship, same-sex parents reported having significantly better relationships with their children than did heterosexual parents. Similar findings have been documented in previous studies with children of lesbian parents expressing more positive relationships with their mothers' new partner than children of heterosexual mother families (Tasker & Golombok, 1995). There are several hypotheses that could explain this finding, some of which stem from the limitations inherent in the studies used for the analysis. . . .

Although the variance among studies for children's gender role development could not be adequately explained in the current analysis, the significant variation for this outcome has also been documented in previous research (Green, Mandel, Hotvedt, Gray, & Smith, 1986; Hoeffer, 1981; Steckel, 1987), suggesting that children raised by same-sex parents may exhibit different sex-typed behaviors than do children raised by heterosexual parents. . . . Therefore, gender role development did not only differ among children raised by parents with different sexual orientations, but there was also variation in children's sex-typed behaviors according to the child's gender. Although further research is needed to help confirm these findings, sex-typed behavior differences among children brought up with parents of different sexual orientations should not come as a surprise given current gender theories. Our results, therefore, could suggest that children's gender role development is likely affected by a multitude of complex variables—not solely the parents' sexual orientation (Stacey & Biblarz, 2001), which could possibly explain the significant variation observed between studies. . . .

Although the results must be interpreted with caution, they should also be understood within the larger body of studies that consistently suggest that children with same-sex parents fare just as well as children with heterosexual parents. . . .

References

Allen, M., & Burrell, N. (1996). Comparing the impact of homosexual and heterosexual parents on children: Meta-analysis of existing research. *Journal of Homosexuality, 32,* 19–35.

Allen, M., & Burrell, N. (2002). Sexual orientation of the parent: The impact on the child. In M. Allen & R. W. Preiss (Eds.), *Interpersonal communication research: Advances through meta-analysis* (pp. 125–143). Mahwah, NJ: USum Associates Publishers.

American Psychological Association. (2002). Ethical principles of psychologists and code of conduct. *American Psychologist, 57*(12), 1060–1073.

Anderssen, N., Amlie, C., & Ytteroy, E. A. (2002). Outcomes for children with lesbian or gay parents: A review of studies from 1978 to 2000. *Scandinavian Journal of Psychology, 43(4),* 335–351.

Belcastro, P. A., Gramlich, T., Nicholson, T., Price, J., & Wilson, R. (1993). A review of data based studies addressing the affects of homosexual parenting on children's sexual and social functioning. *Journal of Divorce and Remarriage, 20,* 105–122.

Bigner, J. J., & Jacobsen, R. B. (1989). Parenting behaviors of homosexual and heterosexual fathers. *Journal of Homosexuality, 18,* 173–186.

Bozett, F. (1987). Children of gay fathers. In F. Bozett (Ed.), *Gay and lesbian parents* (pp. 38–57). New York: Praeger.

Cameron, P., & Cameron, K. (1997). Did the APA misrepresent the scientific literature to courts in support of same-sex custody? *Journal of Psychology, 131,* 313–332.

Fitzgerald, B. (1999). Children of lesbian and gay parents: A review of the literature. *Marriage and Family Review, 29,* 57–75.

Green, R., Mandel, J., Hotvedt, M., Gray, J., & Smith, L. (1986). Lesbian mothers and their children: A comparison with solo parent heterosexual mothers and their children. *Archives of Sexual Behavior, 15*(2), 167–184.

Hoeffer, B. (1981). Children's acquisition of sex-role behavior in lesbian-mother families. *American Journal of Orthopsychiatry, 51,* 536–544.

Lambert, S. (2005). Gay and lesbian families: What we know and where to go from here. *The Family Journal: Counseling and Therapy for Couples and Families, 13*(1), 43–51.

Liddle, B. (1996). Therapist sexual orientation, gender, and counseling practices as they relate to ratings of helpfulness by gay and lesbian clients. *Journal of Counseling Psychology, 43*(4), 394–401.

Lipsey, M. W., & Wilson, D. B. (2001). *Practical meta-analysis.* Thousand Oaks, CA: Sage.

Perrin, E. C. (2002). Technical report: Coparent or second-parent adoption by same-sex parents. *American Academy of Pediatrics, 109*(2), 341–344.

Pilkmgton, N., & Cantor, J. (1996). Perceptions of heterosexual bias in professional psychology programs: A survey of graduate students. *Professional Psychology: Research and Practice, 27*(6), 604–612.

Ryan, D., & Martin, A. (2000). Lesbian, gay, bisexual, and transgender parents in the school systems. *The School Psychology Review, 29*(2), 207–216.

Schumm, W. R. (2004). What was really learned from Tasker and Golombok's (1995) study of lesbian and single parent mothers? *Psychological Reports, 94*(2), 422–424.

Stacey, J., & Biblarz, T. (2001). (How) Does the sexual orientation of parents matter? *American Sociological Review, 66,* 159–183.

Steckel, A. (1987). Psychological development of children of lesbian mothers. In F. Bozett & W. Bozett (Eds.), *Gay and lesbian parents* (pp. 75–85). New York: Praeger.

Tasker, F. (2005). Lesbian mothers, gay fathers, and their children: A review. *Journal of Developmental & Behavioral Pediatrics, 26*(3), 224–240.

Tasker, F., & Golombok, S. (1995). Adults raised as children in lesbian families. *American Journal of Orthopsychiatry, 65*(2), 203–215.

ALICIA CROWL is an assistant professor of school psychology at the University of Kentucky. Her research interests focus on the interactions between various school curricula and children's academic, behavioral, and mental health outcomes; and understanding the effects of specific training programs for lesbian, gay, and bisexual (LGB) school children with LGB parents. She has given many national presentations on the topic of LGB parents and child development and has several publications pertaining to this issue. She received her PhD from Michigan State University.

SOYEON AHN is an assistant professor in the Department of Educational and School Psychology at the University of Miami. Her primary research emphasis is in psychometrics, the study of behavioral data computations, and understanding how to improve existing approaches of meta-analysis research. She received her PhD from Michigan State University.

JEAN BAKER was a former director of the School of Education at Michigan State University. Her research was devoted to understanding what variables contributed to children's educational outcomes. Various scholars have cited several of her publications in more than 100 different articles. Jean Baker passed away on January 10, 2008.

EXPLORING THE ISSUE

Does Parent Sexual Orientation Affect Child Development?

Critical Thinking and Reflection

1. The two studies presented approach the issue in different ways (meta-analysis versus a large random sample). In your opinion, which study provides the best approach for assessing this issue and explain why. In addition, discuss how the approach influences your stance on the issue.
2. Crowl et al. discuss reasons for the variance observed in children's gender role development between the compared groups. What factors other than parent sexual orientation might play a role in a child's gender role behavior? Explain how.
3. The Regnerus study collected its data from one particular time point. Does this technique provide enough insight about the lives of those being studied and the subsequent effects of their family experience? List three reasons explaining your opinion.
4. Choose a current policy in the media pertaining to this issue and discuss how the results from either study might be used to support or oppose the policy.
5. Crowl et al. reaffirm the findings of previous research suggesting "that parent sexual orientation was not a salient predictor of children's development" (Crowl et al., p. 398). Consider what other evidence might be needed to support their findings and explain your reasoning.

Create Central

www.mhhe.com/createcentral

Additional Resource

Spitzer, R. L. (2003). Can some gay men and lesbians change their sexual orientation? 200 participants reporting a change from homosexual to heterosexual orientation. *Archives of Sexual Behavior, 32*(5), 403–417.

An oft-cited and highly controversial landmark study claiming an observed change in sexual orientation.

Internet References . . .

The APA's Official Stance on Sexual Orientation

www.apa.org/helpcenter/sexual-orientation.aspx

The APA's Report on "Appropriate Therapeutic Responses to Sexual Orientation"

www.apa.org/pi/lgbt/resources/therapeutic -response.pdf

Unit 4

Cognitive–Emotional Issues

*A*long with behavior, our cognitive and emotional abilities are of vital interest to psychologists. Many people, for example, are concerned with a particular emotion—how to become and remain happy. Could psychological research on the factors that facilitate and maintain well-being help us to be happier? What about emotions in general? Is there a skill or sensitivity regarding emotions that is akin to intelligence? Are some people better than others at empathizing, reading emotions, or knowing how to manipulate them?

Selected, Edited and with Issue Framing Material by:
Brent Slife, *Brigham Young University*

ISSUE

Can Positive Psychology Make Us Happier?

YES: Julia K. Boehm and Sonja Lyubomirsky, from "The Promise of Sustainable Happiness." In *The Oxford Handbook of Positive Psychology*, 2nd ed. (Oxford University Press, 2009)

NO: Laurel C. Newman and Randy J. Larsen, from "How Much of Our Happiness Is Within Our Control?" An original essay written for this text (2009)

Learning Outcomes

After reading this issue, you should be able to:

- Determine if it is possible to adapt strategies to improve one's happiness.
- Discuss how the manipulation of environmental variables could impact happiness.

ISSUE SUMMARY

YES: Health researcher Julia Boehm and psychologist Sonja Lyubomirsky argue that empirical research has established that people can use multiadaptive strategies to increase their levels of happiness.

NO: Psychologists Laurel Newman and Randy Larsen challenge the external validity and sustainability of the effects of these strategies, arguing that most of what influences our long-term happiness is outside our control.

Who wants to be happy? Or perhaps the empirical question is, how *can* we be happy? The U.S. Declaration of Independence lists the pursuit of happiness as an unalienable right, but no psychological researcher was around in 1776 to teach U.S. citizens how best to pursue it. Nor is the quest for happiness an exclusively U.S. business; the country Bhutan, for instance, has a Gross National Happiness (GNH) index to help guide government policy. Still, in the Western world of psychological research, Maslow's hierarchy of needs seems to be at play. In Maslow's hierarchy, we must satisfy our most basic needs (e.g., hunger) before we can concern ourselves with higher level needs, such as happiness and flourishing. If this is true, then only the more affluent countries, those that have satisfied their citizens' more basic needs, can even afford to ask the happiness question.

With this affluence, the positive psychology movement has risen during the last decade with the study of human flourishing as its major aim. Its focus on examining and nurturing what is best in humans is grounded in ancient Greek philosophies and more recent humanistic psychological theories, such as that of Carl Rogers. Recently, happiness has become a popular emphasis of the movement, with a host of psychological researchers attempting to answer many important questions. Is happiness biologically based? Is it environmental? How much

is under our personal control? Sonja Lyubomirsky's early book described research that she contended would achieve lasting happiness, but many critics examined her results with skepticism. Is the research now substantial enough for psychologists to finally tell people how they can become happy?

Julia Boehm and Sonja Lyubomirsky seem to think so. In the YES article, they argue that there are individual differences in "hedonic adaptation," a term that means people return to previous happiness levels after positive or negative events. Julia Boehm and Sonja Lyubomirsky believe that these differences imply that some people enhance and sustain their own happiness by strategizing the way they construe the world, make decisions, and self-reflect. They hold that genes determine about half of personal happiness, and circumstances may account for another 10 percent, but the other 40 percent may be within individual control. They contend that less happy people can not only learn strategies (e.g., doing acts of kindness, expressing gratitude, and visualizing best possible selves), but also apply these strategies to increase their levels of happiness. Indeed, psychological studies seem to show that careful interventions can be effective in facilitating happiness.

Laurel Newman and Randy Larsen believe that psychologists should be cautious before making public announcements about how we can make ourselves happier. For them, psychologists are misleading when they say that 40 percent of happiness is within our control. Although Laurel Newman and Randy Larsen agree that roughly half of the difference in happiness scores (within a group) may be attributed to genetics, they also believe that most life-changing events (those that affect happiness) are out of a person's control. This means, perhaps most importantly, that strategies and techniques for increasing happiness are not likely to endure, because people have a surprising tendency to return to preexisting levels of happiness after good and bad events have produced temporary changes in happiness levels. Moreover, Laurel Newman and Randy Larsen contend that the experimental effects of the most oft-cited happiness interventions are at best weak and require very specific circumstances to produce any effect.

POINT

- According to some models, 40 percent of happiness may be within our control.
- Circumstantial factors do not adequately explain different levels of happiness.
- Studies with happiness-inducing strategies show people can increase their levels of happiness.
- Individual differences in adaptation show that people can use strategies to help themselves stay happy, even after a less-than-happy event.

COUNTERPOINT

- Heritability estimates describe variations in groups and do not apply to individuals.
- A variety of environmental variables predict happiness, and many of them are uncontrollable.
- These strategies have weak statistical effects that show up only under very specific circumstances.
- People adapt quickly to negative and positive changes, returning to previous levels of happiness.

YES

Julia K. Boehm and Sonja Lyubomirsky

The Promise of Sustainable Happiness

"How to gain, how to keep, how to recover happiness is in fact for most men at all times the secret motive of all they do, and of all they are willing to endure."

—William James

The quest for ever-greater happiness has existed since antiquity. Interest has not abated in today's society, whose preoccupation with becoming happier is evident in countless books and magazine articles promising the secret to a happy life. Indeed, the pursuit of happiness is not without reward, as empirical support is accumulating for the notion that happiness promotes multiple successful life outcomes (including superior health, higher income, and stronger relationships). Nonetheless, conflicting evidence raises questions about whether it is even possible for people to realize and then sustain meaningful changes in well-being.

In this chapter, we examine several issues with respect to sustainable happiness. To begin, we describe what happy and unhappy people are like, paying particular attention to the strategies that chronically happy people appear to use to foster and preserve their well-being. Next, we address some of the scientific community's reservations and uncertainties with respect to the possibility of sustainably increasing happiness. Finally, we review evidence suggesting that people can indeed learn strategies to achieve durable increases in well-being.

What Are Happy and Unhappy People Like?

Why are some people happier than others? Is it due to their marital status or the salary they earn? Is it because of the experiences they have or the culture they grow up in? Hundreds of empirical articles to date have examined how these and other so-called "objective" circumstances relate to happiness. Surprising to many laypeople, such objective factors (including marriage, age, sex, culture, income, and life events) explain relatively little variation in people's levels of well-being.

Given that circumstantial factors do not tell a satisfactory story to account for the differences between happy and unhappy people, one must look elsewhere to understand them. We propose that happy and unhappy individuals[1] differ considerably in their *subjective experience and construal* of the world. In other words, happy people

are inclined to perceive and interpret their environment differently from their less happy peers. This construal theory prompts us to explore how an individual's thoughts, behaviors, and motivations can explain her happiness over and above the mere objective circumstances of her life. A growing body of research suggests that happy people successfully enhance and maintain their happiness through the use of multiple adaptive strategies vis-à-vis construal of themselves and others, social comparison, decision making, and self-reflection.

Construal

Indeed, research suggests that happy individuals tend to view the world relatively more positively and in a happiness-promoting way. For example, when describing their previous life experiences, self-nominated happy people retrospectively evaluated the experiences as more pleasant at both the time of occurrence and when recalling them. Unhappy people, however, evaluated their past life events relatively unfavorably at both time points. Interestingly, objective judges did not rate the events described by happy people as inherently more positive than those described by unhappy people, suggesting that happy and unhappy people experience similar events but interpret them differently. Further supporting this finding, when participants were asked to evaluate hypothetical situations, dispositionally happy people rated the situations more positively compared with their less happy peers, even after current mood was controlled.

Self-nominated chronically happy people also have been found to use a positive perspective when evaluating themselves and others. For example, in one study, students interacted with a female stranger in the laboratory and were then asked to evaluate her personality. Happy students rated the stranger more positively, and expressed a stronger interest in becoming friends with her, compared with unhappy students. Furthermore, happy people tend to judge almost everything about themselves and their lives favorably, including their friendships, recreation, self-esteem, energy levels, and purpose in life.

Social Comparison

At its most basic level, the general finding from the social comparison domain is that happy people are less sensitive to feedback about other people's performances, even when that feedback is unfavorable. An illustrative study from our laboratory involved participants solving anagrams in the presence of a confederate who was performing the same task either much quicker or much slower. When exposed to a slower confederate, all participants (regardless of how happy they were) reacted the same way to the experience—that is, performing the task bolstered confidence in their skills. In the presence of a faster confederate, however, happy students did not change their judgments of how good they were at the task, but unhappy participants derogated their own skills. This finding supports the argument that the self-perceptions of happy individuals are relatively invulnerable to social comparisons.

In another study, students were asked to "teach" a lesson about conflict resolution to a hypothetical audience of children while presumably being evaluated by experts. After this teaching task, participants were supplied with an expert evaluation of their own—and a peer's—teaching performance. The results showed that happy people responded to the situation in a predictable and adaptive manner—they reported more positive emotions when told that their performance was excellent (even when a peer had done even better) than when told that their performance was poor (even when a peer had done even worse). Unhappy people's reactions, by contrast, were surprising and even dysfunctional. They reported more positive emotions after receiving a *negative* expert evaluation (accompanied by news that a peer had done even worse) than after receiving a positive expert evaluation (accompanied by news that a peer had done even better). Again, this suggests that happy people's emotions and self-regard are much less impacted by comparisons with others than those of their unhappy peers.

Happy individuals' inclinations to deemphasize social comparison feedback have been observed in a group context as well. For example, in one study, students competed in 4-person groups (or "teams") in a relay race involving word puzzles. The announcement of the winning team—or their individual rank on their team—did not influence happy participants' moods. In contrast, unhappy participants showed depressed moods after their team supposedly lost, and bolstered moods after learning that they had individually placed 1st on their losing team. The results of this study suggest that unhappy students are more responsive to both group and individual information, particularly in "failure" situations. Whereas unhappy people use individual ranking information (i.e., 1st place on their team) to buffer against unfavorable group comparisons (i.e., their team's underperformance), happy people do not appear to need such a buffer.

Decision Making

Besides using different strategies in the social comparison domain, happy and unhappy people also respond distinctively when making decisions. For example, empirical evidence suggests that happy and unhappy individuals show divergent responses to both inconsequential decisions (e.g., selecting a dessert) and momentous ones

(e.g., selecting a college). Happy people tend to be more satisfied with all of their available options (including the option they eventually choose) and only express dissatisfaction in situations when their sense of self is threatened. For example, when self-reported happy students were asked to rate the attractiveness of several desserts before and after learning which dessert they would get to keep, they increased their liking for the dessert they got and didn't change their liking for the dessert they couldn't get. This seems to be an adaptive strategy. In contrast, unhappy students found the option they were given to be minimally acceptable (derogating that dessert after learning they could keep it), and the forgone options to be even worse.

Similar patterns have been observed for happy and unhappy people facing a more significant decision-making situation—namely, the choice of a university. After being accepted by individual colleges, self-described happy students boosted their liking and judgments of those colleges. To protect themselves, however, these happy students decreased their overall ratings of the colleges that had rejected them. This dissonance reduction presumably allowed the happy participants to maintain positive feelings and self-regard. By contrast, unhappy participants did not use the same strategy to maintain positivity; instead, they (maladaptively) maintained their liking for the colleges that had rejected them.

Happy and unhappy people also differ in how they make decisions in the face of many options. Research suggests that happy individuals are relatively more likely to "satisfice"—namely, to be satisfied with an option that is merely "good enough," without concern for alternative, potentially better options. Unhappy individuals, by contrast, are more likely to "maximize" their options—that is, they seek to make the absolute best choice. Although maximizers' decisions may ultimately produce objectively superior results (e.g., a more lucrative job), maximizers experience greater regret and diminished well-being relative to satisficers. The maximizing tendencies of unhappy individuals may thus serve to reinforce their unhappiness.

Intrusive Dwelling

Happy people are much less likely than their unhappier peers to excessively self-reflect and dwell upon themselves. For example, in several studies, unhappy students led to believe that they had failed at a verbal task experienced negative affect and intrusive negative thoughts, which interfered with their concentration and impaired their performance on a subsequent intellectually demanding test. These findings suggest that unhappy people engage in negative (and maladaptive) dwelling more so than do happy people, and their excessive dwelling not only makes them feel bad, but brings about significant detrimental outcomes. Notably, another study revealed that manipulating a person's focus of attention (i.e., reflecting versus distracting) could eliminate the differences between the cognitive strategies and processes shown by happy and unhappy individuals. This finding hints at a critical mechanism underlying differences between happy and unhappy people—namely, that one could "turn" a happy person into an unhappy one by instructing her to ruminate about herself. Conversely, one could make an unhappy person "look like" a happy person by directing his attention away from himself.

The way that people consider their past life events also may differentially impact happiness. A recent set of studies in the U.S. and Israel examined the relationship between well-being and two different thought perspectives that can be used to consider autobiographical experiences—namely, "endowing" (or reflecting on) life events versus "contrasting" them with the present. Happy people are relatively more likely to report endowing (or savoring) past positive life experiences and contrasting negative life experiences (i.e., considering how much better off they are today), whereas unhappy people are relatively more likely to report endowing (or ruminating about) negative experiences and contrasting positive experiences (i.e., considering how much worse off they are today). This evidence suggests that happy people's strategies of processing life events serve to prolong and preserve positive emotions, whereas the strategies of unhappy individuals serve to dampen the inherent positivity associated with positive events and to enhance the negative affect associated with negative events.

Can Less Happy People Learn Strategies to Achieve Sustainable Happiness?

Our current understanding of the differences between chronically happy and unhappy people suggests that happy people think and behave in ways that reinforce their happiness. Given these findings, is it possible for unhappy people to learn deliberate strategies to achieve ever-greater well-being? Evidence suggests that in naturalistic settings people do try to become happier. For example, college students report a variety of strategies that they use to increase happiness, including social affiliation, pursuing goals, engaging in leisure activities, participating in religion, and "direct" attempts (e.g., act happy, smile). Although some of these techniques—especially social affiliation and direct attempts—are positively correlated with happiness, it is unclear whether such strategies *cause* increases in happiness or whether already happy people are simply more likely to practice them.

Sources of Pessimism Regarding Happiness Change

Doubts about the possibility of increasing and maintaining happiness have dominated the area of well-being and personality. To begin with, twin and adoption studies suggest that genetics account for approximately 50% of the

variation present in well-being. For example, Tellegen and colleagues investigated the well-being of identical and fraternal twins who had been raised together or apart. The happiness levels of the identical twin pairs were strongly correlated, and this correlation was equally high regardless of whether such twins had grown up under the same roof ($r = .58$) or miles apart ($r = .48$). Pairs of fraternal twins, however, showed much smaller correlations between their levels of well-being, even when they shared the same upbringing and household ($rs = .23$ vs. $.18$). Longitudinal studies of changes in well-being over time bolster these data even further. For example, although positive and negative life experiences have been shown to increase or decrease happiness in the short-term, people apparently rapidly return to their happiness baselines. These lines of evidence indicate that each person may have a unique set point for happiness that is genetically determined and immune to influence.

Another concern regarding sustainable changes in well-being is rooted in the concept of hedonic adaptation. Brickman and Campbell argued that after positive or negative life experiences, people quickly become accustomed to their new conditions and eventually return to their baseline happiness. This notion of a "hedonic treadmill" suggests that people adapt to circumstantial changes, especially positive ones. Many people still believe, however, that an incredibly exciting experience or major positive life change, such as winning the lottery, would make them considerably happier. In fact, a study comparing lottery winners and people who experienced no sudden windfall demonstrated that the lottery winners were no happier—and even appeared to obtain less pleasure from daily activities—than did non-winners. This suggests that hedonic adaptation is another potent barrier to sustainably increasing well-being.

A final source of pessimism about the possibility of real change in happiness is the strong association between happiness and personality. Personality traits are characterized by their relatively fixed nature and lack of variation across time. Thus, some researchers conceptualize happiness as part of a person's stable personality and, by extension, as a construct that is unlikely to undergo meaningful change.

The Sustainable Happiness Model

In their model of the primary determinants of happiness, Lyubomirsky, Sheldon, and Schkade challenge these reservations, and offer an optimistic perspective regarding the possibility of creating sustainable increases in happiness. According to their model, chronic happiness, or the happiness one shows during a specific period in life, is influenced by three factors—one's set point, one's life circumstances, and the intentional activities in which one engages. As mentioned, the set point is thought to account for approximately 50% of the variance in individual differences in chronic happiness. Unfortunately, however, because the set point is "set" or fixed, it is resistant to change. Given its relative inflexibility, the set point is unlikely to be a fruitful direction to pursue increases in happiness.

Counter to many lay notions of well-being, a person's circumstances generally account for only about 10% of individual differences in chronic happiness. Life circumstances include such factors as a person's national or cultural region, demographics (e.g., gender, ethnicity), personal experiences (e.g., past traumas and triumphs), and life status variables (e.g., marital status, education level, health, and income). Given that such circumstances are relatively constant, they are more susceptible to adaptation and, hence, have comparatively little impact on happiness. Thus, circumstantial factors also do not appear to be a promising route through which to achieve sustainable well-being.

Interestingly, however, although the average person easily adapts to positive changes in her life, like getting married, winning the lottery, or acquiring sharper vision, individual differences have been found in degrees of adaptation. For example, in a study of reactions to marriage, some newlyweds reported substantial boosts in life satisfaction after the wedding and remained very satisfied even years later, while others rapidly returned to their baseline happiness and others still actually became less happy and stayed relatively unhappy. These findings suggest that people vary in how they *intentionally behave* in response to changing circumstances—for example, the extent to which they might express gratitude to their marriage partner, put effort into cultivating their relationship, or savor positive experiences together.

The most promising factor for affecting change in chronic happiness then, is the approximate 40% portion represented by intentional activity. Characterized by committed and effortful acts in which people choose to engage, intentional activities can be behavioral (e.g., practicing random acts of kindness), cognitive (e.g., expressing gratitude), or motivational (e.g., pursuing intrinsic significant life goals). The benefits of intentional activities are that they are naturally variable and tend to have beginning and ending points (i.e., they are episodic). These two characteristics alone have the potential to work against adaptation. That is, it is much more difficult to adapt to something that is continuously changing (i.e., the activities that one pursues) than to something that is relatively constant (i.e., one's circumstances and situations).

Supporting this argument, when people were asked to rate various aspects of recent positive changes in their activities (e.g., starting a new fitness program) versus positive changes in their circumstances (e.g., moving to a nicer apartment), they described their activity-based changes as more "variable" and less prone to adaptation. Furthermore, activity-based changes predicted well-being both 6 and 12 weeks after the start of the study, whereas circumstance-based changes only predicted well-being at 6 weeks. It appears that by the 12th week of the study, students had already adapted to their circumstantial changes, but not to their intentional activities.

Using Intentional Activities as the Basis of Happiness Interventions

Preliminary evidence suggests that happiness interventions involving intentional activities can be effective in increasing and sustaining happiness. One of the first researchers to teach volitional strategies to increase happiness was Fordyce. Fordyce taught his "14 Fundamentals" of happiness (e.g., socializing, practicing optimism, being present-oriented, reducing negativity, and not worrying) to different classrooms of students. Across seven studies, students who were taught the happiness-increasing strategies demonstrated increases in happiness compared with students who received no training.

Fordyce's pioneering studies provide preliminary evidence that people have the potential to increase their short-term happiness through "training" programs. Extending this work, we have examined in depth several intentional happiness-enhancing activities in the laboratory, and have sought to identify significant moderators and mediators of their effectiveness.

Committing Acts of Kindness

A randomized controlled intervention from our laboratory involved a behavioral intentional activity—in a 10-week experiment, participants were invited to regularly practice random acts of kindness. Engaging in kind acts (e.g., holding the door open for a stranger or doing a roommate's dishes) was thought to impact happiness for a variety of reasons, including bolstered self-regard, positive social interactions, and charitable feelings towards others and the community at large. In this study, happiness was measured at baseline, mid-intervention, immediately post-intervention, and one month later. Additionally, two variables were manipulated: 1) the frequency with which participants practiced acts of kindness (either three or nine times each week) and 2) the variety with which participants practiced acts of kindness (either varying their kind acts or repeating the same acts weekly). Finally, a control group merely listed events from the past week.

Interestingly, the frequency with which kind acts were performed had no bearing on subsequent well-being. The variety of the kind acts, however, influenced the extent to which participants became happier. Those who were asked to perform a wide variety of kind acts revealed an upward trajectory for happiness, even through the 1-month follow-up. By contrast, the control group showed no changes in their happiness throughout the 14 weeks of the study, and those not given the opportunity to vary their kind acts actually became less happy midway through the intervention, before eventually rebounding to their baseline happiness level at the follow-up assessment.

In another kindness intervention from our laboratory, students were asked to perform five acts of kindness per week over the course of 6 weeks, and those five acts had to be done either within a single day (e.g., all on

Monday), or across the week. In this study, happiness levels increased for students performing acts of kindness, but only for those who performed all of their kind acts in a single day. Perhaps when kind acts were spread throughout the week, the effect of each kind act was dispersed, such that participants did not differentiate between their normal (and presumably habitually kind) behavior and the kindnesses prompted by this intervention. Taken together, our two kindness interventions suggest that not only can happiness be boosted by behavioral intentional activities, but that both the timing and variety of performing such intentional activities significantly moderates their impact on well-being.

Expressing Gratitude

Another intervention from our laboratory—one examining the effect of expressing gratitude (or "counting one's blessings") on changes in well-being—conceptually replicated the kindness studies. Being grateful was predicted to bolster happiness because it promotes the savoring of positive events and situations, and may counteract hedonic adaptation by allowing people to see the good in their life rather than taking it for granted. In this study, which was modeled after Emmons and McCullough, participants were asked to keep gratitude journals once a week, three times a week, or not at all (a no-treatment control). In their journals, participants wrote down up to five things for which they were grateful in the past week. The "blessings" recounted included relatively significant things (e.g., health, parents), as well as more trivial ones (e.g., AOL instant messenger).

Well-being was measured both before and after the gratitude manipulation. Corroborating the results of our 6-week kindness study, the role of optimal timing again proved decisive. Accordingly, increases in well-being were observed only in participants who counted their blessings once a week rather than three times a week. This finding provides further evidence supporting the argument that not only can an intentional activity successfully increase happiness, but that the way that activity is implemented is critical.

Visualizing Best Possible Selves

Sheldon and Lyubomirsky investigated yet another intentional activity that might be effective at elevating happiness—namely, the practice of visualizing and writing about one's best possible selves (BPS). This 4-week intervention also included a gratitude condition (in which participants counted their blessings) and a control condition (in which they recalled daily events). In the BPS condition, participants were encouraged to consider desired future images of themselves. King had previously demonstrated that writing about one's best future selves—a process that presumably enhances optimism and helps integrate one's priorities and life goals—is related to boosts in well-being. Results of our 4-week intervention indicated

that participants in both experimental conditions reported increased positive feelings immediately after the intervention; however, these increases were statistically significant only among those who visualized best possible selves.

Processing Happy Life Experiences

Another series of happiness intervention studies focused on the way that people consider positive life experiences. We hypothesized that systematically analyzing and structuring one's thoughts and feelings associated with the happiest moments in life would reduce some of the inherent joy associated with such experiences. In contrast, re-experiencing or savoring such moments (without attempting to find meaning or organization in them) was expected to preserve positive emotions and generally increase happiness. Two experiments tested these ideas using Pennebaker's expressive writing paradigm. In the first study, participants were asked to write about their life experiences (versus talk into a tape recorder or think privately about them) for 15 minutes on each of 3 days. The findings revealed that those who thought about their happiest event reported higher life satisfaction relative to those who talked or wrote about it.

In the second study, participants wrote or thought about their happiest day by either systematically analyzing or repetitively replaying it. The combination of writing and analysis was expected to be the most detrimental to well-being, whereas thinking and replaying was expected to be the most beneficial to well-being. Indeed, those participants who repetitively replayed their happiest day while thinking about it showed increases in positive emotions 4 weeks after the study was over, when compared with the other groups. In sum, the evidence suggests that, when considering the happiest moments in one's life, strategies that involve systematic, planful integration and structuring (e.g., the processes naturally engendered by writing or talking) may diminish the accompanying positive emotions. A successful happiness-increasing strategy, by contrast, involves replaying or reliving positive life events as though rewinding a videotape.

Current and Future Directions

An important caveat to the happiness intervention research conducted to this date is that participants practicing a particular happiness-enhancing activity have not yet been followed in the long term. To be sure, a complete investigation of the sustainable impact of activity-based interventions on happiness must use a longitudinal perspective (i.e., assessing well-being many months and even years post intervention). Although some studies have measured happiness 6 months, 9 months, and even 18 months later, it is unclear whether participants were still engaging in their assigned exercises for that period of time. Indeed, after the prescribed intervention period—when researchers are not encouraging, let alone enforcing, participants to practice their happiness-inducing activity—participants may or may not continue with the activity on their own accord. The committed effort shown by those who use happiness-enhancing strategies should be systematically measured and tested for the extent to which it moderates the effectiveness of strategy enactment.

Empirical evidence suggests, for example, that the participants likely to show long-term benefits of a happiness intervention are those who continue to implement and integrate the intervention activity into their lives, even after the active intervention period has ended. For example, in our study that asked students to either express gratitude or visualize their best futures, positive affect was predicted 4 weeks later by *continued performance* of the intervention activity. Furthermore, those students who found the happiness-enhancing activity rewarding were the most likely to practice it. Similarly, a recent intervention study from our laboratory revealed that the well-being benefits of engaging in a happiness-inducing exercise (either gratitude or optimism) accrued only to those participants who were motivated to become happier, and this effect was in evidence even 9 months later. More to the point, 3 months after completing our intervention, participants who were still practicing their previously assigned exercise reported greater increases in well-being relative to others.

Future researchers also might find it valuable to investigate a variety of specific intentional activities that serve to enhance and sustain well-being. Fordyce proposed as many as 14 different strategies to increase happiness, and dozens of other candidates undoubtedly exist. Thus far, only a subset of strategies has been tested experimentally (e.g., expressing gratitude, imagining best possible selves, practicing kind acts, adjusting cognitive perspective). Although additional happiness exercises have been examined in web-based interventions (e.g., applying personal strengths or thinking positively, the investigation of specific intervention strategies in a controlled laboratory setting is critical, as it allows the testing of theory-based hypotheses about how and why a particular strategy "works."

The variety of questions that controlled laboratory studies can address include the role of variables that potentially moderate the effectiveness of any particular happiness-enhancing strategy. Exploring such moderators may be crucial to understanding the relationship between intentional activities and subsequent well-being. Several moderators, described briefly here, already have begun to be examined (e.g., timing, variety, effort), but many others are untested or unknown. For example, one important moderator to consider in future studies is the "fit" between a person and an appropriate intentional activity—that is, the notion that not every activity is likely to benefit every person. Supporting the critical role of fit, preliminary findings reveal that individuals who report a relatively high degree of fit with the activity they practice (i.e., performing it for self-determined reasons) report bigger gains in happiness.

Happiness interventions also may be more effective when the participant has the support of close others.

When training for a marathon, runners who are part of a "team" have others to provide encouragement and to share both the challenges and rewards of their endeavor. As a result, runners with emotional and tangible support are likely to be more successful than those training alone. Likewise, people practicing strategies to enhance well-being are also likely to benefit from social support.

Another important moderator to consider is culture. The individualist notion of personal happiness distinctive to North America and Europe actually may run counter to the values and prescriptives of collectivist nations. Indeed, the pursuit of happiness in general—or specific strategies in particular—may not be as accepted or well-supported in non-Western cultures. Thus, cultural differences are critical to recognize when evaluating the effectiveness of well-being interventions. Indeed, the results of a recent study support the intriguing idea that foreign-born Asian Americans may benefit less—and differently—from practicing grateful and optimistic thinking than their Anglo-American peers.

Happiness in the Spotlight

This review of the sustainable well-being literature illustrates positive psychology's increasing focus on the causes, correlates, variations, and consequences of happiness. Why has happiness rapidly emerged into the scientific spotlight? Throughout the history of Western individualist societies, both laypeople and intellectuals alike have been preoccupied with attaining greater well-being. Indeed, people in a wide array of cultures report the pursuit of happiness as one of their most meaningful, desirable, and significant life goals. It is not surprising then that happiness should become a topic of tremendous research interest. Furthermore, whereas earlier thinkers, lacking in the proper scientific tools, could only philosophize about the nature and roots of happiness, advances in assessment and methodology have enabled current researchers to investigate subjective well-being with greater confidence and increased precision. Finally, as ever more people around the globe, and especially in the West, have their basic needs met, they have begun to enjoy the "luxury" of focusing on psychological fulfillment—that is, on psychological well-being rather than only on material well-being. And, for those with non-essential wealth, there may be a dawning recognition that material consumption—possessing the latest gadget or living in the grandest house—is not rewarding in and of itself.

Are there any costs to devoting energy and resources to the scientific study of well-being? We believe the costs are avoidable and few. Certainly, a single-minded obsession with the pursuit of happiness may obscure or preclude other important goals or activities for the individual—activities that may be "right," virtuous, or moral, but not happiness-inducing. Furthermore, although many characteristics of happy individuals help them achieve success in many areas of life, some of their characteristics (e.g., reliance on heuristics or diminished attention to the self) may be detrimental in certain contexts. In sum, happiness may be a necessary condition of the good life—a healthy, well-lived life—but it is not a sufficient condition. Other concerns should motivate people too, like cultivating self-acceptance and nourishing strong social relationships. Then again, it is notable that many, if not most, important, worthy, and socially desirable life activities, which sometimes appear to be incongruent with the pursuit of happiness—like caring for a sick family member, cramming for the MCATs, or turning the other cheek—can all be used as strategies to ultimately enhance well-being.

Concluding Remarks

"Man is the artificer of his own happiness."

—Henry David Thoreau

We have reviewed a number of cognitive, judgmental, and behavioral strategies that happy people use to maintain their high levels of well-being and have suggested that less happy people can strive successfully to be happier by learning a variety of effortful, happiness-enhancing strategies and implementing them with determination and commitment. Lyubomirsky, Sheldon, and Schkade's model of the determinants of happiness suggests that, despite historical sources of pessimism regarding change in well-being, people *can* become sustainably happier by practicing intentional activities—but only with concerted effort and under optimal conditions. We believe that hedonic adaptation to positive changes in people's lives is one of the most significant barriers to happiness. The intentional activities described here, and likely many others, can work to inhibit, counteract, or slow down the adaptation process.

Although empirical validation of our model is in the preliminary stage, increasing evidence suggests that engaging in purposeful activities leads to meaningful changes in well-being. Future researchers would do well to consider not only what strategies may successfully enhance happiness, but also under what conditions intentional activities are most effective.

Future Questions

1. Besides happiness, what other outcomes related to the "good life" might be affected by the practice of intentional activities?

2. Which additional intentional activities might serve to enhance happiness?
3. Would certain strategies to increase happiness be more effective in a collectivist versus an individualist culture?
4. Although the variable and episodic nature of intentional activities may serve to counteract adaptation, could people grow accustomed to a certain level of positivity in their lives and hence need more positive experiences just to maintain the same level of well-being?
5. Are activities to increase happiness more effective for happy people (who presumably already implement similar strategies in their daily lives) or unhappy people (who presumably have more to gain in happiness)? Are some strategies a better fit for one group versus the other?

Note

1. In the majority of the studies reported here, happy and unhappy people were identified using a median or quartile split on the widely used 4-item Subjective Happiness Scale. In other words, those scoring in the top half (or quarter) of the happiness distribution were classified as chronically happy, whereas those in the bottom half (or quarter) were classified as chronically unhappy.

JULIA K. BOEHM is a postdoctoral research fellow at Harvard School of Public Health. She received her BA from Lewis & Clark College and her MA and PhD from the University of California, Riverside, where she also received the Chancellor's Dissertation Fellowship. Her research focuses on mental and physical well-being.

SONJA LYUBOMIRSKY is a professor of psychology at the University of California, Riverside, and associate editor of *The Journal of Positive Psychology*. She received a BA from Harvard and a PhD from Stanford. Her research on happiness has been widely featured in journals and the popular media.

Laurel C. Newman and Randy J. Larsen    **NO**

How Much of Our Happiness Is Within Our Control?

In reviewing articles for the "no" side of this issue, there were several individual perspectives on why we psychologists should take caution before announcing to the public that we know how to make people happier. However, there was no culminating piece containing the variety of lines of logic and research that inspire this warning. Thus, the purpose of this piece is not to insist that we have absolutely zero control over our own happiness. Rather, it is to summarize the evidence suggesting that we have much less control over it than positive psychologists typically espouse.

1. **The heritability of happiness:** In 1989, a group of researchers began a wildly ambitious and comprehensive study of twins called the Minnesota Twin Family study. They used comparisons of identical twins, fraternal twins, and other family members to determine the proportion of the variation in the public's happiness scores that is caused by genetic factors, which is called the *heritability* of happiness. In 1996, two of the researchers (David Lykken and Auke Tellegen) published a paper reporting that the heritability is around .50, which means about half of the variability we see in the population's happiness scores is caused by people's genes, and about half by other things. Most psychologists would concede that a person cannot change his or her genes, so it follows that at least one major cause of happiness lies outside of our control.
2. **The hedonic treadmill:** In 1978, Brickman, Coates, and Janoff-Bulman published a well-cited study showing that people who had befallen great fortune (lottery winners) or great tragedy (recent paraplegics) returned to their preexisting levels of happiness within a year following the event. A re-analysis of the data from the study showed that the paraplegics' level of happiness really never fully returned to baseline. Nevertheless, follow-up research has been done on the topic, and most psychologists agree that people do adapt emotionally to most of the good and bad events in life and have a surprising tendency to remain very near their preexisting level of happiness despite life's slings and arrows. This has been called the "hedonic treadmill theory"

because no matter how fast or slow people "run," they stay in the same place (emotionally, of course). This is good news because it means we have the capacity to adapt to the inevitable tragedies and problems of life, but it is also bad news because, for most people, it precludes ever attaining everlasting bliss.

The two points made thus far comprise the portion of this "no we cannot make ourselves happier" argument that is generally accepted, and even pointed out, by most positive psychologists. The points that follow may be viewed as more controversial.

3. **The famous 40 percent:** Sonja Lyubomirsky is most often cited by positive psychologists and the media as the person who has cracked the happiness code and made the fruits available to all. In her book, *The How of Happiness: A New Approach to Getting the Life You Want,* she summarizes the research showing that happiness is 50 percent heritable and 10 percent due to well-studied demographic variables. She claims *that means* the remaining 40 percent of happiness is within our control. To illustrate this concept, the cover of her book contains a pie with 40 percent removed and the claim, "this much happiness—up to 40 percent—is within your power to change." Her book has been touted by many as scientific evidence of great news: We have a surprisingly high level of control over our own happiness. There are a few problems with this conclusion, though.

   a. She misuses heritability estimates. Heritability estimates estimate the proportion of individual differences, or variation, in scores *among a group of people* that can be attributed to their genes. They describe variation in a group, and cannot be applied to any individual person.[1] There are undoubtedly people whose happiness lies largely within their control, and others who suffer from life circumstances that will likely cause lasting and inescapable misery. It is the job of positive psychologists to study these sorts of distinctions rather than making the misleading claim that everyone

An original essay written for this volume.

has an equal capacity for increasing his or her happiness.

b. Even if the 40 percent estimate were valid (which, as I just explained, it isn't), it is not accurate to claim that whatever portion of our happiness is not due to genetics and not due to as-of-yet carefully studied demographic variables is by default within our control. That 40 percent estimate would simply include *everything else*—everything besides genes and the demographic variables that have been carefully studied. That leaves room for many situational and personality variables that likely have a strong impact on our emotional state. Home foreclosures, lost jobs, unfaithful spouses, chronic illness, unplanned pregnancies, miscarriages, broken down cars and other daily hassles, work/life conflict, marital discord—the list is practically endless of things that would be included in that "everything else" portion, and the very important question remains as to which of those variables matter most, and to what extent those variables are actually within our control.

c. The evidence for the effectiveness of existing happiness interventions is shaky and unclear. Several positive psychologists have their own prescriptions for how to increase one's own happiness. These prescriptions are generally based on scientific research,[2] and most involve happiness exercises you can do easily at home to boost your happiness. There are currently two lines of research that have received the most attention that claim to increase happiness. In her book, Sonja Lyubomirsky describes exercises such as a *gratitude exercise* (wherein you contemplate 5 things you are grateful for at the end of each week), committing regular acts of kindness toward others, and distracting yourself when things are going badly rather than ruminating. Seligman and colleagues have tested 5 similar strategies and found scattered effects with 3 of them (though they also found temporary effects with an unconvincing placebo exercise). Although these interventions are often referred to by positive psychologists as promising evidence that we can boost our own happiness, the actual effects of these interventions are unimpressive. Though Lyubomirsky's book does not include actual data from her studies, a careful reading of the original journal articles reporting her results shows that many of the strategies have weak, improperly derived, or even unreported statistical effects that only show up at all under a very specific set of circumstances. Her 2005 paper is most commonly cited as scientific evidence that happiness-boosting interventions can work. However, in the actual paper, the *gratitude exercise* only mattered for people

who did it once per week (not three times per week) and the *acts of kindness* exercise only mattered for people who did 5 acts of kindness all in one day for 6 weeks straight (not people who spread the acts out). Additionally, I use the term "mattered" rather than "worked" because the data were not reported in the article, nor were the results of any statistical tests.[3] Indeed, Boehm and Lyubomirsky's chapter in the *Handbook of Positive Psychology* reviews 8 studies, each testing several of what they call successful activities for increasing happiness. But the whole of the chapter contains mention of only one statistically significant result. The situation is surprisingly bleak considering the methodological features of her studies that should stack the results in her favor.[6] Nevertheless, her book has been translated into 11 languages and she is cited by positive psychologists and the media alike as having uncovered lasting keys to happiness. Several crucial questions remain: Do these exercises really increase happiness at all? If so, what boundary conditions are necessary for them to work? Are they ineffective for some people, and can they even have drawbacks?[4] Will any boost to happiness resulting from these exercises be long-lasting?[5] Given what we know about the hedonic treadmill, and given that emotional adaptation is even faster for good events than for bad ones, it seems likely that any benefits that people might gain from these interventions would dissipate quickly over time.

4. **The trouble with the denominator:** It might be surprising to most people to learn that personality psychologists have found that positive and negative affect (PA and NA) are independent of each other. This means the people who experience the most positive emotions are not necessarily the people who experience the least negative emotions. Furthermore, most psychologists accept the proposition that our subjective well-being is defined, in emotional terms, as our ratio of positive to negative affect. So to make a person happier, you could increase the numerator (PA) *or* decrease the denominator (NA). Unfortunately, there is also a well-documented pattern of findings across various subfields of psychology that "bad is stronger than good." Bad events have a deeper and longer lasting impact on us emotionally than good events. This is called the *negativity bias*, and it is interpreted by most as having an evolutionary purpose: avoiding threats helps us survive; relishing accomplishments does not. What all this suggests is that people would get more bang for their buck by trying to eliminate the causes of negative emotion in their lives than by trying to increase the positive. This has been pointed out in the positive psychology literature,[7] but it remains largely ignored or even dismissed by most positive

psychologists, as their "declaration of independence" depends on their determination to focus on increasing the positive and not dwelling on the negative. To make matters worse, while bad is stronger than good, it also seems evident that many key sources of negative affect (such as those listed in paragraph 3b) are largely if not fully outside of people's control. Indeed, Diener and colleagues recently stressed the need for a *revised adaptation (hedonic treadmill) theory* based on results from a large longitudinal study investigating whether or not people's life satisfaction levels are stable across time. They concluded that most people's were largely stable (which fits with hedonic treadmill theory), but that a portion of people (about 25 percent) have more fluctuating levels of life satisfaction. What variables did they find have a significant and lasting impact on life satisfaction? Unemployment and widowhood (both negative and outside of our control) had the strongest effects, with divorce having significant but smaller effects (an event most people view as negative and often outside of their control). It was in this article that they pointed out that paraplegics and other disabled people (again, negative and outside of their control) actually do not return fully to baseline. The lottery winners did not gain any lasting happiness from their wins (a positive event outside of their control). In fact, almost all the data cited in their review shows that, though life satisfaction may fluctuate, it seems to be lastingly influenced primarily by events that are negative and outside of our control. Another comprehensive study by Diener and colleagues compared well-being data from large samples of people from 55 nations and found that subjective well-being was higher among people who lived in nations that were wealthier, individualistic, and that protected their citizens' human rights. Few people in countries that lack these characteristics are there by choice.

There is some debate as well among psychologists as to whether we *should* be trying to increase happiness in the American public, most of whom report being pretty happy already. That is an issue for another day. The question here is, *if* we concede that boosting happiness is a worthwhile goal to pursue for psychologists, to what extent is doing so *possible*? Careful research has shown that happiness is by no means predetermined or "fixed" by genetics. Psychologists have uncovered a variety of environmental variables that predict (correlate with or cause) happiness. However, we must not confuse prediction with control. Nobody chooses to become a widow, be confined to a wheelchair, live in an impoverished nation, or lose their job. Many of the most influential environmental variables in our lives are every bit as uncontrollable as our genes.

In the field of psychology, unbridled enthusiasm often gives way to skepticism, and this is a good thing for the field. Psychology has a long history of demonstrating that people like to be in control of their surroundings, and they like to be happy. It comes as no surprise that they would embrace the finding that they are in control of making themselves happy. But the job of psychologists is to make claims based on objective interpretation of scientific evidence. Objective interpretation seems to point more to the idea that most of what influences our happiness in large and lasting ways lies outside the realm of the controllable.

Notes

1. See Diener, 2008, for a lengthier explanation of this concept.
2. Psychologists agree that any finding in the field of psychology as well as any claims for treatment or intervention must be based on scientific research, so this is a good thing. However, claiming that one's opinions are based on scientific research has become somewhat of a free pass to say whatever you want as long as there is at least some trend in your data that is consistent with your theory. Most psychologists are not going to take the time to sift through the details of others' (often unpublished) data and publish purposeful criticisms of others' work, and most laypersons do not have the skills to judge the quality of research. Therefore, whether or not the quality and results of the research actually warrant the claims being made is a question that often goes unchecked.
3. The results were described by bar graphs, which showed increases in well-being of .4 points for the acts of kindness exercise and .15 points (identical to the magnitude of change for the control group, incidentally) for the gratitude exercise. However, because there was no information on the scale or its end points and no statistical analyses were presented, it is impossible to judge what these values mean. One can only assume the results were not statistically significant, in which case it is misleading to refer to this article as evidence that these two activities increase happiness.
4. For example, the advice to stop ruminating probably has a lot of cash value for a chronic ruminator, but for most normal, well-adjusted people, ruminating can signal to us that we need to do something about a problem in our environment. Indeed, evolutionary and personality psychologists agree that negative emotions exist because they serve a purpose. Stifling the emotion, though more affectively pleasant, may not always be in our best interest.
5. Occasionally, researchers do conduct follow-up studies several months down the road. When they do, they often find mixed success, meaning that people are still a little happier who engaged in some of the exercises, but people

who completed other exercises have returned to baseline (if they ever budged at all).

6. For example, lack of a convincing placebo control group (even though there is evidence that placebos have an effect in these types of studies), multiple measures of happiness and subjective well-being as dependent variables (which increases the overall probability of finding a significant result due to chance), and instructions telling participants that the researchers *expect* the exercises to boost people's moods (which can influence participants' responses).

7. Larsen and Prizmic estimate that bad events impact us about 3.14 times as strongly as good events.

LAUREL C. NEWMAN is an assistant professor and director of psychology at Fontbonne University in St. Louis. She received a BA from Lindenwood University in Missouri and her MS and PhD from Washington University. She conducts research on the influence of self-perceptions, values, and goals.

RANDY J. LARSEN is chairman of the Psychology Department at Washington University and the William R. Stuckenberg Professor of Human Values and Moral Development. He received his MA from Duquesne University and a PhD from the University of Illinois. He was elected a Fellow of the American Psychological Association and the Association for Psychological Science.

EXPLORING THE ISSUE

Can Positive Psychology Make Us Happier?

Critical Thinking and Reflection

1. Imagine you are an unhappy person who wishes to become happier. How would each of these viewpoints influence your decision of whether or not to seek therapy? What might you expect from therapy in each case?
2. Which of these viewpoints do you agree with most? How does your choice make a difference in how you, as a hypothetical therapist, might address an unhappy client's needs?
3. Larsen and Newman say psychologists should take caution before making public announcements about how we can make ourselves happier. What might result from a lack of caution?
4. Psychologists debate whether or not we should try to increase happiness in the American public. What arguments might either side make?
5. Given that people usually adapt emotionally to good and bad events in life (e.g., their previous happiness levels return), how would you study why unemployment, widowhood, and other circumstances seem to durably lower happiness levels?

Create Central

www.mhhe.com/createcentral

Additional Resources

Niemiec, R., and Wedding D. (2008). *Positive Psychology at the Movies: Using Films to Build Virtues and Character Strengths*. Cambridge, MA: Hogrefe.

Held, B. S. (2004). The negative side of positive psychology. *Journal of Humanistic Psychology, 44* (1), 9–41.

McMahon, Darrin M. (2006). *Happiness: A History*. Boston: Atlantic Monthly Press.

Internet Reference . . .

New York Times

www.nytimes.com/2010/06/01/health
/research/01happy.html?_r=1

Selected, Edited and with Issue Framing Material by:
Brent Slife, *Brigham Young University*

ISSUE

Is Emotional Intelligence Valid?

YES: **John D. Mayer, Peter Salovey, and David R. Caruso,** from "Emotional Intelligence: New Ability or Eclectic Traits?" *American Psychologist* (September 2008)

NO: **Edwin A. Locke,** from "Why Emotional Intelligence Is an Invalid Concept," *Journal of Organizational Behavior* (June 2005)

Learning Outcomes

After reading this issue, you should be able to:

- Discuss whether the narrowing of the definition of Emotional Intelligence (EI) has reduced its misinterpretation.
- Understand whether discriminating between emotions is a learned skill.

ISSUE SUMMARY

YES: Psychologists John Mayer, Peter Salovey, and David Caruso maintain that some individuals have a greater emotional intelligence (EI), a greater capacity than others to carry out sophisticated information processing about emotions.

NO: Social science professor Edwin A. Locke argues that "emotional intelligence" is not a form of intellectual ability.

Do you have a friend who seems to get along with everyone? Is it simply a phenomenon of personality, or do some individuals possess a type of intelligence that facilitates this social skill? Could there be a social or emotional intelligence apart from that measured by standard intelligence tests? From as early as the 1920s, psychologists such as Thorndike, Wechsler, and Gardner have sought to explain performance outcomes that could not be explained by traditional intelligence models. The term emotional intelligence (EI) was coined as early as 1966 to account for some of that unexplained portion, but it was not until the 1990s that psychologists developed models and tests for measuring EI. After *Time* magazine ran a 1996 cover story on EI, the term became a buzzword in the popular media and among professionals, some of whom assert that EI may be more important to business success than standard intelligence.

The concept has taken on a life of its own since Harvard psychologist Daniel Goleman's 1995 book on EI promised to redefine what it means to be smart. Seminars and books appeared advising leaders about the importance of EI in the workplace, and some psychologists attempted to incorporate EI into their models of intelligence. However, many other psychologists disagreed. Apart from the confusion of what exactly EI means, some researchers insisted that the original definition of EI is not a true form of intelligence but rather a matter of awareness and introspection. They argued that intelligence factors have to be part of a single, general mental ability.

In the YES article, John Mayer, Peter Salovey, and David Caruso concede that the popularization of EI has led to considerable confusion as to what EI is or should be. They argue, however, that their own scientific conception of EI qualifies as a valid intelligence because it refers to a mental ability that may exist apart from general intelligence or personality. Further, EI reliably and uniquely predicts behaviors, such as the ability to maintain positive personal commitments. They note that individuals high in EI have a differentiated ability to comprehend and use emotions to benefit themselves and others. Even when personality traits are controlled, EI measurements can predict deviancy and problem behaviors.

In the NO article, Edwin Locke argues that the concept of EI departs from scientific rationality in that its many definitions and claims render it unintelligible. He contends that the purpose behind theories of multiple intelligences, such as EI, is political rather than scientific because EI redefines what it means to be intelligent so that everybody is intelligent. Further, the claim that individuals high in EI can reason with emotion is contradictory; instead, he argues that one simply applies standard intelligence to emotional information. What EI models claim

to predict, according to Locke, belongs to an introspective skill or a personality trait, not an intellectual ability.

POINT

- The earliest model of EI was in some respects overly broad and therefore interpreted incorrectly.
- Emotions are signals that convey information, so one can use them to facilitate thinking.
- Measures of EI significantly increase the prediction of standard intelligence tests.
- Whereas emotional knowledge (the *information* that EI operates on) can be learned easily, EI is a stable aptitude not easily learned.

COUNTERPOINT

- Most definitions are so all-inclusive that they make the concept unintelligible.
- One cannot reason with emotion. Reason and emotion are two distinct processes.
- What is termed emotional intelligence is simply intelligence applied to emotions.
- Discriminating between emotions is a learned skill, just as is detecting a given emotion.

YES

**John D. Mayer, Peter Salovey,
and David R. Caruso**

Emotional Intelligence: New Ability or Eclectic Traits?

The notion that there is an emotional intelligence (EI) began as a tentative proposal (Mayer, DiPaolo, & Salovey, 1990; Salovey & Mayer, 1990). The original idea was that some individuals possess the ability to reason about and use emotions to enhance thought more effectively than others. Since 1990, EI has grown into a small industry of publication, testing, education, and consulting (Matthews, Roberts, & Zeidner, 2004; Matthews, Zeidner, & Roberts, 2002). Matthews et al. (2002) have outlined the dramatic growth of the psychological literature concerning an EI. Yet the apparent size of the field dwarfs what we regard as relevant scientific research in the area. In fact, one commentator recently argued that EI is an invalid concept in part because it is defined in too many ways (Locke, 2005, p. 425).

The original definition of EI conceptualized it as a set of interrelated abilities (Mayer & Salovey, 1997; Salovey & Mayer, 1990). Yet other investigators have described EI as an eclectic mix of traits, many dispositional, such as happiness, self-esteem, optimism, and self-management, rather than as ability based (Bar-On, 2004; Boyatzis & Sala, 2004; Petrides & Furnham, 2001; Tett, Fox, & Wang, 2005). This alternative approach to the concept—the use of the term to designate eclectic mixes of traits—has led to considerable confusion and misunderstandings as to what an EI is or should be (Daus & Ashkanasy, 2003; Gohm, 2004; Mayer, 2006). Many features, such as self-esteem, included in these models do not directly concern emotion or intelligence or their intersection (Matthews et al., 2004, p. 185). We agree with many of our colleagues who have noted that the term *emotional intelligence* is now employed to cover too many things—too many different traits, too many different concepts (Landy, 2005; Murphy & Sideman, 2006; Zeidner, Roberts, & Matthews, 2004). "These models," wrote Daus and Ashkanasy (2003, pp. 69–70), "have done more harm than good regarding establishing emotional intelligence as a legitimate, empirical construct with incremental validity potential." In this article, we explore these key criticisms of the field, contrasting what we believe to be a meaningful theory of EI with models describing it as a mix of traits.

Our principal claim is that a valid EI concept can be distinguished from other approaches. This valid conception of EI includes the ability to engage in sophisticated information processing about one's own and others' emotions and the ability to use this information as a guide to thinking and behavior. That is, individuals high in EI pay attention to, use, understand, and manage emotions, and these skills serve adaptive functions that potentially benefit themselves and others (Mayer, Salovey, & Caruso, 2004; Salovey & Grewal, 2005). As we use the term, *emotional intelligence* is an instance of a standard intelligence that can enrich the discussion of human capacities (Mayer, Salovey, Caruso, & Sitarenios, 2001).

The deeper question raised by Locke's (2005) and others' assertions that EI has become overgeneral is "How does one decide something ought or ought not to be called emotional intelligence?" To address this question, in the first section of this article, The Schism in the Field, we examine the central conception of EI and the current confusion in the field. In the second section, The Four-Branch Model of EI, we further describe our approach to EI. In the third section, The Significance of EI, we examine the various reasons why EI is important as a discrete variable. Finally, in the Discussion and Recommendations section, we consider how the term *emotional intelligence* has come to be so misused and the steps that can be taken to improve terminology and research in the area.

The Schism in the Field
Initial Ideas

Our initial view of EI was that it consists of a group of related mental abilities. For example, we first defined EI as "the ability to monitor one's own and others' feelings and emotions, to discriminate among them and to use this information to guide one's thinking and actions" (Salovey & Mayer, 1990, p. 189). An empirical companion piece operationalized aspects of EI as an ability: Participants examined a set of colors, faces, and designs and had to identify each one's emotional content (Mayer et al., 1990). In a subsequent editorial in the journal *Intelligence*, we discussed the difference between traits such as extraversion, self-confidence, and EI, noting,

> Although a trait such as extraversion may depend on social skill, or result in it, [it] is a . . . preference rather than an ability. Knowing what another person feels, in contrast, is a mental ability. Such knowledge may stem from *g,* or be somewhat independent of it. The way in which we have defined

emotional intelligence—as involving a series of mental abilities—qualifies it as a form of intelligence. (Mayer & Salovey, 1993, p. 435) . . .

External Factors

A journalistic rendering of EI created and also complicated the popular understanding of it. Goleman's (1995) best-selling book *Emotional Intelligence* began with the early version of our EI model but mixed in many other personality traits including persistence, zeal, self-control, character as a whole, and other positive attributes. The book received extensive coverage in the press, including a cover story in *Time* magazine (Gibbs, 1995). Because the book included, in part, the theory we developed, some investigators wrongly believed that we endorsed this complex and, at times, haphazard composite of attributes as an interpretation of EI.

The journalistic version became the public face of EI and attracted further attention, in part, perhaps, owing to its extraordinary claims. Goleman (1995, p. 34) wrote of EI's importance that "what data exist, suggest it can be as powerful, and at times more powerful, than IQ." A few years later, Goleman (1998a, p. 94) remarked that "nearly 90% of the difference" between star performers at work and average ones was due to EI. Although these ideas appeared in trade books and magazine and newspaper articles, they influenced scientific articles as well. For example, one refereed journal article noted that "EI accounts for over 85% of outstanding performance in top leaders" and "EI—not IQ—predicts top performance" (Watkin, 2000, p. 89). Our own work never made such claims, and we actively critiqued them (Mayer, 1999; Mayer & Cobb, 2000; Mayer & Salovey, 1997; Mayer, Salovey, & Caruso, 2000). More recently, Goleman (2005, p. xiii) wrote that others who believed that EI predicts huge proportions of success had misunderstood his 1995 book.

The Advent of Mixed Models

With EI defined in the public mind as a variety of positive attributes, subsequent approaches continued to expand the concept. One defined EI quite broadly as, "an array of noncognitive capabilities, competencies, and skills that influence one's ability to succeed in coping with environmental demands and pressures" (Bar-On, 1997, p. 14). Although the model included emotion-related qualities such as emotional self-awareness and empathy, into the mix were added many additional qualities, including reality testing, assertiveness, self-regard, and self-actualization. It was this mixing in of related and unrelated attributes that led us to call these *mixed models* of EI (Mayer et al., 2000). A second mixed model of EI included such qualities as trustworthiness, adaptability, innovation, communication, and team capabilities as emotional competencies (Goleman, 1998b). The additions of this model led to the characterization of such an approach as "preposterously all-encompassing" (Locke, 2005, p. 428).

Still another research team defined a trait EI as referring to "a constellation of *behavioral dispositions* and *self-perceptions* concerning one's ability to recognize, process, and utilize emotion-laden information. It encompasses . . . empathy, impulsivity, and assertiveness as well as elements of social intelligence . . . and personal intelligence" (Petrides & Furnham, 2003, p. 278). At this point, the pattern is clear: A large number of personality traits are amassed, mixed in with a few socioemotional abilities, and the model is called one of EI or trait EI. (The "trait" designation is particularly confusing, as *trait* is typically defined as a distinguishing quality, or an inherited characteristic, and could apply to any EI model.) Generally speaking, these models include little or no justification for why certain traits are included and others are not, or why, for that matter, certain emotional abilities are included and others are not, except for an occasional mention that the attributes have been chosen because they are most likely to predict success (e.g., Bar-On, 1997).

Such approaches are disappointing from a theoretical and construct validity standpoint, and they are scientifically challenging in that, with so many independent qualities, it is hard to identify a global theme to these lists of attributes. There is, however, an alternative to such a state of (what we see as) disorganization. We believe that our four-branch model of emotional intelligence, for example, provides one conceptually coherent approach (Mayer & Salovey, 1997). It is to this model that we turn next.

The Four-Branch Model of EI
General Introduction to EI

Intelligence Considered

It is possible to develop a coherent approach to the concept of EI. In order to describe an EI, we need first to define intelligence. From the beginning of intelligence theorizing and testing, debates have raged regarding not only the nature of intelligence but also how many intelligences exist (Neisser et al., 1996). However, even the fiercest of *g* theorists, those proposing that intelligence is best described as consisting of a single, general mental ability factor, allow for the existence of more specific ability factors (e.g., Carroll, 1993).

Intelligences can be divided up in different ways, for example, according to whether they address crystallized (memory-dependent) or fluid (process-dependent) abilities or, alternatively, according to the type of information that is their focus. The approach that divides intelligences into information areas, for example, yields a verbal/propositional intelligence that deals with words and logic and a spatial intelligence that deals with arranging and rotating objects in space, among others. Analogously, an EI would address (a) the capacity to reason with and about emotions and/or (b) the contribution of the emotions system to enhancing intelligence.

One longstanding grouping of intelligences divides them into verbal/propositional and perceptual/

organizational areas (e.g., Kaufman, 2000). For decades, researchers have searched for an elusive third intelligence, believing that these two core intelligences by themselves were insufficient to describe individual differences in mental abilities (Walker & Foley, 1973; Wechsler, 1943). In 1920, Thorndike (p. 228) suggested the existence of a social intelligence, which involved "the ability to understand and manage men and women, boys and girls—to act wisely in human relations" (see also Bureau of Personnel Administration, 1930; Thorndike & Stein, 1937). Social intelligence began to be investigated, although it had vocal critics—whose criticisms may have impeded the field's growth (Cronbach, 1960).

None of the proposed earlier intelligences, however, explicitly concerned an EI—reasoning validly about emotions and then using emotions in the reasoning process. By the early 1980s, there was a greater openness to the idea of specific (or multiple) intelligences (Gardner, 1983; Guilford, 1959; Sternberg, 1985), and at the same time, research in emotions was blossoming. Ekman (1973) and others had resurrected Darwin's ideas that some types of emotional information—for example, human facial expressions of certain emotions—are universal; others examined how events lead to cognitive appraisals that in turn generate emotions (Dyer, 1983; Roseman, 1984; Scherer, 1993; Sloman & Croucher, 1981; Smith & Ellsworth, 1985).

Perhaps the elusive intelligence that could complement the traditional dichotomy of verbal/propositional and perceptual/organizational might be one of EI. An EI after all, when compared with social intelligence, arguably could have a more distinct brain locus in the limbic system and its cortical projections (Damasio, 1994; LeDoux, 2000; MacLean, 1973; TenHouten, Hoppe, Bogen, & Walter, 1985). An initial theory of EI developed these ideas along with a first demonstration study to indicate how aspects of it might be measured (Mayer et al., 1990; Salovey & Mayer, 1990).

Emotions as Signals

To describe convincingly what it means to reason with emotions, however, one must understand their informational content. Initially, some people express surprise that emotions convey information at all. Emotions often are viewed as irrational, will-o'-the-wisp states—even pathological in their arbitrariness (Young, 1943). Although this does describe the operation of emotion at times, it is far from a complete picture of a normal, functioning emotion system.

. . . [T]here is compelling evidence that many emotion meanings are in large part universal—and play a key role in helping people to understand their own and others' actions (e.g., Dyer, 1983; Ekman, 1973).

By the 1990s, the significance of emotions and their meanings were better appreciated and were increasingly studied empirically. The functional role of emotions as communication signals became widely accepted, although further issues remain to be explored, such as the meanings of affective dimensions and how social influences may modify emotional expression (Averill, 1992; Barrett & Russell, 1999). . . .

EI and the Four-Branch Model

Emotional abilities can be thought of as falling along a continuum from those that are relatively lower level, in the sense of carrying out fundamental, discrete psychological functions, to those that are more developmentally complex and operate in the service of personal self-management and goals. Crucial among lower level, fundamental skills is the capacity to perceive emotions accurately. Higher level skills include, for example, the capacity to manage emotions properly. These skills can be arranged in a rough hierarchy of four branches (these branches refer to a treelike diagram; Mayer & Salovey, 1997). These include the abilities to (a) perceive emotions in oneself and others accurately, (b) use emotions to facilitate thinking, (c) understand emotions, emotional language, and the signals conveyed by emotions, and (d) manage emotions so as to attain specific goals (Mayer & Salovey, 1997). . . .

Measuring EI

Ability Measures of EI

Individual differences exist in each of these four processes. For example, some people are more accurate in initially perceiving how each individual . . . might be feeling, recognizing their feelings from faces and postures. Such individual differences can be measured. Each ability area of our four-branch model of EI can be operationalized formally as a set of to-be-solved problems, and test takers' responses can be checked against a criterion of correctness. There are a number of ability-based scales of emotional perception (Archer, Costanzo, & Akert, 2001; Matsumoto, LeRoux, & Wilson-Cohn, 2000), emotional identification and understanding (Geher, Warner, & Brown, 2001), and emotional integrative complexity (Lane, Quinlan, Schwartz, Walker, & Zeitlin, 1990).

One measure that spans these areas is the Mayer-Salovey-Caruso Emotional Intelligence Test (MSCEIT). It consists of eight tasks, two for each of the four branches of our EI model (Mayer, Caruso, & Salovey, 1999; Mayer, Salovey, & Caruso, 2002; Mayer, Salovey, Caruso, & Sitarenios, 2003). For example, Perceiving Emotions is assessed by asking participants to identify emotions in pictures of faces, in one task, and in photographs and artwork, in another. . . .

Theory of the Measurement of EI

There are two powerful theoretical reasons why only such a clearly focused, ability-based approach can best measure EI. First, intelligences most generally are defined as mental abilities, and measuring mental abilities involves asking test takers relevant questions and then evaluating their answers against a criterion of correctness (e.g., Carroll, 1993). The MSCEIT expert scoring system identified correct answers by using the pooled responses of 21 emotions researchers (Mayer et al., 2003). . . .

*Key Findings Concerning EI and Other
Psychological Traits*

If, as we claim, EI involves a unique source of variation
that reflects a new intelligence, then it should exhibit
some overlap with other intelligence scales. Studies indicate that EI, as measured by the MSCEIT and its precursor
test the Multifactor Emotional Intelligence Scale (MEIS),
correlates about .35 or so with verbal intelligence, and
lower with perceptual/organizational IQ (Ciarrochi, Chan,
& Caputi, 2000; Mayer et al., 1999). Most of the overlap with verbal intelligence is accounted for by the third
branch of the MSCEIT, Understanding Emotions.

EI also should be relatively independent of more traditional personality scales. To test this, one can correlate
scales of EI with the Big Five personality traits. The Big Five
traits are Extraversion–Introversion, Neuroticism–Stability,
Openness–Closedness, Agreeableness–Disagreeableness, and
Conscientiousness–Carelessness. Each of the Big Five traits
can be divided into more specific traits. For example, one
approach to the Big Five divides Extraversion–Introversion
into such facets as gregariousness, assertiveness, and
warmth (Costa & McCrae, 1992). The Big Five represents
a good starting point for frequently studied personality dimensions, although some traits arguably are not
measured by the Big Five (e.g., educated–uneducated,
diplomatic–humorous, religious–unreligious; Saucier &
Goldberg, 1998).

EI, defined here as an ability, should have minimal correlations with Big Five traits such as Extraversion or Neuroticism: Whether or not people are sociable or emotional,
they can be smart about emotions. We did predict that
EI would have a modest relation to Openness, as Openness often correlates with intelligences (Mayer & Salovey,
1993). The scale correlated .25 with Openness and .28 with
Agreeableness, a trait that includes empathic and interpersonally sensitive content, and had lower correlations with
the rest (Brackett & Mayer, 2003). . . .

A number of observers and commentators on the field
have expressed reservations about whether such tests are
adequate measures of EI and whether they predict important outcomes (e.g., Brody, 2004; Oatley, 2004; Zeidner,
Matthews, & Roberts, 2001). The recent *Annual Review of
Psychology* examination of EI and its measurement covers such concerns in greater detail and summarizes many
of the central, continuing issues (Mayer et al., 2008). To
date, however, we believe that ability scales provide the
best benchmark for this new construct, although existing
scales still have room for substantial improvement.

The Significance of EI

General Considerations of the Validity
of an EI Measure

We recognize that the MSCEIT has important limitations
(see, e.g., our Recommendation 5 below), and yet we consider it among the better and most widely used of the valid

measures available. As such, we focus on it in this section.
The measurement issues surrounding EI are elements of
broader questions: Is a measure such as the MSCEIT a
valid assessment of EI? And can a test such as the MSCEIT
account for new variance in important outcomes? In the
mid-20th century, psychologists believed that such questions about validity could be answered on the basis of findings from key correlational and experimental studies of
the test itself (e.g., Barley, 1962). . . .

Thus far, the measurement evidence tends to favor
the ability-based EI approach described here over other
research alternatives (such as dismissing EI or using mixed
models). Valid approaches to EI can be divided into two
central areas: specific-ability approaches, such as the study
of accurate emotional perception, and integrative models of EI, one example of which is the four-branch model
and the MSCEIT (see Mayer et al., 2008, for other measures). Drawing on revised criteria for test validity (AERA,
APA, & NCME, 1999), a research team (including one of
the present authors) surveyed such EI measures and concluded that tests based either on specific or integrative
ability approaches to measurement exhibited generally
good evidence for their validity. Tests based on mixed
models, by contrast, did not adequately measure EI (Mayer
et al., 2008). . . .

EI and Understanding Feelings

Higher EI does appear to promote better attention to physical and mental processes relevant to clinical outcomes. For
example, people higher in some EI skills are more accurate in
detecting variations in their own heartbeat—an emotion-
related physiological response (Schneider, Lyons, & Williams,
2005). Higher EI individuals also are better able to recognize
and reason about the emotional consequences of events. For
example, higher EI individuals are more accurate in affective
forecasting—that is, in predicting how they will feel at some
point in the future in response to an event, such as the outcome of a U.S. presidential election (Dunn et al., 2007).

EI and Subjective Symptoms

Abilities such as affective forecasting are important, for
example, because psychotherapy patients from a wide
diversity of backgrounds seek help with the hope of gaining insight into their feelings and motives (Evans, Acosta, &
Yamamoto, 1986; Noble, Douglas, & Newman, 1999). If EI
increases an individual's attention to and accuracy about his
or her feelings under various conditions, this could, in turn,
minimize the individual's psychiatric symptoms. David
(2005) examined EI and psychiatric distress on the Symptom
Checklist–90–Revised (SCL-90-R). The higher a person's
EI, the lower their reports of symptoms on the Positive
Symptom Total ($r = -.38$), including, for example, fewer
headaches and less trouble concentrating. Scores on the
Symptom Distress Index, which measures symptom intensity, also declined as EI rose ($r = -.22$). After she controlled
for the Big Five personality dimensions, EI still accounted

for between 1% and 6% of the variance in SCL-90-R scales—supporting the incremental validity of EI. Other reports have indicated that, for example, those diagnosed with dysthymia have lower EI scores than other psychiatric groups (Lizeretti, Oberst, Chamarro, & Farriols, 2006).

EI and Understanding Social Relationships

Many psychotherapy clients hope to improve what have become problematic social behaviors and relationships (Evans et al., 1986; Noble et al., 1999). Research on EI indicates that people with high EI tend to be more socially competent, to have better quality relationships, and to be viewed as more interpersonally sensitive than those lower in EI (Brackett et al., 2006; Brackett, Warner, & Bosco, 2005; Lopes et al., 2004; Lopes, Salovey, Côté, & Beers, 2005; Lopes, Salovey, & Straus, 2003). Many associations between EI and these kinds of variables remain significant even after one controls for the influence of traditional personality variables and general intelligence on the measured outcome.

In one study of friendships, the relationship between EI and participants' engagement in destructive responses to life events experienced by their friends was often significant, even after the researchers controlled for the Big Five, psychological well-being, empathy, life satisfaction, and Verbal SAT scores, but for men only (Brackett et al., 2006); MSCEIT correlations ranged from −.02 to −.33.

Although the findings described above were based on self-evaluated outcome criteria, similar findings have come from observer reports of the same individuals. For example, judges' positive ratings of a videotaped "getting acquainted" social interaction were predicted by the MSCEIT, although again, only for men and not for women. Ratings of the ability to work well with others as well as overall judged social competence correlated .53 and .51, respectively, with EI. The authors noted that significant correlations remained after they partialed out the Big Five (Brackett et al., 2006).

Just as higher EI predicts better social outcomes, lower EI predicts interpersonal conflict and maladjustment. Teenagers lower in EI were rated as more aggressive than others and tended to engage in more conflictual behavior than their higher EI peers in two small-sample studies (Mayer, Perkins, Caruso, & Salovey, 2001; Rubin, 1999). Lower EI also predicted greater drug and alcohol abuse. For example, levels of drug and alcohol use are related to lower EI among males (Brackett, Mayer, & Warner, 2004). Inner-city adolescents' smoking is also related to their EI (Trinidad & Johnson, 2002).

EI and Understanding Work Relationships

High EI correlates with better relationships in business settings as well. Managers higher in EI are better able to cultivate productive working relationships with others and to demonstrate greater personal integrity according to multirater feedback (Rosete & Ciarrochi, 2005). EI also predicts the extent to which managers engage in behaviors that are supportive of the goals of the organization, according to the ratings of their supervisors (Côté & Miners, 2006). In one study, 38 manufacturing supervisors' managerial performance was evaluated by their 1,258 employees. Total EI correlated .39 with these managerial performance ratings, with the strongest relations for the ability to perceive emotions and to use emotions (Kerr, Garvin, & Heaton, 2006). . . .

Discussion and Recommendations
EI as a Valid and Significant New Concept

In this article, we have argued that there exists a valid and conceptually important new variable for investigators and practitioners. EI can be defined as an intelligence that explains important variance in an individual's problem solving and social relationships. Yet the acceptance of the construct is threatened less by its critics, perhaps, than by those who are so enthusiastic about it as to apply the term indiscriminately to a variety of traditional personality variables (as pointed out by Daus & Ashkanasy, 2003, and Murphy & Sideman, 2006).

Why Do Some Investigators and Practitioners Use the Term Emotional Intelligence Overly Broadly?

Expansion of the Emotional and Cognitive Areas of Thinking

Why are traits such as the need for achievement, self-control, and social effectiveness (let alone character and leveraging diversity) sometimes referred to as EI? Perhaps one contributing cause is a lack of perspective on personality as a whole. Psychology needs good overviews of the central areas of mental function—models that define personality's major areas. Yet few such overviews reached any level of currency or consensus in the psychology of the 1980s and 1990s. Hilgard (1980) indicated that psychology is thrown out of balance by the absence of such models. Indeed, the cognitive revolution of the 1960s and 1970s (Miller, 2003), followed by the intense interest in affective (emotional) sciences in the 1980s and 1990s (e.g., Barsade, Brief, & Spataro, 2003), contributed to a sense that cognitive and emotional systems were dominant aspects of the whole of personality. Many psychologists and other investigators began to refer to cognition, affect, and behavior, as though they provided complete coverage of the study of mental life (e.g., Thompson & Fine, 1999). In that impoverished context, the term emotional intelligence could be mistaken as a label for much of mental processing. In fact, however, the three-legged stool of cognition, affect, and behavior underemphasizes such areas of personality as representations of the self, motivation, and self-control processes; more comprehensive models have since been proposed (Mayer, 2003, 2005; McAdams & Pals, 2006). . . .

Our Viewpoint

We agree with a number of observers of this area of study that the term emotional intelligence is used in too all-inclusive a fashion and in too many different ways (Landy, 2005; Locke, 2005; Matthews et al., 2004; Murphy, 2006). Referring in particular to the broadened definitions of EI, Locke (2005) remarked, "What does EI . . . not include?" (p. 428). We believe that there is a valid EI concept. However, we certainly agree that there is widespread misuse of the term to apply to concepts that simply are not concerned with emotion or intelligence or their intersection. The misuses of the term are, to us, invalid in that they attempt to overthrow or subvert the standard scientific language in psychology, with no apparent rationale for doing so. Other investigators similarly have pointed out that it is important to distinguish between valid and invalid uses of the concept (Daus & Ashkanasy, 2005; Gohm, 2004); to date, however, this message has not been heeded as we believe it should be.

Recommendations

. . . Those investigators interested in EI increasingly are asking for clarification of what is and is not legitimate work in the field. Murphy and Sideman (2006, p. 296) put it as a need to "succeed in separating the valid work from the hype." One central concern of ours (and of others), here and elsewhere, has been to distinguish better from poorer approaches to EI.

From our perspective, renaming the Big Five and other classic personality traits as "emotional intelligence" reflects a lack of understanding of personality theory and undermines good scientific practice. It obscures the meaning of EI, and EI is an important enough new construct as to make that unfortunate and problematic. Only when researchers revert to using the term to refer to its legitimate meaning within the conceptual, scientific network can it be taken seriously (AERA, APA, & NCME, 1999; Cronbach & Meehl, 1955). There are a good number of researchers who understand this and who have used the term consistently in a meaningful fashion. As for the others, one of our reasons for writing this article is to convince them of the common sense of using the current personality terminology. On a very practical level, it is often impossible to evaluate a journal article purporting to study EI on the basis of keywords or the abstract: The study may examine well-being, assertiveness, self-perceptions of emotional abilities, or actual abilities.

We have provided an overview of EI in particular with an eye to helping distinguish EI from other more traditional personality variables. We have attempted to make it clearer than before where EI begins and ends and where other personality approaches pick up. Much of the mixed-model research on EI (sometimes called EQ), can be described by what Lakatos (1968, cited in G. T. Smith, 2005, p. 401) referred to as a "degenerating research program," which consists of a series of defensive shifts in terminology and hypotheses "unlikely to yield new knowledge or understanding."

We realize that the recommendations below may be obvious to many, even to those who have not read our article. To be as clear as we can be, however, we propose a set of simple recommendations that we believe will help to safeguard the field and foster its progress.

Recommendation 1

In our opinion, the journalistic popularizations of EI frequently employ inadequate and overly broad definitions of EI, implausible claims, and misunderstandings of the concepts and research more generally. We urge researchers and practitioners alike to refer to the scientific literature on emotions, intelligence, and emotional intelligence to guide their thinking. Simply put, researchers need to cite the research literature rather than journalistic renderings of scientific concepts, which serve a different purpose.

Recommendation 2

Referring to the diverse approaches to EI, one research group observed, "It is precisely because of this heterogeneity that we need clear conceptualization and definition" (Zeidner et al., 2004, p. 247). To restore clarity to the study of EI, we recommend that the term *emotional intelligence* be limited to abilities at the intersection between emotions and intelligence—specifically limited to the set of abilities involved in reasoning about emotions and using emotions to enhance reasoning.

Recommendation 3

We recommend that those interested in EI refocus on research relevant to the ability conception of EI. This includes studies using emotional knowledge measures, emotional facial recognition ability, levels of emotional awareness, emerging research on emotional self-regulation, and related areas (e.g., Elfen-bein & Ambady, 2002b; Izard et al., 2001; Lane et al., 1990; Mayer et al., 2003; Nowicki & Mitchell, 1998).

Recommendation 4

We recommend that groups of widely studied personality traits, including motives such as the need for achievement, self-related concepts such as self-control, emotional traits such as happiness, and social styles such as assertiveness should be called what they are, rather than being mixed together in haphazard-seeming assortments and named emotional intelligence.

Recommendation 5

Much remains unknown about EI (Matthews, Zeidner, & Roberts, 2007). Our final recommendation is that, following the clearer terminology and conceptions above, good theorizing and research on EI continue until more is known about the concept and about human mental abilities more generally. Enough has been learned to indicate that EI is a promising area for study but also that significant gaps in knowledge remain. For example, there needs to be greater attention to issues of culture and gender and their impact on theories of EI and the measurement of EI. Further progress in the measurement of EI generally also is required. Applications of EI must be conducted with much greater attention to the research literature, be grounded in good theory, and reject outlandish claims. . . .

In this article, we hope to have separated this EI from other constructs that may be important in their own right but are ill-labeled as *emotional intelligence*. By clarifying our model and discussing some of the confusion in the area, we hope to encourage researchers and practitioners to distinguish EI from other domains of study. Such distinctions will help pave the way for a healthier, more convincing, and better understood EI, one that best can serve the discipline of psychology and other fields.

John D. Mayer is professor of psychology at the University of New Hampshire. He received his PhD and MA in psychology at Case Western Reserve University and his BA from the University of Michigan. Dr. Mayer has served on the editorial boards of *Psychological Bulletin,* the *Journal of Personality and Social Psychology,* and the *Journal of Personality,* among others, and has been an Individual National Institute of Mental Health postdoctoral scholar at Stanford University. He has published extensively in emotional intelligence, integrative models of personality, and the effects of personality on an individual's life.

Peter Salovey, provost at Yale University, is the Chris Argyris Professor of Psychology and a professor of management and of epidemiology and public health at Yale University. He directs the Health, Emotion and Behavior Laboratory. He also has affiliations with the Yale Cancer Center and the Institution for Social and Policy Studies. Dr. Salovey received an BA in psychology and a coterminal MA in sociology from Stanford University in 1980. He holds three Yale degrees in psychology: an MS (1983), an MPhil (1984), and a PhD (1986). He was president of the Graduate and Professional Student Senate at Yale in 1983–1984. He joined the Yale faculty as an assistant professor in 1986 and has been a full professor since 1995.

David R. Caruso is a research affiliate in the Department of Psychology at Yale University and the coauthor of the Mayer, Salovey, Caruso Emotional Intelligence Test (MSCEIT). He was a National Institute of Child Health and Human Development predoctoral fellow and received a PhD in psychology from Case Western Reserve University. He was then awarded a National Institute of Mental Health fellowship and spent two years as a postdoctoral fellow in Developmental Psychology at Yale University.

Edwin A. Locke

 **NO**

Why Emotional Intelligence
Is an Invalid Concept

Summary In this paper I argue that the concept of emotional intelligence (EI) is invalid both because it is not a form of intelligence and because it is defined so broadly and inclusively that it has no intelligible meaning. I distinguish the so-called concept of EI from actual intelligence and from rationality. I identify the actual relation between reason and emotion. I reveal the fundamental inadequacy of the concept of EI when applied to leadership. Finally, I suggest some alternatives to the EI concept. Copyright © 2005 John Wiley & Sons, Ltd.

 The concept of intelligence refers to one's ability to form and grasp concepts, especially higher-level or more abstract concepts. The observations on which the concept of intelligence is formed are that some people are simply able to 'get' things better than others; that is, they are able to make connections, see implications, reason deductively and inductively, grasp complexity, understand the meaning of ideas, etc., better than other people. Motivation obviously plays a role in understanding concepts and can partly compensate for low ability, but even highly motivated people differ in intellectual ability. Those who are better able to grasp higher-level concepts are better able to handle complex tasks and jobs.

Intelligence must be clearly distinguished from rationality. Whereas intelligence refers to one's *capacity* to grasp abstractions, rationality refers to how one actually *uses* one's mind. A rational individual takes facts seriously and uses thinking and logic to reach conclusions. A person can be very intelligent and yet very irrational (cf. many modern philosophers; Ghate & Locke, 2003). For example, a person's thinking may be dominated by emotions, and they may not distinguish between what they feel and what they can demonstrate to be true.

The concept of emotional intelligence (EI) was introduced by Salovey and Mayer (1990), although related ideas such as 'social intelligence' had been introduced by earlier writers—originally by E. L. Thorndike. Salovey and Mayer (1990, p. 189) defined emotional intelligence as '*the ability to monitor one's own and others' feelings and emotions, to discriminate among them and to use this information to guide one's thinking and actions.*' (Note: definitions of EI are

constantly changing, an issue I will return to later.) There are several problems with this definition. First, the ability to monitor one's emotions does not require any special degree or type of intelligence. Monitoring one's emotions is basically a matter of where one chooses to focus one's attention, outwards at the external world or inward at the contents and processes of one's own consciousness. (This claim obviously implies that people have volitional control over focusing their minds. For a detailed discussion and defense of the claim that people possess volition or free will, see Binswanger, 1991; and Peikoff, 1991.) Focusing inwards involves introspection. Similarly, the ability to read the emotions of others is not necessarily an issue of intelligence. It could simply be a matter of paying attention to others and being aware of one's own emotions so that one can empathize with others. For example, if one is unaware, due to defensiveness, that one can feel fear, one will not be able to empathize with fear in others.

Second, discriminating between emotions is a learned skill, just as is detecting a given emotion. A highly intelligent person may be better able to make very subtle distinctions between similar emotions (e.g., jealousy and envy), but for basic emotions (e.g., love, anger, fear, desire) it just a matter of focusing inwards so as to develop one's introspective skill.

Third, whether one *uses* one's knowledge in everyday action is not an issue of intelligence per se. Many factors may come into play here. Among them are rationality (vs. emotionalism), being in (vs. out of) focus, integrity (including courage in the face of opposition), and the nature of one's purpose. In sum, the definition of EI indicates that it is really some combination of assorted habits, skills and/or choices rather than an issue of intelligence.

It is simply arbitrary to attach the word 'intelligence' to assorted habits or skills, as Howard Gardner and EI advocates do, on the alleged grounds that there are multiple types of intelligences. This extension of the term simply destroys the meaning of the concept—which, in fact, is the hidden agenda of the advocates of multiple intelligences. The ultimate motive is egalitarianism: redefining what it means to be intelligent so that everyone will, in some form, be equal in intelligence to everyone else. The agenda here is not scientific but political. However, arbitrary redefinitions do not change reality. Some people

Locke, Edwin A. From *Journal of Organizational Behavior*, vol. 26, no. 4, June 2005, pp. 425–431. Copyright © 2005 by Wiley-Blackwell. Reprinted by permission via Rightslink.

actually are more intelligent, in terms of their ability to grasp concepts, than others, but this ability is not necessarily reflected in every skill that people choose to develop. If one wants to group a set of related phenomena into a single concept, there must be a conceptually identified, common element among them. Otherwise, the concept has no clear meaning.

As another case in point, consider how Salovey and Mayer, in the same article cited above (Salovery & Mayer, 1990, p. 190), expand their conceptualization of EI. It is said to include the appraisal and expression of emotions in the self, both verbal and non-verbal; the appraisal and identification of emotions in others through non-verbal identification and empathy; the regulation of emotions in oneself and in others; and the utilization of emotions so as to engage in flexible planning, creative thinking, direction of attention, and motivation.

Observe that the concept of EI has now become so broad and the components so variegated that no one concept could possibl[y] encompass or integrate all of them, no matter what the concept was called; it is no longer even an intelligible concept. What is the common or integrating element in a concept that includes: introspection about emotions, emotional expression, non-verbal communication with others, empathy, self-regulation, planning, creative thinking and the direction of attention? There is none.

Following Salovey and Mayer, Daniel Goleman (1995) popularized the concept of EI. According to Goleman, EI involves self-motivation and persistence; skill at introspection; delay of gratification; self-control of impulses, moods and emotions; empathy; and social skills (the ability to make friends). These elements overlap considerably with those of Salovey and Mayer and are equally un-integratible by means of a single concept. Most of the actions involved actually require the use of reason.

To add to the confusion, in another article, Mayer (1999, p. 50) defines EI as, 'the capacity to reason with emotion in four areas: to perceive emotion, to integrate it in thought, to understand it and to manage it'. The fundamental problem here is that one cannot 'reason with emotion'. This is a contradiction in terms. Reason and emotion are two very different cognitive processes, and they perform very different psychological functions. To reason means to observe reality starting with the material provided by the senses, to integrate, without contradiction, sensory material into concepts and concepts into principles. Reason is the means of gaining and validating one's knowledge. It is a volitional process guided by the conscious mind.

In contrast, emotions entail an automatic process based on subconsciously held knowledge and values. Emotions reflect one's stored beliefs about objects, people or situations, and one's subconscious appraisal of them based on one's values. Emotions are the form in which one experiences automatized value judgments (Peikoff, 1991). Every emotion reflects a specific type of value judgment.

For example, fear is the automatic response to the judgment of a physical threat. Anger is the response to the judgment that a wrong has been done to you or valued others. Joy is the result of having achieved some important value. Desire results from appraising some object that one does not possess or some person who one does not yet have a relationship with as a positive value.

Because emotions are automatic and based on subconsciously stored beliefs and values, they cannot be assumed to be valid assessments of reality. One's beliefs might be wrong; one's values might be irrational. Emotions—automatic productions of the subconscious mind—are not tools of knowledge. The psychological function of emotions is not to know the world but to make automatic evaluations and motivate action. Emotions contain, as part of the experience, felt action tendencies. Positive emotions entail the felt tendency to approach, possess, or retain the appraised object; negative emotions entail the felt tendency to flee, harm, or destroy the appraised object. This does not mean, however, that emotions have to be acted on. Through the power of reason we can decide whether action in a given case is appropriate or not and, if appropriate, what action is most suitable given the total situation.

One cannot, therefore, 'reason with emotion'; one can only reason about it. It is through reason that one identifies what emotion one is experiencing, discovers the beliefs and values that gave rise to it, and decides what action, if any, to take on the face of it. It is also through reason, which, as noted earlier, is an active, volitional process, that one determines whether the beliefs behind an emotion are valid and if the values that underlie it are rational. Reason also enables one to reprogram the subconscious so that the automatized appraisals (beliefs, values) that give rise to specific emotions are changed. Further, reason is used to identify defense mechanisms which may distort or prevent one from experiencing emotions, and thus stultify their motivating power.

Reason is also the key to self-regulation, not only of one's emotions in the sense described above, but also of one's life in general. Regulating one's life requires being purposeful, which means setting long-range goals and identifying plans which will enable one to achieve them. This process is not divorced from emotions, since one has to identify what one wants (e.g., in one's career, in romance) before setting a goal to pursue it, but reason must be used to identify one's desires and ensure that they are rational if one is to achieve one's long-range goals. In short, reason, the volitional, active part of one's mind, has to be in charge or one is left at the mercy of the emotions of the moment.

Some EI advocates might agree with all this and argue that EI, despite the definitions usually given, *really* means being intelligent *about* emotions, that is, recognizing their nature and proper function, their relationship to reason, and the need for introspection. If this is what EI advocates mean by their concept, then what they are actually referring to is not another form or type of intelligence but *intelligence (the ability to grasp abstractions) applied to a particular life domain*: emotions. Intelligence, of course, can be applied to any of thousands of life domains, but it does not follow that there are thousands of types of intelligences. If we want to talk about how well a person has *mastered* a certain domain, we already have a word for it: skill.

There is one more aspect to the EI story. In a later book, *Primal Leadership*, Goleman, Boyatzis, and McKee (2002) take EI theory a step further, into the realm of leadership. Effective leadership traits which they claim to be based on EI include:

- Objective self-assessment
- Self-confidence and self-esteem
- Moral character (e.g., honesty and integrity)
- Adaptability and flexibility
- Achievement motivation
- Initiative and self-efficacy
- Organizational awareness (e.g., of organizational politics)
- Customer service
- The use of persuasion tactics
- Developing the ability of followers
- Initiating change
- Conflict management
- Team building
- The use of humor

Goleman et al. (2002) also argue that EI includes the use [of] any or all of the six following leadership styles:

- Visionary
- Coaching
- Affiliative
- Democratic
- Pacesetting
- Commanding

The question one must ask here is, given that leadership based on EI allegedly encompasses such a long list of characteristics that people have associated with effective leadership, what does EI *not* include? One thing is missing from the list: actual intelligence!

In addition to making the concept of EI–leadership preposterously all-encompassing, Goleman et al. (2002, p. ix) seriously misconstrue what organizational leadership involves. They claim that 'The fundamental task of leaders is to create good feelings in those they lead'. This is simply not true. The function of organizations is to attain goals; in the case of private organizations the goal is long-term profitability. Organizations, other than psychotherapy clinics, are not in the 'feel-good' business. Employee morale is important, but as a means to an end not as an end in itself divorced from effectiveness.

It is ironic that Goleman et al's EI approach to leadership, despite its long list of elements, omits any discussion of the *intellectual* aspects of leadership—aspects which are

critical to organizational success, including business success. These aspects require the leaders of profit-making organizations to focus not inwards but outwards, at the business environment. For example, does the leader know or understand:

- Where the company should be heading?
- The role of the different corporate functions?
- The big picture? (Is there an integrating vision?)
- How to fit the different parts and processes of the organization together?
- The strategic and technological environments?
- How to attain a competitive advantage?
- How to achieve cash flow?
- How to prioritize?
- How to balance the short term with the long term?
- How to judge talent when hiring and promoting?
- How to build a culture?
- How to formulate and enforce core values?

Note that performing these very complex tasks requires, among other qualities, *actual* intelligence. Making oneself or other people feel good will not substitute for intellectual deficiencies. Good leadership requires consistent rational thinking by a mind that is able to grasp and integrate all the facts needed to make the business succeed.

Michael Dell (1999, p. 206) makes an important observation regarding the relation of emotions and knowledge:

> there are countless successful companies that are thriving now despite the fact that they started with little more than passion and a good idea. There are also many that failed, for the very same reason. The difference is that the thriving companies gathered the knowledge that gave them a substantial edge over their competition, which they used to improve their execution . . . those that didn't simply didn't make it.

Leadership is not primarily about making people feel good; it's about knowing what you are doing and knowing what to do.

Conclusion

Despite the insuperable problems with the various definitions of EI, there is no denying the importance of one element of EI in human life: introspection. Introspection is a very important human skill; it involves identifying the contents and processes of one's own mind. It is only through introspection that one can monitor such things as one's degree of focus, one's defensive reactions, and one's emotional responses and their causes. Such monitoring has important implications for self-esteem and mental health. Given their emphasis on introspection, it is ironic that advocates of EI show virtually no understanding of the actual nature of emotions. For example, while granting that emotions entail impulses to action, Goleman's (1995) discussion of their causes is confined almost entirely to neurophysiology, especially brain structure. But psychology cannot be reduced to neurophysiology (Bandura, 1997); ideas do not have the same attributes as neurons. Especially unfortunate—and mistaken (see Peikoff, 1991)—is his claim that, like a Frankenstein monster, we have an innate mind–body dichotomy, two clashing brains, one rational and one emotional. This is reminiscent of Freud's arbitrary division of the personality into opposing parts (id, ego and superego)—a notion which originated with Plato.

What is the error here? If EI advocates actually used introspection themselves, they would observe that emotions, as noted earlier, are the product of subconscious ideas—stored knowledge about the objects and automatic value appraisals based on that knowledge. Thus there is no inherent clash between reason and emotion (Peikoff, 1991). As noted, it is through reason that we are able to acquire the knowledge and the values which cause our emotions. It is through reason that we can identify and, through reprogramming, change our emotions. It is through reason that we have the power to decide whether and how to act in the face of emotions. Emotions obviously have a neurophysiological aspect, but brain structure does not determine the content of our knowledge nor of our values. Nor does it determine whether and how we use our reason, since reasoning is a volitional process (Binswanger, 1991).

EI's extension into the field of leadership is even more unfortunate. By asserting that leadership is an emotional process, Goleman denigrates the very critical role played by rational thinking and actual intelligence in the leadership process. Given all the add-ons to the concept proposed by Goleman et al. (2002), any associations between leadership effectives and an EI scale that included these add-ons would be meaningless.

What, then, are we to conclude about EI?

1. The definition of the concept is constantly changing.
2. Most definitions are so all-inclusive as to make the concept unintelligible.
3. One definition (e.g., reasoning with emotion) involves a contradiction.
4. There is no such thing as actual emotional intelligence, although intelligence can be applied to emotions as well as to other life domains.

A more productive approach to the EI concept might be to replace it with the concept of introspective skill. (This would be a prerequisite to emotional self-regulation.) Alternatively, it might be asked whether EI could be relabeled and redefined as a personality trait—possibly, provided it was (re)defined intelligibly and that it was differentiated from skills and from traits that have already been identified (e.g., empathy). However, it is not at all clear at this point what such a trait would be called.

Ayn Rand (1975, p. 77) stated that 'Definitions are the guardians of rationality, the first line of defense against the chaos of mental disintegration.' With respect to the concept of EI, not to mention many other concept[s] in psychology and management (Locke, 2003), we are more in need of rational guardians tha[n] ever.

EDWIN A. LOCKE is Dean's Professor of Leadership and Motivation (Emeritus) at the R. H. Smith School of Business at the University of Maryland, College Park. He received his BA from Harvard in 1960 and his PhD in industrial psychology from Cornell University in 1964. He has published more than 240 chapters, notes, and articles in professional journals. Dr. Locke has been elected a fellow of the American Psychological Association, of the American Psychological Society, and of the Academy of Management. He is interested in the application of the philosophy of objectivism to the behavioral sciences.

EXPLORING THE ISSUE

Is Emotional Intelligence Valid?

Critical Thinking and Reflection

1. Consider Locke's statement that the ultimate motive for advocates of multiple intelligence is egalitarianism. If EI is accepted as intelligence, what real-life changes might take place toward egalitarianism?
2. What is the difference between personality and emotional intelligence? How would you devise tests to measure one while excluding the other?
3. Consider people you know who seem to handle social situations well. Do they differ from others in ability, or is it simply a difference in personality? If ability, does it correlate positively with other abilities? Support your answers.
4. How might the motives of each of these authors be considered political?
5. What social benefits, if any, might result from restricting the scientific definition to the traditional model of a single type of intelligence?

Create Central

www.mhhe.com/createcentral

Additional Resources

Fiori, M., and Antonakis, J. (2011). The ability model of emotional intelligence: Searching for valid measures. *Personality and Individual Differences, 50* (3), 329--334.

Salovey P and Grewal D (2005) The science of emotional intelligence. *Current Directions in Psychological Science, 14*(6).

Internet References . . .

About.com

http://psychology.about.com/od /personalitydevelopment/a/emotionalintell.htm

Emotional Intelligence Information

www.unh.edu/emotional_intelligence/

Unit 5

UNIT

Mental Health Issues

A mental disorder is often defined as a pattern of thinking or behavior that is either disruptive to others or harmful to the person with the disorder. This definition seems straightforward, yet there is considerable debate about whether some disorders truly exist. For example, does a child's disruptive behavior and short attention span unquestionably warrant that he or she be diagnosed with attention-deficit hyperactive disorder (ADHD)? When does "curiosity" and "fidgetiness" become pathological and warrant medication? When, also, are life events, such as elective abortions, considered sufficiently traumatic that they can cause mental health issues, such as posttraumatic stress disorder?

Selected, Edited and with Issue Framing Material by:
Brent Slife, *Brigham Young University*

ISSUE

Does an Elective Abortion Lead to Negative Psychological Effects?

YES: **Priscilla K. Coleman, Catherine T. Coyle, Martha Shuping, and Vincent M. Rue,** from "Induced Abortion and Anxiety, Mood, and Substance Abuse Disorders: Isolating the Effects of Abortion in the National Comorbidity Survey," *Journal of Psychiatric Research* (May 2009)

NO: **Julia Renee Steinberg and Nancy F. Russo,** from "Abortion and Anxiety: What's the Relationship," *Social Science & Medicine* (July 2008)

Learning Outcomes
After reading this issue, you should be able to:
• Discuss the factors that influence the likelihood of developing negative psychological effects following an abortion.

ISSUE SUMMARY

YES: Associate Professor Priscilla K. Coleman and colleagues argue that the evidence suggests that abortion is causal to psychological problems.

NO: Researchers Julia R. Steinberg and Nancy F. Russo counter that other factors, common to women who abort, are responsible for later psychological problems.

The practice of abortion is one of the most widely debated issues in the public sphere. Mere discussion has not seemed to resolve the problems. Would objective studies from psychology help to address the contentious issues surrounding the abortion debate? A recent (2008) task force from the American Psychological Association was especially commissioned to help answer this question. The task force produced a detailed, 91-page report summarizing the psychological literature on the subject.

As this report clarifies, the area of abortion that psychologists have primarily studied is the potential for negative emotional and mental effects on women who terminate their pregnancy. If women who abort are more likely to experience depression and anxiety later in life, as several national surveys appear to indicate, does it necessarily follow that abortion is the *cause* of these psychological problems, or could other factors influence both the likelihood of abortion and negative mental health? Prominent researchers have argued both approaches.

In the first article, authors Coleman, Coyle, Shuping, and Rue seem to argue that abortion leads directly to important psychological problems. They collected data from a nationally representative study (National Comorbidity Survey). Even after accounting for personal, situational, and demographic variables, they found that abortion was related to an increased risk for mental health problems such as panic attacks, agoraphobia, posttraumatic stress disorder (PTSD), and major depression. These authors also found an increased risk for drug abuse among women who underwent an abortion. They concluded that abortion is implicated in between 4.3 and 16.6 percent of these disorders. In addition, they suggested that abortion negatively impacts more mental health outcomes than many other impactful life events such as rape, abuse, and neglect.

In contrast, Steinberg and Russo performed their own analysis of the national data, including the data from National Comorbidity Survey, and came to quite a different conclusion—that abortion cannot be held responsible for negative psychological consequences. They argue that analyses and conclusions, such as those of Coleman and her coauthors, fail to take into account the specific life histories of the women involved in abortion, such as their experience with violence. Steinberg and Russo also believe that many such studies fail to control for important factors such as number of pregnancies, intentions to get pregnant, and prior abortions. They conclude that most of the apparent connection between abortion and anxiety disorders could be attributed to other factors such as violence in the lives of aborting women.

POINT

- Abortion can be considered a trauma.

- When removing the effect of other factors, abortion has a significant relationship to anxiety disorders.
- There is sufficient evidence to conclude that abortion is at least partially responsible for poor mental health outcomes.
- More research is needed to understand the particular ways in which abortion contributes to anxiety.

COUNTERPOINT

- Abortion is often confounded with other life events associated with trauma.
- When removing the effect of other factors, abortion does not have a significant relationship to anxiety disorders.
- There is not sufficient evidence to conclude that abortions rather than life events are responsible for negative outcomes.
- More research is needed to understand how factors other than abortion are responsible for increased anxiety.

YES ↵

Priscilla K. Coleman et al.

Induced Abortion and Anxiety, Mood, and Substance Abuse Disorders: Isolating the Effects of Abortion in the National Comorbidity Survey

1. Introduction

Does induced abortion carry the potential to adversely affect the psychological well-being of women? This seemingly straightforward question is complicated by a number of characteristics inherent in the variables of interest as well as external factors surrounding investigative efforts. Diverse personal, relational, situational, and cultural forces converge in every woman's decision to abort and adjustment afterwards is likewise embedded in a multifaceted context rendering it difficult to tease out effects of the procedure. The private, sensitive, and frequently distressing nature of the abortion experience also introduces challenges to data collection with many women declining to participate or dropping out mid-study resulting in potentially skewed results. Finally, as a topic of academic study with bearing on a divisive social issue that engenders strong emotion, the socio-political views of researchers, reviewers, and journal editors may compromise objectivity in data collection, analysis, interpretation, and publication.

Despite these obstacles, the international literature pertaining to abortion as a predictor of adverse mental health outcomes has grown considerably in the past several decades and the rigor of the published studies has increased. Bradshaw and Slade, authors of an extensive review of published studies on abortion and emotional experiences, concluded "There has been increasing understanding of abortion as a potential trauma" (p. 929) and "The quality of studies has improved, although there are still some methodological weaknesses" (p. 929). In a review by Thorp et al. employing strict inclusion criteria related to sample size and length of time before follow-up, the researchers concluded that induced abortion increased the risk for "mood disorders substantial enough to provoke attempts of self-harm" (p. 67).

Employment of national data sets with reproductive history and mental health variables collected for broad investigative purposes greatly minimizes the potential for bias in data collection and low consent-to-participate rates which might otherwise compromise research on abortion. Large government funded data collection efforts have the benefit of employing professionally trained researchers or clinicians who are blind to the hypotheses of potential studies generated from the data. Further, the integrity and utility of data are maximized when trained professionals interview respondents to determine if they have experienced the symptoms of various disorders. Large-scale, national data sets also typically contain numerous personal and family history background variables that can be conveniently used as control variables.

Unfortunately the number of studies employing large representative samples with controls for third variables likely to be related to both the choice to abort and to the development of mental health problems remains rather small or non-existent for some disorders. Nevertheless, there are studies with nationally representative samples and a variety of controls for extraneous variables indicating an induced abortion puts women at risk for depression. Only one of these studies incorporated a comprehensive measure of mental health problems, leading to insight regarding the likelihood that women who have an abortion will develop an actual diagnosable psychological disorder.

There are a few studies employing national samples that have failed to detect significant associations between abortion and subsequent mental health. However, in the Gilchrist et al. study, very few controls were applied for confounding third variables. As a result, the comparison groups may very well have differed systematically with regard to income, relationship quality including exposure to domestic violence, social support, and other potentially critical factors. The attrition rate in this study was very high and there were additional methodological shortcomings. In the Schmiege and Russo study central analyses lacked controls for variables identified as significant predictors of abortion (higher education, income, and smaller family size). Without the controls, the delivery group, which was associated with lower education and income and larger families, had more depression variance erroneously attributed to pregnancy resolution.

In a recently published qualitative paper by Goodwin and Ogden, the authors concluded that "women's responses to their abortion do not always follow the suggested reactions of grief, but are varied and located

Coleman, Priscilla K., et al. From *Journal of Psychiatric Research*, vol. 43, issue 8, May 2009, pp. 770–773, 775–776 (refs. omitted). Copyright © 2009 by Elsevier Inc. Reprinted by permission via Rightslink.

within the personal and social context" (p. 231). This reality underscores the necessity of employing sufficient controls for confounding variables. All the large-scale studies described above controlled for an assortment of basic demographic variables including age, marital status, social support, number of children, and education. Many of these studies also included control variables indicative of pre-abortion mental health. However, a handful of very recent studies have gone a step beyond and included experiential variables that may be related to the choice to abort and to mental health outcomes. Among the variables in this latter category are relationship problems and childhood or adult history of physical and/or sexual abuse.

There is ample evidence indicating adverse interpersonal experiences, particularly abuse of various forms, predisposes individuals to emotional problems and mental illness. Women who experience intimate partner violence are also more likely to abort compared to women who were not victimized, necessitating the advent of controls for these personal history variables in studies of abortion and mental health.

No existing studies of abortion and mental health have included all the above categories of potential third variables in addition to incorporating variables suggestive of other sources of significant stress in women's lives. One obvious factor that should be controlled is history of miscarriage or stillbirth as non-voluntary forms of perinatal loss have been linked with mental health problems including anxiety and depression. Miscarriages are common, with estimates ranging from 25% to 43% of women experiencing at least one in their lifetime, underscoring the need to collect data on involuntary perinatal loss and control for it in research on the mental health effects of abortion. Serious accidents or life threatening illnesses, chronic health problems, heavy familial demands, and difficulty paying bills are relatively common stressors that should be controlled as well. Social support is another variable that may differ systematically based on abortion choice and/or mental health status and there is research indicating that women who have a strong support system are less likely to be harmed by an abortion.

The purpose of the current study was to explore associations between abortion history and a wide range of anxiety (panic disorder, panic attacks, PTSD, agoraphobia), mood (bipolar disorder, mania, major depression), and substance abuse disorders (alcohol and drug abuse and dependence) using a nationally representative sample. In line with current research trends, the present study incorporates controls for 22 personal history and sociodemographic characteristics. Data from the national comorbidity survey were selected because the data base provides the most comprehensive epidemiological data on the prevalence of psychological disorders in the US. Given that most of the previously reviewed large-scale studies employing a variety of controls have detected an independent contribution of abortion to a variety of mental health concerns, abortion was hypothesized to

have a similar effect with the present survey data, which employed more comprehensive assessments and a more expansive list of controls.

A few of the diagnoses examined herein have not been actively explored in the previous literature on abortion and mental health and inclusion will expand the range of outcomes that have been investigated. Although only one study has identified an association between abortion history and bipolar disorder an extensive literature review conducted by Alloy et al. revealed that individuals with bipolar disorder often experience an increase in stressful events before the onset and recurrences of mood episodes. Similarly no studies to date have examined a potential link between abortion and panic attacks or panic disorder, yet panic disorder is twice as common in women compared to men and research indicates a history of psychosocial stressors including trauma in many who experience panic episodes.

Most of the diagnoses examined in this report have been identified as significant correlates of abortion; however, the effects have not been isolated effectively due to insufficient controls for third variables. In the context of surveying and controlling for potential third variables, this study has the added benefit of providing useful data regarding the magnitude of a large number of individual and situational predictors of several different mental disorders. Oftentimes when the available evidence pertaining to abortion and mental health is debated, there is an assumption that the correlational evidence could likely be explained away by uncontrolled third variables. For example, some may argue it is not the abortion per se, but exposure to intimate partner violence that is behind both the abortion choice and ensuing mental health struggles. Quantification of these risks should bring some clarity to the debate.

2. Method

2.1. Data Source

The national comorbidity survey (NCS) is widely recognized as the first nationally representative survey of mental health in the United States. The general purpose of the NCS was to study the prevalence and correlates of DSM III-R disorders and service utilization trends for these disorders. The structured psychiatric interviews were administered by the Survey Research Center at the University of Michigan (UM), Ann Arbor, between September 14, 1990 and February 6, 1992.

2.2. Participants

The NCS employed a stratified, multi-stage area probability sample of individuals between the ages of 15 and 54 years who represented the non-institutionalized civilian population in the 48 coterminous United States. A response rate of 82.6% was achieved with a total of 8098 respondents participating in the survey. The NCS data relevant to this study include the following: a Diagnostic Interview administered to the entire study sample ($n = 8098$) and a Risk Assessment Interview administered to a subsample ($n = 5877$). Several of the study variables including abortion history and other potential risk factors for the various disorders were only assessed in the subsample. The current sample was therefore confined to the subsample and included all women for whom there were data available on all variables of interest: 399 women who had either one (77%) or more (23%) abortions and 2650 women who did not report an abortion. The average age for the first abortion was 21.8 (SD = 5.49) years with first abortion age spanning 14–37 years.

2.3. Procedure

The NCS employed 158 interviewers with an average of 5 years of prior experience interviewing at the Survey Research Center. Diagnoses were based on a modified version of the Composite International Diagnostic Interview (the UM-CIDI), developed at the University of Michigan and based on the diagnostic criteria of the DSM-III-R. The NCS interviewers went through an intensive training program in the use of the UM-CIDI.

In addition to interview responses, a series of indicator variables for psychiatric diagnoses were created by the staff. These are referred to as "DXDM variables" and were employed as the dependent variables in the current study. Some of these variables were created from items in the Diagnostic interview while others were created from items in the Risk Assessment Interview. The psychiatric illnesses were assessed as "present" or "absent" at the time of data collection providing assurance that in most cases, the abortion preceded the diagnosis.

Abortion history served as the independent variable in the current study. Twenty two different demographic, history, and personal/situational variables operated as control variables in the logistic regression analyses performed to assess independent contributions of abortion history to mental disorders from those most frequently linked to abortion in previous research (anxiety, mood, and substance abuse). The choice of control variables was driven by the literature reviewed previously indicating factors likely to predict the choice to abort and/or mental health problems.

Deriving accurate results from the NCS requires application of correct sample weights. In this study, necessary weighting was conducted as advised by the NCS authors in order to achieve nationally representative results.

3. Results

... Significance tests (chi-square for dichotomous variables and t-tests for continuous dependent variables) revealed differences between women with and without abortion experience relative to marital status, race, number of residents in the respondent's household, employment status, educational attainment, feelings of being worthy/equal to others, history of miscarriage/stillbirth, rape, having been sexually molested in childhood, physically attacked in adulthood, and having experienced a life threatening accident. No differences were observed between the two groups relative to the degree to which the respondent relies on relatives for problems, the frequency with which relatives make demands on the respondent, number of children, having been physically abused as a child, another terrible experience, difficulty paying bills, and health problems.

... For every disorder, the abortion group had a higher frequency that was statistically significant. The disorders with the highest frequencies across both groups were alcohol abuse and drug abuse "with or without dependence" and major depression. Lower frequencies were obtained for bipolar disorder and mania.

... A series of 15 logistic regression analyses with one mental health outcome operating as the criterion variable in each model were conducted. In each analysis the 22 control variables ... were entered into the equation. What is reported ... for every mental health diagnosis is the strength of each significant predictor after the effects of all other predictors were removed. For the induced abortion variable both adjusted and unadjusted effects are provided. For 12 out of 15 of the mental health outcomes examined, abortion made a significant contribution independent of all control variables. For the anxiety disorders, which included panic disorder, panic attacks, PTSD, agoraphobia with or without panic disorder, agoraphobia without panic disorder, a history of abortion when compared to no history was associated with [a] 111%, 44%, 59%, 95%, and a 93% increased risk, respectively. With regard to substance abuse disorders, an induced abortion was associated with a 120%, 145%, 79%, 126% increased risk for alcohol abuse with or without dependence, alcohol dependence, drug abuse with or without dependence, and drug dependence, respectively. Finally, for the mood disorders, the experience of an abortion increased risk of developing bipolar disorder by 167%, major depression without hierarchy by 45% and major depression with hierarchy by 48%. The term "hierarchy" was applied to indicate that the condition was not better accounted for by another disorder.

The abortion variable made a significant independent contribution to more mental health outcomes than a history of rape, sexual abuse in childhood, physical assault in adulthood, physical abuse in childhood, and neglect which contributed to between four and ten different diagnoses. Other variables that made significant contributions to several disorders included age, the respondent's family making frequent demands, health problems, experiencing a life threatening accident, race, lower income, feeling less worthy than others, religion, difficulty paying bills, employment, number of children with the majority of effects showing fewer children was a risk factor, more people in the household, miscarriage/stillbirth, experiencing other terrible life events, marital status, and education. The tendency to feel as though one could not rely on family for problems was only associated with one outcome. . . .

Population attributable risk (PAR) percentages were calculated for each mental health problem. In order to calculate PAR when employing a retrospective design, population exposure must be estimated and odds ratios employed. The adjusted odds ratios . . . which reflect controls for the 22 potential third variables were used. . . . Abortion accounted for between 4.3% and 16.6% of the incidence of the various disorders in the population for which the procedure made an independent contribution.

4. Discussion

The results of this study revealed that women who have aborted are at a higher risk for a variety of mental health problems including anxiety (panic attacks, panic disorder, agoraphobia, PTSD), mood (bipolar disorder, major depression with and without hierarchy), and substance abuse disorders when compared to women without a history of abortion after controls were instituted for a wide range of personal, situational, and demographic factors. As noted above there were a number of demographic and personal history variables that differed systematically between women who had aborted and those who had not. In general, women with an abortion history were more likely to be older, more highly educated, black, separated, divorced, or widowed, live in smaller households, to have been working, to have reported a personal history of more sexual trauma in childhood and adulthood, and they identified more unusually stressful events in adulthood (miscarriage, having been physically attacked, and life threatening accident). Controlling for these variables is an essential design feature of studies pertaining to the mental health correlates of voluntary termination. Consider for example, one of these factors, history of miscarriage/ stillbirth. In this study the abortion group when compared to the no abortion group was considerably more likely to have experienced a non-voluntary loss (31% versus 18.7%) and very few previous studies have included this control. The effects of miscarriage/stillbirth are well documented with approximately 25% likely to suffer from persistent, serious psychological problems. With the variance associated with miscarriages/stillbirths and the number of children statistically removed, the groups in the present study were effectively equated relative to reproductive history. Interestingly non-voluntary losses only had an independent effect on 4 of the 15 psychiatric illnesses examined (drug abuse with or without dependence, drug dependence, mania, and depression without hierarchy).

What is most notable in this study is that abortion contributed significant independent effects to numerous mental health problems above and beyond a variety of other traumatizing and stressful life experiences. The strongest effects based on the attributable risks indicated that abortion is responsible for more than 10% of the population incidence of alcohol dependence, alcohol abuse,

drug dependence, panic disorder, agoraphobia, and bipolar disorder in the population. Lower percentages were identified for 6 additional diagnoses.

Of the 15 disorders examined the only diagnoses not significantly associated with abortion after removing the effects of confounding variables were alcohol and drug abuse without dependence and mania. The mania diagnosis had fewer than 15 cases in each group, far too few to have confidence in the results. A lack of effects for alcohol or drug abuse without dependence is not surprising in that people periodically abuse substances for widely varying reasons including boredom, rebelliousness, curiosity, recreation, etc. without dependency and substance dependence is more likely to be related to emotional difficulties.

The linkages between abortion and substance abuse/ dependence, major depression, bipolar disorder, and PTSD add to the existing body of literature. However, no previous studies have identified links between abortion and panic disorder, panic attacks, and agoraphobia. Some studies have identified biochemical similarities between PTSD and panic disorder, indirectly suggesting related processes may be involved in the associations between abortion and PTSD and between abortion and other anxiety disorders. Taylor and Arnow found that in adults the onset of most panic disorders begins with a spontaneous panic attack within six months of [a] major stressful event. If women experience the abortion as a trauma, the event may trigger a psychological and/or physiological process that culminates in an anxiety disorder. More research is needed to understand the precise process mechanisms linking abortion with various anxiety disorders. Both the abortion and no abortion groups had higher than average rates of trauma of various forms and this may explain the relatively high proportion of women who met criteria for PTSD and other diagnoses.

There are several limitations of this research. Due to data constraints the subsample reported here included only 37.6% of the full NCS. Further, the NCS data do not include a variable related to pregnancy intendedness/ wantedness, therefore it was not possible to compare women who aborted to women who carried an unintended/unwanted pregnancy to term. Although on the surface this may seem like an ideal control group to employ when examining the mental health effects of abortion, the utility of the intendedness and wantedness variables becomes nebulous when examined more closely. According to Finer and Henshaw, "women's pregnancy intentions cannot always be accurately ascertained or neatly dichotomized" (p. 95). Santelli et al. also concluded: "traditional measures of pregnancy intentions did not readily predict a woman's choice to continue or abort the pregnancy" (p. 2009). Pregnancies that are aborted may have been initially intended by one or both partners and pregnancies that are initially unintended may become wanted as the pregnancy progresses. Moreover, after controlling for maternal age, education, marital status, number of people residing with the respondent, trimester in which prenatal care was sought, number of prior births, and all forms of reproductive loss, Coleman et al. found that experiencing an unwanted pregnancy was not related to excessive drug or alcohol consumption. Similarly, Joyce et al. reported that associations between pregnancy wantedness and negative maternal behaviors like substance abuse tend to be minimal after controlling for a comprehensive set of socio-demographic variables.

Most women are likely to experience a variety of reproductive events encompassing multiple pregnancies that continue or are terminated voluntarily or involuntarily with each characterized by distinct levels of intendedness over the course of their lives. Statistically controlling for all reproductive events may be the optimal method given the complex reproductive histories of most women. Controlling only for the intendedness of one pregnancy that is the focus of a study provides no assurance that the proportion of women in the abortion vs. delivery group is equivalent in terms of the intendedness and/or resolution of past or subsequent pregnancies. Future research might however address the mental health trajectories of women with varying combinations of wanted and unwanted pregnancies continued and terminated over an extended period of time. In this way, assessing both positive and negative aspects of a pregnancy in a woman's life might also provide improved understanding of these complex interrelationships.

The problem of women concealing a past abortion which plagues most studies on this topic was also potentially operative here. Additional limitations, the most important of which is probably recall error, are also obviously associated with retrospective data collection. Further, the results provided did not identify the percentage of women with an abortion history who may have suffered from more than one diagnosis. The data pertaining to the number of women who experience post-abortion mental health problems may be somewhat inflated by the failure to account for multiple diagnoses in one individual.

The strengths of this study included the use of a reasonably large nationally representative sample, quantification of risks, professional data collection, well-developed measures of numerous mental disorders examined as correlates of abortion history, and employment of a broad set of control variables. Research with these methodological

features is essential to the process of clarifying the mental health risks unique to abortion.

Future research is needed to shed light on mediating mechanisms linking abortion to various disorders and to decipher the characteristics of women most prone to developing a particular mental health problem. For example, women who have considered their options thoroughly yet remained ambivalent about an abortion based on personal beliefs and/or moral or religious proscriptions may become particularly prone to anxiety or depression when social support is lacking. Or alternatively, women who go through an abortion without much thought or difficulty initially may later find themselves battling a substance abuse problem as a way of numbing thoughts or feelings that emerge in the months or years following an abortion.

The topic of abortion and mental health has been vastly understudied and the progress of research in this area was stalled for a number of years as the literature contained a great deal of conflicting data regarding the basic question of whether or not abortion increases risk for mental health problems. The academic debate was fueled by socio-political agendas that impeded and at times contaminated scientific efforts. Recent years have however ushered in large scale, methodologically sophisticated studies, some of which were reviewed in the introduction segment of this article. These studies have now clearly established an increased risk for a variety of mental health problems in conjunction with abortion. To fully understand the documented risks and move toward developing professional therapy protocols for addressing mental health needs prior to, during, and in the years following an abortion, research efforts need to move beyond dated battles and become devoted to achieving a more substantive understanding of the meaning of abortion in women's lives.

PRISCILLA K. COLEMAN is an associate professor in the School of Family and Consumer Sciences at Bowling Green State University. Dr. Coleman's research interests include the development, expression, and effects of individual differences in parenting, socioemotional development in early childhood, and postabortion emotional sequelae.

Julia Renee Steinberg and Nancy F. Russo  **NO**

Abortion and Anxiety:
What's the Relationship?

Abortion is a common life circumstance for women, with an estimated 1 in 5 women experiencing at least 1 abortion in their lifetime. Recently, concerns have been raised about the impact of having an abortion on women's risk for anxiety as well as other mental health outcomes. A number of researchers have reported an association between pregnancy outcome and anxiety.

Compared to men, women have higher rates of anxiety. Given that an estimated 43% of females will experience at least one anxiety disorder in their lifetime, it is not surprising that some women who have had an abortion also report having anxiety symptoms. The questions addressed here are do women who have abortions have higher rates of anxiety than other women, and if so, how might this abortion–anxiety relationship be understood?

Answering these questions is difficult because abortion is confounded with many life events that have been associated with negative mental health outcomes, in particular unintended pregnancy. An estimated 92% of the pregnancies ending in abortion are unintended, compared to 31% of all births. Differences between women who have an abortion and other groups of women must be interpreted in light of this fact. One way to address the association of pregnancy outcome and pregnancy intention is to examine pregnancy outcome among groups of women who have had unintended pregnancies. Another is to control for experiences that are associated with anxiety and with unintended pregnancy or abortion. In this article we use both strategies and present two studies that examine the relationship of abortion to anxiety symptoms and disorders. Our goal is to ascertain whether the relationship of abortion to anxiety can be explained by pre-existing anxiety, violence exposure, and other relevant covariates.

Abortion and Anxiety

Several studies have examined the relationship between abortion and anxiety in samples of patients as well as non-patients. Although some women do experience post-abortion anxiety, the prevalence of post-abortion anxiety is low, and generally lower than that found pre-abortion. For instance, Lowenstein et al. found that women's anxiety significantly declined after having an abortion. In a review of the post-1990 literature on abortion and mental health, Bradshaw and Slade concluded that most studies found a decrease in anxiety or distress after having an abortion. More recently, however, two studies have been used as evidence that abortion increases risk for subsequent anxiety. . . .

Several factors limit the conclusions of the Fergusson et al. study, however. First, it did not have an appropriate comparison group of women who delivered an unintended pregnancy. Second, small numbers precluded conducting prospective analyses specifically on anxiety or separating out the 21.6% of the sample who reported having multiple abortions. Third, the data were not broken out by specific disorder. Unfortunately the pathways from abortion to anxiety disorder may differ depending on the disorder, and the definition of anxiety disorder used in the study encompassed generalized anxiety disorder, social anxiety disorder, specific phobia, panic disorder, and agoraphobia. Finally, New Zealand's legal requirements use mental health grounds for screening women who have abortions. These laws require that women must first be referred to two certifying specialist consultants who must agree that (1) the pregnancy would seriously harm the life, physical or mental health of the woman or baby; or (2) the pregnancy is the result of incest; or (3) the woman is severely mentally handicapped. An abortion will also be considered on the basis of age, or when the pregnancy is the result of rape. Given that mentally healthy women are less able to obtain abortions in this legal context, it is not surprising to find higher rates of mental disorders in the abortion group. Thus, the Fergusson et al. study does not provide strong evidence for an abortion–anxiety relationship.

Violence, Unintended Pregnancy, and Anxiety

A substantial body of research has established that the rates of violence in the lives of women who have unintended pregnancies—whether or not those pregnancies end in abortion—are higher than rates for other women.

For instance, of 39,348 women in 14 states, Goodwin et al. found that among mothers of newborns, women with unintended pregnancies were 2.5 times more likely to experience physical abuse compared to women whose pregnancies were intended. Additionally, in a meta-analysis of the relation of intimate partner violence and sexual health, Coker found that intimate partner violence was associated with unwanted pregnancy in 3 of 4 studies. Intimate partner violence was associated with abortion in 6 of 8 studies that addressed this association. Two studies also noted an association between abortion and both physical and sexual abuse. Finally, in a multi-national population-based study of 10 countries, Garcia-Moreno, Jansen, Ellsberg, Heise, and Watts found that in 8 of the countries, compared to women who had not experienced violence, women who had experienced some violence in their lives were more likely to have had an abortion. Hence, research consistently finds a relationship of violence with unintended pregnancy, whether terminating in delivery or abortion.

There is also empirical research to support the relation of violence and anxiety. First, violence is a known cause of post-traumatic stress disorder. Second, studies show that both childhood sexual and physical abuse are associated with anxiety disorders such as post-traumatic stress disorder (PTSD) or generalized anxiety disorder. Given violence is strongly and consistently related to both abortion and anxiety, controlling for violence when investigating the relationship of abortion and anxiety is warranted. . . .

In summary, previous research suggests an association between abortion and anxiety, but assessment of anxiety symptoms vs. a specific diagnosis (GAD, social anxiety, PTSD) is lacking. We hypothesize that the relation of anxiety symptoms or disorders and abortion can be explained by pre-pregnancy anxiety and the higher rates of violence in the lives of women who have abortions.

The Case of Multiple Abortions

Most sexually active women are at risk for having an unintended pregnancy, with the risk for more than one such pregnancies increasing over her lifetime. However, researchers have found that the more severe the adversity in childhood, the greater the likelihood of unintended pregnancy. Further, there is evidence that a history of childhood physical or sexual abuse is associated with repeat abortion, which is an indicator of repeated unintended pregnancy. Thus, we hypothesize that the experience of repeat abortions is related to higher rates of violence in women's lives, which in turn puts a woman at greater risk for anxiety. . . .

Study 1: The National Survey of Family Growth (NSFG)
. . .

Results

Do women who terminate a first pregnancy have significantly higher rates of experiencing anxiety symptoms (EAS) compared to women who deliver a first pregnancy?

The answer is yes. . . . The results from logistic regression analyses . . . used first pregnancy outcome to predict subsequent anxiety symptoms among *unintended first pregnancies* and among *all first pregnancies*, respectively, with no covariates controlled. For this model, in both samples pregnancy outcome was significant, with abortion found to be associated with a greater likelihood of having subsequent anxiety symptoms.

To what extent are differences in post-pregnancy rates of anxiety symptoms explained by pre-pregnancy anxiety symptoms, rape experience, and demographic characteristics known to co-vary with anxiety and abortion?

Controlling for pre-pregnancy anxiety symptoms, rape experience, and the other covariates was sufficient to explain the relationship of pregnancy outcome to anxiety symptoms; abortion was no longer found to be associated with increased risk for anxiety symptoms in either sample. . . .

Is there a significant relationship of abortion status (0, 1, or repeat abortion) to rates of anxiety symptoms after first pregnancy?

The answer is a qualified no. . . . [In women with post-pregnancy anxiety symptoms and whoever experienced rape], post-pregnancy anxiety symptoms increased with levels of abortion status, the difference in prevalence of anxiety symptoms between women having repeat (2 or more) abortions and 1 abortion is not statistically significant. Specifically, in this model where no covariates are controlled, logistic regression analyses found that women who reported having repeat abortions were significantly more likely to be identified as having anxiety symptoms than those who reported 0 abortions (*unintended first pregnancies:* $t = 3.48$, $p = 0.001$; *all first pregnancy:* $t = 4.74$, $p < 0.0005$), but not significantly more so than women who reported 1 abortion (*unintended first pregnancies:* $t = 1.40$, $p = 0.16$; *all first pregnancy:* $t = 1.70$, $p = 0.09$). Women who reported experiencing 1 abortion were also significantly more likely to be identified as having anxiety symptoms than those who reported experiencing 0 abortions (*unintended first pregnancies:* $t = 2.58$, $p = 0.01$; *all first pregnancy:* $t = 4.04$, $p < 0.0005$). . . .

Discussion

The finding that women who terminated a first pregnancy had a greater likelihood of subsequent anxiety symptoms than women who delivered a first pregnancy—regardless of intention—is congruent with previous research that has reported an association between abortion and anxiety when relevant variables are not controlled. One contribution of this study is to show that this relation can be accounted for by other factors, particularly pre-pregnancy anxiety and violence. Similar to Major et al.'s findings, for both samples, the strongest predictor of post-pregnancy anxiety was the occurrence of pre-pregnancy anxiety. No relation between abortion on the first pregnancy and anxiety symptoms was found in either NSFG sample when pre-pregnancy anxiety, rape experience, and other relevant covariates were controlled. The significant and independent contributions of pre-pregnancy anxiety symptoms and rape experience to post-pregnancy anxiety symptoms suggest that a more fruitful line of investigation would be to focus on understanding both the pathways of pre-existing conditions and violence exposure to pregnancy outcome among women.

The findings with regard to repeat abortion are problematic due to the lack of information about the timing of the predictor and outcome variables. For women having 1 abortion that occurred on their first pregnancy event, we could assess when anxiety occurred relative to that abortion. However, for women who had abortions after their first pregnancy event, we do not know the timing of those abortions with respect to post-pregnancy anxiety. Consequently, a thorough examination of the relationship of repeat abortion status to anxiety was beyond the scope of this study. Thus, in interpreting our findings with regard to repeat abortions, it must be kept in mind that lack of information about timing of the relevant variables makes speculation about causal inferences particularly inappropriate.

Keeping these caveats in mind, we can say that women who reported having repeat abortions were more likely to experience rape at some time in their lives, as predicted, and were more likely to have higher rates of anxiety symptoms than women who reported 0 abortions, even when covariates were controlled. Similarly, women who experienced 1 vs. 0 abortions were more likely to experience anxiety symptoms, even when controlling for the study variables. However, the fact that the non-significant difference between women who reported repeat abortions compared to women reporting 1 abortion emerged as significant when covariates were controlled suggests that more needs to be known about the women's characteristics to understand what is going on, and that general statements about the relation of "abortion" to mental health are not sufficiently informative to inform clinical practice or public policy. In particular, future research is needed to learn more about how women who have repeat abortions differ in experience from women who report 1 abortion, and how both groups differ from women who report 0 abortion[s].

The ability to identify pregnancy intention in the NSFG provided an opportunity to examine the extent to which pregnancy intention contributes independently to variation in post-pregnancy anxiety symptoms beyond that associated with pre-pregnancy anxiety and pregnancy outcome (abortion vs. delivery). The finding that pregnancy intention continued to make an independent contribution to post-pregnancy anxiety when the other 2 variables were controlled underscores the importance of controlling for pregnancy intention in studies seeking to understand the relation of abortion to mental health. If a study reports a significant correlation between abortion and a mental health outcome such as anxiety, even if

pre-existing mental health factors are carefully controlled, unless pregnancy intention is also controlled the explanation for that correlation is problematic.

In addition to limitations common to retrospective survey research, the major limitations of this particular study include limited assessment of exposure to violence and the inability to define a clinically diagnosed anxiety disorder. Moreover, we determined that among all women, the lifetime prevalence of the variable used to assess generalized anxiety symptoms in the NSFG was more than twice as high (14.8%) as the lifetime prevalence for women in the NCS, a population survey in which a clinical diagnosis of GAD was assessed (6.6%). Thus, it is likely that the anxiety symptoms in the NSFG were reflecting more than generalized anxiety. It may be that effects of pregnancy outcome may emerge for specific clinically diagnosed anxiety disorders. To investigate this possibility, as well as to provide a more thorough examination of the relation of violence exposure to pregnancy outcome, we examined the relation of abortion to selected anxiety disorders using data from the National Comorbidity Survey.

Study 2: The National Comorbidity Survey (NCS)

. . .

Results and Discussion

Do women who terminate a first pregnancy have significantly higher rates of experiencing anxiety disorder, social anxiety, or PTSD compared to women who deliver a first pregnancy?

The answer is no. [In the study,] although the rates of anxiety disorder and social anxiety were higher in the delivery group and the rate of PTSD was higher in the abortion group, these differences were not statistically significant; thus, only the first model is presented.

For the first model we conducted logistic regression analyses with outcome of first pregnancy (abortion vs. delivery) predicting subsequent anxiety disorder, social anxiety, and PTSD, respectively. In contrast to NSFG results, first pregnancy outcome was not related to anxiety disorder, social anxiety, or PTSD. In other words, in the NSFG there was an association between anxiety symptoms and abortion on the first pregnancy that was subsequently explained by the presence of covariates. In the NCS data, however, there was no such association to be explained.

Is there a significant relationship of abortion status (0, 1, or repeat abortion) to rates of each disorder after first pregnancy?

The answer depends on the disorder. . . . For generalized anxiety disorder, the answer is no. There is no relation between first pregnancy outcome and subsequent generalized anxiety disorder. For social anxiety and PTSD, the answer is yes, but the relationships differ for each disorder.

Specifically, in parallel to the approach to the NSFG analyses, a series of logistic regressions were conducted to determine the relationship of abortion status to generalized anxiety disorder, social anxiety, and PTSD. When no covariates were controlled, no relationship of abortion status to generalized anxiety disorder was found, but abortion status was related to rates of social anxiety and PTSD after first pregnancy.... Women who reported repeat (2 or more) abortions had higher rates of social anxiety than those who reported 0 abortions, but the difference was not statistically significant ($p < 0.09$). However, they were significantly more likely to have social anxiety than those who reported 1 abortion ($p = 0.008$). Further, ... women who had repeat abortions were significantly more likely to have PTSD than those who reported 0 abortions, but not 1 abortion. Women who reported 1 abortion did not differ significantly from women who reported 0 abortions with regard to rates of social anxiety or PTSD, respectively (social anxiety: $t = -1.01$, $p = 0.32$; PTSD: $t = 0.70$, $p = 0.49$).

To what extent is the relationship of multiple abortions to anxiety disorder explained by pre-pregnancy anxiety disorder, violence exposure, and demographic characteristics known to co-vary with anxiety and abortion?

Given the limited assessment of violence exposure in the NSFG, we were particularly interested in investigating whether relations found between abortion status and anxiety disorder could be explained with a more thorough assessment of violence exposure. Logistic regression analyses revealed that women who experienced repeat abortion were more likely to be exposed to certain forms of violence than other women.... Compared to women who reported having 0 abortions, women who reported having multiple abortions were significantly more likely to report experiencing rape ($t = 3.765$, $p < 0.01$) or any type of violence ($t = 2.360$, $p < 0.05$), being held captive/ kidnapped/threatened with a weapon ($t = 3.367$, $p < 0.01$), or being physically attacked ($t = 4.539$, $p < 0.0005$). They were more likely to report experiencing molestation, but the difference did not achieve conventional levels of statistical significance ($t = 1.961$, $p = 0.057$). They were equally likely to report experiencing child physical abuse ($t = 0.516$, $p = 0.609$).

Compared to women who had 1 abortion, women who reported having multiple abortions were significantly more likely to report being physically attacked ($t = 2.847$, $p < 0.01$). Although not statistically reliable, they were also more likely to report being held captive/kidnapped/ threatened with a weapon ($t = 1.910$, $p < 0.08$). They were equally likely to report experiencing rape ($t = 1.346$, $p = 0.136$), molestation ($t = 0.349$, $p = 0.729$), child physical abuse ($t = 0.640$, $p = 0.526$), or any type of violence ($t = 0.489$, $p = 0.628$).

Compared to women who reported 0 abortions, women who had 1 abortion were significantly more likely to report experiencing any type of violence ($t = 2.161$, $p = 0.036$)....

Specifically, women who experienced repeated, 1, or 0 abortions were all equally likely be identified as having PTSD ($ts < 0.47$, $ps > 0.63$) and social anxiety ($ts < 1.57$, $ps > 0.12$). However, women who were raped, kidnapped/held captive/threatened with a weapon or physically attacked and those with PTSD before their pregnancy were significantly more likely to have PTSD; and women who had social anxiety before their pregnancy were more likely to have social anxiety afterwards.

Thus, no evidence was found in the NCS data for the claim that abortion on the first pregnancy leads to higher risk for any of the anxiety diagnoses studied, even though it was not possible to control for unintended pregnancy. This finding underscores the importance of careful assessment of outcome variables if an accurate portrait of women's post-abortion mental health is to be developed. The strengths of this study lie in its assessment of multiple forms of violence and the measurement of 3 clinical anxiety disorders. It shares a number of problems with Study 1, however (described below), and wantedness of pregnancy was not assessed.

General Discussion

In both the NSFG and the NCS, two samples that are representative of the United States, we found that women who have abortions on their first pregnancy are more likely to experience violence in their lives, congruent with other research finding an association between violence and abortion. The results also provide additional documentation of the association between violence exposure and anxiety outcomes in the lives of women regardless of pregnancy outcome.

Moreover, the congruence of the findings in the 2 separate studies provides strong support for our hypothesis that confounding factors, including pre-existing anxiety and violence exposure, can explain the abortion–anxiety relationship. The differences in the pattern of findings are informative for interpreting contradictions across studies as well, for they establish that the findings regarding the relation of abortion and mental health will depend on type of violence exposure controlled (e.g., rape vs. physical attack) and clinical significance of the outcome variable (i.e., general symptoms vs. a diagnosis) and warrant limitations on generalization.

The results do not support the use of abortion history as a marker for identifying patients at risk for GAD— women who terminated their first pregnancy were not at higher risk for having an actual diagnosis of GAD. Indeed, such a practice is ill-advised given that being raped, physically attacked, and held captive/threatened with a weapon remained significant predictors of PTSD when pregnancy outcome and other covariates were in the model....

Limitations

... The use of these national data sets to study the relationship of abortion and anxiety disorders (and other measured mental health outcomes) has several limitations in addition to the standard problems associated with retrospective self-report methods, including underreporting of stigmatized conditions and unreliability of memory for timing of events. The length of time from the woman's first pregnancy outcome to the onset of anxiety symptoms (in the NSFG) or to the diagnosis of anxiety disorders (in the NCS) varied from 1 to 6 months to 20 years later. In addition to the standard issues related to reliability of memory, personal (divorce, infertility) and societal (e.g., rising influence of fundamentalist religions, stigmatization of abortion) events that occur subsequent to first pregnancy outcome (and that were not assessed in the survey) may differentially affect anxiety experience or alter the meaning and memory of women who chose to deliver vs. terminate a previous pregnancy. . . .

Whether or not pregnancy intention is controlled, it should be remembered that research on pregnancy outcome, even when prospective and longitudinal, cannot determine that abortion is the *cause* of psychological disorder. This limitation is inherent in abortion outcome research because it is unethical to randomly assign women to the conditions of conceiving and then terminating vs. delivering an unintended pregnancy.

Conclusion

The body of findings reported here suggests that the associations between abortion and anxiety reported previously in the literature may be explained by the fact that in previous research the outcome variable was not a specific clinical anxiety diagnosis, pre-pregnancy anxiety was not controlled, or that women who have unintended pregnancies have higher rates of violence exposure in their lives than women who have intended pregnancies. More theory-based research based on complex models and directed towards understanding the interrelationship among violence, unintended pregnancy, pregnancy outcome (abortion vs. delivery), and mental health is needed. For research having the goal of creating a body of knowledge that will be useful in providing informed consent to women seeking abortion, pregnancy intention should serve as a defining variable in the creation of comparison groups.

Meanwhile, given the lack of evidence that abortion increases risk for anxiety disorder, emphasizing abortion as a marker or screening factor may itself be harmful because focusing on abortion may distract attention from factors that do. The women who experience violence—regardless of pregnancy outcome—are the ones who are at higher risk and who need assistance. It is important that clinicians explore the effects of violence in women's lives to avoid mis-attribution of the negative mental health outcomes of victimization to having an abortion. To do otherwise may be to impede full exploration and understanding of the origins of women's mental health problems and prolong their psychological distress.

JULIA RENEE STEINBERG, PhD, is a postdoctoral fellow in the Department of Obstetrics, Gynecology and Reproductive Sciences at the University of California, San Francisco. Her research interests are in gender and the psychology of women.

NANCY F. RUSSO, PhD, Regents Professor of Psychology and Women and Gender Studies, Arizona State University, is editor or author of more than 200 publications related to gender and the psychology of women. Former editor of the *Psychology of Women Quarterly*, she has received the American Psychological Association's (APA) award for Distinguished Contributions to Psychology in the Public Interest, and is a fellow of the APA, the Association for Psychological Science, and the New York Academy of Sciences.

EXPLORING THE ISSUE

Does an Elective Abortion Lead to Negative Psychological Effects?

Critical Thinking and Reflection

1. Given that only correlating data can be collected on this topic (it being unethical to randomly assign women to either pregnancy or abortion conditions), what are the method limitations for any research on abortion? How do these limitations hinder psychological researchers from settling the abortion debate?
2. Both articles agree that more research on this issue needs to be done. In your view, what type of research is needed and why?
3. The studies presented here used similar data sets, similar methods of analysis, and similar demographic controls. What, then, could account for their opposite conclusions? (Hint: Read the introduction to this book.)
4. How should psychological research impact public decision making and national laws? Can psychology contribute to a public debate if it has disagreements on the conclusions of its data? If so, how can it best make a contribution?
5. Both of these articles look exclusively at the impact of abortion on women. What would you hypothesize might be the impact of an abortion on the man who fathered the fetus? How might a woman's decision to abort (or not) impact her family and other relations? How might the answers to these questions influence the research conclusions on abortion and anxiety?

Create Central

www.mhhe.com/createcentral

Additional Resources

Major, B., Appelbaum, M., Beckman, L., et al. (2009). Abortion and mental health: Evaluating the evidence (PDF). *American Psychologist, 64*(9), 863–890.

Charles, V. E., Polis, C. B., Sridhara, S. K., et al. (2008). Abortion and long-term mental health outcomes: A systematic review of the evidence. *Contraception, 78*(6), 436–50.

Internet Reference . . .

American Psychological Association

www.apa.org/pi/women/programs/abortion/

Selected, Edited and with Issue Framing Material by:
Brent Slife, *Brigham Young University*

ISSUE

Is Attention-Deficit Hyperactivity Disorder (ADHD) a Real Disorder?

YES: **National Institute of Mental Health,** from *Attention Deficit Hyperactivity Disorder* (NIH Publication No. 3572, 2006)

NO: **Rogers H. Wright,** from "Attention Deficit Hyperactivity Disorder: What It Is and What It Is Not," in Rogers H. Wright and Nicholas A. Cummings, eds., *Destructive Trends in Mental Health: The Well Intentioned Path to Harm* (Routledge, 2005)

Learning Outcomes

After reading this issue, you should be able to:

- Understand whether ADHD is a legitimate disorder.
- Discuss what could lead to the over diagnosis of ADHD.

ISSUE SUMMARY

YES: The National Institute of Mental Health asserts that ADHD is a real disorder that merits special consideration and treatment.

NO: Psychologist Rogers H. Wright argues that ADHD is not a real disorder, but rather a "fad diagnosis" that has resulted in the misdiagnosis and overmedication of children.

Diagnosis presents considerable challenges for mental health professionals. The *Diagnostic and Statistical Manual (DSM),* now in its fifth edition, defines widely recognized disorders in terms of clusters of symptoms that typically characterize these disorders. Because mental disorders are usually defined in terms of symptoms, there has been significant room for debate as to which groupings of symptoms constitute legitimate disorders that merit professional attention. Indeed, through its multiple revisions the *DSM* has added some disorders, redefined others, and set aside yet others as these diagnostic debates have shifted the ways we understand mental disorders.

Attention-Deficit Hypractivity Disorder, or ADHD, has been a particularly controversial diagnosis from the time it first appeared in the *DSM-III* nearly 30 years ago. Parents, teachers, psychologists, legislators, and even celebrities have debated not only whether ADHD is a real disorder but also whether the pharmacological treatments that are frequently prescribed are appropriate. Some people worry that we are pathologizing behaviors that are normal and typical of young children (e.g., curiosity, exploration, fidgetiness). Others worry that dismissing the diagnosis and leaving affected children untreated will place these children at a social, academic, and emotional disadvantage.

In the first selection, the National Institute of Mental Health (NIMH) argues that ADHD is a neurologically based disorder that affects 3–5% of school-age children. According to the NIMH, we can all be occasionally distracted, impulsive, and hyperactive. However, the scientists at the NIMH assert that children with ADHD struggle not only with these sorts of behaviors in greater frequency and intensity but also in a manner that is inappropriate for their age group. Moreover, the NIMH argues that there are treatments, which typically should include medicine, that will prevent greater problems in a child's later life.

In the second article, psychologist Rogers H. Wright contends that ADHD is not a real disorder, but rather a "fad diagnosis." According to Wright, there are a number of complex reasons why a child may show distractibility and/or hyperactivity other than ADHD. Wright discusses how stress and fatigue in children can produce these symptoms as well as neurological and/or emotional problems. Wright argues that the diagnosis of ADHD can distract mental health professionals from assessing for these other possible causes of distractibility and hyperactivity, leading to misdiagnosis and inappropriate treatments.

POINT

- There is mounting research evidence that ADHD is a diagnosable disorder that is neurologically based and strongly linked to genetics.

- Hyperactivity and distractibility are common among all children, but these symptoms are more pervasive and inappropriate in children with ADHD.

- ADHD can be diagnosed by assessing whether a person's behavior matches the criteria indicated by the DSM-IV-TR for ADHD.

- Research suggests that the best treatments for ADHD should include medication as part of their regimen.

COUNTERPOINT

- ADHD is a "fad diagnosis" that does not exist, like other similar diagnoses that have come and gone.

- Even when symptoms are more pervasive and inappropriate, these are more often signs of excessive fatigue or stress.

- The cluster of symptoms attributed to ADHD leads mental health professionals to treat a diverse group of people as having a single problem that requires a single solution.

- Pharmaceutical treatments for ADHD can create problems and are often unnecessary when the true cause of symptoms is understood.

YES

National Institute of Mental Health

Attention Deficit Hyperactivity Disorder

Attention Deficit Hyperactivity Disorder (ADHD) is a condition that becomes apparent in some children in the preschool and early school years. It is hard for these children to control their behavior and/or pay attention. It is estimated that between 3 and 5 percent of children have attention deficit hyperactivity disorder (ADHD), or approximately 2 million children in the United States. This means that in a classroom of 25 to 30 children, it is likely that at least one will have ADHD.

A child with ADHD faces a difficult but not insurmountable task ahead. In order to achieve his or her full potential, he or she should receive help, guidance, and understanding from parents, guidance counselors, and the public education system.

Symptoms

The principal characteristics of ADHD are inattention, hyperactivity, and impulsivity. These symptoms appear early in a child's life. Because many normal children may have these symptoms, but at a low level, or the symptoms may be caused by another disorder, it is important that the child receive a thorough examination and appropriate diagnosis by a well qualified professional. Symptoms of ADHD will appear over the course of many months, often with the symptoms of impulsiveness and hyperactivity preceding those of inattention that may not emerge for a year or more. Different symptoms may appear in different settings, depending on the demands the situation may pose for the child's self-control. A child who "can't sit still" or is otherwise disruptive will be noticeable in school, but the inattentive daydreamer may be overlooked. The impulsive child who acts before thinking may be considered just a "discipline problem," while the child who is passive or sluggish may be viewed as merely unmotivated. Yet both may have different types of ADHD. All children are sometimes restless, sometimes act without thinking, sometimes daydream the time away. When the child's hyperactivity, distractibility, poor concentration, or impulsivity begin to affect performance in school, social relationships with other children, or behavior at home, ADHD may be suspected. But because the symptoms vary so much across settings, ADHD is not easy to diagnose. This is especially true when inattentiveness is the primary symptom.

According to the most recent version of the Diagnostic and Statistical Manual of Mental Disorder (DSM-IV-TR),

there are three patterns of behavior that indicate ADHD. People with ADHD may show several signs of being consistently inattentive. They may have a pattern of being hyperactive and impulsive far more than others of their age. Or they may show all three types of behavior. This means that there are three subtypes of ADHD recognized by professionals. These are the predominantly hyperactive-impulsive type (that does not show significant inattention); the predominantly inattentive type (that does not show significant hyperactive-impulsive behavior) sometimes called ADD—an outdated term for this entire disorder; and the combined type (that displays both inattentive and hyperactive-impulsive symptoms).

Hyperactivity-Impulsivity

Some signs of hyperactivity-impulsivity are:

- Feeling restless, often fidgeting with hands or feet, or squirming while seated
- Running, climbing, or leaving a seat in situations where sitting or quiet behavior is expected
- Blurting out answers before hearing the whole question
- Having difficulty waiting in line or taking turns.

Inattention

The DSM-IV-TR gives these signs of inattention.

- Often becoming easily distracted by irrelevant sights and sounds
- Often failing to pay attention to details and making careless mistakes
- Rarely following instructions carefully and completely losing or forgetting things like toys, or pencils, books, and tools needed for a task
- Often skipping from one uncompleted activity to another.

Is It Really ADHD?

Not everyone who is overly hyperactive, inattentive, or impulsive has ADHD. Since most people sometimes blurt out things they didn't mean to say, or jump from one task to another, or become disorganized and forgetful, how can specialists tell if the problem is ADHD?

National Institute of Mental Health. From *Attention Deficit Hyperactivity Disorder*, NIH Publication No. 3572, 2006. Published by The National Institutes of Mental Health. www.nimh.nih.go

Because everyone shows some of these behaviors at times, the diagnosis requires that such behavior be demonstrated to a degree that is inappropriate for the person's age. The diagnostic guidelines also contain specific requirements for determining when the symptoms indicate ADHD. The behaviors must appear early in life, before age 7, and continue for at least 6 months. Above all, the behaviors must create a real handicap in at least two areas of a person's life such as in the schoolroom, on the playground, at home, in the community, or in social settings. So someone who shows some symptoms but whose schoolwork or friendships are not impaired by these behaviors would not be diagnosed with ADHD. Nor would a child who seems overly active on the playground but functions well elsewhere receive an ADHD diagnosis.

To assess whether a child has ADHD, specialists consider several critical questions: Are these behaviors excessive, long-term, and pervasive? That is, do they occur more often than in other children the same age? Are they a continuous problem, not just a response to a temporary situation? Do the behaviors occur in several settings or only in one specific place like the playground or in the schoolroom? The person's pattern of behavior is compared against a set of criteria and characteristics of the disorder as listed in the DSM-IV-TR.

Diagnosis

Professionals Who Make the Diagnosis

If ADHD is suspected, to whom can the family turn? What kinds of specialists do they need?

Ideally, the diagnosis should be made by a professional in your area with training in ADHD or in the diagnosis of mental disorders. Child psychiatrists and psychologists, developmental/behavioral pediatricians, or behavioral neurologists are those most often trained in differential diagnosis. Clinical social workers may also have such training. The family can start by talking with the child's pediatrician or their family doctor. Some pediatricians may do the assessment themselves, but often they refer the family to an appropriate mental health specialist they know and trust. In addition, state and local agencies that serve families and children . . . can help identify appropriate specialists.

Within each specialty, individual doctors and mental health professionals differ in their experiences with ADHD. So in selecting a specialist, it's important to find someone with specific training and experience in diagnosing and treating the disorder.

Whatever the specialist's expertise, his or her first task is to gather information that will rule out other possible reasons for the child's behavior. Among possible causes of ADHD-like behavior are the following:

- A sudden change in the child's life—the death of a parent or grandparent; parents' divorce; a parent's job loss.

- Undetected seizures, such as in petit mal or temporal lobe seizures
- A middle ear infection that causes intermittent hearing problems
- Medical disorders that may affect brain functioning
- Underachievement caused by learning disability
- Anxiety or depression

Next the specialist gathers information on the child's ongoing behavior in order to compare these behaviors to the symptoms and diagnostic criteria listed in the DSM-IV-TR. This also involves talking with the child and, if possible, observing the child in class and other settings.

The child's teachers, past and present, are asked to rate their observations of the child's behavior on standardized evaluation forms, known as behavior rating scales, to compare the child's behavior to that of other children the same age.

The specialist interviews the child's teachers and parents, and may contact other people who know the child well, such as coaches or baby-sitters. Parents are asked to describe their child's behavior in a variety of situations. They may also fill out a rating scale to indicate how severe and frequent the behaviors seem to be.

In most cases, the child will be evaluated for social adjustment and mental health. Tests of intelligence and learning achievement may be given to see if the child has a learning disability and whether the disability is in one or more subjects.

The specialist then pieces together a profile of the child's behavior.

A correct diagnosis often resolves confusion about the reasons for the child's problems that lets parents and child move forward in their lives with more accurate information on what is wrong and what can be done to help. Once the disorder is diagnosed, the child and family can begin to receive whatever combination of educational, medical, and emotional help they need. This may include providing recommendations to school staff, seeking out a more appropriate classroom setting, selecting the right medication, and helping parents to manage their child's behavior.

What Causes ADHD?

One of the first questions a parent will have is "Why? What went wrong?" "Did I do something to cause this?" There is little compelling evidence at this time that ADHD can arise purely from social factors or child-rearing methods. Most substantiated causes appear to fall in the realm of neurobiology and genetics. This is not to say that environmental factors may not influence the severity of the disorder, and especially the degree of impairment and suffering the child may experience, but that such factors do not seem to give rise to the condition by themselves.

The parents' focus should be on looking forward and finding the best possible way to help their child. Scientists are studying causes in an effort to identify better ways to treat, and perhaps someday, to prevent ADHD. They are finding more and more evidence that ADHD does not stem from home environment, but from biological causes. Knowing this can remove a huge burden of guilt from parents who might blame themselves for their child's behavior.

Genetics. Attention disorders often run in families, so there are likely to be genetic influences. Studies indicate that 25 percent of the close relatives in the families of ADHD children also have ADHD, whereas the rate is about 5 percent in the general population. Many studies of twins now show that a strong genetic influence exists in the disorder.

Researchers continue to study the genetic contribution to ADHD and to identify the genes that cause a person to be susceptible to ADHD. Since its inception in 1999, the Attention-Deficit Hyperactivity Disorder Molecular Genetics Network has served as a way for researchers to share findings regarding possible genetic influences on ADHD.

Recent Studies on Causes of ADHD. Some knowledge of the structure of the brain is helpful in understanding the research scientists are doing in searching for a physical basis for attention deficit hyperactivity disorder. One part of the brain that scientists have focused on in their search is the frontal lobes of the cerebrum. The frontal lobes allow us to solve problems, plan ahead, understand the behavior of others, and restrain our impulses. The two frontal lobes, the right and the left, communicate with each other through the corpus callosum (nerve fibers that connect the right and left frontal lobes).

The basal ganglia are the interconnected gray masses deep in the cerebral hemisphere that serve as the connection between the cerebrum and the cerebellum and, with the cerebellum are responsible for motor coordination. The cerebellum is divided into three parts. The middle part is called the vermis.

All of these parts of the brain have been studied through the use of various methods for seeing into or imaging the brain. These methods include functional magnetic resonance imaging (fMRI), positron emission tomography (PET), and single photon emission computed tomography (SPECT). The main or central psychological deficits in those with ADHD have been linked through these studies. By 2002 the researchers in the NIMH Child Psychiatry Branch had studied 152 boys and girls with ADHD, matched with 139 age-and gender-matched controls without ADHD. The children were scanned at least twice, some as many as four times over a decade. As a group, the ADHD children showed 3–4 percent smaller brain volumes in all regions—the frontal lobes, temporal gray matter, caudate nucleus, and cerebellum.

This study also showed that the ADHD children who were on medication had a white matter volume that did not differ from that of controls. Those never-medicated patients had an abnormally small volume of white matter. The white matter consists of fibers that establish long-distance connections between brain regions. It normally thickens as a child grows older and the brain matures.

The Treatment of ADHD

Every family wants to determine what treatment will be most effective for their child. This question needs to be answered by each family in consultation with their health care professional. To help families make this important decision, the National Institute of Mental Health (NIMH) has funded many studies of treatments for ADHD and has conducted the most intensive study ever undertaken for evaluating the treatment of this disorder. This study is known as the Multimodal Treatment Study of Children with Attention Deficit Hyperactivity Disorder (MTA).

The MTA study included 579 (95–98 at each of 6 treatment sites) elementary school boys and girls with ADHD, randomly assigning them to one of four treatment programs: (1) medication management alone; (2) behavioral treatment alone; (3) a combination of both; or (4) routine community care.

In each of the study sites, three groups were treated for the first 14 months in a specified protocol and the fourth group was referred for community treatment of the parents' choosing. All of the children were reassessed regularly throughout the study period. An essential part of the program was the cooperation of the schools, including principals and teachers. Both teachers and parents rated the children on hyperactivity, impulsivity, and inattention, and symptoms of anxiety and depression, as well as social skills.

The children in two groups (medication management alone and the combination treatment) were seen monthly for one-half hour at each medication visit. During the treatment visits, the prescribing physician spoke with the parent, met with the child, and sought to determine any concerns that the family might have regarding the medication or the child's ADHD-related difficulties. The physicians, in addition, sought input from the teachers on a monthly basis. The physicians in the medication-only group did not provide behavioral therapy but did advise the parents when necessary concerning any problems the child might have.

In the behavior treatment-only group, families met up to 35 times with a behavior therapist, mostly in group sessions. These therapists also made repeated visits to schools to consult with children's teachers and to supervise a special aide assigned to each child in the group. In addition, children attended a special 8-week summer treatment program where they worked on academic, social, and sports skills, and where intensive behavioral therapy was delivered to assist children in improving their behavior.

Children in the combined therapy group received both treatments, that is, all the same assistance that the medication-only received, as well as all of the behavior therapy treatments.

In routine community care, the children saw the community-treatment doctor of their parents' choice one to two times per year for short periods of time. Also, the community-treatment doctor did not have any interaction with the teachers.

The results of the study indicated that long-term combination treatments and the medication-management alone were superior to intensive behavioral treatment and routine community treatment. And in some areas—anxiety, academic performance, oppositionality, parent-child relations, and social skills—the combined treatment was usually superior. Another advantage of combined treatment was that children could be successfully treated with lower doses of medicine, compared with the medication-only group.

Medications

For decades, medications have been used to treat the symptoms of ADHD.

The medications that seem to be the most effective are a class of drugs known as stimulants.

Some people get better results from one medication, some from another. It is important to work with the prescribing physician to find the right medication and the right dosage. For many people, the stimulants dramatically reduce their hyperactivity and impulsivity and improve their ability to focus, work, and learn. The medications may also improve physical coordination, such as that needed in handwriting and in sports.

The stimulant drugs, when used with medical supervision, are usually considered quite safe. . . . [T]o date there is no convincing evidence that stimulant medications, when used for treatment of ADHD, cause drug abuse or dependence. A review of all long-term studies on stimulant medication and substance abuse, conducted by researchers at Massachusetts General Hospital and Harvard Medical School, found that teenagers with ADHD who remained on their medication during the teen years had a lower likelihood of substance use or abuse than did ADHD adolescents who were not taking medications.

The stimulant drugs come in long- and short-term forms. The newer sustained-release stimulants can be taken before school and are long-lasting so that the child does not need to go to the school nurse every day for a pill. The doctor can discuss with the parents the child's needs and decide which preparation to use and whether the child needs to take the medicine during school hours only or in the evening and weekends too.

About one out of ten children is not helped by a stimulant medication. Other types of medication may be used if stimulants don't work or if the ADHD occurs with another disorder. Antidepressants and other medications can help control accompanying depression or anxiety.

Side Effects of the Medications

Most side effects of the stimulant medications are minor and are usually related to the dosage of the medication being taken. Higher doses produce more side effects. The most common side effects are decreased appetite, insomnia, increased anxiety and/or irritability. Some children report mild stomach aches or headaches.

When a child's schoolwork and behavior improve soon after starting medication, the child, parents, and teachers tend to applaud the drug for causing the sudden changes. Unfortunately, when people see such immediate improvement, they often think medication is all that's needed. But medications don't cure ADHD; they only control the symptoms on the day they are taken. Although the medications help the child pay better attention and complete school work, they can't increase knowledge or improve academic skills. The medications help the child to use those skills he or she already possesses.

Behavioral therapy, emotional counseling, and practical support will help ADHD children cope with everyday problems and feel better about themselves.

Facts to Remember about Medication for ADHD

- Medications for ADHD help many children focus and be more successful at school, home, and play. Avoiding negative experiences now may actually help prevent addictions and other emotional problems later.
- About 80 percent of children who need medication for ADHD still need it as teenagers. Over 50 percent need medication as adults.

The Family and the ADHD Child

Medication can help the ADHD child in everyday life. He or she may be better able to control some of the behavior problems that have led to trouble with parents and siblings. But it takes time to undo the frustration, blame, and anger that may have gone on for so long. Both parents and children may need special help to develop techniques for managing the patterns of behavior. In such cases, mental health professionals can counsel the child and the family, helping them to develop new skills, attitudes, and ways of relating to each other. In individual counseling, the therapist helps children with ADHD learn to feel better about themselves. The therapist can also help them to identify and build on their strengths, cope with daily problems, and control their attention and aggression. Sometimes only the child with ADHD needs counseling support. But in many cases, because the problem affects the family as a whole, the entire family may need help. The therapist assists the family in finding better ways to handle the disruptive behaviors and promote change. If the child is young, most of the therapist's work is with the parents, teaching them techniques for coping with and improving their child's behavior.

Several intervention approaches are available. Knowing something about the various types of interventions makes it easier for families to choose a therapist that is right for their needs.

Psychotherapy works to help people with ADHD to like and accept themselves despite their disorder. It does not address the symptoms or underlying causes of the disorder. In psychotherapy, patients talk with the therapist about upsetting thoughts and feelings, explore self-defeating patterns of behavior, and learn alternative ways to handle their emotions. As they talk, the therapist tries to help them understand how they can change or better cope with their disorder.

Behavioral therapy (BT) helps people develop more effective ways to work on immediate issues. Rather than helping the child understand his or her feelings and actions, it helps directly in changing their thinking and coping and thus may lead to changes in behavior. The support might be practical assistance, like help in organizing tasks or schoolwork or dealing with emotionally charged events. Or the support might be in self-monitoring one's own behavior and giving self-praise or rewards for acting in a desired way such as controlling anger or thinking before acting.

Social skills training can also help children learn new behaviors. In social skills training, the therapist discusses and models appropriate behaviors important in developing and maintaining social relationships, like waiting for a turn, sharing toys, asking for help, or responding to teasing, then gives children a chance to practice. For example, a child might learn to "read" other people's facial expression and tone of voice in order to respond appropriately. Social skills training helps the child to develop better ways to play and work with other children.

Attention Deficit Hyperactivity Disorder in Adults

Attention Deficit Hyperactivity Disorder is a highly publicized childhood disorder that affects approximately 3 to 5 percent of all children. What is much less well known is the probability that, of children who have ADHD, many will still have it as adults. Several studies done in recent years estimate that between 30 percent and 70 percent of children with ADHD continue to exhibit symptoms in the adult years.

Typically, adults with ADHD are unaware that they have this disorder—they often just feel that it's impossible to get organized, to stick to a job, to keep an appointment. The everyday tasks of getting up, getting dressed and ready for the day's work, getting to work on time, and being productive on the job can be major challenges for the ADHD adult.

Diagnosing ADHD in an Adult

Diagnosing an adult with ADHD is not easy. Many times, when a child is diagnosed with the disorder, a parent will recognize that he or she has many of the same symptoms the child has and, for the first time, will begin to understand some of the traits that have given him or her trouble for years—distractability, impulsivity, restlessness. Other adults will seek professional help for depression or anxiety and will find out that the root cause of some of their emotional problems is ADHD. They may have a history of school failures or problems at work. Often they have been involved in frequent automobile accidents.

To be diagnosed with ADHD, an adult must have childhood-onset, persistent, and current symptoms. The accuracy of the diagnosis of adult ADHD is of utmost importance and should be made by a clinician with expertise in the area of attention dysfunction. For an accurate diagnosis, a history of the patient's childhood behavior, together with an interview with his life partner, a parent, close friend or other close associate, will be needed. A physical examination and psychological tests should also be given. Comorbidity with other conditions may exist such as specific learning disabilities, anxiety, or affective disorders.

A correct diagnosis of ADHD can bring a sense of relief. The individual has brought into adulthood many negative perceptions of himself that may have led to low esteem. Now he can begin to understand why he has some of his problems and can begin to face them.

The National Institute of Mental Health has the mission to transform the understanding and treatment of mental illnesses through basic and clinical research, paving the way for prevention, recovery, and cure.

Rogers H. Wright

Attention Deficit Hyperactivity Disorder: What It Is and What It Is Not

It is almost axiomatic in the mental health field that fads will occur in the "diagnosis" and treatment of various types of behavioral aberrations, some of which border on being mere discomforts. Although the same faddism exists to some degree in physical medicine, its appearance is not nearly as blatant, perhaps in part because physical medicine is more soundly grounded in the physical sciences than are diagnoses in the mental health field. These fads spill over into the general culture, where direct marketing often takes place. One has to spend only a brief period in front of a television set during prime time to discover ADHD (Attention Deficit Hyperactivity Disorder), SAD (Social Anxiety Disorder), or IBS (Irritable Bowl Syndrome). Even when purporting to be informational, these are more or less disguised commercials, inasmuch as they posit a cure that varies with the drug manufacturer sponsoring the television ad.

The other certainty is that these "diagnoses" will fall from usage as other fads emerge, as was the case a decade or so ago with the disappearance of a once-common designation for what is now sometimes called ADHD. That passing fad was known as minimal brain syndrome (MBS) and/or food disorder (ostensibly from red dye or other food additives). From this author's perspective, these fad "diagnoses" don't really exist. Other writers in this volume (e.g., Cummings, Rosemond, and Wright) have commented on the slipperiness of these "diagnoses"—that is, the elevation of a symptom and/or its description to the level of a disorder or syndrome—and the concomitant tendency to overmedicate for these nonexistent maladies.

Children and ADHD

Certainly, there are deficiencies of attention and hyperactivity, but such behavioral aberrancies are most often indicative of a transitory state or condition within the organism. They are not in and of themselves indicative of a "disorder." Every parent has noticed, particularly with younger children, that toward the end of an especially exciting and fatiguing day children are literally "ricocheting off the walls." Although this behavior may in the broadest sense be classifiable as hyperactivity, it is generally pathognomonic of nothing more than excessive fatigue, for which the treatment of choice is a good night's sleep. Distractibility (attention deficit) is a frequent concomitant of excessive fatigue, particularly with children under five years of age, and can even be seen in adults if fatigue levels are extreme or if stress is prolonged. However, such "symptoms" in these contexts do not rise to the level of a treatable disorder.

Conversely, when distractibility and/or hyperactivity characterize the child's everyday behavior (especially if accompanied by factors such as delayed development, learning difficulties, impaired motor skills, and impaired judgment), they may be indicative of either a neurological disorder or of developing emotional difficulties. However, after nearly fifty years of diagnosing and treating several thousand such problems, it is my considered judgment that the distractibility and hyperactivity seen in such children is not the same as the distractibility and hyperactivity in children currently diagnosed as having ADHD. Furthermore, the hyperactivity/distractibility seen in the non-ADHD children described above is qualitatively and quantitatively different, depending on whether it is caused by incipient emotional maldevelopment (functional; i.e., nonorganic) or whether it is due to neurological involvement.

It is also notable that most children whose distractibility and/or hyperactivity is occasioned by emotional distress do not show either the kind or degree of learning disability, delayed genetic development, poor judgment, and impaired motor skills that are seen in children whose "distractibility/hyperactivity" is occasioned by neurological involvement. Only in children with the severest forms of emotional disturbance does one see the kind of developmental delays and impaired behavioral controls that are more reflective of neurological involvement (or what was known as MBS until the ADHD fad took hold). Differentiating the child with actual neurological involvement from the child that has emotionally based distractibility is neither simple nor easy to do, especially if the behavioral (as opposed to neurological) involvement is severe.

A major and profound disservice occasioned by the current fad of elevating nonspecific symptoms such as anxiety and hyperactivity to the level of a syndrome or disorder and then diagnosing ADD/ADHD is that we lump together individuals with very different needs and very different problems. We then attempt to treat the problem(s) with a single entity, resulting in a one-pill-fits-all response. It is also unfortunately the case that many mental health providers (e.g., child psychiatrists, child psychologists, child social workers), as well as many general care practitioners (e.g., pediatricians and internists), are not competent to make such discriminations alone. Therefore, it follows that such practitioners are not trained and equipped to provide ongoing care, even when an appropriate diagnosis has been made.

To add to an already complicated situation, the symptom picture in children tends to change with time and maturation. Children with neurological involvement typically tend to improve spontaneously over time, so that the symptoms of distractibility and hyperactivity often represent diminished components in the clinical picture. Conversely, children whose distractibility and hyperactivity are emotionally determined typically have symptoms that tend to intensify or be accompanied/replaced by even more dramatic indices of emotional distress.

Management of Children Exhibiting "ADHD" According to Etiology

It is apparent that somewhat superficially similar presenting complaints (i.e., distractibility and hyperactivity) may reflect two very different causative factors, and that the successful treatment and management of the complaint should vary according to the underlying causation. Neurological damage can stem from a number of causative factors during pregnancy or the birth process, and a successful remedial program may require the combined knowledge of the child's pediatrician, a neuropsychologist specializing in the diagnosis and treatment of children, and a child neurologist. In these cases appropriate medication for the child is often very helpful.

Psychotherapy for the child (particularly younger children) is, in this writer's experience, largely a waste of time. On the other hand, remedial training in visual perception, motor activities, visual—motor integration, spatial relations, numerical skills, and reading and writing may be crucial in alleviating or at least diminishing the impact of symptoms. Deficits in these skills can be major contributors to the hyperactivity and distractibility so frequently identified with such children. Counseling and psychotherapeutic work with the parents is very important and should always be a part of an integrated therapeutic program. Such children need to be followed by an attending pediatrician, a child neurologist, a child neuropsychologist, and an educational therapist, bearing in mind that treatment needs change throughout the span of remediation. For example, medication levels and regimens may need to be adjusted, and training programs will constantly need to be revised or elaborated.

It is also noteworthy that so-called tranquilizing medication with these children typically produces an adverse effect. This writer remembers a situation that occurred early in his practice, a case he has used repeatedly to alert fledgling clinicians to the importance of a comprehensive initial evaluation and ongoing supervision in the development of neurologically involved children.

John, a two-and-a-half-year-old boy, was referred by his pediatrician for evaluation of extreme hyperactivity, distractibility, and mild developmental delay. The psychological evaluation elicited evidence of visual perceptual impairment in a context of impaired visual motor integration, a finding suggestive of an irritative focus in the parietal-occipital areas of the brain. This finding was later corroborated by a child neurologist, and John was placed on dilantin and phenobarbital. A developmental training program was instituted, and the parents began participation in a group specifically designed for the parents of brain-injured children. Over the next couple of years, the patient's progress was excellent, and his development and learning difficulties were singularly diminished. The parents were comfortable with John's progress and with their ability to manage it, so they decided to have a long-wanted additional child. In the meantime, the father's work necessitated moving to another location, leading to a change of obstetrician and pediatrician.

The second pregnancy proceeded uneventfully and eventuated in the birth of a second boy. Shortly after the mother returned home with the new infant, John began to regress, exhibiting a number of prior symptoms such as hyperactivity and distractibility, as well as problems in behavioral control. The new pediatrician referred the family to a child psychiatrist, who promptly placed John on a tranquilizer. Shortly thereafter, John's academic performance began to deteriorate dramatically, and his school counseled the parents about the possibility that he had been promoted too rapidly and "could not handle work at this grade level."

At this point, the parents again contacted this writer, primarily out of concern for John's diminished academic performance. Because it had been more than two years since John had been formally evaluated, I advised the parents that another comprehensive evaluation was indicated. The parents agreed, and a full diagnostic battery was administered to John, the results of which were then compared to his prior performance. It immediately became apparent that he was not functioning at grade level, and that the overall level of his functioning had deteriorated dramatically.

In his initial evaluation, John's functional level had been in the Bright Normal range (i.e., overall IQ of 110 to 119), whereas his current functioning placed him at the Borderline Mentally Retarded level (IQ below 60). The history revealed nothing of significance other than the behavioral regression after the birth of the sibling and the introduction of the new medication. I advised the parents that I thought the child was being erroneously medicated, with consequent diminution of his intellectual efficiency, and that the supposition could be tested by asking the attending child psychiatrist to diminish John's medication to see if the child's performance improved.

The attending child psychiatrist was quite upset by the recommendations and the implications thereof and threatened to sue me for "practicing medicine without a license." I informed the physician that I was not practicing medicine but rather neuropsychology, along with deductive reasoning known as "common sense," which we could test by appropriately reducing John's dosage level for a month and then retesting him. Faced with the alternative of a legal action for slander or libel for having accused this neuropsychologist of a felony, the child psychiatrist agreed.

Upon retesting a month later, the child's performance level had returned to Bright Normal, and his academic performance and behavior in school had improved dramatically. By this time approximately six to eight months had elapsed since the birth of the sibling, and John had become accustomed to his new brother. All concerned agreed that the medication had not been helpful and that the child should continue for another three to six months without medication. Subsequent contact with the parents some six months later indicated that John was doing well at school. The parents were quite comfortable with the behavioral management skills they had learned, which enabled them to handle a child with an underlying neurological handicap.

As noted earlier, the marked distractibility and/or hyperactivity in children with neurological involvement tends to diminish through adolescence, especially after puberty, as do many of the other symptoms. As a consequence, these children present a very different clinical picture in adolescence and adulthood. Typically, they are characterized by impulsivity, at times poor judgment, and excessive fatigability. It is generally only under the circumstances of extreme fatigue (or other stress) that one will see fairly dramatic degrees of distractibility and hyperactivity. Thus, an appropriate diagnosis leading to productive intervention is difficult to make.

Conversely, children who exhibit the symptoms of distractibility and hyperactivity on an emotional basis typically do not show the diminution of symptomatology with increasing age. In fact, the symptoms may intensify and/or be replaced by even more dramatic symptoms, especially during puberty and adolescence. It should also be emphasized that the kind of distractibility and hyperactivity exhibited by the emotionally disturbed youngster is very different in quality and quantity from that of a youngster whose hyperactivity and distractibility has a neurological basis. Unfortunately, it is also frequently the case that a youngster with a neurological handicap may have significant emotional problems overlaying the basic neurological problems, making diagnosis even more complicated. But the overriding problem confronting parents today is the misdiagnosis of emotionally-based symptoms that brings the recommendation of unwarranted medication.

In the largest study of its kind, Cummings and Wiggins retrospectively examined the records of 168,113 children and adolescents who had been referred and treated over a four-year period in a national behavioral health provider operating in thirty-nine states. Before beginning treatment, sixty-one percent of the males and twenty-three percent of the females were taking psychotropic medication for ADD/ADHD by a psychiatrist, a pediatrician, or a primary care physician. Most of them lived in a single-parent home, and lacked an effective father figure or were subjected to negative and frequently abusive male role models. Behavioral interventions included a compassionate but firm male therapist and the introduction of positive male role models (e.g., fathers, Big Brothers, coaches, Sunday school teachers, etc.) into the child's life. Counseling focused on helping parents understand what constitutes the behavior of a normal boy.

After an average of nearly eleven treatments with the parent and approximately six with the child, the percentage of boys on medication was reduced from sixty-one percent to eleven percent, and the percentage of girls on medication went from twenty-three percent to two percent. These dramatic results occurred despite very strict requirements for discontinuing the medication, which seems to point to an alarming overdiagnosis and overmedication of ADD/ADHD and greater efficacy of behavioral interventions than is generally believed to be the case by the mental health community.

Adult ADHD

The wholesale invasion of ADHD in childhood and adolescence is accompanied by a concurrent explosion of such diagnoses into adulthood. One cannot watch television without being bombarded by the direct marketing that asks: "Do you find it difficult to finish a task at work? Do you frequently find yourself daydreaming or distracted? You may be suffering from ADD. Consult your physician or WebMD." Of course, adult ADD exists; children with real ADD will grow into adulthood. But the symptoms described in this aggressive TV marketing are more reflective of boredom, the mid-day blahs, job dissatisfaction, or stress than a syndrome or disorder requiring treatment.

Unfortunately, treatment interventions focused primarily on medication and based on such ethereal and universal symptoms promise an instant "cure" for the patient who now does not have to confront possible unhappiness or stress. Such simple solutions also find great favor with the insurers and HMOs that look for the cheapest treatment. Persons exhibiting "symptoms" are more likely to benefit from a variety of behavioral interventions ranging from vocational counseling for job dissatisfaction and marital counseling for an unhappy marriage, to psychotherapy for underlying emotional stress, anxiety, or depression. Such interventions tend to be time-consuming and costly, with the consequence that the patients may inadvertently ally themselves with managed care companies devoted to the principle that the least expensive treatment is the treatment of choice.

Distractibility and hyperactivity of the type that we have called the "real ADHD" does exist in adults. However, in general, symptoms are much more subtle and, in many if not most cases, overshadowed by other symptoms. Thus, if mentioned at all, distractibility and hyperactivity are rarely significant presenting complaints. Such things as poor judgment, behavioral difficulties, forgetting, difficulties in reading/calculating, and getting lost are typically pre-eminent in the adult patient's presenting complaints. These usually become apparent in adulthood after an accident, strokes (CVA), infections of the brain, and other such events. The very drama of the causative factor typically makes the diagnosis apparent, and treatment providers are "tuned in" to anticipate sequellae secondary to neurological damage: intellectual and/or judgmental deficits, behavioral change, impulsivity, and motor impairment.

It should be emphasized that hyperactivity and distractibility, although present, are less dramatic symptoms that are understandably of less concern to the patient. Furthermore, they often diminish rapidly in the first eighteen months following the neurological event. Even then, the major constellation of symptoms may not be sufficiently dramatic to alert attending medical personnel as to the primary cause of the patient's complaints. This is particularly true of contrecoup lesions occurring most frequently in auto accidents.

Although circumstances resulting in contrecoup damage are frequent and often missed, there are also other, even more significant, types of neurological involvement that may also pass unnoticed. These include early-onset Alzheimer's disease beginning at age fifty and cerebral toxicity resulting from inappropriate medication in the elderly, which is usually misdiagnosed as incipient Alzheimer's. Expectation can unfortunately contribute not only to a misdiagnosis, but also failure to order tests that might elicit the underlying condition. In addition, the converse may infrequently occur: Neurological involvement may be anticipated but is not demonstrable and does not exist. Three illustrative cases follow.

Case 1

Bill, a young construction worker, received notice of his imminent induction into the armed services. Right after lunch on a Friday afternoon, a large section of 2 × 4 lumber dropped from the second story of a work site, striking him butt-first in the right anterior temporal region of the head. He was unconscious for a short period of time, quickly recovered consciousness, and showed no apparent ill effects from the blow. He refused hospitalization, and was taken by his employer to his home.

On the following Monday, Bill phoned his employer saying that he was still "not feeling too good," and given the imminence of his induction into the Army, he "was just going to goof off" until he was "called up." The employer had no further contact with Bill, who was inducted into the Army, where he almost immediately began to have difficulty, primarily of a behavioral type. Throughout his basic training, he tended to be impulsive and to use poor judgment, and he was constantly getting into fights with his companions. He barely made it through training and was shipped overseas where he was assigned to a unit whose primary duty was guard duty.

Throughout his training and his subsequent duty assignment, Bill was a frequent attendee at sick call with consistent complaints of headache, earning him the reputation of "goof-off." His military career was terminated shortly after an apparently unprovoked attack on the officer in charge of the guard detail to which Bill was assigned. After a short detention in the stockade, he was discharged from the Army. His headaches and impulsivity continued into civilian life and prompted Bill to seek medical assistance through the Veterans Administration. The VA clinic's case study included neurological screening tests that were strongly suggestive of brain involvement. Consequently, he was given a full psychological work-up, which revealed intellectual impairment attendant to temporal lobe damage.

Subsequent neurological and encephalographic studies were consistent with the neuropsychological conclusions, and indicated a major focus in the anterior temporal area of the brain. A careful and detailed history was taken, and the incident of the blow to the head was elicited. This case suggests that even though Bill refused hospitalization, because of the severity of the blow it would have been prudent for the employer to insist on a thorough evaluation.

Case 2

James, a man in his late forties, was the son of a Southern sharecropper. Upon graduation from high school, he attended the Tuskegee Institute for a short period before he was drafted into the armed forces. James had a productive military career and upon his discharge moved to California, got married, and proceeded to raise his family. He had trained himself as a finish carpenter and cabinetmaker. His work was highly regarded, and his annual income was well above the average for his field. One of his three children was a college graduate, a second was well along in college, and the third was graduating from high school. James owned his own home and enjoyed a fine reputation as a contributing citizen of his community.

While at work installing a complicated newel post and banister, James became disoriented and tumbled from a stair landing, falling some five feet and landing primarily on his head and shoulders but experiencing no apparent loss of consciousness. He was taken to a hospital for evaluation but was released with no significant findings. Almost immediately thereafter, he began to have difficulty at work. He would become disoriented, could not tell left from right, and made frequent mistakes in measuring, sawing, and fitting even simple elements. Before the accident he seldom if ever missed work, but now he became a frequent absentee. The quality of his work deteriorated and his income plummeted. He sought medical advice and was given a small stipend under the Workers Compensation program.

Over several weeks, he demonstrated no progress, and the attending neurologist and neurosurgeon referred him for neuropsychodiagnostic evaluation as a possible malingerer. The neuropsychologist noted that James' current status was completely at odds with his prior history, and not at all consistent with malingering. For example, the evaluation revealed that this highly skilled cabinetmaker, to his embarrassment, could no longer answer the question, "How many inches are there in two and a half feet?" The neuropsychological finding of pervasive occipital-parietal involvement was subsequently corroborated by electroencephalographic study.

Case 3

An airline captain driving along Wilshire Boulevard in Los Angeles lost consciousness when he experienced a spontaneous cerebral hemorrhage. He was immediately taken to a nearby major hospital where he received immediate and continuing care. Subsequently, a subdural hematoma developed, requiring surgical intervention. The captain recovered and showed no clinically significant signs of neurological involvement. An immediate post-recovery issue was the possibility of being returned to flight status. The attending neurosurgeon referred the patient for a comprehensive neuropsychological evaluation that found no indication of residual neurological deficit. Consequently, the neuropsychologist and the attending neurosurgeon recommended return to flight status.

In summary, in none of the foregoing situations was attention deficit or hyperactivity a significant presenting complaint, although the presence of both was clinically demonstrable at various times in the posttraumatic period. Yet the failure to recognize their presence would not have had a negative impact on treatment planning and or management in any of the three cases. Conversely, if excessive focus on the possible "attention deficits and/ or hyperactivity disorder" dictated the nature of the therapeutic intervention, a significant disservice to each of these patients would have resulted.

Traditionally when distractibility and/or hyperactivity are prominent parts of the presenting complaint, the mental health provider directs diagnostic energies toward ascertaining the underlying source of these dysphoric experiences. The distractibility and hyperactivity would have been viewed as secondary symptoms to be tolerated, if possible, until the resolution of the underlying problem resulted in their alleviation. In situations where the symptoms were so extreme as to be significantly debilitating, the mental health provider might reluctantly attempt to provide some symptom relief. However, in such cases this was done with the certain knowledge that it was an expedient, and was not addressing causation.

Times have changed dramatically, reflecting the interaction of a number of factors such as competition and cost controls. With the emergence of a plethora of mental health service providers, psychiatry opted to "remedicalize," essentially abandoning what it refers to as "talk therapy" in favor of medicating questionable syndromes and disorders. Psychology, pushed by its academic wing, could never decide what level of training was sufficient for independent mental health service delivery (i.e., master's versus doctoral degrees), and graduate-level training programs began to turn out hordes of master's-level providers in counseling, social work, education, and school psychology.

Meanwhile, the inclusion of mental health benefits in pre-paid health programs broadened consumption and brought about managed care as a means of reducing consumption of all kinds of health services, including behavioral health services. When the American public's impatience with time-consuming processes is added to managed care's limiting of services in the context of a glut of mental health providers the scene is set for considerable mischief. Add to this brew the fact that psychiatry holds a virtual medication-prescribing monopoly in mental health and that drug manufacturers are constantly developing and marketing new magic pills, it all adds up to an environment that encourages the "discovery" of yet another syndrome or disorder for which treatment is necessary.

Summary

When hyperactivity and/or distractibility is truly one of the presenting symptoms, it is indicative of a complex situation that warrants extensive and thoughtful evaluation, and, more often than not, complex and comprehensive treatment planning from the perspective of a variety of specialists. In situations where the attention deficit and/or hyperactivity reflects problems in parenting, chemotherapeutic intervention for the child is likely to be, at best, no more than palliative and, at worse, may succeed in considerably complicating the situation. In this writer's experience, chemotherapeutic intervention for emotionally disturbed children is a last resort and of minimal value in addressing the overall problem. Psychotherapeutic intervention with the parents, which may or may not include the child, is more often than not the treatment of choice. This is a judgment that is best made only after exhaustive study by pediatrics, psychology, neurology, and perhaps, last of all, psychiatry, which so often seems all too eager to overmedicate. . . .

Where the presenting complaints of hyperactivity and distractibility are in a context of delayed development, excessive fatigability, learning deficits, and other such signs, the complexity of the diagnostic problem is substantially increased. In such circumstances, it is absolutely not in the child's best interest to limit the diagnostic evaluation to a single specialty. With the increasing evidence that neurological involvement can follow any number of prenatal and postnatal exposures, wise and caring parents will insist on a comprehensive evaluation by specialists in pediatrics, child neurology, and child neuropsychology. More often than not, if medication is indicated, it will be of a type quite different than what is used in the management of so-called ADHD.

Furthermore, treatment intervention and case management will likely involve skilled educational training of the specialized type developed for use with the brain-injured child. In the case of a friendly pediatrician, a concerned psychologist, or a caring child psychiatrist, any or all attempting unilaterally to diagnose and/or manage the treatment regimen, the concerned and caring parent is well advised to promptly seek additional opinions. For a comprehensive description of the type of evaluation that is most productive in the management of children of this kind.

ROGERS H. WRIGHT is a past president of Division 12 and founding president of Division 31 of the APA. He was founding and cofounding president of the Council for the Advancement of the Psychological Professions and Sciences.

EXPLORING THE ISSUE

Is Attention-Deficit Hyperactivity Disorder (ADHD) a Real Disorder?

Critical Thinking and Reflection

1. According to these authors, how does normal distractibility differ from disordered distractibility? What motivations might some people have to label normal distractibility as a disorder?
2. Wright argues that medication can often create problems whereas NIMH suggests that medication might be necessary to treat ADHD. What are the risks and benefits of pharmacological treatment? What are the risks and benefits of eschewing pharmacological treatment?
3. Based on your readings, do you believe that ADHD is a real disorder? Why or why not? What does it mean if ADHD is or is not a real disorder?
4. There are many people involved in the question of ADHD's legitimacy as a disorder, including children themselves, parents, doctors, psychologists, politicians, and the media. Who should decide whether ADHD is a real disorder? Might any of these groups have motives that could bias them toward one conclusion or the other?

Create Central

www.mhhe.com/createcentral

Additional Resources

Kessler, R. C., Adler, L., Ames, M., et al. (2005). The World Health Organization Adult ADHD Self-Report Scale (ASRS): A short screening scale for use in the general population. *Psychological Medicine, 35*(2), 245–256.

Polanczyk, G., de Lima, M. S., Horta, B. L., et al. (2007). The worldwide prevalence of ADHD: A systematic review and metaregression analysis. *The American Journal of Psychiatry, 164*(6), 942–948.

Faraone, Stephen, V. (2003). *Straight Talk About Your Child's Mental Health: What to Do When Something Seems Wrong*. New York, NY: Guilford Press.

Internet References . . .

Centers for Disease Control and Prevention

www.cdc.gov/ncbddd/adhd/

WebMD

www.webmd.com/add-adhd/default.htm

Selected, Edited and with Issue Framing Material by:
Brent Slife, *Brigham Young University*

ISSUE

Are Fathers Necessary for Children's Well-Being?

YES: Natasha J. Cabrera, Jacqueline D. Shannon, and Catherine Tamis-LeMonda, from "Fathers' Influence on Their Children's Cognitive and Emotional Development: From Toddlers to Pre-K," *Applied Developmental Science* (vol. 11, pp. 208–213, 2007)

NO: Jane Waldfogel, Terry-Ann Craigie, and Jeanne Brooks-Gunn, from "Fragile Families and Child Well-Being," *The Future of Children* (vol. 20, pp. 87–112, 2010)

Learning Outcomes
After reading this issue, you should be able to: • What is the difference between family structure and family stability?   • Can certain family structures affect some child outcomes but not others?   • Is one sex naturally better at parenting than the other? Are there essential characteristics of fathering versus mothering?   • Is having a parent of each sex necessary for the well-being of children?

ISSUE SUMMARY

YES: Professor of human development Natasha J. Cabrera and colleagues report that father engagement has positive effects on children's cognition and language, as well as their social and emotional development.

NO: Jane Waldfogel, Terry-Ann Craigie, and Jeanne Brooks-Gunn, in a detailed analysis of various family structures, find that family instability has a negative effect on children's cognitive and health outcomes, regardless of structure, meaning that children with single or cohabiting parents are not necessarily at risk.

On Father's Day, June 21, 2009, President Obama gave a speech in which he said, "We need fathers to step up." He used his own experiences as a child growing up without a father, as well as his observations as a community organizer and legislator as a basis for his plea. His concerns reflect long-standing assumptions that fathers are necessary for children's well-being. But are they? For decades there has been active debate about parenting roles and responsibilities. Traditionalists assume that there is a maternal instinct and that children will just naturally fare better if there is a mother in the home and a father who fulfills the role of breadwinner. Myths abound about single mothers. These include: Today's family problems are due to the increase in single parenthood; the increase in unwed motherhood was due to the sexual revolution; children of unwed or divorced mothers are doomed to fail; and the male-breadwinner family is the best model. Another myth is reflected in the claim that so many young, poor urban males are involved with gangs, drugs, and guns because they lack a father figure.

The twentieth century saw significant changes in the American family. Well over half of mothers are currently in the paid workforce. More than half of all new marriages end in divorce. One-third of all births are to single women. The traditional family ideal in which fathers work and mothers care for children and the household characterizes less than 10 percent of American families with children under the age of 18. Mothers' increased labor force participation has been a central catalyst of change in the culture of fatherhood. Mothers began to spend less time with children, and fathers began to spend more time. Thus, the cultural interest in fatherhood increased, and it was assumed that fathers were becoming more nurturing and more essential. The history of the ideals of fatherhood reveals that fathers have progressed from distant breadwinner to masculine sex-role model to equal co-parent. Despite changes in the *ideals* of fatherhood, some family scholars observe that fathers' behavior has not changed. Rather, it appears that mothers' behavioral change may be responsible for the change in the culture of fatherhood.

A recent review of comparisons of fathers' and mothers' involvement with their children (in "intact" two-parent families) reveals a gap: fathers' engagement with their children is about 40 percent that of mothers'; fathers' accessibility is about two-thirds that of mothers. Fathers' lesser involvement is even more characteristic of divorced and never-married families. Nearly 90 percent of all children of divorced families live with their mothers. Most single-parent fathers are "occasional" fathers. More than one-third of children in divorced families will not see their fathers at all after the first year of separation. Only 10 percent of children will have contact with fathers 10 years after divorce. Yet, at the same time, research has documented the important ways in which fathers influence their children. But does this mean that fathers are essential? Some contend that fathers are not mothers; fathers are essential and unique. Many reject a gender-neutral model of parenting, arguing that mothers and fathers have specific roles that are complementary; both parents are essential to meet children's needs. Proponents of this model assert that fatherhood is an essential role for men and pivotal to society. They maintain that fathers offer unique contributions to their children as male role models, thereby privileging their children. Moreover, fathers' unique abilities are necessary for children's successful development. However, some scholars have shown that boys raised without fathers, even when their mothers are of low income, can turn out remarkably well. Such findings challenge traditional views of fathering, that is, boys can thrive without fathers. Responsible parenting can occur in a variety of family structures, including single parents and same-sex parents.

At least four contextual forces challenge a redefinition of fathering: (1) Legal notions of fatherhood disregard nurturing. Adequate fathering is primarily equated with financial responsibility. (2) Concepts of masculinity conflict with nurturant parenting. Nurturant fathers risk condemnation as being "unmanly." How can nurturant fatherhood fit into notions of maleness and masculinity? (3) Homophobic attitudes further obstruct nurturant fatherhood. Ironically, active legal debate about sexual orientation and parenting might be influential in reconstructing fatherhood. Is there a model of shared parenting within the gay community? (4) Whether with a two-parent marriage or with parents living in separate households, one parent usually does most, if not all, of the nurturing. Interestingly, it is the case that nurturance is a better predictor of effective parenting than is sex.

Gender neutrality and equality in parenting is undefined. How would you conceptualize a model of shared parenting (taking care not to discriminate against single-parent families)? What would parental equality look like in practice? Is it essential that children be exposed to both female and male role models? If so, why? If women and men were not expected to conform to a specific set of expectations associated with their sex, would the sex of the people raising children matter? Which benefits the child more, a heterosexual set of parents who are bound by strict gender-related conventions, which results in an overbearing, abusive father, or a loving single father or loving, nurturing gay parents?

The following selections advance two models. In the YES selection, Natasha Cabrera and her colleagues' paper suggest that a father's presence has positive effects on children's cognition and language, as well as their social and emotional development, and that the timing of these effects is important. They believe programs that increase fathers' education in particular can contribute to fathers developing positive parenting skills. In contrast, in the NO selection, Jane Waldfogel and her colleagues show that it is the stability within a family structure that is more important than the structure itself.

POINT

- Children with participatory fathers have better developmental outcomes.
- Certain styles of parenting demonstrated by the father are connected with more positive outcomes.
- Fathers' positive parenting is linked with healthier childhood development.
- There is an additive benefit from having two parents with different styles working in unison.

COUNTERPOINT

- Family stability can provide even stronger predictive power than just the presence of a father.
- It is not just the presence of the father, but also the relationship between father and mother which influences the child.
- The presence of a father with abusive parenting can predict more harm than good for children.
- The addition of another parent to an existing family could decrease the stability of the family.

YES

Natasha J. Cabrera, Jacqueline D. Shannon,
and Catherine Tamis-LeMonda

Fathers' Influence on Their Children's Cognitive and Emotional Development: From Toddlers to Pre-K

In recent years, scholarship on *resident low-income fathers* has made important contributions to our understanding of how fathers affect children's development. It has shown that men are involved with their young children in multiple ways through their accessibility, responsibility, and engagement; the quality of father engagement, or father–child interactions, can be positive and supportive; positive father–child interactions matter for children's development, with different effects emerging at different points in development; and, that father–child interactions are embedded in a larger ecology that includes mother–father relationship and the family human and financial resources. This article presents an integration of findings across several of our recent studies that have contributed to each of these areas.

First, we present findings that address the question of how resident fathers are engaged with their young children at 2 years, 3 years, and pre-kindergarten (pre-K). These findings are important because they are based on observed rather than survey data and show that the quality of father–child interactions is consistent across time and that fathers, like mothers, can be sensitive and supportive to their children.

Second, we highlight central fathers' personal and contextual characteristics that affect fathers' engagement. In particular, we focus on fathers' human and financial resources and mother–child interactions. These findings shed light onto particular personal and contextual factors that are central to positive parenting over time, which programs and policies can target for effective interventions.

Third, we focus on how fathers' engagements affect their young children's cognitive, language and social, and emotional outcomes over and above mothers' contribution. The extant literature on low-income fathers has focused on the effects of absent fathers and men's lack of resources on children's development. In contrast, our findings show that fathers who engage with their children in positive ways have significant effects on their cognition and language at 2 and 3 years and their social and emotional development at 2 and 3 years and at pre-kindergarten. These findings are important because they show that fathers uniquely contribute to children's

cognitive and social and emotional development above the effects on mothers' engagement on children.

These studies are guided by the Dynamics of Paternal Influences on Children over the Life Course Model that stipulates the important contribution of parent characteristics, child, and context to parenting and children's outcomes. These findings add to the literature in several ways: First, they focus on an ethnically/racially diverse, low-income sample of fathers who reside with their young children. Second, they show that low-income fathers can make significant contributions to their children's development. Third, these findings are based on observations of fathers and their children and hence move us beyond methodologies that rely on mothers as proxy respondents for fathers.

Methods

Participants

Participants were drawn from research sites that participated in both the National Early Head Start Research and Evaluation Project (EHS study) and the EHS Father Study's Project. Ten of 17 EHS sites participated in the father component of the main study at 2 and 3 years, and 12 participated at pre-K time point. Families ($N = 1,685$ at 2/3 years, $N = 2,115$ at pre-K) were enrolled into the study when they initially applied to have their children receive childcare and parenting services at the local Early Head Start program that is partners in the EHS study. Written consent to participate in the EHS study and family baseline data (e.g., maternal age, race/ethnicity) were obtained from mothers at the start of the research and from fathers at their initial visit.

Because the majority of fathers who participated in the video portion of the study were biological and resident (i.e., 85% at 2 and 3 years, 75% at pre-K), we only include families with a resident biological father at each age point. For the 2 and 3 year time points, we report on a sample of 290, and at pre-K we report on a sample of 313. These samples include families for whom we had father video data on at least one assessment.

Given the design of the study (mothers identified fathers, but not all identified fathers agreed to participate in the study), the fathers who ultimately participated in study 1 (2 and 3 year time point) and study 2 (pre-K time point) of the EHS father study are a select group of men. Compared with those who did not participate in the father study, participating fathers and their children's mothers were more likely to be married and/or cohabiting, White or Latino, completed more years of education, and were more likely to be employed. Additionally, their children had higher scores on cognitive and social and emotional tests than children from nonparticipating families.

The majority of fathers in these reported studies were White (60%, 60%, and 51%, respectively); the remaining fathers were largely African American followed by Latino. Across the three ages, approximately 1/3 to 1/2 of fathers had less than high school degree; remaining fathers had high school degrees or more. Almost all fathers reported working full-time or part-time at the various ages, ranging from 84% to 96%. However, the annual income for families at pre-K was larger ($59,459) than it was at 2 and 3 years ($18,820 and $25,440, respectively). Children averaged 25 months at the time of the 2-year visit, 37 months at the 3-year visit, and 64 months at the time of the pre-kindergarten visit; about half at all three ages were boys.

Procedures

Once fathers had been identified by the child's mother, they were contacted to participate in the study. Participating fathers were administered a father questionnaire and mother–child and father–child dyads were videotaped in separate home visits when children were 2 and 3 years, and about to enter kindergarten. Children's cognitive, language, and social and emotional development were assessed by a trained tester at the mother visit. Fathers were given $20 at the 2- and 3-year visits and $30 at the pre-K visit, and children were given a gift.

Father–child interactions were videotaped during three activities, including 10 or 15 min of semi-structured free play, which was the focus of the investigation. During free play, toys were presented to fathers in three separate bags. Toys were selected to be age appropriate and to offer dyads the opportunity to engage in both concrete and symbolic forms of play (e.g., at 2 years, the father toys included: bag #1—a book, bag #2—a pizza set and telephone, and bag #3—a farm with farm animals). Fathers were asked to sit on a mat with his child, try to ignore the camera, and to do whatever felt most natural. They were instructed to only play with the toys from the three bags and to start with bag #1, move on to bag #2, and finish with bag #3. They were told that they could divide up the 10 min or 15 min as they liked.

Measures

Parent Characteristics

The majority of demographic characteristics were collected from the father interview. Family income was gathered from standards measure of employment. Measures to assess children's development included mental and behavior ratings scales (i.e., emotional regulation and orientation/engagement factors) . . . and children's sociability and emotional regulation.

Parent–Child Interactions

The quality of father–child interactions as well as mother–child interactions were assessed. . . . We assessed three dimensions of positive parenting (i.e., sensitivity, positive regard, and cognitive stimulation) as indicators of fathers' and mothers' *Supportiveness*, which represents parenting that is characterized by emotional support and enthusiasm for the child's autonomous work, responsiveness, and active attempts to expand the child's knowledge and abilities. We included one negative aspect of parenting: *Intrusiveness*, which indicates that the parent is over-controlling and over-involved. All coders were unaware of children's scores on child assessments and father interviews.

Results

Findings from these studies are organized around the three research questions: (1) How do resident fathers engage with their young children? (2) How do human and financial resources and mothers' engagements predict the quality of fathers' engagements with their young children? (3) How do resources and father engagements affect their young children's development, over and above mother engagement?

Fathers' Engagements with Their Young Children

Building on past research that fathers and mothers engage with their children in distinct but also similar ways, our work offers further evidence of the similarities between some parents. Fathers were as sensitive as mothers, and both parents showed low levels of intrusiveness, countering common stereotypes of fathers as aloof. At all child ages studied, fathers and mothers received comparably high scores on their supportiveness . . . and equivalently low scores on their intrusiveness. . . . As observed in the videotaped father–child interaction episodes, children experienced supportive and positive parenting from both their parents.

Financial Resources and Mother–Child Interactions to Father Engagement

Although the samples in our studies represented all resident fathers who were generally higher functioning than nonparticipating fathers, for example, the majority were employed and obtained at least a high school degree, there was variation in the sample that accounted for differences in father engagements.

In terms of human and financial resources, fathers were more supportive at all three ages and less intrusive at

2 years when they had at least a high school education. . . . Income was positively related to fathers' supportiveness at 2 years and pre-K, but not at 3 years . . . , whereas income negatively related to fathers' intrusiveness at these same two ages. . . . At all three ages, mother supportiveness to her child related to father supportiveness. . . . Mother intrusiveness with her child related to father intrusiveness at 2 and 3 years . . . , but not at pre-K. . . .

In summary, fathers' resources and mother supportiveness are significantly related to supportive father engagement at most ages. Also, the finding of covariation between father and mother engagement quality underscores the need to covary mothers' engagement when considering the unique influence of fathering on children's outcomes.

Human and Financial Resources and Parent Engagement in Relation to Children's Development

Children's scores on the mental scale . . . , language scores . . . and word-recognition and applied problems . . . averaged .5 to 1.0 SD below the national norms. However, children were highly regulated and interactive during the administration of child assessments as indicated by their high scores on the orientation/engagement and emotional regulation factors . . . and on the cognitive-social and emotional regulation composite scales. . . .

Predictors to Children's Cognition and Language

Fathers' education (*more* than high school) was significantly related to children's scores. . . . Family income was significantly related to all child outcomes at pre-K. . . .

After accounting for financial and human resources (and mother engagement), the association between father engagement and child outcomes varied slightly over time depending on type of father engagement. In general, mothers' supportiveness related to children's cognitive outcomes at 2 and 3 years, and at pre-K. . . . Fathers' supportiveness related to children's outcomes at 2 and 3 years, but not at pre-K. . . . Intrusiveness varied in its relation to child outcomes by child age. Neither mother nor father intrusiveness were related to child outcomes at 2 and 3 years. . . .

Predictors to Children's Social and Emotional Behaviors

. . . As with cognitive outcomes, fathers' education (more than high school) consistently predicted children's emotional regulation at 2 and 3 years. . . . Family income, on the other hand, mattered only for children's orientation-engagement at 3 years and emotional regulation at pre-K . . . and approached significance to their cognitive-social behaviors at pre-K. . . .

In terms of parent engagement, surprisingly, maternal supportiveness was unrelated to children's outcomes at all ages . . . , however, father supportiveness was positively associated with children's emotional regulation at 2 years . . . and marginally related to their orientation-engagement at both 2 and 3 years. . . . Expectedly, maternal intrusiveness was negatively related to children's emotional regulation at 2 years and pre-K as well as their cognitive-social scores at pre-K. At 2 years, father intrusiveness was positively related to orientation-engagement but inversely related to emotional regulation. . . . Father intrusiveness was unrelated to children's social and emotional outcomes at 3 years and pre-K. . . .

Discussion

To date, studies of how fathers matter to their children have produced inconsistent findings. Some studies have reported that father engagement has no direct effect on children's outcomes. First, it is less likely to find an association between father *report* of engagement and child outcomes than when the quality of father engagement is observed. Second, it is possible that fathers have different effects on children's development across time. Findings from this study support both explanations. We also find that fathers' education and income are key predictors of positive father engagement.

It is noteworthy that the quality of fathers' and mothers' parenting is very similar to each other. Insofar as the brief videotape of parent–child interaction provides a window to how children are parented, we find that both parents are more sensitive than intrusive. In line with prior research, we also find that the most consistent predictors of supportive fathering across children's ages are fathers' education and income. It might be that fathers who have more than high school education are more motivated to parent and are more aware of the developmental needs of children than those with less education.

The next question we were interested in was whether parenting has an effect on children's outcomes. Although children in our study scored .5 to 1.0 SD below national norms of cognitive tests, they were highly regulated across ages. As with predictors to father engagement, in general, fathers who have more than high school education have children performing better in all developmental domains—cognition, language, and social and emotional development. Family income, however, matters more at later ages than earlier; presumably as children get older they need more stimulating materials and opportunities to promote learning. This is consistent with resource theories that posit that parents who have more resources are more likely to invest on their children by providing a stimulating environment that promotes growth and learning than fathers with fewer resources.

Once we accounted for the effect of resources on children's development, we examined the unique contribution that parenting had on children's outcomes. For cognitive development, mothers' and fathers' supportiveness were positively related to children's language and cognitive outcomes across ages, although fathers' supportiveness did not matter at pre-K. For social and emotional development, fathers' supportiveness mattered only at earlier ages, while mother supportiveness was not related at any age. It might be that supportive mothering alone might not be enough to teach children to regulate and pay attention. Perhaps supportive parenting coupled with other dimensions of parenting, not measured here, such as discipline, might be more effective, especially with older children. It is also possible parents in our study were not intrusive enough to have a negative effect on children. Our findings are consistent with past research that supportive parenting is important for children's cognitive development across time and it adds to the literature by showing that *supportive fathering* has similar effects on children's cognitive functioning and emotional development especially with younger children, whereas *supportive mothering* only affects cognitive development across ages.

Our results also shed light on the effects of one dimension of negative parenting. We found parent intrusiveness less consistently related to children's development across domains and ages. In contrast to our findings for supportive parenting, intrusive parenting has an expected negative effect on children's cognition and language, but only for older children. Perhaps over controlling parents tend to inhibit older children's autonomy to verbalize and ask questions hence diminishing opportunities for learning. However, parent intrusiveness related to children's emotional regulation differently depending on child's age and gender of parent. At 2 years, both parents' intrusiveness mattered. Parents who are over controlling and over-involved have young children who are less regulated (i.e., less attentive, less able to stay on task) than non-intrusive mothers and fathers. At 3 and pre-K, maternal intrusiveness was almost consistently related to less emotional reg-

ulation whereas paternal intrusiveness was not related at all. It is possible that children, especially older children, interpret paternal intrusiveness in a more positive way than they do maternal intrusiveness.

In summary, fathers who have at least a high school education were more supportive and less intrusive than parents with fewer resources. Over and above mother engagements, fathers' supportiveness matters for children's cognitive and language development across ages as well as children's social and emotional behaviors, but less consistently. In contrast, father intrusiveness is not related to older children's social and emotional behaviors; it matters only at 2 years. These findings have important implications for policy and programs. Programs that aim at increasing fathers' education and that promote and encourage father's positive parenting will yield large benefits for children.

NATASHA J. CABRERA is a professor of psychology at the University of Maryland. She received a PhD in educational and developmental psychology from the University of Denver, Colorado. Dr. Cabrera is now the director of the University of Maryland's Family Involvement Laboratory.

JACQUELINE D. SHANNON is an associate professor of early childhood education at Brooklyn College. She received a PhD in developmental psychology from New York University. Dr. Shannon is a member of the National Early Head Start Research Consortium, and researches parenting and child cognitive and social-emotional development.

CATHERINE TAMIS-LEMONDA is a professor of applied psychology at New York University. She holds a PhD from New York University. Her research interests include cognitive and social development in infants, and child interactions with parents and family members.

Jane Waldfogel, Terry-Ann Craigie,
and Jeanne Brooks-Gunn

Fragile Families and Child Well-Being

For much of the nation's history, the vast majority of American children were born into and spent their childhood in intact married-couple families. Almost the only exceptions were children whose families suffered a parental death. Over the course of the twentieth century, however, as divorce became more common, an increasing share of children experienced a breakup in their families of origin and went on to spend at least some portion of their childhood or adolescence living with just one parent or with a parent and stepparent. A large research literature developed examining the effects of such living situations on child outcomes.

More recently, as unwed births have risen as a share of all births, family structure in the United States has increasingly featured "fragile families" in which the mother is unmarried at the time of the birth. Children born into fragile families spend at least the first portion of their lives living with a single mother or with a mother who is residing with a partner to whom she is not married. For simplicity, we will refer to the first of these types of fragile family as single-mother families and the second as cohabiting-couple families.

An astonishing 40 percent of all children born in the United States in 2007 were born to unwed parents and thus began life in fragile families. That share was more than twice the rate in 1980 (18 percent) and an eightfold increase from the rate in 1960 (5 percent). Half of the children born to unwed mothers live, at least initially, with a single mother who is not residing with the child's biological father (although about 60 percent of this group say they are romantically involved with the father), while half live with an unwed mother who is cohabiting with the child's father. These estimates imply that today one-fifth of all children are born into single-mother families, while another fifth are born into cohabiting-couple families. Therefore, in examining the effects of unwed parenthood on child outcomes, it is important to consider both children living with single mothers and those living in cohabiting-couple families.

Single parenthood and cohabitation have lost much of their stigma as their prevalence has increased. But there are still many reasons to be concerned about the well-being of children in fragile families, and, indeed, research overwhelmingly concludes that they fare worse than children born into married-couple households. What remains unclear is how large the effects of single parenthood and cohabitation are in early childhood and what specific aspects of life in fragile families explain those effects.

In this article, we review what researchers know about the effects of fragile families on early child development and health outcomes, as well as what they know about the reasons for those effects. Many underlying pathways or mechanisms might help explain the links between fragile families and children's cognitive, behavioral, and health outcomes. Identifying these mechanisms is important to efforts by social scientists to understand how family structure affects child outcomes and to develop policies to remedy negative effects. A challenge that must be addressed is the role of "selection." The characteristics of young women and men who enter into single parenthood or cohabiting relationships differ from those of men and women in married-couple families, and those pre-existing characteristics might lead to poorer outcomes for children regardless of family structure. Parents in fragile families, for example, tend to be younger and less educated than those in married-couple families, and they may also differ in ways that cannot readily be observed even using detailed survey data. A final question is the degree to which the stability of the family setting affects how well children fare. In fact, recent research holds that it is in large part the stability of the traditional family structure that gives it its advantage.

We highlight new answers to these questions from studies using data from the Fragile Families and Child Wellbeing Study (FFCWS)—a data set designed specifically to shed new light on the outcomes of children born into single-mother and cohabiting families and how they compare with those of children in married-couple families. The study follows children from birth and collects data on a rich array of child health and developmental outcomes, thus providing evidence on how children's outcomes differ depending on whether they grow up in single and cohabiting versus married-couple families and on the factors that might underlie those differences.

We review the evidence on the effects of fragile families on child well-being by comparing outcomes for three types of families. The first type is families where children live with two married parents (for simplicity, we refer to

Waldfogel, Jane; Craigie, Terry-Ann; Brooks-Gunn, Jeanne From *The Future of Children*, vol. 20, 2010, pp. 87–112, a collaboration of the Woodrow Wilson School of Public and International Affairs at Princeton University and the Brookings Institution. Copyright © 2010 Princeton University, all rights reserved.

these as traditional families). In this category are children living with their married biological parents as well as children living with married stepparents. (Research has documented differences in outcomes between these two subgroups of children, but those differences are not our focus here.) Rather, we are interested in two other types of families—both fragile families—that have become increasingly prevalent in recent years. One is single-mother families in which the mother was not married at the time of the birth and in which she is not currently living with a boyfriend or partner. The other is cohabiting-couple families in which the mother was not married at the time of the birth but is currently cohabiting with a boyfriend or partner, who might be either the child's biological parent or a social parent (someone who is not biologically related to the child but who functions at least partially in a parental role). We do not distinguish between families that share and do not share households with extended family members or with other families or friends. We also do not distinguish between single mothers who are in a dating or visiting relationship and those who are not. Such distinctions likely matter, but our focus is on the three more general family types: traditional married-couple family, single-mother family, and cohabiting-couple family.

Explaining the Links between Fragile Families and Poorer Child Well-Being

Many studies, reviewed below, concur that traditional families with two married parents tend to yield the best outcomes for children. But the specific pathways by which growing up in traditional families lead to this advantage are still being debated. The key pathways, or mechanisms, that likely underlie the links between family structure and child well-being include: parental resources, parental mental health, parental relationship quality, parenting quality, and father involvement. As noted, the selection of different types of men and women into the three different family types also likely plays a role, as does family stability and instability. We discuss each of these mechanisms in turn. . . .

Past Research on the Links between Family Structure and Child Outcomes

An extensive body of work has examined the effects of parental divorce on child outcomes. As noted, however, most of this work was published before the massive increase in unwed parenthood that now characterizes American families. Thus, informative as it was about the effects of divorce, this early wave of research lacked data to explain how unwed parenthood might affect child outcomes.

The classic study by Sara McLanahan and Gary Sandefur, published in 1994, bridged the gap by bringing together an array of evidence on how growing up in various types of nontraditional families—including both divorced families and unwed-mother families—affected child well-being. Even after controlling for the selection of different types of individuals into different types of family structure, the authors concluded that children who spent time in divorced- or unwed-mother households fared considerably worse than those remaining in intact two-parent families throughout their childhood and adolescence. While they were still in high school, they had lower test scores, college expectations, grade-point averages, and school attendance, and as they made the transition to young adulthood, they were less likely to graduate from high school and college, more likely to become teen mothers, and somewhat more likely to be "idle" (a term that refers to those who are disengaged from both school and work). . . .

With regard to mechanisms, McLanahan and Sandefur found that income was an important explanatory factor for the poorer outcomes of children in single-parent families (but not for children in stepparent families). On average, single-parent families had only half the income of two-parent families, and this difference accounted for about half the gap between the two sets of children in high school dropout and nonmarital teen birth rates (in regression models that also controlled for race, sex, mother's and father's education, number of siblings, and residence). The other important mechanism was parenting. When McLanahan and Sandefur entered parenting into the regressions (instead of income), they found that the poorer parenting skills and behaviors in single-parent families explained about half the gap in high school dropout rates, but only a fifth of the gap in teen birth rates (again controlling for race, sex, mother's and father's education, number of siblings, and residence). Because the authors did not control for income and parenting in the same models, the question of how much overlap there was in their effects remains.

Although child health was not a focus in the McLanahan and Sandefur analysis, other analysts have consistently found effects of family structure on children's health outcomes. Janet Currie and Joseph Hotz found that children of single mothers are at higher risk of accidents than children of married mothers, even after controlling for a host of other demographic characteristics. Anne Case and Christina Paxson showed that children living with stepmothers receive less optimal care and have worse health outcomes than otherwise similar children living with their biological mothers (whether married or single). An extensive body of research also links single-parent and cohabiting-family structures with higher risk of child abuse and neglect.

As McLanahan and Sandefur noted at the time, their findings were worrisome given the burgeoning growth in unwed parenthood in the United States at the time. Although an earlier generation of researchers had debated whether or not divorce affected children's well-being, McLanahan and Sandefur's findings left little doubt that children of unwed parents were worse off than other groups. Concern about how children would fare in unwed families ultimately led to the Fragile Families and Child Wellbeing Study.

The Fragile Families and Child Wellbeing Study

The Fragile Families and Child Wellbeing Study is a new data set that follows a cohort of approximately 5,000 children born between 1998 and 2000 in medium to large U.S. cities.

Approximately 3,700 of the children were born to unmarried mothers and 1,200 to married mothers. The study initiated interviews with parents at a time when both were in the hospital for the birth of their child and therefore available for interviews. As a consequence, FFCWS is able to comprehensively detail the characteristics of both parents and the nature of their relationship at the time of the child's birth.

The study also contains extensive information on early child developmental and health outcomes. . . .

Interviewers gather data on children's behavior problems by asking mothers questions from the Child Behavior Checklist about both externalizing and internalizing behaviors—that is, both outward displays of emotion, including violence and aggression, and introverted behavioral tendencies, including anxiety, withdrawal, and depression. The study assesses prosocial behavior (which includes the child's ability to get along in social situations with adults and peers). . . .

Finally, FFCWS includes several measures of child health. The initial survey records whether a child had a low birth weight. In addition, at the age-three and age-five in-home assessment, the interviewer records physical measurements of the child's height and weight to make it possible to calculate the child's BMI and to determine whether the child is overweight or obese. At the same interviews, the mother is asked about four other health outcomes: whether the child has ever been diagnosed with asthma; the child's overall health, from the mother's perspective; whether the child was hospitalized in the past year; and whether the child had any accidents or injuries in the past year. The study also includes fairly extensive information on child abuse and neglect, which captures another aspect of child health and well-being. The primary caregiver's use of discipline strategies is measured by the Conflicts Tactics Scale (including the child neglect supplement). Parents are also asked whether their family has ever been reported to child protective services for child abuse or neglect.

Studies using data from FFCWS have found that in general, children in traditional married-couple families fare better than children living in single-mother or cohabiting families. We summarize separately below the evidence on cognitive development, child behavior, and child health.

Fragile Families and Child Cognitive Development

. . . [A]mong couples unmarried at the time of the child's birth, marriage improved cognitive scores for children whose parents later married. . . . [However, there is] no difference in children's vocabulary scores at age three between stable two-parent families (whether cohabiting or married) and stable single-mother families, but . . . scores are lower in unstable families (whether cohabiting or married) than in stable families. . . .

Fragile Families and Child Behavior Problems

. . . [C]hildren living with cohabiting parents have more externalizing and internalizing behavioral problems than children living with married parents, even at age three. One explanation may be the pre-existing risks that accompany nontraditional families. . . . [W]hen single mothers have more material and instrumental support, children have fewer behavior problems and more prosocial behavior. . . . [R]elationship conflict exacerbates externalized behavioral problems in children regardless of past family structure transitions.

. . . [B]ehavioral problems are intensified with each additional change in family structure the child experiences (changing from single to cohabiting parent, or cohabiting to single, for example), with this association mediated at least in part by differences in maternal stress and parenting quality. . . . [B]oth cohabiting and dating mothers confirm that mothers experiencing instability in their relationships go on to report more stress and to engage in harsher parenting.

It appears, however, that there is an important interaction between family structure and stability. . . . [S]tability seems to matter in cohabiting families, but not in single-mother families, where the risk of behavior problems is elevated even if that family structure is stable. . . . [H]aving a social father involved in a child's life can lower behavioral problems just as having an involved biological father can. . . .

Fragile Families and Child Health

. . . [C]hildren born to unwed mothers have worse health across a range of outcomes, even after controlling for other differences in characteristics such as maternal age, race and ethnicity, and education. Children living with single mothers have worse outcomes on all five health measures than children living with married parents, while children in cohabiting-couple families tend to have worse outcomes on some but not all measures. . . . [I]nstability for the most part does not affect children's health outcomes (the exception is hospitalizations, where they find, unexpectedly, that children who experienced more instability are less likely to have been hospitalized). These findings suggest that what negatively affects health among children in fragile families has to do with living with single or cohabiting parents (rather than experiencing changes in family structure). . . .

[S]ome of the mechanisms that link unwed parenthood with greater risk of low birth weight [include smoking cigarettes and using] illicit drugs during pregnancy, and less [receipt of] prenatal care in the first trimester of their pregnancy. . . . [However,] unwed mothers who received support from the baby's father are less likely to have a low-birth-weight baby, as are those who cohabited with the father.

Studies based on FFCWS also confirm earlier research finding that children living with single mothers are at higher risk of asthma. . . .

A few studies have taken advantage of the data in FFCWS to examine the effects of family structure on child abuse and neglect. . . . [A]lthough marriage appears to be protective in the raw data, that effect disappears in models that control for parental and family characteristics. . . . [B]oth single-mother families and cohabiting families where the mother is living with a man who is not the biological father of all her children are at higher risk of having been reported than are families where the mother is living with the biological father of all her children. . . . [The] presence of a social father in the home is associated with increased risk of abuse or neglect.

Our Own Analyses of FFCWS

The many studies in this area, including the recent ones using FFCWS data, do not always define family structure or stability in a consistent way. Studies also vary in the extensiveness of other controls that are included in the analyses. These differences across studies can make it difficult to generalize across studies and to summarize their results.

Accordingly, we carried out our own analyses of FFCWS data, estimating the effect of a consistently defined set of family structure and stability categories on a set of child cognitive, behavioral, and health outcomes at age five. The family categories we defined account for both family structure at birth and stability since birth. We divide families into the following six categories: stable cohabitation, stable single, cohabitation to marriage, married at birth (unstable), cohabiting at birth (unstable), and single at birth (unstable). We then contrast them with the traditional family reference group (that is, families in which parents were married at the child's birth and have remained so). . . .

Cognitive Outcomes

[A]ll types of nontraditional or unstable families are associated with lower scores, with the exception of the cohabitation to marriage category, which is [not] significantly different from the stable married category. The possible mediators explain some, but not all, of these negative effects.

Aggressive Behavior Outcomes

[A]ll types of nontraditional or unstable families are associated with worse scores. . . . However, in contrast to the results for cognitive outcomes, it appears that for aggressive behavioral problems, growing up with a single mother (stable or unstable) is worse than growing up with a cohabiting mother. The effects of growing up with a single mother . . . remain significant after controlling for demographic differences . . . plus possible mediators.

Health Outcomes

Results for the health outcomes reveal a different pattern. [F]or obesity, the worst outcomes are associated with growing up with a single parent (whether stable or unstable) or an unstable cohabiting parent. This pattern is true as well for asthma, although after controlling for demographic differences (or demographic differences plus the possible mediators), instability appears to be most important (with the worst outcomes found for children of unstable single or unstable cohabiting mothers).

These results suggest that the relative importance of family structure versus family instability matters differently for behavior problems than it does for cognitive or health outcomes. That is, instability seems to matter more than family structure for cognitive and health outcomes, whereas growing up with a single mother (whether that family structure is stable or unstable over time) seems to matter more than instability for behavior problems.

Summary and Conclusions

In this article we summarize the findings from prior research, as well as our own new analyses, that address the question of how well children in fragile families fare compared with those living in traditional married-parent families, as well as what mechanisms might explain any differences. . . .

Until recently, most . . . research focused on divorced parents. The sharp rise over the past few decades in births to unwed mothers, however, has shifted the focus to unmarried single and cohabiting parents. These demographic changes make it difficult to compare research done even ten or fifteen years ago with research on cohorts from the beginning of this century. Rapid changes in the characteristics of parents over time also could result in different selection biases in terms of which parents (both mothers and fathers) have children when married or when unmarried (for example, as the pool of parents having unwed births grows, the characteristics of unwed parents may become more similar to those of married parents, which would result in smaller estimated associations between fragile families and child outcomes). And given that recent cohorts of children born to single and cohabiting parents are relatively young, an additional complication involves comparing outcomes across studies (that is, analysts cannot yet estimate effects of family structure on adolescent and adult outcomes for cohorts such as FFCWS). There-fore, although growing up with single or cohabiting par-ents rather than with married parents is linked with less desirable outcomes for children and youth, comparisons of the size of such effects, across outcomes, ages, and cohorts, is not possible. In addition, analysts have used vastly different controls to estimate family structure effects, again complicating the quest for integration across studies. We addressed this latter problem by carrying out our own analyses using a consistent set of controls across outcomes. . . .

As noted, past research focused mainly on children whose parents were married when they were born but then separated or divorced (and subsequently lived on their own or remarried). Today, an increasing share of American children is being born to unwed mothers and thus the children are spending the early years of their lives in fragile families, with either a single mother or a cohabit-ing mother.

That worrisome change informed the launch of the Fragile Families and Child Wellbeing Study a decade ago. Today FFCWS provides a wealth of policy-relevant data on the characteristics and nature of relationships among unwed parents. . . .

Studies using the FFCWS data have shed new light on how family structure affects child well-being in early child-hood. The findings to date confirm some of the findings in earlier research, but also provide some new insights. In terms of child cognitive development, the FFCWS studies are consistent with past research in suggesting that chil-dren in fragile families are likely at risk of poorer school achievement. Of particular interest are analyses suggesting that some of these effects may be due to family instability as much as, or more than, family structure. That is, some studies find that being raised by stable single or cohabiting parents seems to entail less risk than being raised by single or cohabiting parents when these family types are unsta-ble. Because findings are just emerging, the relative risks of unmarried status and turnover in couple relationships cannot be specified yet. . . .

With regard to child behavior problems, evidence is consistent that children in fragile families are at risk for poorer social and emotional development starting in early childhood. In contrast to the results for cogni-tive outcomes, it appears that behavioral development is compromised in stable single-mother families, but, in common with the results for cognitive outcomes, such problems are aggravated by family instability for children in cohabiting families. The research also sheds a good deal of light on mechanisms, such as maternal stress and men-tal health as well as parenting, that might help explain why behavior problems are more prevalent in fragile families.

FFCWS is also providing some new insights on the effects of family structure on child health. Across a range of outcomes, findings suggest that children of single moth-ers are at elevated risk of poor health; evidence of health risks associated with living with cohabiting parents is less consistent. Findings for child abuse and neglect are also intriguing and suggest that children of single mothers and cohabiting mothers are at elevated risk of maltreatment, although marital status per se may be less consequential than whether a man who is not the child's biological father is present in the home. . . .

To the extent that children in fragile families do have poorer outcomes than children born into and growing up in more stable two-parent married-couple families, what are the policy implications? In principle, the findings summarized here point to three routes by which outcomes for children might be improved. The first is to reduce the share of children growing up in fragile families (for example, through policies that reduce the rate of unwed births or that promote family stability among unwed par-ents). The second is to address the mediating factors that place such children at risk (for example, through policies that boost resources in single-parent homes or that fos-ter father involvement in fragile families). The third is to address directly the risks these children face (for example, through high-quality early childhood education policies or home-visiting policies).

JANE WALDFOGEL is a professor of social work and public affairs at Columbia University. She received her PhD in public policty from Harvard University. Dr. Waldfogel's research centers on the impact of public policy on children and families.

TERRY-ANN CRAIGIE is an assistant professor in economics at Connecticut College. She received a PhD from Michigan State University. Her research interests include economics of the family and consequences of family formation on early childhood.

JEANNE BROOKS-GUNN is a professor of child development at Columbia University and a codirector of the National Center for Children and Families. She received her PhD from the University of Pennsylvania. Her current research evaluates the effect of public policy on enhancing the well-being of children in poverty.

EXPLORING THE ISSUE

Are Fathers Necessary for Children's Well-Being?

Critical Thinking and Reflection

1. Do you think there is such a thing as a maternal instinct?
2. Are fathers essential? Are male role models essential? If so, for whom—boys or girls or both?
3. Even if the two-parent family often has an easier time at effective parenting, does it mean that it is the only acceptable model?
4. Should fathers move beyond the provider or breadwinner role and become more involved in the physical and emotional care of their children? Should fathers emulate mothers' traditional nurturing activities?
5. Can parenting partnerships be truly egalitarian? What might they look like?

Create Central

www.mhhe.com/createcentral

Additional Resources

Esther Dermott, *Intimate Fatherhood: A Sociological Analysis.* New York, NY: Routledge.

Armin A. Brott and Jennifer Ash, *The Expectant Father: Facts, Tips, and Advice for Dads-to-Be* (New Father Series, Abbeyville Press, New York, 2001).

Internet References . . .

Single Mother Assistance

www.singlemoms.org/

National Fatherhood Initiative

www.fatherhood.org/

Unit 6

UNIT

Psychotherapy Issues

*M*any psychologists specialize in treating the mental, emotional, and behavioral difficulties of life and living. Yet there is considerable debate about what difficulties should be treated and how therapy should be conducted. Should difficulties in dealing with Facebook, for example, be treated, or is Facebook a primarily positive social influence? Also, are all types of therapy equally effective, or is there psychological evidence that some therapeutic techniques are more effective than others? What about therapist training? Should therapists specialize in particular approaches and theories of psychotherapy, or should they be more eclectic and train to be ready to administer all approaches and theories for the life problem at hand?

ISSUE

Selected, Edited and with Issue Framing Material by:
Brent Slife, *Brigham Young University*

Are All Psychotherapies Equally Effective?

YES: Benjamin Hansen, from "The Dodo Manifesto," *Australian and New Zealand Journal of Family Therapy* (December 2005)

NO: Jedidiah Siev, Jonathan D. Huppert, and **Dianne L. Chambless,** from "The Dodo Bird, Treatment Technique, and Disseminating Empirically Supported Treatments," *Behavior Therapist* (April 2009)

Learning Outcomes

After reading this issue, you should be able to:

- Discuss the role "technique" plays in the successful outcome of therapy.
- Discuss whether the disorder dictate treatment.

ISSUE SUMMARY

YES: Psychologist Benjamin Hansen agrees that psychotherapeutic techniques clearly differ among the various approaches, but he argues that all such psychotherapy techniques produce similar outcomes.

NO: Psychologists Jedidiah Siev, Jonathan Huppert, and Dianne Chambless assert that outcomes among the various psychotherapies differ primarily because one technique or therapy is better than another.

Have you or a member of your family ever considered psychotherapy? If so, you may have wondered how you would select the best therapist. Are some therapists better than others? Are some techniques or theories better than others? Will just any therapist or technique do? These kinds of concerns have led psychologists to investigate the effectiveness of various elements of psychotherapy. They attempt to examine not only which of these elements—therapists, techniques, and even the clients themselves—are the most influential but also whether certain types of psychotherapy theories are more effective than other theories in relation to these elements.

Most researchers have concluded that the different elements of therapy do come together to prompt positive changes. However, some disagree on the specific features that make one therapy more effective than another. One camp of researchers believes that all psychotherapy techniques are essentially equal in their effectiveness. This position is sometimes called the *Dodo hypothesis*, because the Dodo bird in *Alice's Adventures in Wonderland* arranged a race in which all the contestants won, and "all must have prizes." In other words, all the different therapy techniques "won" or are equally effective, so the differential effects of psychotherapy must be due to other factors (sometimes called "common factors"), such as client relationship and therapist skill. The other camp, by contrast, believes that

therapeutic techniques are crucial to any effective therapy. In fact, for psychologists who oppose the Dodo hypothesis, technique is pivotal because it often interacts with common factors to produce therapeutic change.

In the YES article, Benjamin Hansen is clearly from the first researcher camp. He affirms that the Dodo hypothesis is correct: no one type of therapy is superior to any other. He agrees that psychotherapy is generally helpful to those who receive it, but he believes that there is ample empirical evidence to suggest that those positive effects occur for a variety of patients and disorders irrespective of technique. Those therapists who believe that a particular technique is better than another only do so because they are biased toward a favored theoretical position. He argues, instead, that therapists should rely on a common factors approach to achieve successful therapy results.

By contrast, in the NO article, Jedidiah Siev, Jonathan Huppert, and Dianne Chambless argue that research on the Dodo hypothesis conceals significant differences in treatment outcomes for therapies and techniques. From their perspective, such research is aggregated from so many different populations, disorders, and treatments that it cannot make comparisons on particular treatments for specific disorders. Yet this is what consumers and therapists most need—information about which therapy or technique is most effective for specific problems under certain circumstances. Jedidiah Siev, Jonathan Huppert, and Dianne

Chambless do not deny the significance of "common factors," but they also do not believe that this significance eliminates the importance of therapy strategies. Indeed, it is in the interaction of these factors and these techniques that the greatest effectiveness is achieved.

POINT

- Effects of psychotherapy are due to common factors rather than specific techniques.
- Meta-analyses provide evidence that particular treatments do not significantly differ.
- Therapies are equally effective because all forms share similar technical components.
- Because no one technique is better than another, more therapy options are available to treat distressed persons.

COUNTERPOINT

- Specific techniques interact with and influence common factors to produce the general effects of psychotherapy.
- Meta-analyses confound too many variables to discern specific treatment superiorities.
- Techniques among therapies differ enough to produce different results.
- The disorder should dictate what technique is used. No psychotherapy can be superior for all disorders and all contexts.

YES

Benjamin Hansen

The Dodo Manifesto

There is currently a very strong move in healthcare toward 'outcomes', 'evidence-based practice' and 'standardised treatments'. This appears to be inspired by escalating costs. In such an environment, evidential (rhetorical?) lightweights like family therapy will struggle to compete with interventions such as CBT and medication. Do we have anything real to worry about?

The Dodo Hypothesis and Comparative Studies of Psychotherapy

The Dodo hypothesis originated with the psychologist Saul Rosenzweig in 1936. Rosenzweig published a paper about 'implicit common factors' in psychotherapy. He speculated that the efficacy of all forms of psychotherapy was similar, and that the success of psychotherapy was due to factors such as the therapeutic relationship and aspects of the patient's and therapist's personalities rather than specific techniques. Rosenzweig was reminded of an episode from *Alice's Adventures in Wonderland* where the somewhat deranged Dodo bird organises a race in which the contestants start from different points on the course and at different times. After a while, the Dodo decides that the race is over. When asked who won the race the Dodo declares that 'everybody won, and all must have prizes'.

Some of the earliest empirical support for the Dodo hypothesis came in the late 1950s from the work of the psychiatrist Jerome Frank. Frank conducted research that compared weekly individual therapy, weekly group therapy and fortnightly supportive therapy (1/2 hour) for depressed patients. He found no difference between the conditions with regard to the relief of distress (Frank & Frank, 1993).

In 1975, Luborsky, Singer and Luborsky published an influential paper titled 'Comparative Studies of Psychotherapies: Is It True That Everyone Has Won and All Must Have Prizes?' These authors conducted a review of the available research literature and concluded that psychotherapy was an effective treatment, all psychotherapies were similarly efficacious, and medications were more efficacious than psychotherapy.

In 1977, Smith and Glass published the first meta-analysis of psychotherapy outcomes. This technique, pioneered by Glass, enabled the statistical coding and analysis of a host of relevant variables. The technique was a significant improvement on the subjective reviews of the past, and meta-analysis did much to establish the credibility of psychotherapy as a bona fide treatment for psychological distress (Wampold, 2001). Smith (1982) provided an overview of the original work and some subsequent refinements. The average effect size for psychotherapy was found to be 0.85, a large effect. This meant that the average person who received psychotherapy was better off than 80% of those who did not, assuming that the benefits of psychotherapy were normally distributed. This positive effect held across the spectrum of client variables and disorders. Smith found no significant differences between the various types of psychotherapy, and no significant differences between the efficacies of psychotherapy and medication. Furthermore, she discovered no correlation between therapist effectiveness and their qualifications and experience. These findings have been replicated in more recent meta-analyses (Wampold et al., 1997; Wampold, 2001; Elliott, 2002). Shadish et al. (1995) provided an overview of meta-analytic findings specific to marital and family therapy (MFT). Essentially the news is the same. MFT works. Only modest differences emerge between orientations with regard to outcomes. MFT does not appear to be any more effective than individual therapies.

The National Institute of Mental Health (NIMH) Treatment of Depression Collaborative Research Program compared the efficacy of cognitive behaviour therapy (CBT), interpersonal therapy (IPT), the tricyclic antidepressant Imipramine plus clinical management, and a placebo pill plus clinical management. Elkin (1994) reported on the general effectiveness of the treatments. Overall 24% of patients fully recovered from their depression by the end of the 16-week treatment period and stayed well throughout the 18-month follow-up period. The percentages of patients who recovered and stayed well in each of the conditions were CBT (30%), IPT (26%), placebo (20%), and Imipramine (19%).

The findings reported above are derived from efficacy studies—evaluations of psychotherapy in controlled (to varying degrees) conditions. Seligman (1995) reviewed and summarised the findings of the 'Consumer Reports' survey on psychotherapy. This was an effectiveness study; that is, an evaluation of the usefulness of psychotherapy as it is practised in the real world. The survey revealed that psychotherapy generally appeared to be very beneficial to its recipients, but no one treatment was more effective than any other. Other findings were that long-term therapy was more beneficial than short-term treatment; medication did not enhance the benefits of psychotherapy; psychologists, psychiatrists and social workers were equally effective practitioners of psychotherapy, while marriage counsellors and family GPs were not as effective as mental-health professionals. These results were recently replicated in Germany (Hartmann & Zepf, 2003).

But Wait, There's More . . .

Much of the empirical support for the Dodo hypothesis comes from comparative studies of psychotherapy, but data from client, process and component studies are also supportive. For example Sotsky et al. (1991) reviewed data from the NIMH Treatment of Depression Collaborative Research Program in order to determine which patients might benefit most from particular treatments. They found that the least cognitively impaired subjects appeared to respond most favourably to CBT. Ilardi and Craighead (1994) looked at process data and found that most of the improvement that occurs during the course of cognitive therapy for depression occurs before any cognitive restructuring has begun. And, closer to home, Walsh (2004) conducted a study that involved 100 families who underwent structural family therapy. He found that the type of intervention used was not related to outcome. Structural family therapy apparently does not change family structure. Ahn and Wampold (2001) conducted a meta-analysis of component studies. They found that the key components of various treatment packages appear to add virtually nothing to the effectiveness of therapy.

Further support for the Dodo hypothesis comes from studies of therapist effects vs. treatment effects. Kim (2003) reviewed the data produced by the NIMH Treatment of Depression Collaborative Research Program in order to evaluate therapist effects against treatment effects. Kim found that 12.4% of the outcome variance at termination between the CBT and IPT conditions was due to therapist effects. Treatment effects accounted for 0% of the variance. Huppert et al. (2001) also found that therapist effects were very significant vis-à-vis treatment effects in a study that looked at the treatment of panic disorder. Interestingly, both of these studies involved manualised treatments. It thus appears unlikely that psychotherapy can ever truly be standardised.

The Dodo hypothesis is also supported by studies in which the effectiveness of trained and untrained therapists is compared. Trained therapists would presumably have a better grasp of technique than untrained therapists, and if technique is truly important, be more effective than untrained therapists. The most infamous study in this area is that published by Strupp and Hadley in 1979. The study compared the psychotherapeutic potency of very experienced psychologists and psychiatrists (average length of experience, 23 years) to college professors without a relevant professional background but who appeared to be able to form understanding relationships. The subjects were male college students who exhibited symptoms of mild depression and anxiety. On average, the subjects treated by the professors showed as much improvement as the subjects treated by the professionals. This study, however, raises some concerns. One problem was that the professionals were assigned harder cases. However, the general finding is far from unique. For example, Leonard Bickman's (1999) review concluded that the available evidence did not support the utility of experience or higher degree programs for psychotherapists. In a more recent review, Atkins and Christensen (2001) reached the same conclusion. One review by Stein and Lambert (1995) found a modest effect for training, but the evidence was indirectly derived from the reviewed studies, and the authors concluded their review with a comment about the overall paucity of supporting evidence for graduate training.

CBT Equals Supertherapy?

A key issue in the literature is the relatively large effect sizes often attributed to cognitive and behavioural therapies. Some researchers have attributed such findings to allegiance effects (Smith, 1982; Miller et al., 1997; Wampold, 2001). Others, such as Eysenck (1994), say that this is all nonsense and maintain that cognitive and behavioural treatments are actually much better than the rest. A known tendency toward bias occurs in comparative trials of psychotherapy. This is apparently in the direction of the theoretical orientation of the first senior author (Denman, 1993). Luborsky et al. (1999) assessed that 69% of the variance in outcomes in comparative studies of psychotherapy was due to allegiance effects.

It is hard, however, to prove bias objectively. Robert Matthews' (2004) article about parapsychology provides an interesting parallel. Matthews reported on a number of studies that showed strong evidence for ESP. He was not interested in exploring whether or not ESP existed, but rather looked at the fact that scientific data had little impact on the opinions of believers and non-believers alike. Believers felt that positive data confirmed the obvious—ESP was real. Nonbelievers felt that data must have been contaminated or fraudulently produced because ESP does not exist. Matthews suggested that empirical evidence does not carry as much weight as we often assume, because the data around effects are construed through philosophical frameworks that are inherently subjective.

In any case, one does not have to look hard to find studies that suggest that CBT is nothing special. For example, Parker, Roy and Eyers (2003) concluded in a recent review that the superiority of CBT to other psychotherapies as a treatment for depression had not been proven. Shear et al. (1994) directly compared CBT to nonprescriptive counselling as a treatment for panic disorder. They found that both interventions were equivalently helpful.

And, in a relatively rare instance of a specific finding in a comparative study of psychotherapies, McIntosh et al. (2005) found that nonspecific supportive clinical management was significantly superior to CBT and IPT as a treatment for anorexia nervosa. Another specific finding, very relevant to family therapists, came about through the London Depression Intervention Trial. This study compared systemic therapy, CBT and antidepressant medications for depression. Systemic therapy was clearly the most efficacious treatment (Jones & Asen, 2000). . . .

What Are the Common Factors in Psychotherapy?

We don't really know. Empirically what has been established is that specific effects account for, at best, 8% of outcomes, general effects account for 70%, and the remaining 22% is unexplained but may have something to do with client characteristics (Wampold, 2001).

Frank and Frank (1993) suggested four factors common to all forms of psychotherapy. First, a relationship between the patient and the helper such that the patient had confidence in the helper's competence and desire to help. Second, the therapy took place in a setting designated by society as a place of healing. The setting also offered advantages such as safety and confidentiality. Third, a rationale was offered for the patient's distress that contained the possibility of resolution. Fourth, a task was prescribed by the therapist's rationale or theory that required some sacrifice or effort on the part of the patient. These factors invoked a placebo response. In essence, psychotherapy enhanced the patient's morale and this, in effect, could lead to snowballing changes in the patient's attitudes and behaviour.

Following the above model, it would appear that seeing a psychotherapist is little different to seeing a shaman in another culture. Perhaps you are feeling poorly. You go to see the Great Healer at her Sacred Tent. The healer tells you that you have offended the gods. She hands you a big stick and tells you that you need to take on a bear to make up for it. You narrowly survive your encounter with the bear and soon after start to feel better.

There is some empirical support for the view that psychotherapy is a placebo treatment. Baskin et al. (2003) conducted a meta-analysis of the structural equivalence of placebo controls in psychotherapy. They found that when placebo conditions are structurally equivalent to treatment conditions—that is, same number and duration of sessions, same format of therapy and equivalently trained therapists—the effects of active treatments above placebo appear to be negligible.

One the most popular common-factor models was proposed by Miller, Duncan and Hubble (1997). These authors suggested that the effectiveness of psychotherapy was due to a set of factors—extratherapeutic (40% of any change that occurs), therapeutic relationship (30%), placebo effects (15%) and technique (15%). The percentages in this model obviously involve some guesswork, but the components have substantial empirical support. Extratherapeutic factors refer to client characteristics and chance events. The therapeutic relationship is the most well-supported common factor (Lambert & Barley, 2001). As an aside, it is interesting to note that the therapeutic relationship appears to impact significantly on the efficacy of drug treatments as well (Krupnick et al., 1996). Placebo effects refer to hope and expectancy. Technique is important in the sense that it provides structure. Unstructured therapy is highly correlated with poor outcomes. This model seems to reflect the literature on common factors pretty well.

Sprenkle and Blow (2004) suggested that family therapists had largely ignored common-factors research. This was apparently due to the discipline's proud 'maverick' tradition. The authors also noted, importantly, that family therapy is uniquely complex in that we have to apply common factors to families rather than individuals. Thus, for example, family therapists need to build and maintain a number of therapeutic alliances at any one time.

On the Other Hand . . .

Responses could be made to the Dodo hypothesis. The most salient would likely be that most of the research done tests psychotherapies against each other across broad heterogeneous groups. This means that average effect sizes may be quite meaningless. Parker et al. (2003) make this point in relation to research on CBT as a treatment for depression. Subjects are put into categories that are based on severity rather than aetiology. Treatments are assessed in terms of their universal impact. This means little chance of any specific effects being noted. The authors draw an analogy with oncology—cancers are not classified as belonging to groups such as major cancer, minor cancer or subclinical cancer and neither chemotherapy nor surgery is used as a universal treatment.

In addition to obfuscating potentially very important differences among clients, there is also the reliability problem with psychiatric diagnoses. Kutchins and Kirk (1998) cited an impressive array of evidence to the effect that this issue surfaces even when trained and experienced assessors are used. These authors reported that in DSM field trials, professionals were often unable to agree on the category of disorder from which a particular patient suffered, let alone a specific diagnosis. A number of diagnoses also have validity issues. Here is an example relevant to those of us who work with children and youth—'conduct disorder'. Lambert et al. (2001) found that the diagnostic criteria for conduct disorder had only slightly more internal consistency than symptoms chosen at random from the DSM-IV.

And another problem. How many unique manoeuvres are there in psychotherapy? Miller et al. (1997) suggest a tendency for the proponents of the various schools of psychotherapy to highlight the differences among 'brands'. These authors use solution-focused brief therapy and Narrative therapy as an example. A number of therapeutic moves are common to both approaches but different language is used, and this suggests differences in content. In a study that has dire implications for comparative studies of psychotherapy, Ablon and Jones (2002) looked at data from the NIMH Treatment of Depression Collaborative Research Program. They had hypothesised that manualised psychotherapy regimens in controlled trials overlap considerably in process and technique. When they compared prototypical regimens for IPT and CBT with transcripts from the NIMH study's IPT and CBT conditions they found significant overlap, and indeed therapists in both conditions appeared to be doing CBT. Have we been comparing Coke to Pepsi and puzzling over findings that they both appear to be fizzy cola drinks?

Some authors have suggested that all forms of psychotherapy share effective technical components. Eysenck (1994) suggested that behavioural interventions (relaxation, modelling, suggestion, flooding with response prevention, and so on) were responsible for all of the benefit of psychotherapy, as well as spontaneous remission and placebo responses to psychotherapy. These techniques were sometimes inadvertently used by nonbehavioural therapists.

Gibney (2003) proposed that the essence of all psychotherapy was 'double description'. Gibney's idea was not a response to the Dodo hypothesis, but it is relevant. Double description is about drawing distinctions—comparing one version of events with other possibilities. The idea comes from Gregory Bateson's (1972) observation that the defining quality of mind is the ability to take multiple perspectives. Gibney suggested that the various schools of psychotherapy offered alternate, novel descriptions of the client's issues and thus established contexts in which new ways of thinking and behaving could develop. This is a poetic explanation that may contain some truth.

A third problem with the data that substantiates the Dodo hypothesis is that most of it comes from efficacy studies—subjects usually have one uncomplicated diagnosis, treatment regimens are manualised, supervision is intense and so on. This is, of course, exactly how psychotherapy is not usually practised in the real world. So how relevant is the information from such studies?

Sexton, Ridley and Kleiner (2004) have been highly critical of the idea of grounding MFT practice and research in common factors. These authors made the point, probably correctly, that the so-called common factors are not clearly defined identities and are 'decontextualised'—they are not tied to the process of therapy. Sexton et al. suggested that a common-factors approach is old hat and somewhat primitive. They maintained that family therapists can now draw upon a variety of theoretically sound and well-validated models in the marketplace. Sexton is in fact a developer of one such product—Functional Family Therapy (see Sexton & Alexander, 2003).

What Does It All Mean?

The good thing about science is that it often reveals 'truths' that are not readily apparent. For example, the fact that matter and energy are the same thing is surprising. The fact that the book of life is written in an alphabet of only four letters is also surprising. However, to draw upon the 40-30-15-15 model described above, for example, it is not surprising to find that clients have lives outside of therapy that may impact very significantly on their well-being. It is not surprising that treating clients with sensitivity and respect is helpful. It is not surprising that hope is helpful. It is not surprising that taking a structured approach to solving client's problems is more helpful than just having a chat. Further to this list of not surprising revelations—it is not surprising that these factors would take precedence over the technical aspects of therapy. The utility of a supportive relationship and some hope to a distressed person is patently obvious. And because psychotherapy is conducted *with* intelligent, autonomous human beings rather than *on* inert mechanisms, factors such as the therapeutic relationship will determine the utility of any technical procedures because they will determine the participation of the client in therapy. So it would appear that after more than 40 years of research into psychotherapy, we have arrived at commonsense. And we cannot even say for sure that technical factors have no specific effects, because of significant flaws in the way the basic concepts have been operationalised in efficacy trials.

In my view, the current state of affairs reflects an obsession in Western culture that was originally inspired by Isaac Newton. Prior to Newton, most people had existed in a state of resigned bafflement about the apparendy discontinuous vastness that was the universe.

Newton's genius was to unite a collection of previously disparate phenomena with a few simple 'laws'. Since that time, it has been on for young and old, with generations of thinkers trying to duplicate the great man's feat within their own fields of expertise. Sadly, those of us who work within the 'mind sciences' have been given the short end of the stick. We work with inordinately complex, invisible, indivisible and often inferred entities that elude simple quantification. As a result our 'science' often does not turn out very well. What it all means is this—the positivistic paradigm is not a good paradigm through which to legitimise the practice of family therapy, or any form of psychotherapy for that matter. It has obviously been very useful in other fields, but much less so here.

I am not suggesting that we abandon research, but it may be more useful for family therapists to justify their practice with hard results rather than flashy rhetoric. I am sure that we can all cite very successful psychotherapeutic interventions with our clients. The psychologist Daniel Fishman (1999) has pointed out that while universal solutions do not appear to have adequately met many human problems, there are a plethora of smaller, local, contextual examples of successful interventions.

Fishman suggested a pragmatic approach where psychotherapists and professionals in related fields direct their efforts toward addressing the specific concerns of clients by the most appropriate means available. Such interventions could be incorporated into a database of case studies through which future practice could be informed. (Given the concerns about bias in the outcomes literature, it may be appropriate for future efficacy trials to be run by neutral parties or perhaps teams of ideologically opposed researchers such as psychoanalysts and radical behaviourists.) Fishman's approach seems sensible in light of the Dodo hypothesis. Indeed, it was the approach followed by one of family therapy's folkheroes—Milton Erickson. Erickson's approach was to have an approach for each client (Jackson, 2003). Beels (2002) suggested that Erickson was one of a long line of American pragmatists who provided as much impetus for the development of 'family therapy' as the original Bateson group. To practise pragmatically, we need pluralism in psychotherapy. Therapists would need to be able to draw upon as wide a range of ideas as possible. Family therapy is clearly a useful tool to have at one's disposal when working with children and young people or looking at client problems that have a systemic flavour.

There is a clear way forward here—(1) turn down the positivistic rhetoric, (2) adopt a sceptical attitude to the claims of evidence-based practice proponents, and (3) offer solid pragmatic data in support of our discipline.

Conclusion

The evidence as it stands suggests that no one type of psychotherapy is generally superior to any other. CBT and medication do not appear to be superior technologies. Thus, we have numerous valid approaches through which to assist distressed persons. In the main, the positivistic paradigm in psychotherapy research has not produced many profound insights, but certain commonsense aspects of psychotherapy appear to be very important. Taking a pragmatic approach to therapy and research is a way forward for family therapists.

BENJAMIN HANSEN is a psychologist and the team leader of the Mackay district Child and Youth Mental Health Service in Queensland, Australia. He provides assistance to children and adolescents through development and coordination of a range of early identification, assessment, treatment, and support plans for emotional and behavioral disturbances and/or emerging mental health issues. He also does tutoring work with James Cook University and dabbles in private practice.

Jedidiah Siev, Jonathan D. Huppert, and Dianne L. Chambless

 **NO**

The Dodo Bird, Treatment Technique, and Disseminating Empirically Supported Treatments

In a recent presidential column in *the Behavior Therapist*, Raymond DiGiuseppe observed that efforts to disseminate empirically supported treatments (ESTs), and especially cognitive-behavioral treatments, have been limited by perceptions "that all psychotherapies are equally effective [the Dodo Bird verdict], and . . . that common factors, therapist, and relationship variables account for the majority of the variance in therapy outcome studies" (2007, p. 118). He called for dialogue with proponents of those views, in an effort to understand their perspective and convey the alternative. Ultimately, "either we rebut these conclusions, conduct new research to show they are wrong, or we accept them and change our message" (p. 119). The aim of this article is to provide some historical context in terms of previous attempts to respond to these contentions and to present an update on recent research bearing directly on the Dodo Bird verdict and the assertions regarding variance accounted for by active ingredients (e.g., technique).

Aggregation

Evidence for the claim that all psychotherapies are equally efficacious derives from meta-analyses that combine various treatments for various disorders (e.g., Luborsky et al., 2002; Wampold et al., 1997). At most, these meta-analyses yield small effect sizes for average between-condition comparisons (e.g., $d = 0.21$; Wampold et al.), and the authors infer that, overall, no two psychotherapies are differentially efficacious for treating a disorder. Such a conclusion, however, is based on the fallacious reasoning that because all treatments for all disorders do not differ on average, no particular treatment is superior to another for a specific disorder (see Beutler, 2002; Chambless, 2002; Crits-Christoph, 1997; Hunsley & Di Giulio, 2002; and many others who have argued this point). Even operating with this reasoning, most meta-analyses have found differences between treatment orientations (Luborsky et al.; Shapiro & Shapiro, 1982; Smith & Glass, 1977; Wampold et al.), even when taking into account allegiance. Furthermore, in response to Wampold et al.'s meta-analysis, Crits-Christoph suggested that aggregating various populations, disorders, and treatments would likely obscure real differences in treat-

ment outcomes. Moreover, half of the studies examined by Wampold and colleagues evaluated the treatment of anxiety, and nearly 70% compared cognitive to behavioral therapies, characteristics of the studies that may minimize the likelihood of finding substantial treatment differences. Crits-Christoph demonstrated that 14 of the 29 studies that Wampold and colleagues included that compared two treatments for specific disorders grounded in different orientations yielded large effect sizes. Similarly, Beutler, Chambless, and others (Chambless & Ollendick, 2001; Hunsley & Di Giulio, 2002) have cited multiple studies and reviews that question the Dodo Bird verdict.

As a further challenge to the Dodo Bird verdict, Siev and Chambless (2007) recently conducted meta-analyses comparing CBT and relaxation (two bona fide treatments for anxiety disorders) for panic disorder (PD) and generalized anxiety disorder (GAD). In so doing, we compared two specific cognitive-behavioral interventions in the treatment of two anxiety disorders. The results revealed that for PD, CBT outperformed relaxation at posttreatment on all panic-related measures and indices of clinically significant change. In contrast, for GAD, the two treatments were equivalent on all measures. Furthermore, therapists in all studies were crossed with treatment condition, and most authors assessed client expectations and ratings of treatment credibility, which were high and never differed by treatment group. These methodological strengths bolster the likelihood that treatment techniques affected treatment effects.

In addition to combining various treatments and disorders, many meta-analyses in which the Dodo Bird verdict is advanced do not distinguish between primary and secondary outcome measures (Wampold et al., 1997). Rather, they derive a single effect size for each between-condition comparison by averaging all outcome measures. Their logic for doing so is:

> Given the assumption that researchers choose outcome measures that are germane to the psychological functioning of the patients involved in the study, it is the effect of the treatment on the set of outcome measures that is important. . . . Focusing on a few of many outcome measures to establish superiority causes fishing and error rate

problems (Cook & Campbell, 1979) and distracts the researcher from examining the set of outcome measures, which might have produced a negligible effect size. (Wampold et al., 1997, p. 210)

However, the average of all outcome measures does not accurately capture the efficacy of the treatment for individuals suffering from a specific disorder, and is likely artificially to attenuate the magnitude of the effect size. The extent to which a treatment for a disorder (e.g., PD) affects domains of common comorbidity (e.g., depression) is critical information, but is not of equal import in evaluating the treatment's efficacy as is the extent to which it affects core symptoms of the disorder (e.g., panic symptoms and diagnostic status). Although it is true that researchers should articulate a priori the primary dependent measures, reasonable concerns about post hoc reporting biases (e.g., selectively emphasizing significant findings from a large set of mostly nonsignificant findings) ought not preclude researchers from investigating secondary outcomes. Combining measures of primary and secondary outcomes forces can obscure or mask entirely meaningful differences in treatment effects (see Crits-Christoph, 1997).

Meta-analytic data comparing CBT and relaxation for PD and GAD that were not published in Siev and Chambless (2007) illustrate the importance of considering not only disorders separately, but primary and secondary outcome measures separately, as well. . . .

Rather, in conducting or interpreting these data, one must consider a fundamental issue: What is the question? It is our contention that rarely does the researcher, clinician, or consumer care whether, on average, treatments for all disorders across all domains do not differ. Rather, the consumer (to take one, for example) wishes to know what treatment will best alleviate the distress caused by his or her symptoms (cf. the fundamental psychotherapy question of Paul, who articulated the importance of asking not only whether psychotherapy works, but "What treatment, by whom, is most effective for this individual with that specific problem, and under which set of circumstances?" [1967, p. 111; emphasis in the original]). When the presenting problem is PD, the best answer to that question (if the options are CBT and relaxation) is that CBT is likely to reduce primary panic-related symptoms by approximately half a standard deviation more than is relaxation. Cast as a binomial effect size display,[1] this represents an increase in the rate of success from 38% to 62%. The wise consumer suffering from PD will choose CBT.

Bona Fide Treatments

Even advocates of a common factors approach to psychotherapy acknowledge that not all conceivable interventions are efficacious. Instead, the Dodo Bird verdict extends only to bona fide treatments, meaning those "intended to be therapeutic" (Wampold et al., 1997, p. 205). This distinction between bona fide and sham treatments in

evaluating the relative efficacy of different treatments, while having appeal, also introduces a number of theoretical and conceptual difficulties.

Wampold and colleagues (e.g., Ahn & Wampold, 2001; Messer & Wampold, 2002) conclude that treatment outcome studies are futile because comparisons between bona fide treatments yield clinically insignificant differences and those between bona fide treatments and controls yield uninteresting differences. This contention is somewhat circular, however, because categorization as a bona fide treatment is both a criterion for inclusion in, and an implication of, the results of clinical experience and treatment outcome research (and meta-analyses that synthesize multiple such studies). To illustrate, consider the history of behavioral treatments for obsessive-compulsive disorder (OCD). Forty years ago, behavioral therapists treated OCD with relaxation. As exposure and response prevention (ERP) was developed, clinicians discovered that it was far more efficacious than relaxation, which is now considered a placebo in the treatment of OCD. Does the discovery that one treatment outperforms a second render that very comparison invalid? In fact, in a recent survey of psychologists who treat anxiety disorders and who predominantly favor a CBT approach, more clinicians endorsed using relaxation to treat OCD, than endorsed using ERP (Freiheit, Vye, Swan, & Cady, 2004). Surely those clinicians consider relaxation to be a bona fide treatment. How can it then become something other than a bona fide treatment when a researcher uses it? Wampold and colleagues' concern that comparisons between bona fide treatments and shams are rigged and sometimes uninformative is well taken. Certainly treatments should be compared to real treatments and not trimmed down, three-legged horses. At the same time, to conduct component analyses that evaluate particular techniques often presented together as parts of a larger treatment package, certain treatment elements must be excluded. This is part of the bind.

A related complication stems from the study- or disorder-specific classification of a treatment as bona fide. Although Wampold et al. (1997) formulate an operational definition of bona fide to identify particular studies for inclusion in their meta-analysis, there is little conceptual justification for some resultant distinctions. For example, according to Wampold et al.'s guidelines, whereas relaxation is now considered a placebo for OCD, it is a bona fide treatment for GAD because studies have demonstrated that relaxation works as well as other treatments for GAD (and therefore therapists expect relaxation to be therapeutic), but not for OCD (and therefore [study] therapists now do not expect relaxation to be therapeutic). In other words, researchers expect some treatments to work because they have found them to do so, and others to work less well because they have found them to do so. Herein lies another difficulty with Wampold et al.'s classification of treatments as bona fide: It is circular to discount the superior efficacy of a treatment on the grounds that "I knew it would work better," if that assumption derived from observation of the same superior efficacy. Moreover, if this reasoning is correct, on what other grounds is relaxation a bona fide treatment for one anxiety disorder and not another? Considering that Wampold et al. aggregate across disorders and treatments, this poses a particular theoretical difficulty. Is it reasonable to include comparisons of CBT and relaxation for GAD (as they do), but not for OCD? Wampold et al. use the notion of bona fide treatment to ensure that the patient and the therapist have positive expectancies about outcomes, as expectancies are proposed to be an essential common factor related to outcome. However, if a therapist and a patient expect ERP to work better than relaxation for OCD, for example, then they are correct in their expectation, but it does not mean that expectancy is driving the treatment effect. Are the effects caused by expectancy, or do people expect more from treatments that work better? Finally, Wampold et al.'s criterion of bona fide treatment comparisons creates the potential trap that if consensus were reached that exposure-based CBT is the treatment of choice for OCD, then one could not establish its efficacy, as there could not be a bona fide treatment with which to compare exposure-based CBT.

Relationship and Therapist Variables, Common Factors, and Technique

The notion that the therapeutic relationship, therapist, and/or common factors contribute significantly more to treatment outcomes than do specific techniques has been stated by many (e.g., Levant, 2004; Messer & Wampold, 2002; Wampold, 2001), although with voices of opposition (Beutler, 2004; Huppert, Fabbro, & Barlow, 2006). The claim that technique accounts for approximately 10% to 15% of the variance of therapy outcome, whereas expectancy, relationship factors, and common factors account for closer to 40%, is frequently demonstrated in a pie chart (e.g., Lambert & Barley, 2001; 2002). However, the history of this chart may give the reader pause. Originally published in 1986 by Lambert, Shapiro, and Bergin in the *Handbook of Psychotherapy and Behavior Change* (3rd edition), the pie chart represented a summary of Lambert's reading of the literature from the previous 20+ years; it was not an empirical determination. One would hope that some progress has been made in the 20 years since, especially with regard to understanding mediators, moderators, and processes in therapy, and in CBT in particular. To take one study as exceptional in terms of such progress, Clark et al. (2006) showed that CBT targeting core cognitions and concerns of individuals with social anxiety disorder was more effective than exposure therapy (with a purely behavioral rationale of habituation) plus relaxation. Clark et al. report the effects of technique, alliance, and expectancy (see pie chart in Figure 1). Not only were

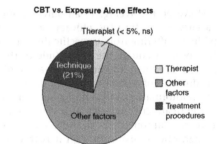

Breakdown of Clark et al.'s (2006) Data by Technique, Therapist Effects, and Unknown

therapist effects not large or significant, but there were no differences between the two treatment conditions in ratings of alliance ($p = .57$), credibility ($p = .26$), or expectancy ($p = .22$), suggesting that these mechanisms were not responsible for the differential treatment outcome between CBT and exposure. Similar data from another research group suggest that these CBT techniques for social anxiety disorder may be more effective than exposure alone (Huppert, Ledley, & Foa, 2007). At the same time, treatment technique did not account for 70% or 80% of the variance, and it is unlikely that any treatment will reach such a threshold.

How large are technique effects likely to be? Even Lambert's pie chart indicates that up to 15% of treatment effects may be due to technique, whereas Wampold (2001) suggests 8%. Before speculating about their magnitude, one needs to consider how best to determine technique effects. One method may be to compare active therapy to placebo. Overall, CBT for anxiety disorders has in fact shown significant superiority to placebo (cf. Hofmann & Smits, 2008), with an average effect size for the magnitude of the difference of 0.33 for intent-to-treat and 0.73 for completer analyses. However, there is variability in these effects, with the strongest evident in the treatment of acute stress disorder and OCD, and the weakest in the treatment of PD. Why might this be? It has been shown previously that OCD is less placebo responsive than is PD or social anxiety disorder (Huppert et al., 2004; Khan et al., 2005), and technique effects are most demonstrable in the disorders that have the smallest placebo effects. In fact, for some disorders (e.g., major depression), significant technique effects are somewhat difficult to demonstrate by comparing placebo to CBT (DeRubeis et al., 2005), although such effects are more prominent when examining follow-up data (e.g., Hollon et al., 2005). Similarly, in the case of PD, for which the magnitude of placebo response also appears to be high (Huppert et al.; Khan et al.), significant between-treatment effects are more evident at long-term follow-up (Barlow, Gorman, Shear, & Woods, 2000). In sum, it is difficult to determine the overall effect of technique without considering disorder and population, a conclusion reinforced by our discussion of the Dodo Bird verdict.

There are other methods by which one may examine technique effects. For example, Ablon and Jones (2002) showed that cognitive therapy techniques accounted for a significant amount of change in depressive symptoms in the NIMH Treatment of Depression Collaborative Research Program in both CBT and interpersonal psychotherapy treatment conditions. In addition, Cukrowicz et al. (2005) reported data suggesting that when a clinic changed its policy to conduct only ESTs, there was significant improvement in patient outcomes. Howard (1999) noted that individuals in a managed care environment who had specialty training in CBT for anxiety disorders were more likely to retain their patients, and those patients were also less likely to receive further treatment 1 year later. It is important to note that studies that simply examine orientation are unlikely to find such effects, as many practitioners who identify their primary orientation as cognitive-behavioral continue to use relaxation as a treatment of choice for OCD and PD (e.g., Freiheit et al., 2004).

But what about the contribution of alliance, common factors, and therapist effects? On average, studies yield a correlation of .22 between measures of alliance and outcome (Martin, Garske, & Davis, 2000), demonstrating that the former accounts for 5% of the variance in the latter. Note that this effect size derives from data aggregated across studies of a range of therapies and treatments, similar to the effect sizes calculated by Wampold and colleagues, and Luborsky and colleagues. Again, looking at specific therapies and specific populations, the verdict is much less clear. For example, Lindsay, Crino, and Andrews (1997) showed that the alliance in ERP and the alliance in relaxation were equal for patients with OCD, but the differences in efficacy were substantial. Similarly, Carroll, Nich, and Rounsaville (1997) showed that alliance was correlated with outcome in a supportive therapy for substance abuse, but not CBT. In CBT for depression, the data from DeRubeis and colleagues' studies have consistently showed that the therapeutic alliance is better for patients whose symptoms and cognitions have already changed for the better (e.g., Tang & DeRubeis, 1999); that is, early improvement in treatment leads to a more positive alliance. However, in Cognitive Behavioral Analysis System of Psychotherapy, where the alliance is an explicit focus of treatment, alliance appears to be predictive of outcome (Klein et al., 2003). Overall, alliance may have the greatest relationship to outcome if the therapist makes it a central focus of treatment. However, in such treatments, the distinction between alliance and technique is blurred. As others have noted (Beutler, 2002; Crits-Christoph et al., 2006), if one addresses alliance directly in treatment sessions, the very focus on alliance becomes a treatment technique. There is only one pilot study to date that attempts to improve alliance by using specific alliance-enhancing

techniques (Crits-Christoph et al.), and the results are equivocal. The effects of alliance-enhancing techniques in certain areas (e.g., change in alliance and improvement in quality of life) are large, but the impact on symptoms is small, and the results are difficult to interpret without a comparison group of new trainees who may have learned to improve alliance without additional techniques. However, the study is seminal in its attempt directly to improve alliance, and further such studies are needed to evaluate the causal impact of alliance on outcome.

Therapist effects have been discussed on and off for over 30 years. More recently, some have shown that differences between therapists in treatment outcome may be decreased with manualized treatments (Crits-Christoph et al., 1991), although not eliminated (e.g., Huppert et al., 2001). How large are therapist effects? Overall, they seem to range from 5% to 15% (see also Crits-Christoph & Gallop, 2006; Lutz, Leon, Martinovitch, Lyons, & Stiles, 2007). However, the question of what makes therapists different from each other remains, and one answer may be technique. Some therapists are likely more adept than others at using some techniques, formulating treatment plans, encouraging their patients to do difficult exposures, etc., even within CBT. Of course, therapists also differ on ability to form an alliance, but the therapist who is able to articulate a strong treatment rationale tailored to the patient's specific presentation and to explain why the treatment can help (or the therapist who is able to provide an example of an imaginal exposure that directly taps into an OCD patient's fears) will likely be experienced by the patient as empathic and understanding. Thus, techniques may be part of therapist effects (or vice versa), and not something that can be truly separated from them.

Just as alliance and therapist effects sometimes may be accounted for by technique, so may other putative common factors (consider, for example, how data on outcome provided during psychoeducation probably influence both therapist and patient expectancy). Indeed, the notion of common factors itself has broadened to the point that some would include the technique of exposure as a common factor (Lambert & Ogles, 2004). However, as Weinberger (1995) noted, common factors may not be so common after all. The extent of focus on alliance differs between treatments, and so does the amount, type, or quality of exposure. And if the goal of psychotherapy research is to determine the best ways to relieve suffering for the most people, researchers need to continue to focus on the areas that are most manipulable, such as technique. In fact, Lambert's latest research is an excellent example of high-quality research that integrates the arguments for the importance of technique, alliance, and therapist factors. In brief, Lambert has improved the quality of treatment outcome in therapy by providing therapists with feedback on patient progress and whether therapists are off track with their patients' predicted trajectories (Lambert, 2007). Notably, the feedback includes specific techniques that may help put them back on track. One may wonder aloud whether use of other types of disorder-specific information could further enhance the efficacy of such interventions.

Overall, many researchers—ourselves included—attempt to quantify the relative contributions of technique and other effects. Frequently such data are presented so as to support the exclusive role of one of the aforementioned effects (e.g., alliance, therapist, common factors, technique) in influencing treatment outcome. It is equally important, however, to demonstrate how such partisan divisions are not reflected in the real world, where all of these effects meet in a complex series of interactions. In fact, the patient's contribution to outcome (including diagnosis, insight, motivation, severity, psychosocial background, etc.) is likely the greatest. One may conclude that effective techniques are likely to positively influence not only treatment outcomes, but also therapy relationships. Few would argue that one should conduct therapy in the context of a hostile or negative therapeutic relationship. However, techniques are ubiquitous and need to be studied in order to determine how to best improve them and, thereby, patient outcomes.

DiGiuseppe (2007) suggested that unless the Dodo Bird verdict and contentions regarding greater effects of therapist, alliance, and common factors are addressed empirically, psychologists who value scientific inquiry must accept the implications of those assertions. In fact, these notions have been argued against for years, and many continue to examine the data. In this review, we have attempted to convey the following. First, the Dodo Bird verdict is predicated on meta-analyses that aggregate data across treatments, disorders, and outcome measures, and such aggregation likely masks or attenuates treatment differences between particular treatments for particular disorders on primary outcomes, even though such differences have the most direct implications for treatment. Second, there are numerous logical difficulties with the classification of treatments as bona fide, a requisite criterion for inclusion in some of the aforementioned meta-analyses. Third, there is empirical evidence that technique effects are sometimes greater than effects of common factors. More generally, the magnitude of technique effects depends on disorder and population, bolstering the assertion that broad judgments about the relative importance of technique and common factors are insufficient and can be misleading. Instead, more nuanced accounts that do not aggregate across moderating variables are necessary to conduct and evaluate psychotherapy outcome research. Finally, putative common factors such as therapist skill, the therapeutic alliance, and treatment expectancy are likely influenced by technique. Hence, their effects are not easily separable from those of active ingredients, but instead are explained by series of complex interactions. Nevertheless, there will always be others who critique the analyses, draw different conclusions, and advocate for those stances, and efforts to disseminate ESTs are limited in part because opponents of ESTs have presented their perspective more aggressively to wide-spread audiences. We must continue to address their arguments with empirically based data and logic and make our voices heard in the broad court of professional opinion.

Note

1. The binomial effect size display is a means of depicting an effect size as a relative success rate. Based on the assumption that the rate of treatment success is 50% overall, the binomial effect size display is used to translate an association between treatment and outcome into the proportion of successes in one treatment group relative to another.

JEDIDIAH SIEV is a clinical fellow in psychology (psychiatry) at the Massachusetts General Hospital/Harvard Medical School. While completing his graduate studies at the University of Pennsylvania, he specialized in empirically supported treatments for obsessive-compulsive disorder and related disorders, as well as other anxiety and internalizing disorders. He is interested in cognitive factors that contribute to the development and maintenance of obsessive-compulsive disorder and related disorders. He also investigates the relationship between psychotherapy outcomes in regard to active ingredients and common factors.

JONATHAN D. HUPPERT is a professor of psychology at The Hebrew University of Jerusalem. His research efforts are aimed at developing the optimal psychosocial treatments for anxiety and related disorders. He conducts studies on the process and outcomes of cognitive-behavioral treatments for anxiety disorders. He also examines the impact of the co-occurrence for other types of psychopathology such as depression or psychosis on anxiety and their impact on treatment outcomes and processes.

DIANNE L. CHAMBLESS is a Merriam Term Professor of Psychology at the University of Pennsylvania. She is also the director of clinical training for the Department of Psychology. Her areas of research include anxiety disorders, expressed emotion, and empirically supported treatments.

EXPLORING THE ISSUE

Are All Psychotherapies Equally Effective?

Critical Thinking and Reflection

1. Assuming that the Dodo hypothesis is correct, would *any* technique—perhaps even a nonsensical or an evil technique—produce equivalent results? Why or why not?
2. How would you know if one technique was superior to another? How do you think the authors of the readings would know?
3. From the perspective of the authors of the NO reading, why is it important to consider whether one technique or therapy is more effective than another?
4. Would the authors of the NO reading say that technique alone is sufficient to produce desired results in psychotherapy? What if the therapist is unskilled or inexperienced? Explain your answer.
5. Assuming that the Dodo hypothesis has been tested and found to be valid, how might it have advantages for the treatment of psychological disorders?

Create Central

www.mhhe.com/createcentral

Additional Resources

Silverman, D. K. (2005). What works in psychotherapy and how do we know? What evidence-based practice has to offer. *Psychoanalytic Psychology, 22* (2), 306–312.

Wampold, B. E. (2006). *The Great Psychotherapy Debate*. PhD dissertation, University of Wisconsin–Madison. Retrieved December 2006.

Internet Reference . . .

The National Council of Psychotherapists

http://thencp.org/

Selected, Edited and with Issue Framing Material by:
Brent Slife, *Brigham Young University*

ISSUE

Should Therapists Be Eclectic?

YES: Jean A. Carter, from "Theoretical Pluralism and Technical Eclecticism," in Carol D. Goodheart, Alan E. Kazdin, Robert J. Sternberg, eds., *Evidence-Based Psychotherapy: Where Practice and Research Meet* (APA, 2006)

NO: Don MacDonald and Marcia Webb, from "Toward Conceptual Clarity with Psychotherapeutic Theories," *Journal of Psychology and Christianity* (Spring 2006)

Learning Outcomes
After reading this issue, you should be able to:
• Determine the potential benefits that could be derived from an eclectic approach to psychotherapy.   • Identify some detrimental effects an eclectic approach could have.

ISSUE SUMMARY

YES: Counseling psychologist Jean Carter insists that the continued improvement and effectiveness of psychotherapy requires that techniques and theories include the different approaches of psychological theory and practice through an eclectic approach.

NO: Professors of psychotherapy Don MacDonald and Marcia Webb contend that eclecticism creates an unsystematic theoretical center for psychological ideas and methods that ultimately limits overall therapeutic effectiveness.

Most psychotherapists acknowledge that they need a good theory or theories to help guide their treatment of clients. If you were a psychotherapist, how would you use these ideas? Would you try to find the *single* best or most favorite theory, or would you pick and choose various parts from among *all* the theories? Some psychotherapists choose the single-theory approach because it seems more systematic and less fragmented. Other psychotherapists choose to work with many theories, because they see it as a way to create comprehensive therapies that are capable of addressing a variety of client situations.

The second approach is usually considered *eclectic* because psychotherapists select or employ individual elements from a variety of sources, systems, and styles. The word "eclectic" is derived from the ancient Greek and literally means "to choose the best." For example, some eclectic psychotherapists choose to subscribe to theories from humanistic psychology for their view of human nature, while practicing techniques derived from the cognitive psychology movement. Eclecticism is a popular way to resolve the varied problems of therapy. Surveys report that roughly two-thirds of all psychotherapists endorse some form of eclecticism. Still, its merit and validity as a guiding framework for psychological endeavors continues to generate debate.

Counselor Jean Carter is a prominent example of one side of this debate. In the YES selection, she argues that patients and their problems rarely fall into well-defined categories. As such, she believes that psychotherapists must embrace a variety of theories and associated techniques to overcome this challenge—eclecticism. She contends that real-world applications of an eclectic approach is a better treatment model, especially in comparison to single-theory approaches, because it is tailored for each patient and therefore adaptive and flexible across various scenarios. For this reason, she maintains that therapists should add diverse perspectives to their theoretical framework and avoid committing to any one conceptual approach.

Psychotherapists Don MacDonald and Marcia Webb oppose eclectic approaches because they sacrifice clarity in the process of psychotherapy. They argue that many psychotherapists opt for an eclectic approach just to avoid the difficult task of finding a single theory to guide their therapy. However, by sidestepping the process of committing to and thus understanding thoroughly a particular theory, eclectics unknowingly run the risk of understanding very little about the theories they employ. Indeed, this course of action eventually leads to a type of eclectic approach that is called *syncretism*. Syncretism occurs when psychotherapists try to unite aspects of theories and methods that are often contrary to one another. Don MacDonald and Marcia Webb conclude that a return to traditional single-theory approaches is required to achieve better clarity and effectiveness within psychotherapeutic practice.

POINT

- Therapy based on eclectic theories and techniques can manage diversion situations more readily.
- Eclectic systems allow therapists to choose the best methods and ideas for use.
- Therapy becomes more practical because therapists have all the theories and techniques they need.
- Therapists are better able to focus on therapeutic relationship because they do not have to focus on rigid single-theory concepts.

COUNTERPOINT

- Eclectic approaches have weak conceptual bases that fail to create a cogent rationale for clients to understand and trust.
- Without a guiding framework, therapists are less knowledgeable about theories overall.
- Access to a wide variety of theories and techniques does not necessarily ensure that the best option is selected.
- Single-theory therapists are well versed in the techniques and conceptual basis that guide how they form the therapeutic relationship.

YES ⤶

Jean A. Carter

Theoretical Pluralism and Technical Eclecticism

The real world of psychotherapy practice is complex, requiring moment-by-moment decisions about the treatment plan, the techniques being used, the working diagnosis, and even the goals. Patients rarely can be put into neat diagnostic boxes, and there is a great deal about their lives that psychotherapists cannot control. Clinicians know that psychotherapy occurs within a relationship that is personal and interpersonal, deeply textured, and responsive to the patient. Psychologists are trained in both the science and the practice of psychology, and they firmly believe in the value of evidence and the science base for their practice. The integration of these factors in recent calls for greater accountability and quality improvement in health care practice creates important challenges for both the scientists and the practitioners within psychology. Although the two groups share the goals of improving the effectiveness of psychotherapy and enhancing outcomes for patients, the tools and methods each uses to approach these goals may reflect quite different viewpoints. Like the blind men exploring an elephant, the part of psychotherapy one touches shapes how one understands the nature of the endeavor.

Although psychology has been committed to the integration of science and practice throughout its history, current initiatives to articulate and implement evidence-based practice principles highlight both that commitment and the difficulties inherent in integrating disparate views (American Psychological Association [APA], 2005). From a scientific perspective, psychologists seek greater control of variables, clarity of questions and methods, and general principles that are valid and reliable. From a practice perspective, they are committed to enhancing the lives of patients, drawing on general psychological principles, treatment-oriented research, and their experience in the multilayered world of practice.

Inevitably, divergent perspectives result in conflicts as psychologists attempt to bring together different approaches to the same shared goal of more effective practice. The significance of these conflicts, and the tension surrounding them, rises as funding and policy implications are increasingly based on demonstrable effectiveness and its evidence base. Practitioners are concerned about the limitations required by scientific methodologies and the direct application of research findings to any particular individual or treatment, as well as funding and treatment constraints arising out of misapplications of methodologies and results. . . .

Clinicians know the impact of psychotherapy; they experience it as they sit with their patients hour after hour, struggling with the anguish and difficulties patients bring into their offices. A long history of evidence supports the effectiveness and durability of psychotherapy (Ahn & Wampold, 2001; Barlow, 2004; Elkin et al., 1989; Lambert & Barley, 2002; Lambert & Bergin, 1994; Lipsey & Wilson, 1993; Roth & Fonagy, 1996; Sloane, Staples, Cristol, Yorkston, & Whipple, 1975; Smith, Glass, & Miller, 1980; Wampold et al., 1997). These reports include psychotherapy studies, literature reviews, and meta-analyses and represent many theoretical perspectives, patient and treatment types, and a variety of outcome measures. The picture is clear—psychotherapy works, and works well, much of the time.

At the same time, no particular form or model of therapy has been found to consistently work better than others (Wampold, 2001). In recent research designed to evaluate psychological interventions to relieve specific target problems in well-defined treatment populations using controlled treatment protocols (Barlow, 2004), the data support the efficacy of specific treatments but do not clearly support differential treatment effects (Wampold, 2001; Westen, Novotny, & Thompson-Brenner, 2004). In addition, questions about the applicability of the results of these studies to the general treatment population and therapeutic realities abound. One cannot conclude that particular treatments are clearly better than other treatments or clearly better than treatment as usual in the community. The research literature thus supports clinicians' experiential knowledge that psychotherapy works but does not offer them specific information about what to do when or with whom to provide effective psychotherapy.

Practitioners value the grounding of practice within evidence, including the evidence that they collect and draw on as they engage in a version of science within the hour (Carter, 2002; Strieker & Trierweiler, 1995). They continually ask questions about what is or is not working and why, and they attempt to understand how to enhance the multilayered practice that occurs within a specific interpersonal context (Samstag, 2002) and with its own unique demands. . . . Within this continually changing world of practice, clinicians rely on the therapeutic relationship; a broad knowledge of individual differences, psychological principles, and change processes; a theoretical grounding that offers cogent explanations; and techniques that provide the necessary tools for change.

This chapter offers a perspective on the importance of maintaining multiple theoretical formulations for effective psychological practice and on the role of related techniques in the psychotherapy process. Evidence-based practice in psychology has as its background the complex factors that affect the psychotherapy process and the history of research demonstrating the effectiveness of psychotherapy. It reflects an understanding of the contextual model of psychotherapy with its emphasis on common factors. I propose the essential integration of theoretical pluralism and technical eclecticism as significant components of real-world applications of evidence-based practice in psychology.

The Multilayered Real World of Psychotherapy

Psychotherapy is complex and requires continual responsiveness. Many factors operate at any given moment, all of which may call for the clinician's attention, and many of which are not within his or her control. Clinicians look for ways to understand psychological distress and to effect change in a way that takes into account this complexity. Although this chapter does not primarily address the wide range of presentations and problem types or specific treatments designed to be effective with the variety of clients clinicians face, it is important that the reader understand the psychotherapy process as an ongoing complex interplay of factors in which the clinician makes frequent decisions within an uncertain context, using their own clinical expertise and probabilistic research evidence to guide them in the moment. . . .

[P]atients present dramatically different pictures, even those who meet the same diagnostic criteria from the *Diagnostic and Statistical Manual of Mental Disorders* (American Psychiatric Association, 1994). Clinicians attend to disorder-related issues, including presenting problem, level of distress, level of function, co-occurring problems, and attachment style (see Norcross, 2002). They attend to life circumstances (e.g., available resources and support systems, medical concerns, social skills), individual and group characteristics (APA, 2002, 2003; Sue, 2003; Sue & Lam, 2002), and values. These factors are what patients bring into treatment and what influences their lives outside of treatment as well as the treatment itself (see Miller, Duncan, & Hubble, 1997). In addition, these patient factors do not remain static and do not follow neat lines of development or change and may be affected by

happenstance, or things that occur in people's lives that may not be under their control but that significantly affect their lives and the treatment.

In addition to patient factors, there are a number of factors related specifically to the therapist that operate throughout treatment (see Norcross, 2002, for a discussion of clinician factors). Clinicians vary in interpersonal skills and abilities, experience, training, values, personal characteristics, knowledge base, and worldview, as well as other factors. Just as no two patients are exactly the same, clinicians are not interchangeable.

Structural aspects of the clinical situation affect what can or does occur within treatment. These factors may include the resources available and costs related to engaging in treatment (Yates, 1994, 1995, 2000). The payer or agency may impose session or treatment limits. Moves, job changes, and other life events may affect the length or nature of treatment independent of patient preference or clinician recommendation.

Theoretical models also play a significant role in psychotherapy. Clinicians may rely on theory to explain change processes, and in the contextual model (Wampold, 2001) theories are valuable because they provide rationales for treatment, help organize it, and guide appropriate therapeutic goals for the particular clinical context. Clinicians also rely on a range of techniques drawn from multiple theoretical perspectives that research has found to be effective for particular symptom pictures or particular patient types and that the clinicians have found to be effective through their own experience and expertise (e.g., Arnkoff, Glass, & Shapiro, 2002; Beutler, Alomohamed, Moleiro, & Romanelli, 2002; Norcross, 2002).

The Contextual Model of Psychotherapy

Psychotherapy practice is inextricable from the context in which it occurs. Psychotherapy is an interpersonal experience, with a patient who is in distress and a treatment based on psychological principles and offered by a therapist. Wampold (2001), in *The Great Psychotherapy Debate*, presented a compelling differentiation between the medical model of psychotherapy and the contextual model of psychotherapy and described the research foundation on which the contextual model rests. Although not all clinicians or researchers see this model as a more accurate fit for psychotherapy process and outcomes data, the presentation closely matches the lived experience of many clinicians. It also provides the foundation for the remainder of this chapter. . . .

The Therapeutic Relationship

The therapeutic relationship is foundational to the psychotherapy endeavor. Just as psychotherapy cannot proceed without patients, it cannot proceed without a clinician,[1] and the therapeutic relationship is built by the two participants. The therapeutic relationship accounts for 30% of the variance in outcome in psychotherapy, second only to patient factors, which represent 40% of the variance (Assay & Lambert, 1999; Lambert, 1992; Lambert & Barley, 2002). . . .

The Working Alliance

The *therapeutic relationship* and the *working alliance* are often referred to synonymously, particularly in the research literature. The working alliance (originally conceptualized by Bordin, 1975) includes a bond between patient and therapist, agreement on goals, and consensus on therapeutic tasks. The alliance has repeatedly been found to be significantly related to outcome; Wampold (2001) and Horvath and Bedi (2002) provided summaries of this research. Given the large proportion of variance in outcome accounted for by the alliance, it is clearly important for clinicians and researchers to be continually attentive to the role and impact of the alliance and to the ways in which the alliance as a relationship can be enhanced.

The agreement on tasks and consensus on goals that are components of the alliance are significant in any consideration of the role of theory in evidence-based practice in psychology. Although well-designed research supports the effectiveness of psychotherapy, it does not offer clear support for relative effectiveness—that is, of one form of treatment over another, including treatment as usual in the community (Westen et al., 2004). . . .

The working alliance includes clinician and patient agreement on goals and tasks as major components of a successful alliance, and positive working alliance is related to better outcomes. The question may arise, however, about which goals and tasks the clinician and patient may agree on and how they come to the definition and the agreement. There are many possible goals and expected or desirable outcomes from psychotherapy, and it sometimes appears that there are as many measures of goals and outcomes as there are possible outcomes. Some examples included in studies of outcomes are self-esteem, premature termination, global change, symptom severity, interpersonal functioning, addiction severity, change in distress, drug use, alleviation of depressive symptoms, social adjustment, specific symptoms, social relationships, indecision, personal growth, relations with others, social or sexual adjustment, interpersonal problems, defense style, employment status, legal status, self-concept, anxiety symptoms, medication compliance, quality of life, hospitalization, productivity, and satisfaction with treatment (Horvath & Bedi, 2002). It is clear that the range of possible outcomes is huge. At the same time, the clinician and patient must identify outcomes they believe to be desirable and goals to be achieved and must reach agreement on these goals as an essential part of the alliance. The definition of outcomes arises from a shared perspective held by the clinician and patient.

Typically, the desirable goals for any particular psychotherapy are derived from patient need and problem type and patient and clinician worldviews. They are consistent with the theoretical framework from which the treatment was developed. Thus, agreement on goals implies agreement (whether implicit or explicit) on the theoretical framework (cogent and coherent explanation or rationale) from which the clinician operates. Therefore, the theoretical framework provides an important structure within which psychotherapy occurs and is significantly related to one of the components of psychotherapy outcome (agreement on goals as part of the alliance).

Patient Belief in the Treatment

According to Frank (1973; Frank & Frank, 1991) and Wampold (2001), the patient's belief in the treatment, its context, and the clinician is a component shared by all psychotherapy approaches. Indeed, it is hard to imagine how a patient without some belief and hope in the effectiveness of treatment could be an active participant in psychotherapy or could share an agreement on goals or outcome with the clinician. The participation of patients is essential, of course. Duncan (2002) described patients as the heroes of the treatment; it is the patient's therapy, and he or she makes whatever changes are to be made. Successful collaboration between clinician and patient (Tryon & Winograd, 2002) and lower levels of resistance (Beutler, Moleiro, & Talebi, 2002) are related to positive outcomes. Patient factors such as positive expectation, motivation, and openness to treatment (Grencavage & Norcross, 1990) account for 40% of the variance (Assay & Lambert, 1999). These factors, which are central to the patient's belief in the treatment, make patient characteristics and values the most potent component of successful treatment. These findings support the importance of agreement on goals and consensus on tasks, which are part of the alliance and part of the patient's belief in the healing benefit of psychotherapy. When there are difficulties in collaboration and resistance to the treatment is high (both reflect difficulties in the alliance), existing evidence suggests that acknowledging the patient's concerns, attending to the relationship, and renegotiating goals and roles may be effective in ameliorating problems in the alliance (Beutler & Harwood, 2002; Beutler, Moleiro, et al., 2002; Safran & Muran, 2002).

The Value of Flexible Theoretical Frameworks

Effective treatment clearly needs a cogent rationale, and clinician and patient need to agree on goals and tasks based on that rationale. At the same time, the complexity of psychotherapy may require renegotiating goals and roles to better align patient and clinician and to better match patient characteristics and worldview. Renegotiation and realignment call for flexibility in the theoretical framework guiding the treatment designed for the specific patient and his or her situation, as well as flexibility in the use of techniques derived from various theoretical approaches. The clinician needs to be adaptive and conversant with multiple theoretical perspectives that may guide his or her ability to integrate clinician worldview and patient worldview to match the particular patient. The clinician must be prepared to incorporate additional or different theoretical components to achieve better fit for the patient. In other words, the clinician's effectiveness rests in part on maintaining theoretical pluralism and the ability to be integrative in those theories.

A Conceptual Scheme

Rosenzweig (1936/2002) and Frank (Frank & Frank, 1991) supported the importance of an ideology or rationale provided by the clinician that presents a cogent, coherent, and plausible explanation for both the patient's distress and the approach the clinician will take to help the patient. This ideology engages the patient. It offers the patient hope and expectation (remoralization through positive expectation) in the treatment, as well as a way to understand the goals and tasks of treatment, which in turn enhance outcomes. Ideology, rationale, and coherent and cogent explanation are all different words for the *theoretical formulation* that guides the clinician in the treatment.

Patient Expectancy

Patient expectancy and hope are potent contributors to positive outcomes. Assay and Lambert (1999) suggested that the accumulation of research puts the contribution of patient expectancy for outcomes at about 15% of the variance. Expectation is typically cast as a placebo effect in medical model approaches, but the contextual model includes it as a central component of effective treatment. Placebo effects are essentially psychological effects and thus are undesirable in a model that attempts to minimize extrinsic factors through tight control and adherence to the treatment as defined. However, increased psychological effects as a result of psychological treatments seem desirable—not undesirable—outcomes and should be supported, and factors that increase positive expectations should be promoted. For example, a patient who moves into a hopeful state and no longer exhibits hopelessness (one of the primary symptoms of depression) because of his or her belief in the treatment demonstrates the effectiveness of nonspecific psychological factors in the treatment. The clinician wants to enhance the patient's belief in what he or she is offering to enhance expectancy effects. Therefore, the clinician would promote the importance of the theoretical framework to engage and encourage patients and heighten expectancy effects, as well as to take advantage of the positive contribution theory makes to agreement on goals and tasks.

Allegiance

Trust is a significant part of therapy; patient belief in and openness to treatment and the patient-clinician bond component of the alliance rely on trust (Horvath & Bedi, 2002). Clinicians' belief in their therapeutic models or theories is related to outcomes through its impact on clinician–patient agreement on goals and desirable outcomes and the extent to which it engages the patient. Therefore, the clinician must believe in his or her own treatment model, just as the patient does. The theoretical framework must therefore be cogent, coherent, and explanatory for the clinician as well as for the patient. Theory also provides the clinician with an underlying organization for the large amounts of information that are relevant to psychotherapy and that must be available for the clinician's use in the treatment.

To the extent that the clinician believes the theory to be explanatory for the patient's distress and to provide a rationale for the treatment plan and its implementation, one would expect the clinician to have considerable allegiance to the theoretical model he or she is using. Wampold (2001) offered extensive evidence regarding clinician allegiance to an espoused theoretical model and its strong positive relationship to outcomes.

It is important to note that the relationship between allegiance and outcomes appears to hold regardless of the truth value of the theory. One might think that this would lead to rampant development of a vast array of untested and untestable theoretical models. Despite frequent counts of theoretical models that number several hundred (e.g., Bergin & Garfield, 1994), the major models remain largely consistent categories.[2] At the same time, consistent with the importance of the theoretical model to both clinician and patient, clinicians would be expected to do one of two things: either endorse one of the existing general theoretical models or endorse an approach that draws from more than one model. Both seem to occur simultaneously, however. Clinicians choose one model as primary (often with a secondary choice when that is an alternative) and may also espouse an integrative perspective (drawing on multiple models) or eclecticism as their theoretical perspective (Garfield & Bergin, 1994; Jensen & Bergin, 1990; Norcross, Prochaska, & Farber, 1993; Wampold, 2001). Typically, *eclectic* draws the largest endorsement as a single category. Norcross et al. (1993) found that 40% of the members of the Division of Psychotherapy of the APA who responded to a survey of theoretical orientation chose *eclectic*, reflecting individualized versions based on experience, training in multiple models, and alterations in response to patient need. Clinicians' choice of eclectic as a theoretical perspective needs attention to understand its meaning, impact, and role as an explanatory system and the extent to which it is a well-developed individualized model versus a process for integrating multiple models (Carter, 2002).

Currently, theoretical integration, technical eclecticism, and common factors are receiving considerable attention, reflecting dissatisfaction with individual theoretical approaches and attempts to develop more flexible approaches. Theoretical integration is problematic if it becomes its own model, because it then has all of the problems that are associated with a single theoretical model (Feixas & Botella, 2004; O'Brien, 2004). However, it provides a useful framework if it provides procedures for integrating diverse perspectives into a system that is applicable for the particular clinician-patient pair, to the particular patient problems, and in the particular context (Feixas & Botella, 2004).

Technical eclecticism alone as a response to the poor fit of theoretical models is limited, because it takes only interventions into account and ignores the relevance and role of theoretical models. From an integrative or theoretically eclectic perspective, however, it is important for clinicians to be skilled in techniques drawn from the multiple theories from which their own theoretical perspective is derived. Because allegiance to a cogent rationale is important and clinicians and patients rely on theories to organize and guide their work, clinicians are expected to modify models as needed to be responsive to patients. Thus, psychologists must continue to develop and teach multiple models, to understand the components of the theories as explanatory tools, and to understand and effectively implement the techniques derived from the models.

Rituals and Procedures (Otherwise Known as Techniques)

Frank and Frank (1991), drawing on Rosenzweig's formulation (1936/2002), focused on the importance of rituals and procedures that are consistent with the rationale given for the treatment. The rituals and procedures that Frank and Frank suggested may best be understood as the interventions or techniques that are logically derived from the theoretical formulation of the causes of the patient's distress and the approach to ameliorating the dysfunction. Clinicians design techniques, then, to have a specific impact on symptoms, behaviors, or other components as defined by the theory from which they arise and with which they are consistent. Rosenzweig believed that an impact on any subsystem (or aspect) of personality affects all of the personality, suggesting that effective treatment may occur with any one of multiple symptoms as the target of interventions. If Rosenzweig was correct, techniques should have a positive impact on outcomes, but the impact should account for a relatively small portion of the variance. According to Assay and Lambert (1999), techniques overall account for only 15% of the variance, and specific techniques appear to make little additive difference in outcome (Wampold, 2001). Valuable research using designs that offer well-controlled and targeted interventions for specific symptom pictures demonstrates their effectiveness in both absolute and relative terms (Barlow, 2004). Although application of these results may call for adaptation to the particular treatment picture, these are useful tools for the clinician to have readily available. It is interesting to note that Westen et al. (2004), in a review of the current status of what have been known as empirically supported treatments, offered a hypothesis on the role of negative diatheses as an underlying principle that may be common to all psychological disorders and explanatory for varied presentations and comorbidity. The relationship between specific techniques for specific symptoms and the complex symptom picture in a typical clinical practice offers great opportunities for collaboration between research and practice.

Nevertheless, techniques do matter. Interventions are the tools through which psychotherapy occurs within the context previously described. They are the expression of the belief system arising from theoretical models. They operationalize the therapeutic tasks that are part of the alliance. They are the medium by which the relationship is developed and maintained. They build hope in the patient through active engagement in the tasks of therapy. They effectively alter specific symptoms. Hence, it is essential for clinicians to be technically eclectic and prepared with a wide range of tools to address the needs of patients in the continually changing world of psychotherapy. The contextual model, which reflects the deeply complex interpersonal world of psychotherapy, supports the importance of techniques as tools in trade (Wampold, 2001), with clinicians having the ability to apply multiple techniques in the service of an individually tailored psychotherapy.

Conclusion

Most clinicians strongly support models of psychotherapy that are context centered, that place a strong value on the relationship and alliance, and that are embedded in theoretical models. At the same time, clinicians rely on eclectic or integrative models, and their work reflects theoretical pluralism. In addition, experienced clinicians from different theoretical perspectives are more similar than different within the psychotherapy hour, using techniques drawn from a variety of theoretical approaches and reflecting technical eclecticism in the application of psychotherapy.

Psychological scientists and psychological practitioners have a number of areas of agreement about the evidence base underlying practice. The therapeutic relationship, a central component to practice, has strong evidentiary support as an essential factor in successful outcomes. Therefore, clinicians should devote considerable attention to building and maintaining a strong therapeutic relationship in the implementation of evidence-based practice. Evidence drawn from research on psychotherapy supports the importance of coherent and cogent explanations for distress, dysfunction, and treatment to positive outcomes. Therefore, clinicians who engage in evidence-based practice should devote time, energy, and attention to strengthening the cogency and clarity of their theoretical formulations, including both the major theoretical perspectives and the variants that are consistent with their own worldviews and psychology's scientific base. Theoretical pluralism is an important part of evidence-based practice.

The therapeutic alliance (which is part of the relationship) rests on agreement on goals and tasks and is positively

Should Therapists Be Eclectic? by Slife   **207**

related to outcomes. Agreement on goals and tasks is drawn from agreement on and belief in the explanations for and implementation of the treatment (the theoretical model the clinician uses and the techniques drawn from that model). The alliance necessarily takes into account the therapist's role, the patient's role, and the relationship between them. Clinicians who integrate principles of evidence-based practice devote energy to learning techniques that emanate from their own theoretical model. In addition, they should maintain openness to techniques that may complement or supplement those derived from their model, that may enhance the relationship, and that may fit the patient's desired goals, problems, and characteristics.

Placebo or expectancy effects are essentially belief in or hope for the treatment that rests on the patient's and the therapist's belief that the explanation is valid and that it will work—again, the important role of theory. Clinicians demonstrating evidence-based practice should support patients' hopes and beliefs, as well as their own, which requires a somewhat different approach to the evidence foundation for psychotherapy that draws on a context of discovery rather than a context of justification for the scientific thinking occurring within the hour.

Skill with a range of techniques is important as an expression of the theory (agreement on tasks), as a way to effectively manage the alliance and relationship, as rituals, and as ways to accommodate multiple problems, worldviews, and expected outcomes. Technical eclecticism is an important component of evidence-based practice in psychology.

Psychological research underlying evidence-based practice in psychology

- supports the use of theoretical pluralism and technical eclecticism to enhance the alliance and strengthen the therapeutic relationship;
- supports a coherent, cogent, and organized explanation for patient distress and its amelioration;
- fosters patient hope; and
- uses a range of techniques to maximize effectiveness.

Evidence-based practice in psychology has at its core an effort to enhance patient involvement and choice, as well as participation in his or her own health care. Implementing evidence-based practice requires the continuous and deliberate incorporation of both a scientific attitude and empirical research into an understanding and appreciation for the unique demands of psychotherapy practice. Commitment to evidence-based practice continues a strong belief in the integration of science and practice in psychology. Embracing it reflects psychology's past and supports its future.

Notes

1. Some computer models of intervention do not require the active participation of a clinician. However, psychotherapy is commonly understood to be an interpersonal process between a patient and a therapist.

2. The major models are behavioral and cognitive-behavioral, psychodynamic, humanistic or experiential, systems theory, and feminist theory. All of them have multiple variants that reflect shifts in perspective or incorporation of new knowledge drawn from general psychological principles or research on the treatment model itself.

JEAN A. CARTER is currently a member of the board of directors of the American Psychological Association. She began a psychotherapy practice in Washington, D.C., after receiving her PhD in counseling psychology from the University of Maryland in 1980 and continues her practice. At the Washington Psychological Center, she focuses on psychotherapy with individuals and couples, emphasizing aspects of serious trauma, relationship issues, depression, and work stress/vocational adjustment. Other areas of interest for her include grief and loss and issues related to sexual orientation for both individuals and couples. She also serves as an adjunct faculty member at the University of Maryland in counseling psychology.

Don MacDonald and Marcia Webb

 **NO**

Toward Conceptual Clarity with Psychotherapeutic Theories

The proliferation of theories for conducting psychotherapy makes it easy for a therapist to become lost in the welter of ideas. In particular, clarity about the criteria for and the evaluation of theories lags. The present article discriminates between syncretism and eclecticism. As part of the discrimination, it provides 14 interrelated criteria by which to assess a theory. It also distinguishes between theories and treatment models. Finally, it presents a proposal for the reciprocal development of both. These 14 criteria come from a broad array of professional literature, and provide an approximation of a holistic perspective of humanity. They also describe theories in a complex and comprehensive manner, and offer therapists the opportunity to make indepth attempts toward the integration of one's personal faith commitments and one's professional identity. Even with responsible efforts toward conceptual clarity, the authors describe the high potential for syncretism, due to the multitude of theories, models, and criteria currently available to psychotherapists. The authors further propose strategies to prevent the conceptual compromises associated with a syncretistic approach to the conceptualization and conduct of psychotherapy.

Psychotherapists look to theories to help them develop treatment goals, assessments, methods, and evaluations of processes and outcomes. Theory is a map and, as such, is an indispensable tool. Cherry, Messenger, and Jacoby (2000) and Striker (2002) identified psychotherapy as an important professional function, regardless of the preparation orientation of the therapist, viz., clinical scientist, scientist-practitioner, and practitioner-evaluator. Psychotherapeutic theories as maps, however, are only as helpful as their clarity permits. This article explores major sources of compromise for theoretical clarity and discusses means for fostering clarity. It makes no claims for achieving clarity. Rather the article proposes criteria that will hopefully stimulate discussion about the intentional development of theory. Thus, it is meant to be heuristic.

Theories of psychotherapy abound. Literally hundreds of theories exist and the number is growing (Corsini, 2000; Miller, Duncan, & Hubble, 1997). Naturally, it is impossible for a psychotherapist to know all or even most of them. Given that meta-analyses on the comparative effectiveness of many different therapeutic approaches indicate most are similar in being generally helpful (Shadish, Matt, Navarro, & Phillips, 2000; Smith & Glass, 1977; Wampold et al., 1997), it is unnecessary for psychotherapists to know multiple theories in order to work effectively. Rather, it seems that the therapist must be thoroughly grounded in the concepts and methods that he or she uses.

While knowledge of multiple theories may be unnecessary, it is nevertheless essential for effective psychotherapists to understand at least one theory well in order to apply it. On a continuum for comprehension of theory (McBride & Martin, 1990), one end entails understanding one or more theories thoroughly while the opposite end of the continuum entails understanding very little about even one theory. Limited understanding of even one theory relegates psychotherapists to adding a method here and an idea there, without a systematic conceptual basis to hold those methods and ideas together; this is conceptual *syncretism*. In the worst cases, psychotherapists operate out of syncretism, wherein they unsuccessfully attempt to synthesize different, perhaps contradictory, ideas and methods, with little or no awareness of their inherent incongruities. A cogent conceptual system, though, would solve this difficulty. . . .

The conceptual formation that psychotherapists go through is tantamount to the development of philosophies of science and practice. It may be a personal philosophy or one shared by colleagues in a department, school, or professional organization. It is nevertheless a conceptual guide to conducting and understanding research as well as clinical practice (Kendall, Butcher, & Holmbeck, 1999; Polkinghorne, 1986).

Arriving at a place of conceptual clarity vis-à-vis psychotherapeutic theories and a Christianity-theories relationship is far from an exact or predictable process. However, the process need not be hopeless or haphazard. We propose three broad approaches to intentionally enhance conceptual clarity. One, a common factors approach, is well established. The second, a rubric for theoretical criteria, is a proposal to establish descriptive criteria for theories of psychotherapy. Third, discriminating between theories and treatment models, is an established issue that is still seldom addressed. Admittedly all are exploratory efforts and will hopefully be heuristic. All are meant to stimulate discussion around how Christian

MacDonald, Don; Webb, Marcia. From *Journal of Psychology and Christianity*, 2006. Copyright © 2006 by Christian Association for Psychological Studies, Inc. Reprinted by permission.

psychotherapists and psychotherapy students can develop clear understandings of the profession and of themselves as persons and professionals.

Common Factors

Some researchers have suggested that common factors across all therapeutic modalities are responsible for treatment effectiveness, more than effects of any particular therapeutic approach (Carkhuff & Berenson, 1967; Corrigan, Dell, Lewis, & Schmidt, 1980; Hubble, Duncan, & Miller, 1999; Weinberger, 2002). Multiple studies confirm, for example, that a psychotherapist's warmth, regardless of the treatment modality employed in sessions, is associated with positive client outcomes. A placebo effect of treatment, or the client's simple expectation of progress, has also been demonstrated to be a catalyst of positive change in therapy, again regardless of the specific treatment approach.

Given the proliferation of multiple treatment modalities from which to choose for positive therapeutic outcomes and the evidence for common factors across various modalities, it is perhaps not surprising that in the last 40 years, movements for psychotherapeutic eclecticism or integration, have developed. Writers proposing the integration[1] of psychotherapies argue that no single theoretical system can account for, and meet, all therapeutic needs. They suggest instead that the use of flexible, varied treatment approaches is necessary to accommodate the multifaceted nature of human experience, rather than strict adherence to one narrowly defined, limited psychotherapeutic modality (Brammer, Shostrom, & Abrego, 1993; Carter, 2002; Prochaska & Norcross, 1999).

The prevalence of these ideas is evident in surveys of psychotherapists. Norcross and his colleagues undertook surveys in 1981, 1991, and 2001 (Norcross, Hedges, & Castle, 2002). Across the three surveys, more than one-third of the psychotherapists who practiced psychotherapy described themselves as eclectic; eclecticism was by far the largest group. Jensen, Bergin, and Greaves (1990) obtained a broad sampling of psychotherapists, including psychologists and psychiatrists. Jensen et al. found that 59% (psychiatrists) to 70% (clinical psychologists) of the groups sampled regarded themselves as eclectic. While the figures vary, it is clear that a substantial number of psychotherapists, including psychologists, draw upon multiple theories to inform their clinical practices. Such a strategy, however, is no solution for syncretism; indeed, it may increase the risk of syncretism.

Eclecticism need not be de facto syncretistic. One of the more widely respected attempts at a form of eclecticism, known as Therapeutic Integration, is found in the writing of Paul Wachtel (1977). Wachtel provides a model for the harmonious interaction among diverse theories of treatment. His efforts toward integration of psychotherapeutic theories helped establish the potential and validity of the integration movement (Prochaska & Norcross,

1999). More recently, he reworked his original formulation to include further developments in psychotherapy, such as general system theory (Wachtel, 1997).

Even with prototypes such as Wachtel (1977, 1997), the task of psychotherapeutic integration is not for the faint of heart; it is more complex than assumed by perhaps too many psychotherapists. Given that the pluralistic praxis of daily experiences for psychotherapists is often complicated and challenging, conceptual clarity is a sine qua non. Unfortunately, more than one observer has noted that attempts at theoretical integration are often haphazard, unsystematic, internally conflicted, and arbitrary (Ginter, 1988; Norcross, 1986; Patterson, 1990). In other words, many psychotherapists function in a syncretistic manner.

The worst results of syncretism are conceptual confusion and ineffectiveness in treatment (McBride & Martin, 1990; Smith, 1982; Travis, 2003). In syncretism, the psychotherapist lacks overall organizing principles to guide treatment—the map is flawed or incomplete. As the descriptions of mental health and goals of therapy can vary across theories of psychotherapy, the syncretistic psychotherapist may unknowingly drift amidst competing, and potentially contradictory, notions of treatment plans and methods.

Understanding theoretical constructs is often difficult. Yet application of theory is even more difficult. Psychotherapy students often complain it is hard to put a theory into practice, as it ideally appears in a text or video. Even an experienced psychotherapist may have trouble clearly describing the theory drawn upon and its appearance in clinical situations. Conceptual clarity is essential, though, if psychotherapy is to fulfill its claim and potential to provide scientifically based services (Deegear & Lawson, 2003; McPherson, 1992; Striker, 2002). . . .

Distinctions Between Theories and Models

A major detraction from theoretical clarity exists around use of the term "theory." It is typically used inaccurately, with vague definitions and criteria (Blocher, 1987). As applied here, a theory is a formally organized collection of facts, definitions, constructs, and testable propositions that are meaningfully interrelated (Kendall et al., 1999; Mullins, 1971; Wallsten et al, 2000).

Few of the hundreds of "theories" meet most of the rubric's fourteen criteria. Probably none fulfill all of the criteria. Most of what are called theories are more accurately called treatment models. They develop in a process parallel to theories and share some features with theories (see Figure 1). A treatment model usually identifies therapy goals, processes, and methods thought to be helpful, but lack clarity about specific, foundational theses and hypotheses that support the use of certain treatment strategies. Instead, the assessment of helpfulness usually follows from clinical experiences of the person(s) who developed the model. While possibly useful and

Figure 1

Major Pieces in the Development of Theories and Models

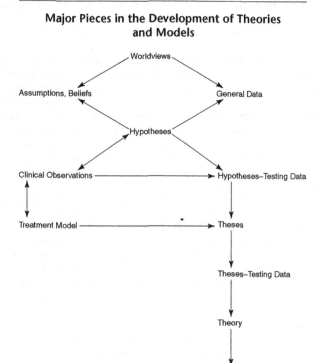

Worldviews relate reciprocally with general life data. Worldviews are influenced by learning experiences and, in turn, affect what people perceive and how they interpret their perceptions. While genetically transmitted temperaments provide broad parameters for worldviews, daily life experiences affect the particular manifestations of these temperaments (Kristal, 2005). Say, for instance, both the psychotherapist and client in the previous paragraph are born with a temperament of approach to human relations or sociability. The psychotherapist's overall life experiences of trust and security in relationships, . . . builds on this inherent tendency. The client's experiences of pain and betrayal in significant relationships, however, prompt an approach-avoidance conflict around relationships (i.e., temperament plus positive experiences prompt formation of relationships, while potent negative experiences signal danger in human relations).

Assumptions and beliefs and general life data, with their worldviews substrate, combine to foster hypotheses about psychotherapy in general and about specific clients (Figure 1). Thus, the personal life of the psychotherapist is an active participant in the conceptualization and execution of treatment processes (Corey, Corey, & Callanan, 2003; Tjeltveit, 1986). Hypotheses, then, have a recursive relationship with clinical observations, wherein the psychotherapist notes how clients act vis-à-vis their personalities, therapeutic issues, and the therapeutic setting (including the psychotherapist), while the personalities, issues, and setting influence the psychotherapist.

Psychotherapy hypotheses are also tested as to their veracity. That is, the psychotherapist checks the validity and reliability of conceptualizations about an individual or a group of clients (e.g., those diagnosed with bulimia). The psychotherapist systematically collects and tests data pertinent to therapeutic hypotheses. This is where the criteria of the rubric may be especially useful. Testing usually involves a few clients and may consist of parametric, nonparametric, or qualitative research designs and statistics (Beutler, 2000; Striker, 2002).

The hypothesis-testing of therapeutic data demarcates the divergence of theory development from treatment model development (Figure 1). With the latter, clinical observations and inferences from them remain the primary data. The treatment model might be a valid and reliable representation of clients and psychotherapy, but subjectivity precludes such determinations (Campbell & Stanley, 1966). Data that are systematically collected and analyzed, plus clinical observations and inferences, afford a broader platform upon which to build theoretical constructs (Kendall et al., 1999). . . .

Well developed and tested hypotheses allow for thesis construction. Theses, of course, guide formal data collection and analyses. From theses-testing, the psychotherapist has a clear data-based foundation for theory building. Theoretical constructions, in turn, are tested, retained, rejected, or modified (Carter, 2002; Mullins, 1971; Persons, 1991). Theory development through theses-testing does

immediately applicable, a treatment model lacks the formal organization and verification of a theory (Blocher, 1987). It is possible for a treatment model to develop into a theory (Figure 1), however few do so.

Figure 1 traces major pieces in the development of theories and models. While a two-dimensional illustration suggests this development is linear and sequential, the actual process is more like a hologram: a three-dimensional sphere with worldviews . . . in the center and the other pieces arranged around the center, linked to each other through reciprocal feedback loops. Ideally, the process is open to new information on a selective basis (i.e., based on theory construction criteria), which balances change with organization and stability (Bertalanffy, 1968; Keeney & Ross, 1985).

Worldviews pervade all other theory development processes, as discussed in the section on theory development criteria. These cognitions directly affect the assumptions and beliefs a psychotherapist applies to creating, interpreting, and applying a theory or model. Insofar as they influence all aspects of theory, conceptual neutrality is impossible (MacDonald, 1991; Sue & Sue, 2003). A psychotherapist, for example, who holds the belief that the world is basically a safe place may tend to draw attention to instances of safety in the life of a client who was physically abused as a child and overlook the client's own view of the world as essentially a dangerous place.

not guarantee unambiguous results, eliminate subjectivity, or partition out worldviews, but effects of these factors are easier to identify and explain when referenced to specific data.

Discussion in this section summarized general conceptual development of psychotherapeutic treatment models and theories. Even though most psychotherapists do not develop a formal theory or model, they either adopt an existing approach to psychotherapy or create a personal one (Corsini, 2000). This process yields optimal conceptual clarity when the psychotherapist manages it in the intentional, explicit manner of theory development.

Choosing a Theory or Model

At some point the psychotherapist chooses one or more theories or models as a means to work with people. This choice typically occurs in a preparation program (Capuzzi & Gross, 1995), although it is not limited to this period of time and the psychotherapist may subsequently add to the choice or even change entirely. Regardless of the timing, psychotherapists often experience direct or de facto pressure to make one of three choices: (a) align with one theory or model, (b) take an intentional eclectic or integration stance, or (c) do not think about it, thereby opening the door to syncretism. The preferred professional route, as discussed shortly, is either aligning with one theory or taking an intentionally eclectic stance. Both of these preferred choices are deliberate, systematic, and have their respective benefits and limitations. Unfortunately, some research suggests that psychotherapists who choose the third option of not thinking about it can be unaware of the degree to which they have adopted a de facto syncretistic approach to treatment.

Researchers have distinguished, for example, between those practitioners who are *explicitly eclectic*, who are aware of and intentional regarding their modalities of preference, and those who do not endorse an eclectic approach, but who nevertheless employ terminology and techniques from a variety of theories. This latter group has been described as *implicitly eclectic* (Hollanders, 1999). Findings surrounding the phenomenon of implicit eclecticism suggest that some practitioners in the process of theory adoption opt for the not-think-about-it stance, as listed above, or invest so little intellectual energy in a single theory or in an eclectic stance that it is almost the same as not thinking about the process altogether (Omer & Dar, 1992). It is this choice that fosters syncretism.

Selecting and staying with one theory or model has a number of benefits. Psychotherapists who commit themselves to the study and application of one theory or model have the potential to achieve a type of professional integrity in their practice of psychotherapy. They may be less prone to alteration by vacillations within the profession arising from, for example, treatment fads or pressures from external sources, such as insurance companies or public opinion (Prochaska & Norcross, 1999). These psychotherapists may be more likely to offer a consistent, balanced vision of treatment via their given modalities of intervention. In addition, adherence to a single theory or model allows for an enriched dialogue among similarly committed professionals who share the common knowledge of its language, ideas and history. This shared dialogue further augments the possibilities for development of the theory or model within professional societies over time. Finally, commitment to one theory or model may foster an appreciation not only of its unique advantages and limitations in psychotherapy, but also of its differences from other theories and models.

Syncretism, with its hodge-podge of multiple treatment elements, increases the possibility for the distinctiveness and organization of each theory or model, with its particular terminology and application, to be lost. This may result, paradoxically, in the lack of appreciation for, or even awareness of, the genuine diversity that exists across conceptual and treatment approaches.

Part of the difficulty in selecting and employing "theories," however, is that many of them are actually treatment models (ref. Figure 1), which are often less articulated than many psychotherapists find useful. The less articulated a model is, of course, the harder a psychotherapist must work to make sense of the model and to apply it. The assumption here is that no treatment strategy optimally coheres outside of the more comprehensive, schematic system afforded by a theory (Kendall et al., 1999). Perhaps the psychotherapist works out a personal resolution to the unexplained parts of a treatment model, creating individual theses and hypotheses where none have been formally articulated by proponents of the model. It is also possible, though, that the psychotherapist remains unclear about what the model means and how to implement it.

While this lack of comprehensiveness in models is problematic for psychotherapists, the adoption of a personal resolution surrounding the missing elements of a model may create other difficulties. This strategy unwittingly encourages the formation by multiple psychotherapists of idiosyncratic conceptualizations around a single model, each of which is tailor-made for and by the therapist in question, yet each of which bears the same name, and is promoted as reflecting the original model upon which it was based. This in itself may serve as a catalyst for some degree of confusion, rather than clear communication, among psychotherapists and consumers of therapeutic services.

Despite these difficulties, going the route of a treatment model has definite appeal. For one, it has fewer steps and is a faster route than theory-building (Omer & Dar, 1992) (Figure 1). Second, the usual datum of proof, "clinical observations," has a way of supporting existing hypotheses (Travis, 2003). That is, the subjectivity and arbitrariness of these observations makes it very difficult to validate their accuracy between observers. The observations are what Campbell and Stanley (1966) called case studies or crude correlations. Case studies or crude correlations may provide nominal data that are helpful in stimulating further research, but neither is sufficient in the long-term for inferring causality or systemic relational patterns.

Research in cognition identifies a tendency to focus upon and recall selectively that information which supports original ideas, a reasoning fallacy known as *confirmation bias*. *Belief perseverance*, a reasoning fallacy similar to confirmation bias, further complicates the problem. According to research examining belief perseverance, people tend to adhere to their original ideas, regardless of the presence of disconfirming evidence. While these studies in cognition considered the problematic reasoning of the average individual in everyday situations, anecdotal evidence also exists to support the existence of these fallacies in academic and scientific reasoning as well (Eysenck & Keane, 2000; Howard, 1985; Reisberg, 1997). As Tjeltveit (1986) demonstrated, psychotherapists also succumb to reasoning fallacies in their practical, daily work with clients and in how they think about working with clients. Theories, with their inherent processes of verification that are involved in their establishment and development, allow for greater challenges to reasoning fallacies such as confirmation bias and belief perseverance.

Knowing What to Believe: Strategies Toward the Prevention of Syncretism

Unfortunately, preparation programs may inadvertently encourage the development of syncretism among students. This implicit encouragement comes about when programs feel appropriately obligated to present students with the widest possible exposure to various treatment theories and models. The syncretistic effect compounds where faculty teach no differentiation between theories and models. At the same time, constraints on programs (e.g., administrative budget, faculty experience) may make it impossible to teach each of these approaches at sufficient depth or breadth to foster conceptual sophistication. Given this challenge, how might preparation programs provide opportunities for students both to grasp the diversity of theories and models available to psychotherapists today, while steering clear of the conceptual compromises accompanying syncretism?

Many programs offer at least one survey course in multiple therapeutic modalities (APA, 2003). In addition to its presentation of various approaches to treatment, this course could also include sections examining the broad distinctions between theories and models, and the relative benefits and challenges of each. Examining and applying the 14 criteria for a theory may help students comprehend significant issues involved when selecting a theory or model, or when considering some form of eclecticism or integration (MacDonald, 1991). Current research on common factors might be included as a topic for this course, allowing the student as well to consider the importance of

factors beyond modality that impact treatment efficacy. In addition, this course might examine the movement for therapeutic integration, with its more sophisticated exemplars (e.g., Watchel, 1977, 1997). Finally, explicit discussion regarding the problems of syncretism might be included in a survey course covering multiple approaches to treatment. Faculty could describe examples of syncretistic analyses in class as an effort to illuminate their limitations.

It might be essential to cover philosophies of science and practice in a preparation program. These broad topics would provide students general worldviews through which they could evaluate theories and models. . . . Inasmuch as psychology and allied professions prematurely truncated the close relationship with its parent discipline, philosophy (MacDonald, 1991, 1996; Miller, 2005), the helping professions have unknowingly suffered from a lack of conceptual breadth and perspective. Addressing philosophy of science in a course or courses should help speak to this lack. . . .

Philosophies of science and practice in psychotherapy courses might consider the strengths and the limitations of the scientific enterprise in general, as well as the many variables which impact the development and application of psychotherapy over time. Such perspectives may allow the Christian therapist greater understanding when examining various psychotherapeutic theories or models. . . .

Following a preliminary course introducing several theories and models, students might be encouraged to focus upon one or two for the remainder of their preparation. This choice would hopefully impact the focus and themes of various papers they construct in classes. . . .

Supervision of therapy is another opportunity for preparation to focus upon one modality (Matarozzo & Garner, 1992). For individual supervision, programs could intentionally assign students to supervisors based on that supervisor's preferred treatment theory or model, allowing the student an extended opportunity to observe the elements of that approach in a mentoring relationship. Supervisors might also assign to supervisees readings composed by the major contributors to the theory or model under consideration. Supervisees could be taught to prepare in their client progress notes a written summary of the components of sessions, specifically utilizing the language and ideas of the specific model, to bring each time to supervision. In group supervision, supervisors might distribute information about one case to supervisees, with each supervisee assigned to describe that case from the perspective of a distinct theory or model before the group.

Fundamental to each of these suggestions is the need to be more intentional with the preparation of psychotherapists in order to foster greater conceptual clarity and to reduce the likelihood of syncretism. The rapid proliferation of new therapies has created a situation in which the explicit discussion of the choice for therapeutic stance becomes all the more important. A student's eventual clinical efficacy as a psychotherapist, and thus even the future direction of psychotherapy as a valid resource for the community, necessitates clarity about communication and choices regarding therapeutic modalities.

Note

1. We realize that some authors distinguish between eclecticism and the more recent term of integration. To complicate matters further, the term integration has been used for several decades to denote efforts to bring Christian faith and psychology together. It is beyond the scope of our article to discern between eclecticism and integration. Since the terms overlap substantially, we use them interchangeably. We also assume that most psychotherapists who are Christians wish to integrate their faith and

their craft, understanding that some differ on this point.

Don MacDonald is a professor of marriage and family therapy in the psychology department at Seattle Pacific University. He received his PhD in counseling psychology at Michigan State University in 1984. His interests include the theological, philosophical, and historical influences of Christianity and psychology.

Marcia Webb is an associate professor in the Department of Clinical Psychology at Seattle Pacific University. She is involved in the Living Well Initiative, a multidisciplinary program providing education and conducting research about severe and persistent mental illnesses. Her research emphasizes forgiveness, the self-conscious emotions of shame and guilt, the integration of psychology and theology, and the psychology of religion.

EXPLORING THE ISSUE

Should Therapists Be Eclectic?

Critical Thinking and Reflection

1. What are the advantages and disadvantages inherent in an eclectic approach and a single-theory approach?
2. Consider how you would go about selecting a theoretical orientation. What factors would be most important in deciding whether to adhere to one theory over another and why?
3. What hidden biases motivate the authors of the YES and NO selections to promote either an eclectic or a single-theory approach?
4. Are eclectic approaches ever truly capable of being systematic if they are created from diverse theories and techniques? State your own position on this issue and describe your justification for endorsing it.
5. Are there instances where a single-theory approach can draw from ideas and techniques that are not traditionally a part of that system?

Create Central

www.mhhe.com/createcentral

Additional Resources

Brooks-Harris, J. E. (2008). *Integrative Multitheoretical Psychotherapy*. Boston, MA: Houghton-Mifflin.

Lazarus, A. A. (2005). Multimodal therapy. In *Handbook of Psychotherapy Integration* (2nd ed., pp. 105–120), J. C. Norcross and M. R. Goldfried (Eds.). New York: Oxford.

Good, G. E., and Beitman, B. D. (2006). *Counseling and Psychotherapy Essentials: Integrating Theories, Skills, and Practices*. New York: W. W. Norton.

Internet References . . .

Psych Central

http://psychcentral.com/therapy.htm

Integrated Psychotherapy

www.integratedpsychotherapy.com/

Selected, Edited and with Issue Framing Material by:
Brent Slife, *Brigham Young University*

ISSUE

Can Psychotherapy Change Sexual Orientation?

YES: Stanton L. Jones and Mark A. Yarhouse, from "Ex-Gays?: A Longitudinal Study of Attempted Religiously Mediated Sexual Orientation Change," *Journal of Sex & Marital Therapy* (pp. 404–427, 2011)

NO: A. Lee Beckstead, from "Can We Change Sexual Orientation?" *Archives of Sexual Behavior* (vol. 41, no. 1, pp. 121–134, 2012)

Learning Outcomes

After reading this issue, you should be able to:

- Understand how individuals wishing to change their sexual orientation should be encouraged to do so.
- Decide if sexual orientation change efforts provide false hope to individuals.

ISSUE SUMMARY

YES: Psychologists Stanton Jones and Mark Yarhouse describe an extensive study they believe demonstrates that sexual orientation can be changed in therapy clients at a faith-based center.

NO: Psychotherapist A. Lee Beckstead reviews current psychological attitudes toward homosexuality and concludes that treatment to change sexual orientation is more likely to harm than to help.

Few contemporary social and political issues are more controversial than those relating to sexual orientation and homosexuality. Opinions on this topic run strong and vary widely based on differing social, political, moral, and religious views. While the debate in today's political landscape often centers on the legality of homosexual marriage, topics relating to homosexuality have a complicated history with psychology and psychiatry. In fact, homosexuality was defined as a mental illness until a 1973 committee decision of the American Psychiatric Association. Today, however, the American Psychological Association states quite straightforwardly that lesbian, gay, and bisexual orientations "represent normal forms of human experience." Yet some aspects of homosexuality still elicit differing professional opinions, in particular the notion of sexual orientation change efforts (SOCE).

SOCE or "reparative therapies" involve individuals seeking help from distress caused by an unwanted sexual orientation and are typically administered in faith-based ministries and clinics. While proponents see these treatments as a valuable option available to those seeking relief from a burden defined within personal moral guidelines, opponents take offense at the notion that homosexuality could or should be treated at all. Conflicting research findings have further complicated the issue. The APA has

attempted to clarify the issues by expressing concern over the safety of any therapy "promoted to modify sexual orientation." A proposed California law would also bar the application of SOCE techniques to minors. On the other hand, supporters of SOCE treatments argue that some research supports the effectiveness and safety of efforts to alter an unwanted sexual orientation.

Psychologists Stanton Jones and Mark Yarhouse, two SOCE researchers, present research that they say demonstrates the possibility of sexual orientation change among individuals seeking it. In this research they tracked measures of homo- and heterosexual identification over a 7-year period among religious individuals who sought to change their homosexual orientation. Jones and Yarhouse found that approximately one-third of the individuals receiving SOCE treatment experienced either a lasting "conversion" of sexual attraction from same-sex to opposite-sex, or a significant decrease in homosexual attraction. An additional one-third of participants experienced moderate but insufficient change in same-sex attraction, while the final third experienced no change or more fully embraced their homosexual identification. The authors cite this evidence to support the possibility that homosexual orientation is changeable.

Psychotherapist A. Lee Beckstead reviews the literature addressing sexual reorientation. He argues that little is known for certain, but the limitations of SOCE therapy are sufficiently significant that efforts would be more productively spent elsewhere. He specifically finds fault with the methods of several studies that seem to support SOCE. For example, he questions the trustworthiness of self-report measures. Beckstead also calls attention to the overall discouraging findings about the possibilities for change in sexual orientation as well as the possibilities for harm in individuals. He concludes that treatment services are better focused on fighting discrimination against non-heterosexuals and helping them to live with the reality of their sexual orientations.

POINT

- SOCE patients have reported significant changes in sexual orientation.
- The specific subjects involved in this research were highly motivated to seek a change and demonstrate the realm of what is possible.
- Clients who desire to change their sexual orientation should be given the opportunity to access the tools to do so.
- Those seeking change reported no negative effects of treatment.

COUNTERPOINT

- Some former SOCE clients report going back to a homosexual orientation after treatment.
- The samples used at religious ministries do not represent a normal population from which to draw conclusions.
- SOCE misrepresents the possibility of successful change, giving false hope of changing what is likely a permanent feature of sexuality.
- Self-report measures are unreliable from those who are religiously motivated and seeking change in sexual orientation.

YES

**Stanton L. Jones and
Mark A. Yarhouse**

Ex-Gays?: A Longitudinal Study of Attempted Religiously Mediated Sexual Orientation Change

The seeming professional consensus that sexual orientation is immutable was asserted for years on the Public Affairs website of the American Psychological Association, where an absolute answer to the question of change was offered: "Can therapy change sexual orientation? No. . . . [H]omosexuality is not an illness. It does not require treatment and is not changeable." The present study was initiated at the time when the prevailing view was that homosexual orientation was not changeable. Claims of immutability have often been paired with expressed concern about harm produced by the attempt to change, such as the American Psychiatric Association's claim that the "potential risks of 'reparative therapy' are great, including depression, anxiety and self-destructive behavior."

The assertion that sexual orientation is immutable was notable in light of the dozens of studies published in professional journals over decades suggesting significant change by at least some of those seeking change via professional psychotherapy or religiously mediated means. Still, reports of some possibility of change in sexual attraction have continued to emerge. For example, Diamond followed a group of 89 young women over a decade across five samplings. Although this was not a study of sexual orientation change as such, Diamond studied several variables, including sexual identity labels, intensity of attraction, and behavior, and whether these variables changed over time. In general, most women who consistently identified themselves as bisexual and unlabeled "reported that attractions to men and women were about equal in intensity." In contrast, most women who identified as lesbian consistently throughout the longitudinal study reported "between 90 and 95 percent of their attractions for women." However, at her 10-year assessment, "10% of the women who had originally identified as lesbian ended up settling down into long-term relationships with men." Showing the complexity of her findings, she further reported, "Among the 12 women who ended up re-identifying as heterosexual during the study (5 of whom returned to a lesbian, bisexual, or unlabelled identity by the 10-year point), only 3 claimed that they no longer experienced attractions for women." Although Diamond's was not a study of intentional attempts to change

orientation, and acknowledging possible profound developmental differences in male and female sexuality, these basic findings stand in dissonance with any absolute declaration that orientation cannot change.

The American Psychological Association's recent pronouncements on the likelihood of change have moderated somewhat from the earlier immutability stance on their website. The Executive Summary of the Report of the American Psychological Association Task Force on Appropriate Therapeutic Responses to Sexual Orientation stated that its review has established that "enduring change to an individual's sexual orientation is uncommon," although in other places the report strikes a stance of agnosticism, stating for example that "there is little in the way of credible evidence that could clarify whether SOCE [sexual orientation change efforts] does or does not work in changing same-sex sexual attractions."

On what basis has immutability been asserted in light of prior published research claiming such change? Anecdotes of failed change (by "ex-ex-gays") have contributed to such pessimism, as has the steady decline of published studies in the last several decades. Most important, the methodological rigor of past research has been challenged, with the lack of longitudinal studies the most frequent concern expressed. The public affairs website of the American Psychological Association stated for many years that "claims [of orientation change] are poorly documented. For example, treatment outcome is not followed and reported over time as would be the standard to test the validity of any mental health intervention." Indeed, many past studies were methodologically limited. They used obscure or idiosyncratic measures of sexual orientation change, relied on therapist ratings rather than client ratings, used reports from memory of past feelings rather than sampling participants prospectively, and/or were cross-sectional snapshots rather than true longitudinal studies. The American Psychological Association Task Force formulated five "best-practice standards for the design of efficacy research" on SOCE:

Research on SOCE would (a) use methods that are prospective and longitudinal; (b) employ sampling methods that allow proper generalization;

(c) use appropriate, objective, and high-quality measures of sexual orientation and sexual orientation identity; (d) address preexisting and co-occurring conditions, mental health problems, other interventions, and life histories to test competing explanations for any changes; and (e) include measures capable of assessing harm.

The present study was designed to address the weaknesses of previous studies, particularly the need for longitudinal studies. Though the design of the present study was conceptualized and implemented many years before the 2009 Task Force Report, this study meets many of the standards proposed by the American Psychological Association Task Force. In particular, and responding to their five recommendations:

1. The present study is prospective and longitudinal.
2. Its quasi-experimental design is adequate to address ("generalize to") the fundamental question of whether sexual orientation change is ever possible, although the design is inadequate, as the Task Force Report points out, because of the "absence of a control or comparison group," to allow for decisive causal attribution of the changes noted to the religious interventions. The design is adequate, however, as a test of the possibility of change.
3. The study used the best validated measures of sexual orientation current in the late 1990s when the design was set.
4. The study did not address competing explanations as proposed by the Task Force because it had an insufficient sample size to make valid inferences.
5. The study included a validated measure of psychological distress as an index of harm.

Measurement of sexual orientation can be construed as one of the most contentious issues in studying the possibility of sexual orientation change. Previous studies of change have been criticized for using unvalidated and/or idiosyncratic measures of sexual orientation. Although a valid concern, this criticism also makes two highly problematic assumptions: (a) that a stable consensus exists around a single definition of sexual orientation and (b) that there exists a consensus about reliable and valid ways to assess it. On the nature of sexual orientation, for example, Cochran argued:

> Sexual orientation is a multidimensional concept including inter-correlated dimensions of sexual attraction, behavior, and fantasies, as well as emotional, social, and lifestyle preferences. . . . I refer to those individuals who experience same-gender sexual desire or behavior or who label themselves with any of a number of terms (e.g., lesbian, homosexual, gay, bisexual, questioning) that reflect a sense of possessing, at least in part, a same-gender sexual orientation.

This definition reflects a modesty, fluidity, multidimensionality, and open-endedness that is well-grounded in the complex realities of sexual orientation. Similarly, despite our intent to use best measures of sexual orientation, Sell was not without basis for his general conclusion that "none of these [sexual orientation measures existing in 1997] are completely satisfactory." We report on two measures of sexual orientation from among the more highly regarded scales available when this study began, focusing on those that appear to most straightforwardly assess basic dimensions of sexual orientation. We did not use psychophysiological measures to assess sexual orientation, because we judged such methods to be (a) pragmatically impossible given the geographically dispersed nature of our sample, our limited control over initial assessment settings and later move to assessment via phone and self-administered questionnaires, and the limitations of our funding; (b) morally unacceptable to the bulk of our research participants because such methods require participants to be exposed to sexually explicit stimulus materials that their moral principles would direct them to refrain from; and (c) not justified in light of current research challenging the reliability and validity of the methods themselves.

There are two sets of methods used by those seeking change in sexual orientation. One set involves professional psychotherapy; these methods are often called reorientation or conversion therapies. Independently, there are religious ministries of various kinds that use a combination of spiritual and psychological methods to seek to produce orientation change. This study addresses the generic questions of whether sexual orientation is changeable and whether the attempt is harmful by focusing only on the religiously mediated approaches to change. We report longitudinal outcomes over a 6-7-year period for a group of individuals seeking sexual orientation change via a diverse cluster of religious ministries under the Christian umbrella organization, *Exodus*. The hypotheses for this study were (a) sexual orientation change is possible for some; and (b) the attempt to change is, on average, not harmful. . . .

Discussion

On a number of standardized quantitative measures of sexual orientation, this population experienced statistically significant change away from homosexual experience and orientation. Although statistically significant, the average changes in absolute terms on the quantitative measures are modest at best, though the qualitative outcomes suggest clinically and personally significant outcomes for a number of individuals. The diversity of outcomes, as portrayed in the cross-tabulation table of raw Kinsey attraction and fantasy scores and in the qualitative outcomes, partially explains the modest absolute magnitudes of the quantitative outcomes, as they depict individuals shifting from more average scores at Tl to both extremes of final outcomes. In other words, the modest if significant average changes are composites of some dramatic shifts to a gay identity, but also of others who report dramatic changes away from homosexual orientation. Results were considerably less dramatic for the Phase 1 subpopulation (i.e., those in the change process for less than 1 year at the Time 1 assessment).

Our first hypothesis was that sexual orientation is changeable. If change is taken to mean a reduction in homosexual attraction and an increase in heterosexual attraction, we found evidence that successful change of sexual orientation occurred for some individuals concurrent with involvement in the religiously mediated change methods of Exodus Ministries (23% of the T6 sample by qualitative self-categorization). Those who report a successful heterosexual adjustment regard themselves as having changed their sexual orientation. For conventionally religious persons, a reduction in homosexual attraction and stable behavioral chastity as reported by 30% of the T6 sample may also be regarded as a successful outcome. Those who report chastity regard themselves as having reestablished their sexual identities to be defined in some way other than by their homosexual attractions. No data emerging from this study suggest that this is a maladaptive or unsustainable outcome.

Phase 1 participants, those inducted into the study early in their change venture, appear to be disproportionately represented among the more negative qualitative outcomes and had more modest quantitative outcomes. This may indicate that positive outcomes for those first initiating the change process are likely less positive than the overall findings of this study would suggest, that the change process is difficult and requires extraordinary persistence to attain success, or other possibilities. There were, however, some Phase 1 participants in all qualitative outcome categories.

The qualitative Success: Chastity outcomes might be regarded legitimately not as change of orientation but rather as a shift in sexual identity. Recent theoretical and empirical work on sexual identity among religious sexual minorities suggests that attributions and meaning are critical in the decision to integrate same-sex attractions into a gay identity or the decision to disidentify with a gay identity and the persons and institutions that support gay identity. Some religious persons attribute their same-sex attraction to who they really are, and they integrate their attractions into a private and public gay identity. Other religious persons, though, attribute their attractions to living in an imperfect world, early parent–child relationships, experiences of childhood sexual abuse, and so on, and form their identity around other aspects of themselves, such as their religious identity, which they may experience as equally or more central to their identity than their experiences of same-sex attraction.

In light of the role of attributions and meaning in sexual identity labeling, is it possible as well that some of what is reported in this study as change of orientation (i.e., the outcomes experienced by the Success: Conversion

participants) is more accurately understood as change in sexual identity? An interesting observation about this data is that most of the change that was reported on the self-report measures occurred early in the change attempt. Our previous report indicated that this change most commonly occurred between T1 and T2, and that the shift that occurred was sustained through T3. The present data suggest such change can be sustained through T6 for those who report successful change. These findings go against the common argument that change of orientation is gradual and occurs over an extended period of time. Some may see these results as reflecting not a change in sexual orientation for most participants who reported such change, but rather a change in sexual identity. Such a change might result from how one thinks of oneself and labels one's sexual preferences (i.e., attributions and meaning making). It is also possible, though, that this data reflects persons who experienced a change in orientation and a change in sexual identity. In some individuals, a shift in sexual identity might subsequently be consolidated as true shift in sexual orientation. The Kinsey measures of sexual attraction and sexual fantasy would seem to measure some of the fundamental dimensions of sexual orientation. The shifts reported appear to be consolidated and sustained over time for those who reported a successful outcome at T6. It certainly appears from this data that the process of change is complex and multifaceted.

The proportion of participants that must be considered unequivocal successes (Conversion) by the standards of Exodus increased from 15% of the sample at T3 to 23% of the sample at T6. Combined with the Chastity outcome participants, 53% of the T6 sample attained a form of success that these individuals consider a successful outcome, this compared to a total of 38% of such successful outcomes at T3. An additional 16% continue 6 and 7 years later to pursue change, and appear to have derived enough benefit from the change attempt to continue down this challenging path despite not attaining the outcomes they desire. In contrast, the outcomes that are regarded by Exodus as failures are not so regarded by many in the professional community nor by these individuals; the Failure: Gay Identity outcome cases are not properly analogous to relapses to worsened manifestations of addictive behavior or heightened psychotic states.

The overall T6 outcomes reported here must be seen as an overly optimistic representation of the possibility of change. What would be the most pessimistic prognostication of outcomes in sexual orientation change from the Exodus process one could make from this data? If one assumed that only the Phase 1 participants were valid representatives of a true prospective study (which might be true), and that all missing cases were failures (which we know not to be true), one could conclude that from 57 initial Phase 1 participants, only five attained Success: Conversion status (9%), six attained Success: Chastity (11%), and four attained Continuing status (7%). One could further insist that only Success: Conversion status represents a successful outcome rigorously construed. By these standards, only 9% of the sample attained success. On the one hand, this outcome refutes any putative claim that sexual orientation is not changeable; on the other hand, this is not an optimistic projection of likelihood of change for one considering that process.

The attempt to change sexual orientation did not appear to be harmful on average for these participants. The only statistically significant trends that emerged for the GSI (global) and PSDI (distress intensity) variables indicated improving psychological symptoms Tl to T6. Despite these findings, we cannot conclude that particular individuals in this study were not harmed by their attempt to change. Specific individuals may claim to have experienced harm from the attempt to change, and those claims may be legitimate, but although it may be that the attempt to change orientation caused harm by its very nature, it may also be that the harm was caused by particular intervention methods that were inept, harsh, punitive, or otherwise ill-conceived, and not from the attempt to change itself. Our findings mitigate against any absolute claim that attempted change is likely to be harmful in and of itself.

The change results documented in this study are generated by a set of diverse, religiously based intervention programs. The diversity of the methods implemented by the various 16 ministries from which we obtained participants, combined with the size of our sample, leaves us unable to determine or even speculate on key elements of the process of change, or to discriminate active from inactive elements of the intervention methods. The study of religious change methods introduces unique uncertainty. Many authors have discussed the poorly understood power of religious and quasi-religious change. The effective ingredients of such change may be explainable in utterly naturalistic terms (i.e., the mundane wrapped up in religious interpretation). Diamond explained the modest change documented in her sample via naturalistic means, saying "stability reliably emerges as new patterns of thought and behavior are repeated and reinforced via internal feedback mechanisms." Perhaps the same happened in this population, but religious change processes could also harness other processes and resources not typically associated with psychological methods and not adequately explained by recourse to naturalistic phenomena.

In conclusion, the findings of this study appear to contradict the commonly expressed view that sexual orientation is not changeable and that the attempt to change is highly likely to result in harm for those who make such an attempt.

STANTON L. JONES is a professor of psychology and the provost of Wheaton College. He has received his MA and PhD in clinical psychology at Arizona State University.

MARK A. YARHOUSE is a professor of psychology at Regent University. His research interests include alternative views of sexuality in psychology. He has completed a PsyD and MA in clinical psychology at Wheaton College.

A. Lee Beckstead

Can We Change Sexual Orientation?

Introduction

Can people intentionally change their sexual orientation? Unfortunately, not much is known to answer this question reliably. However, this article will provide an overview of what we do know about sexual reorientation and what we need to know further to promise such an outcome responsibly. Specifically, this article will present how mental health providers have attempted to help those who experience "unwanted" attractions how researchers have tried to verify or critique such efforts, and how the practice and promise of sexual reorientation affect the public and could inform our understanding of human sexuality.

Contrasting reports of success and harm have spurred debates for many years regarding the possibility of changing sexual orientation. For instance, as Jones and Yarhouse published their "evidence that successful change of sexual orientation occurred for some individuals concurrent with involvement in the religiously mediated change methods of Exodus Ministries," the President of Exodus, Chambers, had a different view: "The majority of people that I have met, and I would say the majority meaning 99.9% of them have not experienced a change in their orientation."

One analogy for understanding the confusion, debates, and lack of reliable information regarding sexual reorientation is the blind men and the elephant. As the story goes, a group of individuals (either blind or in the dark) each touch one particular area of the elephant and, confident in their own perception, argue with the others about what is an elephant. Claims are simplistic and unbalanced and thus mislead. Conflicts and disagreements can turn extreme and become polarizing, fragmented, and dissociative, depending upon the biases of the individuals. Side-taking strategies are employed—and reinforced—to validate world views. Similarly, many have attempted to grasp the "beast" of trying to resolve sexual orientation conflicts, and world views have either limited or helped such attempts. . . .

Research to Verify or Disqualify Sexual Reorientation

Most people are not skilled in evaluating the validity of a research study. Because of this, the general public is vulnerable to being misled into believing one study over another, despite study flaws. The research regarding sexual reorientation is one area in which this type of misunderstanding and misuse can go unbridled. Many authors have described the political "culture wars" influencing the debates of sexual reorientation and warn how unscientific opinions can be elevated to the same level as science. . . . As a result, simplistic, misrepresentative interpretations of complex issues are represented to the public as facts; For example, Nicolosi stated

> We should stop telling young people and others struggling with homosexuality that they're stuck with it. Instead we should say, "If you want to change, you can, like so many others who have.". . . Clearly, [Nicolosi, Byrd, and Potts, 2000] validates homosexuality as a psychological condition, rather than a genetic or hereditary one.

APA grew concerned about the conflicting information available regarding the premises and promise of sexual orientation change efforts (SOCE). Subsequently, it appointed a Task Force in 2007 to review and evaluate the research on such practices and provide recommendations based upon that review. For the sake of disclosure, I was part of that Task Force. The Task Force found that from the early 75 studies (from 1960 to 1985), 6 had adequate design to determine efficacy and safety. These studies concluded that aversive techniques rarely led to change in sexual orientation. Behavioral changes observed outside of the laboratory were rare and participants did not report changes to other-sex attractions that could be empirically validated. A reduction of arousal to all sexual stimuli was an outcome for some. The evaluation of the 8 recent studies (from 1986 to 2009) found that none were methodologically adequate to determine efficacy and safety. Other reviews concluded that the evidence is weak for extinguishing or unlearning sexual arousal responses once they are established.

Methodological errors in SOCE research included the following: (1) results are based on restricted, self-selected samples that represented a socially stigmatized population who affirmed heterocentric biases; (2) methods did not account for participants' interests to manage self-impressions and potential to promote their beliefs and lifestyles and misreport "successes" and "failures"; (3) some results were based on therapists' subjective impressions; (4) researcher biases or lack of expertise were not managed or addressed; (5) comparison or control groups were not used; and (6) longitudinal methods were not utilized to determine the duration or process of any positive changes. Conceptual errors of SOCE research were due to a reliance on non-validated instruments that (1) had no comparable or neutral measurements of heterosexuality, bisexuality, and homosexuality and (2) failed to behaviorally anchor response items. Some studies neglected to use fantasy and arousal to indicate sexual orientation and harms were not measured or were inadequately measured based upon self-reports. The APA report also pointed out how statistical errors made changes in scores unreliable in two typically promoted SOCE research.

Self-reports of reorientation have also not been consistent with objective data and ex-gay leaders have been known to continue their homosexual behaviors, even having sex with those they counsel. These discrepancies in self-report and behavior may be explained by a need to manage impressions for self and others, as illustrated by one former SOCE client:

> I buried the shame I felt for resuming the hoax. In my talks with [my religious leader], I pretended that I was changing so I could be an acceptable member of the LDS church. I tried convincing myself that I was changing.

Several scholars have proposed that some who report positive SOCE results were actually bisexual in nature and capable of enjoying heterosexuality. In SOCE samples, it is unclear who experiences some degree of attractions or aversion toward the other sex, let alone what exactly these attractions and aversions entail. Along these same lines, broad promises of "change" do not consider any selection criteria based on why some same-sex attracted individuals can experience heterosexual relationships as fulfilling and why others will find inevitable dissatisfaction in them.

Ethical concerns exist surrounding the promotion of pro-SOCE research. The first is a failure to consider the social impact that can occur from falsely representing successful outcomes (e.g., homosexuals could choose heterosexuality if they were just motivated). The second is the reinforcement of heterosexism and the harm that can occur by colluding with such beliefs (e.g., homosexuality is a treatable disorder). Spitzer for example, needed to inform the Finnish Parliament that his research could not be used to justify taking away the civil right of LGB individuals, despite its pro-SOCE results.

The hope of sexual reorientation is spreading internationally as ex-gay organizations are establishing branches worldwide through an emphasis on religion and therapy as the cure. Such promises can impact family members and religious leaders, as illustrated by the promise of a leader of the Church of Jesus Christ of Latter-Day Saints (LDS) to those attending as Evergreen International[1] conference. Expressing how honorable they were for their struggle and sacrifice, this leader expressed, "If you are faithful, on resurrection morning—and maybe even before then—you will rise with normal attractions for the opposite sex." Some are advised by their leaders to marry, with high hopes that are unsustainable in the long-term. Moreover, LGB youth can suffer when told by their parents that they should change to fit in. As Rust described:

> The proposition that a malleable core sexual orientation exists is untestable. Its function is not scientific, but psychological; it allows individuals undergoing reparative therapy to hope that they will, ultimately, be able to live without fear that their same-sex desires will resurface.

More extreme is how the promise of sexual reorientation is being used in Uganda to pass a law that documents "the fact that same sex attraction is not an innate and immutable characteristic." The National Association of Social Workers of Uganda backs this bill and defined homosexuality as a "part of a range of feelings individuals ought to learn to bring under control as they mature." Leaders from Exodus International presented in Uganda prior to the bill being written. This bill would enact the death penalty for those who have previous "convictions" and for those who are HIV-positive and would require mandatory reporting of all homosexual "offences." Disclosures made in counseling settings of being homosexual would only be exempt from this death penalty for individuals seeking behavior management. To be licensed, counseling organizations must agree not to dispense pro-LGB advice to clients. The final outcome for this bill was unclear when this article was published.

Anecdotal reports of both harms and benefits of SOCE are available. Harms were described by former clients as due to being misinformed about realistic outcomes; being misled with unsubstantiated theories and treatments; blaming themselves—and being blamed—for not changing and thus internalizing treatment failure; being reinforced that living as LGB must be avoided; restricting education and exploration of options; feeling pressured to be "one way or another"; and rejecting or suppressing core aspects of self. Such aspects were reported as increasing despair, self-hatred, confusion, anxiety, depression, guilt, shame, discrimination, sexual dysfunction, intimacy difficulties, and suicidality. SOCE benefits reported by former clients included being provided with hope, relief, support, and answers that fit their ideology; being able to adopt a positive "non-gay" or repentant identity; finding a place to belong, meet similar individuals, and feel normal; having a place to talk about both the religious and sexual aspect of themselves; enhancing closeness with others; having behaviors congruent with religion, family expectations, and marital needs; enhancing gender identity and competencies, and enhancing self-exploration. However, as some of the participants of Beckstead and Morrow and Shidlo and Schroeder related, harms or ineffectiveness were experienced after a period of benefit, which indicates the need for a long-term analysis of SOCE.

The APA Task Force's final conclusions were that "there is insufficient evidence that SOCE are efficacious for changing sexual orientation. Furthermore, there is some evidence that such efforts cause harm." The APA passed a resolution based on these conclusions, encouraging "mental-health professionals to avoid misrepresenting the efficacy of [SOCE] by promoting or promising change in sexual orientation" and recognizing that the benefits reported by participants (e.g., validation, support) can be gained through approaches that do not attempt to change sexual orientation.

SOCE proponents rebutted by arguing that if we cannot conclude SOCE are effective, then we cannot say SOCE are not ineffective or that sexual orientation cannot be changed; absence of evidence is not evidence of absence. SOCE proponents criticized the APA's conclusions by stating that LGB-affirmative approaches are not held to the same criteria used to evaluate SOCE. Yarhouse further noted that Shidlo and Schroeder's study on harms suffered from similar limitations as Spitzer's study: "To reject one study on methodological grounds means rejecting the other." Moreover, SOCE proponents declared it unethical to ban such treatments because doing so would violate clients' right for self-determination.

Taken at face value, these rebuttals seem reasonable. However, they are unbalanced due to their restricted world view. In SOCE proponents' eyes, LGB individuals are guilty until proven innocent. In other words, SOCE proponents start with an assumption of pathology in how they see homosexuality and expect LGB proponents to disprove their assumption. The impact of homophobia, heterosexism, and sexism seem[s] invisible to SOCE therapists, clients, and researchers, discounting the long history of rejection and its effects. Evidence of data do[es] exist to inform the psychology of LGB individuals, but such information came only after a paradigm shift occurred socially and institutionally. Regarding client self-determination, Gonsiorek warned clinicians about "the assumption of unlimited client choice" and asserted, "Client choice properly functions as an aspect of informed consent and not as a substitute for ethical decision making and practice standards.". . .

Therapeutic Recommendations

Rather than using approaches that advocate for only one aspect of the client (e.g., LGB-affirming or religious-affirming), integrated treatment approaches are needed. Such methods would try to reduce the dichotomies and splitting that have existed in social and therapeutic settings. Along these lines, APA recommended a client-centered framework for those distressed by a homosexual orientation. This approach is based on clinicians' enhancement of their multicultural competence to support all aspects of a client, without an a priori assumption of the final outcome.

Assessing with clients their sources of distress and motivations for SOCE seems the most responsible. Distress with a same-sex erotic orientation may not be due to only one factor (e.g., minority stress) or another (e.g., religious values conflict). For instance, individuals whose religion is intrinsic and who have internalized negative stereotypes may be highly motivated to try to change their sexual orientation. Negative internalized beliefs are associated not only with religion but also with gender and family attachment styles. For non-heterosexuals, religion and family can be sources of power and benefit, as well as distress and prejudice.

With a comprehensive assessment of the person's sexual orientation, sexuality, and lived context, more sophisticated and thus effective treatment approaches could be developed. For instance, it would theoretically make sense that those who experience high or moderate aversion to the body and gender characteristics of the other sex would have a more difficult time, or even an unrealistic chance, extinguishing these attractions and making the significant leap of experiencing high or moderate attractions to the other sex. This may be difficult even if the person had high social attraction, aesthetic attraction, and emotional attraction to the other sex or the person's spouse. Blanchard et al.'s research on alloerotic response makes it apparent to be conservative in hoping for change if the difference in one's preferred arousal is significantly different to the erotic features of other-sex adults. Individuals may experience a potential for arousal, but the difference between their preferred arousal and other-sex adult characteristics may make it erotically unfulfilling. A person would need to make these changes in attraction as they also attempt to manage significant erotic and relationship preferences and needs. Therefore, a timeline could be explored with non-heterosexuals who wish to marry heterosexually that may help them recognize the range of their attractions, aversions, needs, and resources. Evaluating the short- and long-term trajectory of outcomes may produce more informed decisions and self-direction.

Reports of aversion could be explored in therapy regarding etiology and options. For example, if aversion is an indicator of a biological limit, then more information is needed to know if this limit is malleable to change or if treatments that ignore this limit create dissociation, trauma, avoidance, rationalization, and lying. SOCE participants may vary in how they experience such biological aversion, which may be one reason why some report harm and others do not from such interventions. If aversion originates from stigma-related beliefs and feelings, then exploration of such experiences may create change by allowing for reevaluation of such beliefs. Homophobia, instead of homosexuality, becomes the focus of treatment.

The question may not be, however, if someone should "come out of the closet" and adopt an LGB identity, but if that person has the confidence to manage any problems associated with it. Furthermore, coping with minority stress depends not only on personal factors (e.g., resilience and coping styles) but also on group resources (e.g., a positive collective identity and community support)

Increasing self-acceptance and developing a positive self-identity seem essential to counteract societal rejection and neglect. Overall, interventions would focus on helping the client develop internal and external resources to reduce the impact of stigma.

Treatments that reduce clients' fears and shame about their attractions may be an effective route to diminishing the intensity associated with their attractions and thus allow such individuals to make more choices for themselves. For instance, McConaghy, Blaszczynski, and Kidson researched one method that helped sex offenders decrease sexual compulsivity by increasing self-regulating abilities. This approach seems similar to Tan and Yarhouse that utilizes mindfulness skills to help traditional religious, same-sex attracted individuals accept their attractions nonjudgmentally and make personally meaningful choices without needing to reject, minimize, or cultivate their attractions.

Instead of trying to control sexual arousal, APA recommended therapeutic interventions facilitate (1) changes in self-awareness (e.g., increased knowledge, acceptance, self-efficacy, self-concept, and relationships); (2) changes in sexual orientation identity (e.g., private and public identification, sexual stigma, and group affiliation); (3) changes in emotional adjustment (e.g., reducing shame and enhancing ability to grieve losses and face discrimination); and (4) changes in personal beliefs, values, and norms (e.g., exploring and reevaluating religious and sexual beliefs, behaviors, self-expression, and motivations). In working with those who value traditional religion, APA encouraged clinicians to base their work on the psychology of religion that understands the importance of religion and spirituality as it also addresses the harm due to the human errors of such practices. Overall, resolving sexual orientation conflicts seems to entail diverse trajectories, similar to other aspects of identity. These uniquely personal trajectories can involve periods of conformity, attempts to change self, disillusionment, exploration, evaluation, normalization, grieving, acceptance, self-authority, self-efficacy, pride, integration, complexity, and ambiguity, regardless of ultimate identity choice.

Summary

The main "take home" points of this article are for clinicians, researchers, officials, and lay people to consider (1) recognizing that SOCE assumptions and research base provide little basis for concluding whether SOCE has any effect on a non-heterosexual orientation; (2) recognizing the complex issues in researching and helping non-heterosexuals who are unable to adopt a positive and "out" sexual identity; and (3) viewing resolutions of sexual orientation distress not as an outcome, such as heterosexuality, but as an individualized process that allows for exploration and complexity.

Because of the social and personal implications, comprehensive and thus effective treatment plans are needed to help non-heterosexuals live with the reality of their sexual orientation and social identities. Multivariate assessments of sexual orientation and sexuality, including various levels of attraction and aversion, seem appropriate to facilitate realistic and resourceful approaches. Based on the review above, our best efforts may not be in trying to change possibly immutable aspects of sexuality but in trying to reduce the misunderstanding, discrimination, and hostility that exist within non-heterosexuals and their social situations.

Note

1. A lay organization that "helps people who want to diminish same-sex attractions and overcome homosexual behavior" (Evergreen International, 2010).

A. Lee Beckstead has received his PhD from the University of Utah in counseling psychology. He was a member of the 2007–2009 APA task force to evaluate efforts to change sexual orientation. Beckstead currently works in private practice.

EXPLORING THE ISSUE

Can Psychotherapy Change Sexual Orientation?

Critical Thinking and Reflection

1. Jones and Yarhouse describe in detail their efforts to perform an extensive study according to standardized research procedures, while Beckstead cites the flaws of general SOCE research as one of SOCE's major limitations. Why are methods so important in determining the worth of psychological research?
2. How are self-report measures used in these examples of research on sexual orientation? What are their strengths and weaknesses?
3. Much of the SOCE research supporting the possibility of a changeable sexual orientation is conducted at institutions espousing religious values. Do you believe that such values may be a hindrance to scientific research? Why or why not?
4. Imagine a therapist with two clients, both teenage males attracted to men. One client desires to cope with persecution he is feeling at school, while the other finds his attraction to men unwelcome and wants to change it. How do the personal views of the therapist affect the treatment he or she will give to each of these males?
5. Over the years, the APA has changed its stance on homosexuality. What is the role of national psychological organizations such as APA in influencing public opinion? What is the role of the scientific establishment in informing the public?

Create Central

www.mhhe.com/createcentral

Additional Resources

Spitzer, R. L. (2003). Can some gay men and lesbians change their sexual orientation? 200 Participants reporting a change from homosexual to heterosexual orientation. *Archives of Sexual Behavior, 32*(5), 403–417.

An oft-cited and highly controversial landmark study claiming an observed change in sexual orientation.

The APA's report on "Appropriate Therapeutic Responses to Sexual Orientation," to which A. Lee Beckstead contributed. Retrieved from www.apa.org/pi/lgbt/resources/therapeutic-response.pdf

Internet Reference . . .

The APA's Official Stance on Sexual Orientation

www.apa.org/helpcenter/sexual-orientation.aspx

Unit 7

UNIT

Social Issues

*S*ocial psychology is the study of humans in their social environments. For example, a social psychologist might ask how the social environment of torture affects a prisoner. Is coercive interrogation (possibly torture) a good method of gaining important information, or is it a waste of time that only does psychological harm? What can psychologists contribute to these questions? How much are social environments responsible for female mating preferences? Might mating preferences be more influenced by innate genetic and thus evolutionary factors? What about the relatively recent changes in our social environment? Some psychologists have pointed to the recent upsurge of sexually explicit "societal and cultural messages" on the Internet and other media. Could this upsurge lead to problems, such as pornography and sexual addictions in general? Do such addictions even exist?

Selected, Edited and with Issue Framing Material by:
Brent Slife, *Brigham Young University*

ISSUE

Can Sex Be Addictive?

YES: Patrick Carnes, from "Understanding Sexual Addiction," *SIECUS Report* (June/July 2003)

NO: Lawrence A. Siegel and Richard M. Siegel, from "Sex Addiction: Recovering from a Shady Concept," An Original Essay Written for *Taking Sides: Human Sexuality,* 10th edition (2006)

Learning Outcomes

After reading this issue, you should be able to:

• Describe some of the similarities and differences between dysfunctional behavior and addictive behavior.

ISSUE SUMMARY

YES: Sexual addiction expert Patrick Carnes argues not only that sex can be addictive but also that sex can be as addictive as drugs, alcohol, or any other chemical substance.

NO: Sex therapists Lawrence A. Siegel and Richard M. Siegel believe that while some sexual behaviors might be dysfunctional, calling those behaviors "addictive" confuses a moralistic ideology with a scientific fact.

Addiction has become a pervasive feature of modern societies. Of the $666 billion spent for health care in the United States, 25 percent was spent on healthcare problems related to addiction. Of the 11 million victims of the violent crimes that are committed each year in the United States, nearly 3 million reported that the offender had been drinking prior to the crime. Research also suggests that between 6 and 15 million Americans have compulsive shopping behaviors that result in unmanageable debt, bankruptcy, and damaged relationships. These varied examples demonstrate not only the damage addiction does but also the widely varying meanings it has—from drug addiction to shopping addiction.

Should we add "sex addiction" to the list? Few would dispute that certain chemicals, such as cocaine and even alcohol, merit the addiction label, but is it taking the label too far to consider sexual practices that lead to dysfunction an addiction? The term "addiction" is thought to be derived from the Latin word *addicere*, meaning to adore or to surrender oneself to a master. From this perspective, the term might seem to fit because some people appear to "surrender" themselves to the "master" of sexual games, sexual banter, and sexual intercourse. Indeed, sexuality seems to consume our popular culture. On the other hand, would not many adolescents (and even our popular culture itself) be considered "addicts" in this sense? What meaning does

addiction have if everyone is addicted? Would not everyone be addicted to food in the same sense? Obviously, such questions have great importance for whether something should be treated in psychotherapy.

Widely regarded as an expert on sexual addiction, Patrick Carnes has been at the forefront of sexual addiction therapy. Carnes firmly believes that sex can be addictive and dysfunctional sexual practices ought to be treated in therapy. In fact, he promotes the use of a 12-step program, not unlike Alcoholics Anonymous, to help overcome sexual addiction on his website, www.sexhelp.com. He justifies this parallel with chemical dependency and treatment because sexual intercourse has a clear physiological component—sexual pleasure. Carnes claims that compulsively seeking sexual stimulation can lead to many negative consequences in an addict's life.

Sex therapists Lawrence A. Siegel and Richard M. Siegel disagree sharply with Carnes' position. In the NO selection they argue that those who want to call sex addictive have a hidden agenda. Their agenda is to extend society's fairly clear moral condemnation of drug abuse to sexual behaviors. The Siegels ask whether sexual behaviors are not in a different category altogether than drug abuse. If they are, then the unacceptability of drug-related abuse should not be extended to sexual behaviors, at least not in the same way. The Siegels go on to argue that the term "addiction" itself has difficulties. They contend that psychology cannot decide what it means, either to be addicted to something or to have an addictive nature. They conclude by reviewing some of Carnes' early work in sexual addic-

tion, and then they respond to it by attempting to show his moral bias toward any sexual practice other than monogamous intimacy in marriage.

POINT

- Sex can be addictive.

- Sex addiction has physical and chemical components.

- Many deviant sexual behaviors fit the definition of what makes something addictive.
- Sex addicts, like those with eating disorders or alcoholism, cannot control their destructive behavior and need help.

COUNTERPOINT

- Addiction is merely a term for any behavior that falls outside of social norms.
- Chemical dependency should not be confused with mechanisms that drive sexual appetite.
- A consistent clinical definition of "addiction" has not been agreed upon.
- Sexual behavior is an issue of personal responsibility, not personal physiology.

YES

Patrick Carnes

Understanding Sexual Addiction

During the past three decades, professionals have acknowledged that some people use sex to manage their internal distress. These people are similar to compulsive gamblers, compulsive overeaters, or alcoholics in that they are not able to contain their impulses—and with destructive results.

Definition

To facilitate classification and understanding of psychological disorders, mental health professionals rely on the *Diagnostic and Statistical Manual of Mental Disorders* (DSM) published by the American Psychiatric Association and now in its fourth edition.

Each edition of this book represents a consensus at the time of publication about what constitutes mental disorders. Each subsequent edition has reflected changes in understanding. The *DSM's* system is, therefore, best viewed as a "work in progress" rather than the "bible."

The term *sexual addiction* does not appear in *DSM-IV*. In fact, the word *addiction* itself does not appear. It condenses the criteria for addictive disorders—such as substance abuse and pathologic gambling—into three elements:

- *Loss of control (compulsivity).* "There is a persistent desire or unsuccessful efforts to cut down or control substance abuse." "Has persistent unsuccessful efforts to control, cut back, or stop gambling."
- *Continuation despite adverse consequences.* "The substance use is continued despite knowledge of having a persistent or recurrent physical or psychological problem that is likely to have been caused or exacerbated by the substance use." "Has committed illegal acts such as forgery, fraud, theft, or embezzlement to finance gambling."
- *Obsession or preoccupation.* "A great deal of time is spent in activities necessary to obtain the substance, use the substance, or recover from its effects." "Is preoccupied with gambling."[1]

Complex Problem

Typically, individuals in trouble for their sexual behavior are not candid about whatever incident has come to light, nor are they likely to reveal that the specific behavior actually is a part of a consistent, self-destructive pattern. The nature of this illness causes patients to hide the severity of the problem from others, to delude themselves about their ability to control their behavior, and to minimize their impact on others.

Often some event will precipitate a visit to the primary care provider. Sexual excess of some type will create a physical problem. Sexually transmitted diseases, damage to genitals, unwanted pregnancies: all are among the reasons for such a visit. Most patients will say that the event is a unique situation.

The primary care provider will often treat the physical problem without probing for more information. If, however, there is sexual addiction, the problem will not disappear. A wide range of behaviors can be problematic, including compulsive masturbation, affairs, use of pornography, voyeurism, exhibitionism, sexual harassment, and sex offending.

Health care providers must understand that underneath what appears to be an isolated event may be a more complex pathologic problem with a host of related factors such as the following:

- A high incidence of depression and suicide
- The presence of high-risk and dangerous behaviors including self-harm designed to escalate sexual experiences
- The high probability of other addictive behaviors including alcoholism, drug abuse, and pathologic gambling
- Extreme disruption of the family, including battering, sexual abuse, and financial distress

Behaviors

Clinicians should remember that the discovery of something sexual does not make an addictive illness. A long-term affair, for example, would be a problem for a spouse but would not be a compulsive pattern. Likewise, a person with exploitive or violent behavior does not necessarily have an addictive illness.

I have been gathering data on sexual addiction since 1985. In the process, I have found that sexually addictive behavior clusters into 10 distinct types. Patients often will be active in more than one cluster. That is one of the most important lessons of sexual addiction: Patterns exist among behaviors.

Carnes, Patrick. From *SIECUS Report*, vol. 31, no. 5, June/July 2003, pp. 5–7. Copyright © 2003 by Sexuality Information and Education Council of the United States. Reprinted by permission of SIECUS.

The 10 distinctive types of behaviors are:

- *Fantasy sex.* Arousal depends on sexual possibility. The individual neglects responsibilities to engage in fantasy and/or prepare for the next sexual episode.
- *Seductive role sex.* Arousal is based on conquest and diminishes rapidly after the initial contact. It can be heightened by increasing risk and/or number of partners.
- *Voyeuristic sex.* Visual stimulation is used to escape into an obsessive trance. Arousal may be heightened by masturbation or risk (peeping), or violation of boundaries (voyeuristic rape).
- *Exhibitionistic sex.* The individual attracts attention to the body or its sexual parts. Arousal stems from the shock or the interest of the viewer.
- *Paying for sex.* Arousal is connected to payment for sex and, with time, it actually becomes connected to money itself. Payment creates an entitlement and a sense of power over meeting needs. The arousal starts with "having money" and the search for someone in "the business."
- *Trading sex.* Arousal is based on gaining control of others by using sex as leverage.
- *Intrusive sex.* Arousal occurs by violating boundaries with no repercussions.
- *Anonymous sex.* Arousal involves no seduction or cost and is immediate. It has no entanglements or obligations associated with it and often is accelerated by unsafe or high-risk environments such as parks and restrooms.
- *Pain-exchange sex.* Arousal is built around specific scenarios or narratives of humiliation and shame.
- *Exploitive sex.* Arousal is based on target "types" of vulnerability. Certain types of vulnerable people (such as clients/patients) become the focus.

In addition, in recent years people have begun to use cybersex in unexpected numbers, and many are finding themselves accessing sex in problematic ways.

Individuals suffering from sexual addiction have found sex on the Internet a natural extension of what they are already doing. They can act out any of the previously mentioned 10 types of sexual behavior on the Internet. They can find sex partners, be voyeuristic, start affairs, and swap partners, among other things.

There are also many individuals who never would have experienced sexual compulsive behavior had it not been for the Internet. Consider this:

- About 200 sex-related Web sites are added each day, and there are more than 100,000 existing sites.
- Sex on the Internet constitutes the third largest economic sector on the Web (software and computers rank first and second), generating one billion dollars annually.
- A total of 65 million unique visitors use free porn sites, and 19 million unique visitors use pay porn sites each month.

- Approximately one percent of Internet users have a severe problem that focuses almost exclusively on cybersex, with major neglect of the rest of their life's activities.[2]

Successful Treatment

A number of key factors are involved in successful recovery from sexual addition. They include:

- *A good addiction-oriented primary therapist.* Most successful recoveries involve a relationship with a therapist over a three- to five-year period, the first two years of which are very intense.
- *A 12-step sexual addiction group.* The probability of relapse is extremely high if the addict does not attend meetings.
- *A 12-step program for other addictions.* If the addict has other addictions, a 12-step program is necessary for those as well. A suggestion that makes things easier is to find a sponsor or sponsors who attends all of the same meetings your patient does. This way, there is a consolidation of relationships.
- *Program work, not just attendance.* Completing step work, finding a sponsor, and doing service are all key elements of recovery. Individuals should become actively involved in the program's activities. In a recent outcome study of an inpatient program for sexual addiction, researchers discovered that only 23 percent actually complete the first nine of the 12 steps in 18 months. However, of those who did, recidivism was rare.[3]
- *Early family involvement.* Family participation in the patient's therapy improves the chance for success.
- *Spiritual support.* Addicts report that the spiritual work started in their 12-step communities and continued in various spiritual communities was critical to the changes they needed to make.
- *Exercise along with good nutrition and a healthy lifestyle.* Addicts who reduce their stress, start an exercise program, and eat more healthfully do better in their recovery.

In discussing what had helped them in their recovery, over 190 sex addicts indicated that these treatments were the most helpful (in order from most to least): a higher power (87 percent); couples 12-step group based on sexual addiction (85 percent); a friend's support (69 percent); individual therapy (65 percent); a celibacy period (64 percent); a sponsor (61 percent); exercise/nutrition (58 percent); a 12-step group based on subjects other than sexual addiction (55 percent); partner support (36 percent); inpatient treatment (35 percent); outpatient group (27 percent); therapy (21 percent); family therapy (11 percent); and after care (hospital) (9 percent).[4]

Healthy Sexuality

The goal of treatment is healthy sexuality. Some therapists insist on a period of celibacy, which does help to reduce chaos and make patients available for therapy. But recovery from sexual addiction does not mean sexual abstinence.

The objective of treatment is to help individuals develop a healthy, strong sexual life. One of the risks is that the patients may slip to a position of sexual aversion, in which they think all sex is bad. Sexual aversion, or "sexual anorexia," is simply another variant of sexual compulsive behavior.

Patients will sometimes bounce from one extreme to the other. True recovery involves a clear understanding about abstaining from certain sexual behaviors combined with an active plan for enhancing sexuality.

Recovery from sexual addiction is likened to recovery from eating disorders. Food is a necessary part of life, and recovery from eating disorders requires defining what is healthy eating and what is not. Similarly, the goal of recovery from sexual addiction is learning what is healthy sexuality for the individual.

Healthy sexuality for most sexually addicted individuals involves not only a change in behavior but also an avoidance of fantasizing about behaviors that are unhealthy. Sexual fantasizing can be healthy, particularly for a reasonably healthy couple that uses their increased excitement to move toward rather than away from the partner. However, sexual imagery that is not respectful of other human beings increases objectification, depersonalization, and destructive bonding based on hostility rather than affection. Asking patients about his or her "sobriety" definition and about the content of fantasies provides clues to help with treatment and recovery.

Keeping Up

To determine how well the patient is doing in establishing a healthy lifestyle, clinicians can ask some simple questions. Does the patient have tools for avoiding relapse during times of hunger, anger, loneliness, and tiredness? Is the patient attending 12-step self-help meetings? If not, what are the obstacles preventing the patient from doing so? What are the patient's perceptions of what goes on at a meeting? Does he or she have a sponsor (a person longer in recovery who can guide the newer member)?

Is the patient seeking a counselor or therapist who is knowledgeable in addiction recovery? Is there balance between work and recreation? Is the patient exercising or engaging in any sports? Is the patient actively working to improve his or her relationship with a spouse or significant other? Is the spouse also attending a self-help meeting? These are all indicators to determine if the individual is fully engaged in building a healthier lifestyle.

Conclusion

The treatment of sexual addiction has taken a long time to gain recognition and respect as an area of medical specialty.

As with other disorders, such as alcoholism or anorexia, clinicians face many challenges in learning about sexual addiction. Most who take time to learn find patients who are profoundly grateful.

In many ways, the field of sexual addiction lags behind both professional and lay awareness of alcoholism or anorexia. Yet, important strides are being made in both understanding and awareness.

Appreciating the issues and challenges of sexual addiction will help clinicians when their patients' behaviors cross the line from problems of judgment to symptoms of a clinical disorder.

PATRICK CARNES is a nationally known speaker on sex addiction and recovery issues and is currently the executive director of the Gentle Path program at Pine Grove Behavioral Center in Hattiesburg, Mississippi.

Lawrence A. Siegel and
Richard M. Siegel

 **NO**

Sex Addiction: Recovering
from a Shady Concept

It seems, more than ever, that many Americans are more comfortable keeping sex in the dark or, as sex addiction advocates might actually prefer, *in* the shadows. We seem to have gotten no further than the Puritan claims of sex being evil and pleasure being threatening. "The Devil made me do it" seems to be something of a battle cry, especially when someone gets caught cheating on their spouse, having inappropriate dalliances with congressional pages, or visiting prostitutes. Even those not in relationships are easily targeted. We constantly hear about the "dangers" of internet porn and how every internet chat room is just teeming with predators just waiting to devour our children. Daily masturbation is considered by these folks as being unhealthy and a marked pathology. As a society, we seem able to be comfortable with sex only as long as we make it uncomfortable. As one of the leading sexologists, Marty Klein, once wrote:

> "If mass murderer Ted Bundy had announced that watching Cosby Show reruns had motivated his awful crimes, he would have been dismissed as a deranged sociopath. Instead, Bundy proclaimed that his 'pornography addiction' made him do it, and many Right-wing feminists and conservatives treated this as the conclusion of a thoughtful social scientist. Why?"[1]

The whole idea of "sex addiction" is borne out of a moralistic ideology masquerading as science. It is a concept that seems to serve no other purpose than to relegate sexual expression to the level of shameful acts, except within the extremely narrow and myopic scope of a monogamous, heterosexual marriage. Sexual diversity? Interests in unusual forms or frequency of sexual expression? Choosing not to be monogamous? Advocates of "sex addiction" would likely see these as the uncontrollable acts of a sexually pathological individual; one who needs curing.

To be clear, we do not deny the fact that, for some people, sexual behavior can become problematic, even dysfunctional or unmanageable. Our objection is with the use of the term "sexual addiction" to describe a virtually unlimited array of—in fact, practically ANY—aspect of sexual expression that falls outside of the typically Christian view of marriage. We believe that the term contributes to a generally sex-negative,

pleasure-phobic tone in American society, and it also tends to "pathologize" most forms of sexual expression that fall outside of a narrow view of what "normal" sex is supposed to look like. This is a point made clear by sex addiction advocates' own rhetoric. Three of the guiding principles of Sexaholics Anonymous include the notion that (1) sex is most healthy in the context of a monogamous, heterosexual relationship; (2) sexual expression has "obvious" limits; and (3) it is unhealthy to engage in any sexual activity for the sole purpose of feeling better, either emotionally or to escape one's problems. These principles do not represent either science or most people's experience. They, in fact, represent a restrictive and repressive view of sex and sexuality and reflect an arrogance that sex addiction proponents are the keepers of the scepter of morality and normalcy. Moreover, the concept of "sex addiction" comes out of a shame-based, arbitrarily judgmental addiction model and does not speak to the wide range of sexual diversity; both in and outside the context of a committed relationship.

A primary objection to the use of the term "sex addiction," an objection shared with regard to other supposed behavioral "addictions," is that the term *addiction* has long ago been discredited. Back in 1964, the World Health Organization (WHO) declared the term "addiction" to be clinically invalid and recommended in favor of dependence, which can exist in varying degrees of severity, as opposed to an all-or-nothing disease entity (as it is still commonly perceived).[2] This is when we began to see the terms *chemical dependency* and *substance abuse*, terms considered to be much more appropriate and clinically useful. This, however, did not sit well with the addiction industry. Another objection to the concept of "sex addiction" is that it is a misnomer whose very foundation as a clinically significant diagnosis is built on flawed and faulty premises. For example, a common assertion put forth by proponents of sex addiction states that the chemical actions in the brain during sexual activity are the same as the chemical activity involved in alcohol and drug use. They, therefore, claim that both sexual activity and substance abuse share reward and reinforcement mechanisms that produce the "craving" and "addictive" behaviors. This assertion is flawed on several levels, not the least of which is that it is based on drawing conclusions from brain scan imaging that are devoid of any real interpretive foundation; a "leap of faith," so to speak. Furthermore, it is somewhat of a stretch to equate the neurophysiological mechanisms which underlie chemical dependency, tolerance, and withdrawal with the underlying mechanisms of what is most often obsessive-compulsive or anxiety-reducing behaviors like gambling, shopping, and sex. Another example often cited by sex addiction proponents is the assertion that, like alcohol and drugs, the "sex addict" is completely incapable of controlling his or her self-destructive behavior. Of course, this begs the question of how, then, can one change behavior they are incapable of controlling? More importantly, however, is the unique excuse this "disease" model provides for abdicating personal responsibility. "It's not my fault, I have a disease." Finally, a major assertion put out by sex addiction advocates is that anyone who is hypersexual in any way (e.g., frequent masturbation, anonymous "hook ups," infidelity, and cybersex) must have been abused as children or adolescents. Again, the flaws here are obvious and serve to continue to relegate any type of frequent sexual engagement to the pathological and unseemly.

Every clinician knows that "addiction" is not a word that appears anywhere in the *Diagnostic and Statistical Manual*, or "DSM," the diagnostic guidebook used by psychiatrists and psychologists to make any psychopathological diagnosis. Nor does it appear in any of the International Classification of Diseases (ICD-10), codes used for classifying medical diagnoses. "Abuse" and "dependence" do appear in the DSM, relevant only to substance use patterns, but "addiction" does not. Similarly, there is an ICD-10 code for "substance dependence," but not addiction. Why? Perhaps because the word means different things to different people, especially when used in so many different contexts. Even without acknowledging the many trivial uses of the addiction concept, such as bumper stickers that proclaim, *"addicted to sports, not drugs,"* cookies that claim to be *"deliciously addicting,"* Garfield coffee mugs that warn *"don't talk to me until after my first cup,"* or T-shirts that say *"chocoholic,"* there aren't even consistent *clinical* definitions for the concept of addiction. A 1993 study, published in the *American Journal of Drug and Alcohol Abuse*, compared the diagnostic criteria for substance abuse and dependence between the DSM and ICD-10. The results showed very little agreement between the two.[3]

Pharmacologists, researchers who study the effects of drugs, define addiction primarily based on the presence of tolerance and withdrawal. Both of these phenomena are based on pharmacological and toxicological concepts of "cellular adaptation," wherein the body, at the very cellular level, becomes accustomed to the constant presence of a substance, and readjusts for "normal" function; in other words, whatever the "normal" response was before regular use of the substance began returns. This adaptation first accounts for tolerance, wherein an increasing dose of the substance to which the system has adapted is needed to maintain the same level of "normal." Then it results in withdrawal, wherein any discontinuation of the substance disrupts the "new" equilibrium the system has achieved and symptoms of "withdrawal sickness" ensue. This is probably most often attributed to addiction to opiates, such as heroin, because of its comparison to "having a monkey on one's back," with a constantly growing appetite, and its notorious "cold turkey" withdrawal. But perhaps it is most commonly observed with the chronic use of drugs with less sinister reputations, such as caffeine, nicotine or alcohol.

Traditional psychotherapists may typically define addiction as a faulty coping mechanism, or more accurately, the *result* of using a faulty coping mechanism to deal with some underlying issue. Another way to consider this is to see addiction as the symptom, rather than the disease, which is why the traditional therapist, of any theoretical orientation, is likely to want to find the causative issue or issues, and either teach the patient more effective coping mechanisms or resolve the unresolved issue(s) altogether.

Another definition of addiction has emerged, and seems to have taken center-stage, since the development of a pseudo-medical specialty known as "addictionology" within the last twenty or so years. Made up primarily of physicians, but including a variety of "addiction professionals," this field has helped to forge a treatment industry based on the disease model of addiction that is at the core of 12-Step "fellowships," such as Alcoholics Anonymous and Narcotics Anonymous. Ironically, despite the resistance to medical or psychiatric treatment historically expressed in AA or NA, their philosophy has become the mainstay of the addictionological paradigm.

If the concept of chemical addictions, which have a neurophysiological basis that can be measured and observed, yields no clinical consensus, how, then, can we legitimize the much vaguer notion that individuals can be "addicted" to behavior, people, emotions, or even one's own brain chemistry? Other than to undermine responsibility and self-determination, we really can't. It does a tremendous disservice to our clients and patients to brand them with a label so full of judgment, arbitrary opinion, and fatuous science. It robs individuals of the ability to find their own levels of comfort and, ultimately, be the determining force in directing their own lives. There is a significant and qualitative difference between the person who acts because he or she can't (not a choice, but a position of default) and the person who is empowered to choose not to. As clinicians, we should be loathe to send our clients and patients down such a fearful, shameful road.

In 1989, Patrick Carnes, founder of the sex addiction movement, wrote a book entitled *"Contrary to Love."* The book is rife with rhetoric and personal ideology that reveals Carnes's lack of training, knowledge, and understanding of sexuality and sexual expression; not surprising for someone whose background is solely in the disease model of alcoholism. This, while seemingly a harsh judgment, is clearly reflected in his Sex Addiction Screening Test (SAST). Even a cursory glance at the items on the SAST show a deep-seated bias against most forms of sexual expression. Unlike other legitimate screening and assessment tools, there is no scientific foundation that would show this tool to be credible (i.e., tests of reliability and validity). Instead, Carnes developed this "test" by simply culling his own ideas from his book. Annie Sprinkle, America's first adult-film-star-turned-PhD-Sexologist, has written a very good web article on the myth of sex addiction. In it, she also describes some of the shortcomings of the SAST. While not describing the complete test here, a listing of some of the assessment questions are listed below, along with commentary.[4]

1. *Have you subscribed to sexually explicit magazines like* Playboy *or* Penthouse? This question is based on the assumption that it is unhealthy to view images of naked bodies. Does that mean that the millions of people who subscribe to or buy adult magazines are sex addicts? Are adolescent boys who look at the *Sports Illustrated* Swim Suit edition budding sex addicts? By extension, if looking at *Playboy* or *Penthouse* is unhealthy and pathological, then those millions of people who look at hardcore magazines or Internet porn should be hospitalized!

2. *Do you often find yourself preoccupied with sexual thoughts?* This is totally nebulous. What does "preoccupied" mean? How often does one have to think about sex in order to constitute preoccupation? Research has shown that men, on average, think about sex every eight seconds; does that mean that men are inherently sex addicts?

3. *Do you feel that your sexual behavior is not normal?* What is normal? What do they use as a comparison? As sexologists, we can state unequivocally that the majority of people's sexual concerns relate, in one way or another, to the question "Am I normal?" This is incredibly vague, nebulous, and laughably unscientific.

4. *Are any of your sexual activities against the law?* This question is also steeped in a bias that there is only a narrowly acceptable realm of sexual expression. It assumes that any sexual behavior that is against the law is bad. Is being or engaging a prostitute a sign of pathology? What about the fact that oral sex, anal sex, and woman on top are illegal in several states?

5. *Have you ever felt degraded by your sexual behavior?* Again, there is a serious lack of quantification here. Does regretting a sexual encounter constitute feeling degraded? Does performing oral sex for your partner, even though you think it's degrading, constitute a pathology or compromise? What if one's partner does something during sex play that is unexpected and perceived as degrading (like ejaculating on someone's face or body)? What if someone enjoys feeling degraded? This question pathologizes at least half of the S/M and B/D communities. Moreover, anyone who has had a long and active sexual life may likely, at one point, have felt degraded. It is important to note that this question does not ask if one consistently puts oneself in a position of being degraded but, rather, have you ever felt degraded. We suspect that most people can lay claim to that.

6. *Has sex been a way for you to escape your problems?* Is there a better way to escape one's problems temporarily? This is a common bias used against both sex and alcohol use: using sex or alcohol to provide relief from anxieties or problems is inherently problematic. It also begs the question: why are things like sex and alcohol not appropriate to change how one is feeling but Zoloft, Paxil, Xanax, and Klonopin are? The truth of the matter is that sex is often an excellent and healthy way to occasionally experience relief from life's stressors and problems.

7. *When you have sex, do you feel depressed afterwards?* Sex is often a great way to get in touch with one's feelings. Oftentimes, people do feel depressed after a sexual experience, for any number of reasons. Furthermore, this doesn't mean that sex was the depressing part! Perhaps people feel depressed because they had dashed expectations of the person they were involved with. Unfulfilled expectations, lack of communication, and inattentiveness to one's needs and desires often result in post-coital feelings of sadness and disappointment. In addition, asking someone if they "feel depressed" is arbitrary, subjective, and clinically invalid.

8. *Do you feel controlled by your sexual desire?* Again, we are being asked to make an arbitrary, subjective, and clinically invalid assessment. There is an undercurrent here that seems to imply that a strong sexual desire is somehow not normal. Human beings are biologically programmed to strongly desire sex. Our clients and patients might be better served if we addressed not their desires, but how and when they act upon them.

Again, it needs noting that the concept of "sex addiction" is one with very little clinical relevance or usefulness, despite it's popularity. Healthy sexual expression encompasses a wide array of forms, functions, and frequency, as well as myriad emotional dynamics and personal experiences. Healthy behavior, in general, and sexual behavior, in particular, exists on a continuum rather than a quantifiable point. Using the addiction model to describe sexual behavior simply adds to the shame and stigma that is already too often attached to various forms of sexual expression. Can sexual behaviors become problematic? Most certainly. However, we must be careful to not over-pathologize even problematic sexual behaviors because, most often, they are symptomatic expressions rather than primary problems.

For many years, sexologists have described compulsive sexual behavior, where sexual obsessions and compulsions are recurrent, distressing, and interfere with daily functioning. The actual number of people suffering from this type of sexual problem is relatively small. Compulsive sexual behaviors are generally divided into two broad categories: *paraphilic* and *non-paraphilic.*[5] Paraphilias are defined as recurrent, intensely arousing fantasies, sexual urges, or behaviors involving non-human objects, pain and humiliation, or children.[6] Paraphilic behaviors are usually non-conventional forms of sexual expression that, in the extreme, can be harmful to relationships and individuals. Some examples of paraphilias listed in the DSM are pedophilia (sexual attraction to children), exhibitionism (exposing one's genitals in public), voyeurism (sexual excitement from watching an unsuspecting person), sexual sadism (sexual excitement from dominating or inflicting pain), sexual masochism (sexual excitement from being dominated or receiving pain), transvestic fetishism (sexual excitement from wearing clothes of the other sex), and frotteurism (sexual excitement from rubbing up against or fondling an unsuspecting person). All of these behaviors exist on a continuum of healthy fantasy play to dangerous, abusive, and illegal acts. A sexologist is able to view these behaviors in varying degrees, knowing the difference between teacher-student fantasy role play and cruising a playground for victims; between provocative exhibitionist displays (including public displays of affection) and illegal, abusive public exposure. For those with a "sex addiction" perspective, simply having paraphilic thoughts or desires of any kind is reason to brand the individual a "sex addict."

The other category of compulsive sexual behavior is non-paraphilic, and generally involves more conventional sexual behaviors which, when taken to the extreme, cause marked distress and interference with daily functioning. This category includes a fixation on an unattainable partner, compulsive masturbation, compulsive love relationships, and compulsive sexuality in a relationship. The most vocal criticism of the idea of compulsive sexual behavior as a clinical disorder appears to center on the overpathologizing of these behaviors. Unless specifically trained in sexuality, most clinicians are either uncomfortable or unfamiliar with the wide range of "normal" sexual behavior and fail to distinguish between individuals who experience conflict between their values and sexual behavior, and those with obsessive sexual behavior.[7] When diagnosing compulsive

sexual behavior overall, there is little consensus even among sexologists. However, it still provides a more useful clinical framework for the professional trained in sexuality and sexual health.

To recognize that sexual behavior can be problematic is not the same as labeling the behaviors as "sexually compulsive" or "sexual addiction." The reality is that sexual problems are quite common and are usually due to non-pathological factors. Quite simply, people make mistakes (some more than others). People also act impulsively. People don't always make good sexual choices. When people do make mistakes, act impulsively, and make bad decisions, it often negatively impacts their relationships; sometimes even their lives. Moreover, people do often use sex as a coping mechanism or, to borrow from addiction language, medicating behavior that can become problematic. However, this is qualitatively different from the concept that problematic sexual behavior means the individual is a "sexual addict" with uncontrollable urges and potentially dangerous intent. Most problematic sexual behavior can be effectively redirected (and cured) through psychosexual education, counseling, and experience. According to proponents of "sex addiction," problematic sexual behavior cannot be cured. Rather, the "sex addict" is destined for a life of maintaining a constant vigil to prevent the behavior from reoccurring, often to the point of obsession, and will be engaged in a lifelong process of recovery. Unfortunately, this view often causes people to live in fear of the "demon" lurking around every corner: themselves.

LAWRENCE A. SIEGEL practices forensic psychiatry and psychiatry in Valhalla, New York.

RICHARD M. SIEGEL is a Florida-licensed mental health counselor, board-certified sex therapist, and certified addictions professional.

EXPLORING THE ISSUE

Can Sex Be Addictive?

Critical Thinking and Reflection

1. The Siegels see the "diagnosis" of sexual addiction as having a moral basis. Are there other, more conventional diagnoses in the *DSM-IV* that might also be viewed in this manner? If so, what implications would this have for those diagnoses?
2. Examine some of the addiction literature and see what other definitions of "addiction" there might be. What might those definitions imply about the possibility of a sexual addiction? Support your answer.
3. Imagine you are working with a couple in therapy and the husband frequently views pornography. What possible dangers could his behavior present? Should his habit be considered a sexual addiction? Support your answer.
4. What is involved in the process of a 12-step program? How well do these programs address the specific issues involved in sex addiction? What might the Siegels criticize about the application of the Alcoholics Anonymous model to sex?
5. Compare and contrast the physiological mechanisms underlying chemical addiction with the physiological mechanisms underlying sexual stimulation. Are they similar as Carnes seems to believe?
6. What is "healthy sex"? Who should get to define it? Would what is considered "healthy" sexual practices be different for a (recovering) sex addict?

Create Central

www.mhhe.com/createcentral

Additional Resources

Collins, G. N., and Adleman, A. (2011). *Breaking the Cycle: Free Yourself from Sex Addiction, Porn Obsession, and Shame*. New Harbinger Publications.

Carnes, P. (1983). *Out of the Shadows: Understanding Sex Addiction by*. Hazelden.

Goodman, A. (1998). *Sexual Addiction: An Integrated Approach*. International Universities Press.

Internet References . . .

Sex Addiction: Articles and Topics

www.scoop.it/t/sex-addiction

Sexual Addiction Help

http://sexualaddiction.org/

Selected, Edited and with Issue Framing Material by:
Brent Slife, *Brigham Young University*

ISSUE

Is Excessive Use of Facebook a Form of Narcissism?

YES: **Christopher J. Carpenter,** from "Narcissism on Facebook: Self-Promotional and Anti-Social Behavior," *Personality and Individual Differences* (vol. 52, no. 4, pp. 482–486, 2012)

NO: **Bruce C. McKinney, Lynne Kelly,** and **Robert L. Duran,** from "Narcissism or Openness? College Students' Use of Facebook and Twitter," *Communication Research Reports* (vol. 29, no. 2, pp. 108–118, 2012)

Learning Outcomes

After reading this issue, you should be able to:

- Decide if using Facebook could accentuate narcissistic behavior.
- Determine what empirical evidence exists that supports the correlation between Facebook use and narcissism.

ISSUE SUMMARY

YES: Christopher Carpenter, assistant professor of communication at Western Illinois University, argues that elements of narcissistic personality disorder predict specific patterns of Facebook use (including the frequency of certain behaviors).

NO: Bruce McKinney, professor of communication studies at the University of North Carolina Wilmington, Lynne Kelly, professor and director of the School of Communication at the University of Hartford, and Robert Duran, professor in the School of Communication at the University of Hartford, contend that narcissism is unrelated to the frequency of Facebook use.

$\mathbf{I}$t seems that everybody has a Facebook account these days. Facebook has become so commonplace in our society that people are often considered strange for *not* using it regularly. Still, Facebook use has become increasingly controversial in recent years (Anderson, Fagan, Woodnutt, & Chamorro-Premuzic, 2012). Common concerns include the prevalence of inappropriate behaviors, verbal abuse, cyber-bullying, interpersonal conflict, and breaches of privacy (Anderson, Fagan, Woodnutt, & Chamorro-Premuzic, 2012; Aydin, 2012). Though some of these concerns are similar to those regarding general Internet use the controversial nature of Facebook is unique in that Facebook use is just as much about the cultivation and presentation of one's own self-image as it is about interacting with others.

Some recent research suggests that Facebook's uniqueness is positive. Its format—which encourages expanding one's social network (or "audience") as well as encouraging emotional self-disclosure—may facilitate both the development of new friendships and the preservation of

old friendships (Manago, Taylor, & Greenfield, 2012). For this reason, many psychologists regard Facebook as a welcome technological development, a tool for developing and maintaining social relationships in a rapidly evolving world. But is it possible that *excessive* use of Facebook—with its inherent emphasis on cultivating and presenting one's self to others—is associated with *narcissism*? Psychologists consider narcissism to be a personality disorder in which people have an inflated sense of self-importance as well as extreme preoccupation with themselves. Needless to say, this consequence would not be a positive outcome of Facebook use.

The author of the YES selection, Carpenter, tends to agree with this negative consequence. He believes that Facebook is a fertile environment for people to express narcissistic tendencies. Because Facebook provides people with a means to develop and maintain a network of friends and acquaintances, with the express purpose of sharing personal information with that network, it can become an ideal setting for people to display a variety of antisocial behaviors that are commonly associated with narcissistic personality disorder—and may even encourage such behavior. In order to support his claim, Carpenter had nearly 300 college students take a survey designed to determine if two of the more socially disruptive elements of narcissism (i.e., grandiose exhibitionism and entitlement/exhibitionism) predict particular patterns of Facebook use. According to Carpenter, the results of the study suggest that both of these elements are, indeed, related to specific patterns of behavior on Facebook.

The authors of the NO selection take a completely different point of view. McKinney, Kelly, and Duran believe that narcissism is unrelated to the frequency of Facebook use. Though it is likely that narcissism may influence *some* people's behavior on Facebook, McKinney, Kelly, and Duran believe that the majority of young adults use Facebook merely as a tool to communicate with others—independent of narcissistic personality traits. As such, they contend that the frequency of Facebook use *is not* indicative of narcissism. To support this claim, they administered a short survey to 233 college students to assess the frequency and nature of Facebook use among students.

According to their results, narcissism was unrelated to the frequency of Facebook use, one's motivation for using it, and various *types* of posts made on Facebook.

References

Anderson, B., Fagan, P., Woodnutt, T., and Chamorro-Premuzic, T. (2012). Facebook psychology: Popular questions answered by research. *Psychology of Popular Media Culture, 1*(1), 23–37. doi:10.1037/a0026452

Aydin, S. (2012). A review of research on Facebook as an educational environment. *Educational Technology Research and Development, 60*(6), 1093–1106.

Manago, A. M., Taylor, T., and Greenfield, P. M. (2012). Me and my 400 friends: The anatomy of college students' Facebook networks, their communication patterns, and well-being. *Developmental Psychology, 48*(2), 369–380. doi:10.1037/a0026338

POINT

- Facebook is often used as a means of obtaining self-validation.
- Facebook is an ideal setting for the manifestation of narcissistic behaviors.
- The structure of Facebook encourages narcissistic behavior.
- Empirical evidence suggests that narcissistic elements predict Facebook use.

COUNTERPOINT

- Facebook is primarily used as tool for communication.
- Facebook caters to a wide range of individuals, most of whom are not narcissistic.
- Narcissistic behaviors on Facebook are only incidental.
- Empirical evidence suggests that narcissism does not influence the frequency of Facebook use.

YES

Christopher J. Carpenter

Narcissism on Facebook: Self-Promotional and Anti-Social Behavior

Introduction

Facebook is one of the most popular websites in the world with over 600 million users (Ahmad, 2011). Those who use Facebook enjoy many benefits. Some college students use Facebook to seek and receive social support when they feel upset (Park, Kee, & Valenzuela, 2009; Wright, Craig, Cunningham, & Igiel, 2007). Toma and Hancock's (2011) recent experiments found when individuals are feeling distressed, they turn to Facebook to feel better. On the other hand, DeAndrea, Tong, and Walther (2011) argue that although online interaction provides opportunities for positive social interaction, some users abuse the affordances of social networking sites like Facebook to behave in anti-social ways. They argue that researchers need to move past seeking to determine if computer-mediated communication (CMC) has positive or negative effects as a whole but to determine why people use websites like Facebook in ways that promote or harm interpersonal relationships.

This study sought to take a step in that direction by examining one possible predictor of anti-social Facebook use: trait narcissism. The narcissistic personality type will first be briefly explicated. Then the existing research on the relationship between narcissism and Facebook use will be explored to develop hypotheses.

Investigating the relationship between narcissism and Facebook behavior is important because Facebook is becoming an increasingly important part of people's lives. Several researchers have found a relationship between narcissism and frequency of using Facebook (Buffardi & Campbell, 2008; Mehdizadeh, 2010; Ong et al., 2011). Other researchers found that narcissism is associated with the number of friends their participants have on Facebook (Bergman, Fearrington, Davenport, & Bergman, 2011). If these findings are accurate, it suggests that when people are interacting with others on Facebook, they are more likely to be interacting with individuals who are high in trait narcissism than in other contexts. If Facebook users are likely to be engaging in negative behaviors, the quality of the interpersonal interactions people experience on Facebook will be reduced. Furthermore, some research suggests that people are evaluated not just by their own profiles but by the comments others make on their profiles (Walther, Van Der Heide, Kim,

Westerman, & Tong, 2008). The negative behavior of narcissists on Facebook may reflect poorly on the innocent friends of those narcissists. If the relationship between narcissism and various kinds of behaviors can be uncovered, perhaps interventions can be designed to improve the Facebook social skills of trait narcissists.

Narcissism

When they developed the narcissistic personality inventory (NPI) Raskin and Terry (1988) found a great deal of ambiguity in the personality literature concerning the primary aspects of narcissism. They therefore included a variety of heterogeneous traits in their conceptualization of narcissism. These included aspects such as "a grandiose sense of self-importance or uniqueness," "an inability to tolerate criticism," and "entitlement or the expectation of special favors without assuming reciprocal responsibilities" (p. 891).

This definition covers a constellation of concepts and the NPI sought to measure all of them as aspects of a single personality trait.

In contrast, Ackerman et al. (2011) argue that the NPI is really measuring three different traits. They claim that one of the aspects of narcissism measured by the NPI is leadership ability and that aspect is often associated with positive interpersonal outcomes. The leadership aspects of narcissism were not the focus of this investigation as they are associated with pro-social behavior. On the other hand, they argue that the NPI also includes two other aspects of narcissism that they discovered drive the relationship between narcissism and anti-social behavior. These traits were the focus of this investigation.

Ackerman et al. (2011) labeled the first socially toxic element, "Grandiose Exhibitionism" (GE). This aspect of narcissism includes "self-absorption, vanity, superiority, and exhibitionistic tendencies" (p. 6). People who score high on this aspect of narcissism need to constantly be at the center of attention. They say shocking things and inappropriately self-disclose because they cannot stand to be ignored. They will take any opportunity to promote themselves. Simply gaining the interest and attention of others satisfies them.

Attention is not enough for those who possess the other negative aspect of narcissism labeled, "Entitlement/

Exploitativeness" (EE). Ackerman et al. (2011) argue this aspect includes "a sense of deserving respect and a willingness to manipulate and take advantage of others" (p. 6). This tendency goes beyond the need for attention associated with GE as people high in this trait are those who will feel they deserve everything. More importantly, these people do not let the feelings and needs of others impede their goals. Ackerman et al. (2011) found that participants with higher EE scores were increasingly likely to have negative interactions reported by their roommate and their roommate was more likely to be dissatisfied with their relationship.

Narcissism and Facebook

Examination of the interpersonal possibilities offered by Facebook as well as the limited extant research suggests several tentative hypotheses about Facebook behaviors and the two aspects of narcissism under investigation. Initially, individuals who are high in GE will want to gain the attention of the widest audience possible (Ackerman et al., 2011). Therefore, they are predicted to have a high friend count given their drive to seek attention from as many people as possible. If they are seeking a wider audience, they are also predicted to accept friend requests from strangers because they would be seeking an audience rather than using Facebook to engage in social interaction with existing friends. They may also attempt to gain the attention of their audience by frequently offering new content. Posting status updates, posting pictures of themselves, and changing their profile are all methods of using Facebook to focus attention on the self. These different aspects of providing content will be labeled self-promotion and as a group they are predicted to be positively associated with GE.

On the other hand, Ackerman et al. (2011) found that EE tended to be associated with anti-social behaviors that indicate that others should cater to the narcissist's needs without any expectation of reciprocity. In the offline world, people high in EE might expect favors such as time, money, social support, and indications of respect from others. Although time and money might be harder to demand on Facebook, those high in EE should expect social support and respect. Some research suggests that many individuals who gain social support on Facebook feel less stress (Wright et al., 2007). Facebook users who are high in EE would be predicted to demand social support but be unlikely to provide it to others. They feel that others should support them when they are distressed, but they feel no duty to reciprocate.

There are several ways that those high in EE might expect to receive respect from their social network on Facebook. Those high on EE would be likely to use Facebook to determine what others are saying about them. They would be more likely to focus on the status updates from their network for the purpose of determining if their network is speaking as well of them as their inflated sense of self-importance would demand. Some research suggests that when someone high in trait narcissism is slighted, they aggressively retaliate (Bushman & Baumeister, 1998; Twenge

& Campbell, 2003). Ackerman et al. (2011) argue that EE is the subscale is the aspect of narcissism most associated with socially disruptive behaviors such as aggression. Therefore, EE is predicted to be associated with responding to negative comments from others with verbally aggressive responses. Finally, if the EE subscale is tapping into a trait that demands respect from others, they would also be predicted to become angry when they do not get the respect they feel they deserve. One way this might be expressed on Facebook would be becoming angry when others do not comment on their status updates. When people post status updates on Facebook, others have the opportunity to indicate agreement or praise their comments. Someone high in EE would become angry when they did not get this attention. These hypotheses were tested using a survey of Facebook users.

Method

Sample

There were 294 participants in the survey whose ages ranged from 18 to 65 years ($M = 23.26$, $SD = 7.30$). Of this sample, 74.1% were college students and 68% were female. The sample was a convenience sample recruited by the members of an undergraduate research methods course in a medium sized Midwestern, American university. They contacted their social network and solicited volunteers to complete the survey. Participations were uncompensated. All participants were Facebook users.

Procedure

Participants were given a link to the online consent form that described their rights as research participants. If they indicated that they agreed to participate, an online survey appeared. The online survey began with the questions regarding Facebook use, and then they were asked the GE, and EE subscales of the NPI using the items identified by Ackerman et al. (2011). After the NPI subscales was the Rosenberg (1965) self-esteem scale and then basic demographic items.

Instruments

The items for all the original scales are contained in Appendix A. Table 1 contains means, standard deviations, number of items, and reliability estimates for all of the focal constructs. The first set of items concerned the frequency with which the participants engaged in particular Facebook behaviors on a 6-point scale ranging from "never" to "all the time." These include the self-promotion behaviors, accepting strangers as friends, and retaliating against mean comments. The participants were next asked the items from Dillard and Shen (2005) felt anger scale by instructing participants to "Please use the following scale to respond to how you feel when people do not comment as much as you would like on your status updates on Facebook." For each of the four emotions listed (irritated, angry, annoyed, aggravated) they were asked to respond

Table 1

Means, standard deviations, scale reliability, and number of items for constructs

Measure	M	SD	Reliability	Number of items
GE	3.14	2.18	0.83	9
EE	0.89	1.04	0.68	4
Self-esteem	3.16	0.50	0.87	10
Self-promotion	3.23	1.01	0.84	5
Accept strangers' friend requests	1.98	1.34	—	1
Retaliate against mean comments	1.64	1.14	—	1
Seeking support from others	2.71	1.56	0.95	5
Providing support to others	4.21	1.64	0.92	4
Anger at lack of comments	1.43	1.93	0.96	4
Looking to see if others comment about the self	2.85	1.48	0.87	4
Number of friends	652.58	473.36	—	1
Difference between seeking and providing social support	−1.50	1.60	0.87	

using an 11-point scale ranging from "I feel none of this emotion" to "I feel a great deal of this emotion." Most of the remaining Facebook questions utilized a 7-point Likert scale ranging from "strongly disagree" to "strongly agree." The variable representing the difference between the amount of social support they provide and the amount they seek was calculated by subtracting the amount they provide from how much they seek. Finally, the participants were asked how many friends they had on Facebook (range: 12–4655).

In order to determine the construct validity of the new multi-item measures, a confirmatory factor analysis was conducted. AMOS 18.0 was used to estimate the fit of the four factor model containing the items for self-promotion, checking for comments about the self by others, providing social support, and seeking social support. The data were adequately consistent with the model ($CFI = .93$, $RMSEA = .09$).

The participants responded to the items identified by Ackerman et al. (2011) for the two subscales of interest from the NPI. Their scores were calculated by summing the number of narcissism items they chose on the forced-choice NPI items for each subscale. They also responded to the Rosenberg self-esteem scale. The self-esteem scores were calculated by calculating the average score for each participant such that higher scores indicated greater self-esteem. Table 2 contains a correlation matrix of all the measured constructs.

Table 2

Correlation matrix of measured constructs

	1	2	3	4	5	6	7	8	9	10	11	12	13	14
1. GE														
2. EE														
3. SE	0.36													
4. Self-promotion	0.28	−0.09												
5. Number of friends	0.27	0.07	0.04											
6. Accept strangers	0.17	−0.01	0.04	0.33										
7. Seek support	0.25	0.31	−0.16	0.26	0.21									
8. Provide support	0.14	0.19	−0.22	0.39	0.13	0.28								
9. Difference in social support	−0.01	−0.03	−0.10	0.33	0.11	0.10	0.50							
10. Anger	0.14	0.21	−0.11	0.03	0.02	0.17	0.46	−0.54						
11. Check for comments	0.23	0.20	−0.28	0.08	0.02	0.27	0.23	0.06	0.16					
12. Retaliate with mean comments	0.14	0.30	−0.16	0.21	0.16	0.30	0.31	0.30	−0.01	0.32				
13. Sex	0.25	0.36	−0.13	0.32	0.17	0.41	0.34	0.10	0.23	0.30	0.38			
14. Age	−0.13	−0.10	−0.06	0.26	0.06	−0.14	0.03	0.19	−0.17	−0.08	−0.08	−0.04		
15. College student	−0.21	−0.19	−0.02	−0.22	−0.28	−0.13	−0.10	0.02	−0.12	−0.06	−0.19	−0.16	0.06	
	−0.11	−0.10	−0.04	−0.19	−0.20	−0.04	−0.12	0.03	−0.15	−0.05	−0.13	−0.15	0.01	0.46

Note: Correlations such that $r > .11$ are $p < .05$, $r > .14$ are $p < .05$, and $r > .18$ are $p < .001$. Sex is coded male = 0 and female = 1. College student status is coded non-college students = 0 and college students = 1.

Results

Statistical Analysis

Initially, the results concerning self-promotion will be examined. Then the results concerning anti-social behaviors will be discussed. All hypotheses were tested by regressing each Facebook behavior onto GE, EE, and self-esteem, with ordinary least squares estimates. Rhodewalt and Morf (1995) argued that including self-esteem in the regression equation controls for the overlap between healthy self-esteem and narcissism. There is conceptually some overlap between self-esteem and narcissism in that GE is driven partially by the narcissist's belief that he or she is due attention because they are such a valuable person. Similarly EE is partially driven by the narcissist's belief that she or he is entitled to anything she or he wants because they perceive themselves to be a valuable person, Regression analysis partials out the healthy parts of self-regard from the unhealthy aspects that drive GE and EE.

Self-Promotion

Recall that it was predicted that GE would be related positively to self-promoting Facebook behaviors that allow one to present an inflated sense of self to as many people as possible. Examination of Table 3 shows the standardized regression coefficients for the regression of the self-promoting Facebook behavior factor on GE, EE, and self-esteem. GE was the only substantial predictor of the self-promoting Facebook behaviors. Also, it was predicted that GE would be associated with a higher friend count as those high in GE would be seeking a large audience to provide attention. GE was again the only substantial predictor of friend count. Finally, GE was predicted to be positively associated with the frequency with which the participants accept strangers as friends to again expand their audience. GE was positively associated with accepting strangers but surprisingly, EE was a substantial predictor as well.

Anti-Social Behavior

It was also predicted that EE would be positively related to several anti-social behaviors associated with their sense of entitlement to non-reciprocated social support and positive regard. Examination of Table 3 shows the standardized regression coefficients for the regression of each anti-social Facebook behavior on GE, EE, and self-esteem. The regression models showed that EE was a substantial predictor of retaliating against mean comments, seeking more social support than one provides, and checking Facebook to see what others are saying about one. These relationships are consistent with the predicted pattern of a positive association between EE and anti-social behavior. On the other hand, EE did not predict getting angry when people do not comment on one's status. This latter finding was inconsistent with the hypothesis. In general, the data were consistent with the expectation that EE would be associated with behaviors that demonstrated a focus on one's own needs without regard for those of others.

There were also unexpected relationships between GE and anti-social behaviors. In particular, GE was substantially associated with an increased likelihood of retaliating against mean comments about oneself, though the relationship was weaker than the relationship of this behavior with EE. Additionally, GE was predictive of seeking more social support than one provides. Surprisingly, although EE was not a substantial predictor of getting angry about the lack of comments on one's status by others, GE was positively associated with this response.

Table 3

Results of regressing GE, EE, and self-esteem on Facebook behavior with standardized beta weights and R^2 values

Facebook behavior	β			
	GE	EE	SE	R^2
Self-promoting behavior	**.28	−.05	−.03	.07
Number of FB friends	**.21	−.09	−.02	.04
Frequency of accepting stranger as friends	**.23	**.21	**−.20	.16
Retaliate against mean comments	**.19	**.28	**−.15	.17
Seek social support	**.18	.10	**−.26	.10
Provide social support	.04	−.06	−.11	.01
Seek more social support than provide	*.13	*.16	*−.14	.07
See if others are talking about me	.09	**.26	**−.16	.12
Get angry at lack of status comments	*.31	.05	*−.36	.18

*Statistically significant at $p < .05$.
**Statistically significant at $p < .01$.

Self-Esteem

Although self-esteem was not the focus of this investigation, self-esteem tended to be negatively predictive of some of the same behaviors that the two narcissism scales were positively related to. Examination of Table 3 show[s] that self-esteem was not substantially related to the self-promotion behaviors. On the other hand, it was negatively predictive of many of the anti-social behaviors.

Discussion

This study sought to test the prediction that the two socially disruptive elements of narcissism would each predict a particular pattern of Facebook behaviors. Grandiose exhibitionism was predicted to be related to Facebook behaviors that afforded extensive self-presentation to as large an audience as possible via status updates, photos, and attaining large numbers of friends. Entitlement/exhibitionism was predicted to be related to anti-social behaviors such as retaliating against negative comments about oneself, reading others status updates to see if they are talking about oneself, and seeking more social support than one provides. With few exceptions, the data were consistent with these hypotheses. Additionally, in some cases, self-esteem was negatively related to these narcissistic Facebook behaviors.

The anti-social behaviors were predicted to be primarily associated with EE but both aspects of narcissism were predictive of some of these behaviors. Both subscales were related positively to retaliating against mean comments as well as seeking more social support than one provides. Despite EE being identified as the more socially disruptive aspect of narcissism (Ackerman et al., 2011), only GE was related to angry responses to perceived social neglect. Perhaps this finding occurred because people who are seeking attention are more likely to be angered about not getting attention paid to their status updates. This finding suggests that in particular cases, it is GE, not EE that is more strongly anti-social aspect of narcissism. Both GE and EE were associated with angrily retaliating against negative comments about the self. In general, the relationships with both of these two narcissism subscales is consistent with previous research finding that narcissism is negatively predictive of communal orientations to social interaction (Bradlee & Emmons, 1992) and positively predictive of interpersonal deviance (Ackerman et al., 2011).

This study also provided some support for Ackerman et al.'s (2011) contention that these two subscales of the NPI are measuring different constructs. The differential pattern of relationships with the self-promotional behaviors shows that the nomological network of each subscale differs in substantial ways from the other. On the other hand there were several cases in which both subscales were related in the same way to some of the anti-social Facebook behaviors. These findings suggest that although EE does not tap into the desire to self-promote, GE may

include some of the aspects of entitlement that Ackerman et al. (2011) predicted would be more associated with the EE trait. Future researchers examining narcissism would be advised to consider each subscale of the NPI both separately and as a whole to further examine the factor structure of the NPI.

Limitations

The generalizability of the findings in this study is limited because the sample was not representative. Although it was not composed entirely of college students, about three fourths of the participants were college students. Given that Facebook is reaching all over the world and across all demographics (Ahmad, 2011) it is important to replicate this study with a broader sample in order to determine if these relationships can be found with other groups. Perhaps in other cultures, narcissism expresses differently on Facebook.

Additionally, the relationships uncovered in this study may have been inflated by several sources of method bias (Podsakoff, MacKenzie, Lee, & Podsakoff, 2003). It is possible that a consistency motif was operating to inflate the relationship among the Facebook behaviors. Item context effects may also have caused some participants to interpret the NPI items based on their Facebook behavior and hypothesis guessing may have encouraged some participants to intentionally inflate those relationships. Additional research should measure individuals' NPI scores and then have independent coders record many of the Facebook behaviors measured in this study by examining the participants' Facebook accounts.

Future Research

More research is needed on socially disruptive Facebook communication. Additional socially disruptive communication patterns should be uncovered and examined. Furthermore, the effects of anti-social behavior on other users is an important and untapped area of research. In general, the "dark side" of Facebook (DeAndrea et al., 2011) requires more research in order to better understand Facebook's socially beneficial and harmful aspects in order to enhance the former and curtail the latter.

Conclusion

Given the explosion in Facebook's popularity (Ahmad, 2011), this article took a significant first step towards identifying the kinds of people who may create a socially disruptive atmosphere on Facebook. If Facebook is to be a place where people go to repair their damaged ego (Toma & Hancock, 2011) and seek social support (Wright et al., 2007) it is vitally important to discover the potentially negative communication one might find on Facebook and the kinds of people likely to engage in them. Ideally, people will engage in pro-social Facebooking rather than anti-social mebooking.

Appendix A

Self-promotion questions

How often do you post status updates to Facebook?

How often do you post photographs of yourself on Facebook?

How often do you update your profile information on Facebook?

How often do you change your profile picture on Facebook?

How often do you tag pictures of yourself on Facebook?

Accept friend requests from strangers

How often do you accept a friend request from a total stranger on Facebook (assuming they do not appear to be a fake profile)?

Retaliate against negative comments

How often do you make mean comments on someone's status if they said something negative about you on Facebook?

Checking for comments about the self

I use Facebook to see what people are saying about me.

I like to read my Facebook newsfeed to see if my friends have mentioned me.

It is important to me to know if anyone is saying anything bad about me on Facebook.

I usually know what people are saying about me on Facebook.

Offer social support

I use Facebook to offer emotional support to people I know when they are feeling upset about something.

If I see someone post a Facebook status update that indicates they are upset, I try to post a comforting comment on their status.

It is important to me to try to cheer up my friends by commenting on their Facebook status updates when it appears that they feel distressed.

I try to make people feel better by commenting on their Facebook status when I can tell they are having a bad day.

Seek self support

Whenever I am upset I usually post a status update about what is bothering me.

If something made me sad, I usually post a comment about it on Facebook.

Posting a status update to Facebook is a good way to vent when something is bugging me.

If I post a Facebook status update about something that is bothering me, it makes me feel better.

I use Facebook to let people know that I am upset about something.

Number of friends

How many friends do you have on Facebook (total number of people in your "Friends").

References

Ackerman, R. A., Witt, E. A., Donnellan, M. B., Trzesniewski, K. H., Robins, R. W., & Kashy, D. A. (2011). What does the narcissistic personality inventory really measure? *Assessment, 18,* 67–87.

Ahmad, A. (2011). Social network sites and its popularity. *International Journal of Research and Reviews in Computer Science, 2,* 522–526.

Bergman, S. M., Fearrington, M. E., Davenport, S. W., & Bergman, J. Z. (2011). Millennials, narcissism, and social networking: What narcissists do on social networking sites and why. *Personality and Individual Differences, 50*(5), 706–711. doi:10.1016/j.paid.2010.12.022.

Bradlee, P. M., & Emmons, R. A. (1992). Locating narcissism within the interpersonal circumplex and the five-factor model. *Personality and Individual Differences, 13,* 821–830.

Buffardi, L. E., & Campbell, W. K. (2008). Narcissism and social networking web sites. *Personality and Social Psychology Bulleting, 34,* 1303–1314.

Bushman, B. J., & Baumeister, R. F. (1998). Threatened egotism, narcissism, self-esteem, and direct and displaced aggression: Does self-love or self-hate lead to violence? *Journal of Personality and Social Psychology, 75,* 219–229.

DeAndrea, D. C., Tong, S. T., & Walther, J. B. (2011). Dark sides of computer-mediated communication. In W. R. Cupach & B. H. Spitzberg (Eds.), *The dark side of close relationships II* (pp. 95–118). New York. New York: Routledge.

Dillard, J. P., & Shen, L. (2005). On the nature of reactance and its role in persuasive health communication. *Communication Monographs, 72,* 144–168.

Mehdizadeh, S. (2010). Self-presentation 2.0: Narcissism and self-esteem on Facebook. *Cyberpsychology, Behavior, and Social Networking, 13,* 357–364.

Ong, E. Y. L., Ang, R. P., Ho, J. C. M., Lim, J. C. Y., Goh, D. H., Lee, C. S., et al. (2011). Narcissism, extraversion, and adolescents' self-presentation on Facebook. *Personality and Individual Differences, 50,* 180–185.

Park, N., Kee, K. F., & Valenzuela, S. (2009). Being immersed in social networking environment: Facebook groups, uses and gratifications, and social outcomes. *Cyberpsychology & Behavior, 12,* 729–733.

Podsakoff, P. M., MacKenzie, S. M., Lee, J., & Podsakoff, N. P. (2003). Common method variance in behavioral research: A critical review of the literature and recommended remedies. *Journal of Applied Psychology, 88,* 879–903.

Raskin, R. N., & Terry, H. (1988). A principal-components analysis of the narcissistic personality inventory and further evidence of its construct validity. *Journal of Personality and Social Psychology, 54,* 890–902.

Rhodewalt, F., & Morf, C. C. (1995). Self and interpersonal correlates of the narcissistic personality inventory: A review and new findings. *Journal of Research in Personality, 29,* 1–23.

Rosenberg, M. (1965). *Society and the adolescent self-image.* Princeton, NJ: Princeton University Press.

Toma, C. L., & Hancock, J. (2011). *Affirming the self online: Motives and benefits of Facebook use.* Boston,

MA: Paper presented at the annual meeting of the International Communication Association.

Twenge, J. M., & Campbell, W. K. (2003). "Isn't it fun to get the respect that we're going to deserve?" Narcissism, social rejection, and aggression. *Personality and Social Psychology Bulletin, 29,* 261–272.

Walther, J. B., Van Der Heide, B., Kim, S. Y., Westerman, D., & Tong, S. T. (2008). The role of friends' appearance and behavior on evaluations of individuals on Facebook: Are we known by the company we keep? *Human Communication Research, 34,* 28–49.

Wright, K. B., Craig, E. A., Cunningham, C. B., & Igiel, M. (2007). *Emotional support and perceived stress among college students using Facebook.com: An exploration of the relationship between source perceptions and emotional support.* Chicago, IL: Paper presented at the annual meeting of the National Communication Association.

CHRISTOPHER J. CARPENTER is an assistant professor of communication at Western Illinois University. He has received a PhD in communication at Michigan State University.

Bruce C. McKinney, Lynne Kelly,
and Robert L. Duran

Narcissism or Openness? College Students' Use of Facebook and Twitter

With 845,000,000 + Facebook® users worldwide (see http://www.facebook.com/press/info.php?statistics), it is a popular means by which people stay connected to their social network (Ellison, Steinfield, & Lampe, 2007; Hampton, Goulet, Rainie, & Purcell, 2011). Scholars in psychology have studied personality variables of users of social networking sites (SNSs; e.g., Ryan & Xenos, 2011; Wilson, Fornasier, & White, 2010). Perhaps because these sites have ⅄ features enabling individuals to share information about themselves, some scholars (e.g., Buffardi & Campbell, 2008; Mehdizadeh, 2010) have focused on narcissism. Despite the limitations of these studies and some inconsistent findings, popular press articles (e.g., Jayson, 2009; O'Dell, 2010; Rosen, 2007) have proclaimed that SNSs breed narcissism among users.

Critiques of SNSs and branding of users as narcissistic are based on limited empirical evidence, and fail to consider that such sites are inherently communication tools. Hampton et al. (2011) found that Facebook users have more close social ties; that most of what they "do" on Facebook, besides provide status updates about themselves, is comment on others' posts, updates, and photos; and that "Facebook use seems to support intimacy rather than undermine it" (p. 25). These and other study results (e.g., Stern & Taylor, 2007; Urista, Dong, & Day, 2009) calls into question the conclusion that activity on an SNS is narcissistic, and raises the possibility that active self-presentation on an SNS reflects an openness about sharing information about one-self with others to facilitate communication and maintain relationships with one's wide circle of friends and acquaintances. This study investigated whether a communication perspective better explains individuals' activities on SNSs than narcissism does. With so many SNS users, it is important to determine whether their behavior is aberrant (i.e., narcissistic) or appropriate for the relationship maintenance purpose of these sites.

Narcissism and Social Networking

Several studies have examined the association between the usage of SNSs—in particular, Facebook—and narcissism. According to Buffardi and Campbell (2008), "Narcissism refers to a personality trait reflecting a grandiose and inflated self-concept" (p. 1304). The narcissist tends to view him- or herself as intelligent, powerful, physically attractive, unique, and entitled (Buffardi & Campbell, 2008). Some researchers (e.g., Twenge & Foster, 2010; Twenge, Konrath, Foster, Campbell, & Bushman, 2008a, 2008b) have claimed that there has been a significant increase in narcissism among "generation Ys" or "millennials" over the last 2 decades, although others dispute this (Trzesniewski, Donnellan, & Robbins, 2008a, 2008b).

Research studying the association of narcissism with usage of an SNS has generally concluded that there is a positive relationship (e.g., Buffardi & Campbell, 2008; Mehdizadeh, 2010; Ryan & Xenos, 2011), but a closer look reveals limitations and inconsistent findings. Buffardi and Campbell, using the Narcissistic Personality Inventory (NPI; Raskin & Terry, 1988) and coding, had raters examine individuals' Facebook pages. They found that higher scores on the NPI were related to more interactions on Facebook (specifically, number of friends and wall posts); there was no relation between page owners' narcissism and quantity of information they posted about themselves, as had been expected. Narcissism was positively related to coder ratings of self-promoting information, as well as "main photograph attractiveness, self-promotion, and sexiness" (Buffardi & Campbell, 2008, p. 1310).

Consistent with Buffardi and Campbell (2008), Mehdizadeh (2010) found that narcissism scores were positively correlated with the time spent on Facebook and the number of times Facebook was checked per day. Results provided partial support for the hypothesis that narcissism scores are related to self-promoting content, although the study author did the ratings of self-promoting content; thus, the findings are potentially biased and, therefore, suspect.

In contrast to results obtained by Buffardi and Campbell (2008) and Mehdizadeh (2010), Bergman, Fearrington, Davenport, and Bergman (2011) found narcissism was unrelated to the amount of time spent on SNSs or the frequency of status updates. It also was not related to types of SNS activities, with the exception of more posting of self-focused pictures. However, results indicated that narcissism was positively related to the number of, and desire to have, many SNS friends, as well to the belief that others are interested in one's activities and a desire to let others know what one is doing. Ong et al. (2011) found that over and above extraversion, narcissism was positively related to self-ratings of the attractiveness of Facebook profile pictures and to the frequency of status updates (in contrast to Bergman et al.'s, 2011, findings). However, narcissism was unrelated to social network size (also in contrast to Bergman et al.'s, 2011, findings) and number of photos posted, once extraversion was taken into account. Finally, Ryan and Xenos (2011) reported that, although Facebook users were higher on overall narcissism than non-users, narcissism was unrelated to the amount of time spent on Facebook (consistent with Bergman et al., 2011). This study also found that narcissism was associated with a preference for the "photos" feature, and that the exhibitionism dimension, but not the overall NPI score, was related to a preference for the "status updates" feature. However, the study did not distinguish between photos about oneself or viewing others' photos, or between posting status updates or viewing others' updates.

SNS Tools for Communication and Relationship Maintenance

Research by communication scholars on SNSs is limited, and has focused on how such sites form and maintain social capital (e.g., Ellison et al., 2007; Valenzuela, Park, & Kee, 2009) or on why in individuals are drawn to such sites (e.g., Stern & Taylor, 2007; Urista et al., 2009) and how they use them (e.g., Mansson & Myers, 2011). Findings have been consistent that individuals use these sites, particularly Facebook, largely to maintain existing relationships and stay connected to people in their lives (Ellison et al., 2007; Hampton et al., 2011; Stern & Taylor, 2007; Urista et al., 2009). Mannson and Myers focused on how users expressed affection to maintain relationships, finding that many forms of expressed affection transpired on Facebook. Results of these studies, thus, suggest that users view these sites as enabling communication and the sharing of information about one another.

Rationales and Research Questions

The purposes of this study were twofold. First, because studies of narcissism and SNS usage have produced mixed results, additional research is warranted. This study overcame a limitation of published research by distinguishing between self-focused and other-focused SNS activity. Second, this study offered an alternative to narcissism as the motivator of self-focused SNS activity by viewing SNSs as tools for communication and maintaining relationships. From this perspective, self-focused information may be motivated by a positive attitude about sharing such information to stay connected to one's social network.

To the first purpose, studies have produced mixed results pertaining to the relationship between SNS usage

and narcissism. Given these conflicting findings and the lack of research differentiating the focus of Facebook activity (i.e., to promote oneself or check out others), the following research questions were addressed:

> *RQ1: Are there positive relationships between narcissism and both the frequency of using Facebook to provide information about oneself and the number of Facebook friends?*
>
> *RQ2: Is there a negative relationship between narcissism and frequency of using Facebook to find out about others?*

All SNSs are not necessarily used in the same ways; previous research has not distinguished among SNSs or only examined Facebook. One other popular site, Twitter, described as an "information network" (www.twitter.com), has not been studied with respect to narcissism. Twitter would seem to be a perfect venue for narcissists because it allows individuals to answer the question, "What are you doing?," via messages of 140 characters or less. The belief that there is an audience interested in following one's moment-to-moment postings suggests egocentrism, self-aggrandizement, and self-importance—the very characteristics of narcissistic individuals. That one can tweet or follow others' tweets suggests two possible relationships with narcissism. Therefore, we addressed the following research questions:

> *RQ3: Is there a positive relationship between narcissism and both the frequency of using Twitter to provide information about oneself and the number of Twitter followers?*
>
> *RQ4: Is there a negative relationship between narcissism and frequency of using Twitter to follow others?*

Although a "New Narcissism" (Rosen, 2007) may, in part, account for the popularity of SNSs, it is also likely that SNSs are simply one way young adults communicate. Bergman et al. (2011), in explaining their unexpected result that narcissism was unrelated to the amount of time on SNSs and the frequency of status updates, concluded the following: "This suggests that Millennials' SNS usage is not solely about attention—seeking . . . but is also a means of staying connected and communication" (p. 709). In addition, the prevalence, ease, norm, and structure of SNSs may foster a positive attitude about being open about oneself. Providing information about oneself is normal and expected behavior on these sites. Acquisti and Gross (2006) concluded that "Respondents are fully aware that a social network is based on information sharing" (p. 18). Indeed, that is what Twitter is intended for, and the structure of Facebook, with user profiles, status updates, and so forth encourages such sharing. Thus, SNS users likely share information about themselves not because they are narcissistic, but because they have a positive attitude about sharing such information—an attitude consistent with viewing SNSs as means to communicate and stay connected. Therefore, the following research questions were addressed:

> RQ5: Are there positive relationships between attitudes about being open in sharing information about oneself and both the frequency of usage of Facebook overall and the frequency of usage of Facebook to inform friends about oneself?
>
> RQ6: Are there positive relationships between attitudes about being open in sharing information about oneself and both the frequency of usage of Twitter overall and the frequency of usage of Twitter to inform friends about oneself?

Method

Participants

Undergraduate students ($N = 233$) in communication classes at a medium-sized, Southern university and at a medium-sized, Northeastern university were administered an anonymous survey. The sample consisted of 144 women (62%) and 89 men (38%), with an average age of 19.77 years ($SD = 1.55$). Of the respondents, 86.6% were White, 5.2% were Hispanic, 4.7% were African American, 0.4% were Asian, and 3% were "other." There were no significant differences on any variables between the two universities.

Measures

Attitude Toward Being Open

This measure consisted of 20 Likert-type items, with response options ranging from 1 (*strongly disagree*) to 5 (*strongly agree*). The items, which we generated, were designed to tap participants' attitudes about how open they are in sharing information about themselves with others in their social circles (e.g., "I share information about myself with only a few close friends," and "I enjoy letting people know things about me"). Existing measures of self-disclosure did not capture the concept of attitude toward being open in sharing information about oneself with the wider social network. For instance, the Wheeless (1978) Revised Self-Disclosure Scale was designed for respondents to focus on a "specific target individual," and all items tap behavior, whereas the measure we developed incorporated items focused on attitudes. However, the Wheeless *amount* and *valence* dimensions were useful in helping us generate items.

Items were factor analyzed using principal components with varimax rotation, producing a three-factor solution accounting for 54.68% of the variance (see Table 1).[1] The first factor, *reveal*, had six items, and tapped participants' willingness to be open and the enjoyment of sharing information about themselves with a wide circle of friends ($M = 3.03$, $SD = 0.73$). *Privacy*, the second dimension, was defined by four items that referred to a lack of concern for privacy (e.g., "People worry too much about their privacy";

Table 1

Principal Components Factor Analysis of the Attitude Toward Openness Scale

Items	Factor 1: Reveal	Factor 2: Privacy	Factor 3: Valence
1. I let a wide circle of friends know a lot about me.	.79	.10	.04
2. I share information about myself with only a few close friends. (R)	−.68	−.22	.05
3. I like letting people know a lot about me.	.72	.20	.05
4. I let very few people know what I've been up to lately. (R)	−.66	−.12	.08
5. I don't hide much about myself with my wide circle of friends.	.71	.13	.15
6. I enjoy letting people know things about me.	.63	.18	.15
7. Keeping information about myself private is very important to me. (R)	−.29	−.67	.09
8. People worry too much about their privacy.	.18	.73	.02
9. I don't worry about how much information people have about me.	.16	.66	.26
10. People today need to be more concerned about their privacy. (R)	−.13	−.79	.00
11. I generally let people know only good things about me. (R)	−.03	−.02	.73
12. It is okay if people know bad things about me.	.18	.25	.66
13. It is best to let people know only things that make me look good. (R)	−.01	.04	.76
14. I let people know good and bad things about me.	.21	.10	.74
Eigenvalue	4.40	1.86	1.39
Portion of variance	31.46	13.32	9.91
Cronbach's alpha	.82	.73	.71

Note: N = 233. R in parentheses refers to reflected items.

Table 2

Descriptive Statistics

Variable	n	M	SD
Frequency of Twitter use	77	3.10	1.35
Frequency of sending tweets	72	2.71	1.39
Frequency of following tweets	72	3.56	1.42
Number of followers on Twitter	68	72.50	168.49
Frequency of FB use	227	4.41	1.01
Frequency of FB use to tell friends about oneself	210	2.79	1.00
Frequency of FB use to find out about friends	224	3.81	1.06
Frequency of posting photos about oneself on FB	200	1.69	0.71
Narcissism	180	17.74	6.42
Attitude toward openness about sharing information about oneself			
Reveal dimension	229	3.03	0.73
Privacy dimension	232	2.52	0.70
Valence dimension	233	3.35	0.64

Note: N = 233. FB = Facebook®.

$M = 2.52$, $SD = 0.70$). The final factor, valence, consisted of four items focused on willingness to share both positive and negative information about oneself ($M = 3.35$, $SD = 0.64$).

Usage of SNSs.

To measure how frequently participants use Twitter and Facebook, 13 items were generated. Response options for 11 of the items were as follows: 0 (*never*), 1 (*less than a few times a month*), 2 (*a few times a month*), 3 (*a couple of times in a week*), 4 (*1 or 2 times a day*), and 5 (*many times a day*). These items measured the frequency of using Twitter overall and sending tweets about oneself, following others' tweets, and updating one's profile photo and profile information; and the frequency of using Facebook overall and letting friends know what one is doing, finding out about friends, updating one's profile and profile photo, and posting photos of oneself. The other two items asked participants to indicate how many Twitter followers and Facebook friends they have. Table 2 presents descriptive statistics for all variables.

Measure of Narcissism

To assess narcissism, the NPI (Raskin & Terry, 1988) was used. Evidence for construct validity of the NPI is reported by Raskin and Terry and Watson, Grisham, Trotter, and Biderman (1984). The NPI is a 40-item measure in which respondents must choose between two options for each item: an option that is indicative of narcissism (e.g., "I like to be the center of attention") and an option that is not (e.g., "I prefer to blend in with the crowd"). Items were summed to produce a score ($M = 17.74$, $SD = 6.42$); reliability was good ($\alpha = .81$), and the

mean was comparable to that obtained by Buffardi and Campbell (2008).

Results

Table 2 presents descriptive statistics. Large variation was reported in the number of Twitter followers and Facebook friends; the medians were 38 and 700, respectively. Whereas 227 (97.4%) participants use Facebook, only one-third use Twitter.

The first two research questions focused on the relationships between narcissism and the use of Facebook to provide information about oneself (*RQ1*) and to find out about others (*RQ2*). Bivariate correlations revealed no significant relationships (see Table 3). However, narcissism was significantly and positively related to the number of Facebook friends ($r = .16$, $p < .05$), although the correlation was small.

RQ3 and *RQ4* focused on relationships between narcissism and the frequency of using Twitter and the number of Twitter followers. Narcissism had a significant, positive relationship with the use [of] Twitter to send tweets about oneself ($r = .26$, $p = .05$), but not with the number of Twitter followers or the use of Twitter to follow others (see Table 3).

RQ5 and *RQ6* addressed the relationships between attitude toward being open in sharing information about oneself and both Facebook and Twitter use. The *reveal* dimension of attitude toward openness (i.e., willingness to be open and enjoyment of sharing information about oneself with a wide circle of friends) was significantly and positively related to the frequency of Facebook use to tell friends about oneself ($r = .30$, $p < .01$) and the frequency of

Table 3

Correlation Matrix

Variable	(2)	(3)	(4)	(5)	(6)	(7)	(8)	(9)	(10)	(11)	(12)	(13)
(1) Narcissism	.13	.09	−.02	.15	.26*	.07	.04	.04	.06	.05	.12	.16*
(2) Reveal		.47**	.27**	.19	.24*	.01	−.06	.11	.30**	.05	.19**	−.01
(3) Privacy			.24**	.03	.10	−.11	.27*	−.02	.13	.01	.14	.04
(4) Valence				.17	.12	.06	.10	−.08	.04	.00	−.01	.00
(5) Use Twitter					.81**	.85**	.24*	.10	.34**	.15	.32**	.05
(6) Send tweets						.64**	.31*	.09	.45**	.14	.26*	.12
(7) Follow tweets							.18	.04	.11	.07	.24	−.05
(8) Number Twitter followers								−.09	−.08	−.14	−.06	−.02
(9) Use FB									.31**	.61**	.23**	.03
(10) FB about self										.56**	.26**	−.04
(11) FB to find out about friends											.26**	−.06
(12) Post pics about self on FB												.04
(13) Number FB friends												—

Note: N = 233. FB = Facebook®.
*p = .05. **p = .01.

[Handwritten annotations: "Studies into home page? Accuracy v. Fantasy? True v. projected self?" and "Conflict intimacy & fake self — FB perpetuates a fantasy where I reconstruct who I want you to think I am"]

sending tweets about oneself ($r = .24, p < .05$). The *privacy* dimension (i.e., a lack of concern for privacy) obtained a significant, positive relationship with the number of Twitter followers ($r = .27, p < .05$; see Table 3).

Discussion

Results of this study indicated that narcissism is unrelated to the frequency of using Facebook to post about one-self (i.e., status updates or photos) but, consistent with two studies (Bergman et al., 2011; Buffardi & Campbell, 2008), is related to the self-reported number of Facebook friends. However, narcissism was significantly related to using Twitter to send tweets about oneself. Finally, attitude toward being open about sharing information about oneself was significantly related to the frequency of using Facebook and Twitter to provide self-focused updates and photos of oneself.

These findings suggest that Facebook is not dominated by narcissistic millennials, as some have proposed (Jayson, 2009; Rosen, 2007), although, consistent with previous research, those higher on narcissism appear to be driven to amass a larger number of Facebook friends. A contribution of this study is that it examined the attitude toward being open about sharing self-focused information that reflects the communicative and relationship maintenance functions of SNSs. The behavior of posting about oneself on Facebook may be better explained by the attitude that it is appropriate and enjoyable to share

information with a wide circle of friends. One study found that participants reported a greater likelihood of disclosing personal information on Facebook than face to face (Christofides, Muise, & Desmarais, 2009), leading the authors to conclude that there is "something different" about the interaction on Facebook, perhaps because it "creates norms regarding what specific information to disclose based on what others have disclosed" (p. 343). Anderson and Raine (2010) stated that "A solid majority of technology experts and stakeholders said the Millennial generation will lead society into a new world of personal disclosure and information sharing using new media" (p. 2). Indeed, as Livingstone (2008) stated, "[S]ocial networking sites typically display as standard precisely the personal information that previous generations often have regarded as private" (p. 404). In sum, our study suggests that the posting of self-focused information and photos on Facebook reflects a positive attitude about such information sharing, not narcissism. This attitude may result from disclosure norms on Facebook, as well as its primary function to connect with one's social network.

An additional contributor is that this study is the first to examine the relationship between narcissism and Twitter usage. Results suggest that Twitter may be the network of choice for narcissists, which may, in part, account for the substantially lower number of Twitter users, as compared to Facebook users. Respondents with significantly higher scores on the NPI also reported sending more tweets about themselves, but narcissism was not related to the number of Twitter followers (which is not in the user's control) or using Twitter to follow others. Whether Twitter is the preferred tool for narcissists requires future research, but this study suggests that it may be.

A limitation of this study is the use of self-reports to assess the frequency of using SNSs to share information and view others' information, as well as self-reports of the frequency of sending tweets about oneself. Actual usage may differ from self-reported usage. A final limitation is that the attitude toward openness measure was author generated, and has not been systematically tested for validity. However, it has face validity, its dimensional structure was solid, and reliabilities were good. Future research should assess the construct validity of the measure.

Results of this study suggest that the use of SNSs by college students is not evidence of narcissism. It appears that the posting of photos of oneself and updating of one's status on Facebook is more a reflection of young adults' orientation to openness with regard to their daily lives. However, the usage of Twitter does appear to be somewhat narcissistically driven. Thus, it appears that it is not the technology that creates narcissism as much as it is the narcissistic personality that seeks a form of technology allowing one to be the center of attention.

Note

1. An earlier factor analysis revealed weak communalities for six items, which were subsequently dropped; many of the items were negatively worded and, thus, potentially confusing to respondents (i.e., 2 items were dropped from each factor—specifically, "I don't like to reveal much about myself," "It is fine if people I'm not close to know what I've been up to lately," "I don't keep many secrets about myself," "People are too open about themselves with others," "I don't mind revealing things about me that might be embarrassing," and "I don't worry about what others might think about what I say about myself").

References

Acquisti, A. A., & Gross, R. (2006). Imagined communities: Awareness, information sharing, and privacy on the Facebook. *Privacy Enhancing Technologies, 4258,* 1–22. doi:10.1007/11957454_3

Anderson, J., & Raine, L. (2010, July 9). *Millennials will make online sharing in networks a lifelong habit* (Report No.). Retrieved from Pew Internet & American Life Project website: http://www.pewinternet.org/Reports/2010/Future-of-Millennials/Overview.aspx

Bergman, S. M., Fearrington, M. E., Davenport, S. W., & Bergman, J. Z. (2011). Millennials, narcissism, and social networking: What narcissists do on social networking sites and why. *Personality and Individual Differences, 50,* 706–711. doi:10.1016/j.paid.2010.12.022

Buffardi, L. E., & Campbell, W. K. (2008). Narcissism and social networking Web sites. *Personality and Social Psychology Bulletin, 34,* 1303–1314.

Christofides, E., Muise, A., & Desmarais, S. (2009). Information disclosure and control on Facebook: Are they two sides of the same coin or two different processes? *CyberPsychology & Behavior, 12,* 341–345. doi:10.1089/cpb.2008.0226

Ellison, N. B., Steinfield, C., & Lampe, C. (2007). The benefits of Facebook "friends": Social capital and college students' use of online social network sites. *Journal of Computer-Mediated Communication, 12,* 1143–1168.

Hampton, K., Goulet, L. S., Rainie, L., & Purcell, K. (2011, June 16). *Social networking sites and our lives* (Report No.). Retrieved from Pew Internet & American Life Project website: http://www.pewinternet.org/Reports12011/Technology-and-social-networks.aspx

Jayson, S. (2009, August 25). Are social networks making students more narcissistic? *USA Today.* Retrieved from http://www.usatoday.com/news/education/2009-08-24-narcissism-young_N.htm

Livingstone, S. (2008). Taking risky opportunities in youthful content creation: Teenagers' use of social networking sites for intimacy, privacy and self-expression. *New Media & Society, 10,* 393–411. doi:10.1177/1461444808089415

Mansson, D. H., & Myers, S. A. (2011). An initial examination of college students' expressions of affection through Facebook. *Southern Communication Journal, 76,* 155–168.

Mehdizadeh, S. (2010). Self-presentation 2.0: Narcissism and self-esteem on Facebook. *Cyberpsychology, Behavior, and Social Networking, 13,* 357–364.

O'Dell, J. (2010, August 30). Facebook feeds narcissism, survey says. CNN.com. Retrieved from www.cnn.com/2010/TECH/social.media/08/30/facebook.narcissism.mashable/index.html

Ong, E. Y. L., Ang, R. P., Ho, J. C. M., Lim, J. C. Y., Goh, D. H., Lee, C. S., & Chua, A. Y. K. (2011). Narcissism, extraversion and adolescents' self-presentation on Facebook. *Personality and Individual Differences, 50,* 180–185.

Raskin, R., & Terry, H. (1988). A principal-components analysis of the Narcissistic Personality Inventory and further evidence of its construct validity. *Journal of Personality and Social Psychology, 54,* 890–902.

Rosen, C. (2007). Virtual friendship and the new narcissism. *The New Atlantis, 17,* 15–31. Retrieved from http://www.thenewatlantis.com/docLib/TNA17-Rosen.pdf

Ryan, T., & Xenos, S. (2011). Who uses Facebook? An investigation into the relationship between the Big Five, shyness, narcissism, loneliness, and Facebook usage. *Computers in Human Behavior, 27,* 1658–1664. doi:10.1016/chb.2011.02.004

Stern, L. A., & Taylor, K. (2007). Social networking and Facebook. *Journal of the Communication, Speech & Theatre Association of North Dakota, 20,* 9–20.

Twenge, J. M., & Foster, J. D. (2010). Birth cohort increases in narcissistic personality traits among American college students, 1982–2009. *Social Psychological Personality Science, 1,* 99–106.

Twenge, J. M., Konrath, S., Foster, J. D., Campbell, W. K., & Bushman, B. J. (2008a). Egos inflating over time: A cross-temporal meta-analysis of the narcissistic personality disorder. *Journal of Personality, 76,* 875–901.

Twenge, J. M., Konrath, S., Foster, J. D., Campbell, W. K., & Bushman, B. J. (2008b). Further evidence of an increase of narcissism among college students. *Journal of Personality, 76,* 919–927.

Trzesniewski, K. H., Donnellan, M. B., & Robins, W. (2008a). Do today's young people really think they are so extraordinary? An examination of secular trends in narcissism. *Psychological Science, 19,* 181–188.

Trzesniewski, K. H., Donnellan, M. B., & Robins, W. (2008b). Is "generation me" really more narcissistic than previous generations? *Journal of Personality, 76,* 903–918.

Urista, M. A., Dong, Q., & Day, K. D. (2009). Explaining why young adults use MySpace and Facebook through Uses and Gratifications Theory. *Human Communication, 12,* 215–229.

Valenzuela, S., Park, N., & Kee, K. F. (2009). Is there social capital in a social network site?: Facebook use and college students' life satisfaction, trust, and participation. *Journal of Computer-Mediated Communication, 14,* 875–901.

Watson, P. J., Grisham, S. O., Trotter, M. V., & Biderman, M. D. (1984). Narcissism and empathy: Validity evidence for the Narcissistic Personality Inventory. *Journal of Personality Assessment, 48,* 301–304.

Wheeless, L. R. (1978). A follow-up study of the relationships among trust, disclosure, and interpersonal solidarity. *Human Communication Research, 4,* 143–157.

Wilson, K., Fornasier, S., & White, K. M. (2010). Psychological predictors of young adults' use of social networking sites. *CyberPsychology, Behavior, and Social Networking, 13,* 173–176. doi:10.1089/cyber.2009.0094

Bruce C. McKinney is a professor of communication studies at the University of North Carolina Wilmington and former president of the UNCW Faculty Senate. He has received a PhD in speech communication from the Pennsylvania State University.

Lynne Kelly is a professor and director of the School of Communication at the University of Hartford. She has received the 1996–1998 Harry Jack Gray Distinguished Teaching Humanist award, as well as the 1999 Roy E. Larsen Award of Excellence in Teaching. She has received a PhD in speech communication from the Pennsylvania State University.

Robert L. Duran is a professor in the School of Communication at the University of Hartford. He has received the University of Hartford 2003–2004 Award for Outstanding Teaching and the 2010 Roy E. Larsen Award of Excellence in Teaching. He has received a PhD in human communication from Bowling Green State University.

EXPLORING THE ISSUE

Is Excessive Use of Facebook a Form of Narcissism?

Critical Thinking and Reflection

1. The authors of both selections use very similar research methods but arrive at very different conclusions. What are some of the *differences* between their methods that may account for this?
2. Why does Carpenter completely ignore one of the three main aspects of narcissism (i.e., "an inability to tolerate criticism") in his study? Was he justified in his decision to do so?
3. In the "Discussion" section of McKinney et al.'s article, they concede that there *are* a few behaviors on Facebook/Twitter that can be predicted by narcissistic personality. Were the authors justified in disregarding these findings when forming their overall conclusion that narcissism does not influence Facebook/Twitter use?
4. Though not the focus of Carpenter's study, he draws attention to an interesting correlation between self-esteem and narcissistic behaviors on Facebook (see the "Self-Esteem" section of the YES selection). How might you explain this correlation?

Create Central

www.mhhe.com/createcentral

Additional Resources

Nadkarni, A., and Hofmann, S. (2001). Why do people use Facebook? (English). *Personality and Individual Differences, 52*(3), 243–249.

Internet References . . .

Narcissistic Personality Inventory: Narcissism Test

http://personality-testing.info/tests/NPI.php

Facebook and Twitter Are Magnets for Narcissists

www.cbc.ca/news/technology/story/2013/06/11/tech-facebook-narcissism.html